The Nature of the International Firm

The Nature of the International Firm

Nordic Contributions to International Business Research

Edited by

Ingmar Björkman and Mats Forsgren

HANDELSHØJSKOLENS FORLAG

**Distribution: Munksgaard International Publishers Ltd
Copenhagen**

© by the authors and Handelshøjskolens Forlag 1997
Printed in Denmark 1997
Set in Plantin by Grafisk Værk A/S, Denmark
Printed by Reproset, Copenhagen
Cover designed by Kontrapunkt
Book designed by Jørn Ekstrøm

ISBN 87-16-13359-5

Series A
COPENHAGEN STUDIES IN ECONOMICS AND MANAGEMENT, NO. 11.

Preface

The aim of this book is to present an overview of much of the research on international business that is currently carried out in the Nordic countries. Most of the papers in this volume were presented at a workshop arranged at the Institute of International Economics and Management, Copenhagen Business School in June, 1995. The objective of the two-day workshop was to draw together Nordic scholars for informal discussions about international business research. We would like to express our thanks to the participants as well as to the Institute of International Economics and Management for their contributions to the workshop.

During the workshop it was decided to publish a book based on these Copenhagen presentations. In addition, some papers by Nordic scholars not at the workshop have been added subsequently. All the papers have undergone considerable revision since the workshop and none of them have been previously published.

The volume includes contributions from 29 researchers. We are greatly indebted to Gitte Jacobsen and Anne Dystrup Pedersen for their editorial work. Without their efficiency this book could not have appeared.

June 1996

Ingmar Björkman
Swedish School of Economics
Helsinki

Mats Forsgren
Copenhagen Business School
Copenhagen

Contents

Ingmar Björkman &   1. Nordic Contributions to International
Mats Forsgren: Business Research   *11*

Part I
Perspectives on the International Firm

Ulf Andersson &
Jan Johanson: 2. International Business Enterprise   *33*

Steen Thomsen: 3. Comparative Institutional Advantage.
                     – Assessing the Impact of International
                     Differences in Corporate Governance   *51*

Mats Forsgren: 4. The Advantage Paradox of the Multinati-
                     onal Corporation   *69*

Part II
Driving Forces Behind
Internationalisation

The Internationalisation Process

Ivo Zander &   5. The Oscillating Multinational Firm
Udo Zander: – Alfa Laval in the period 1890–1990   *89*

Bent Petersen &   6. Twenty Years After
Torben Pedersen: – Support and Critique of the Uppsala
                     Internationalisation model   *117*

Tine Langhoff: 7. The Influence of Cultural Differences on
                     Internationalisation Processes of Firms
                     – An Introduction to a Semiotic
                     and Intercultural Perspective   *135*

Sara McGaughey,
Denice Welch,
Lawrence Welch: 8. Managerial Influences and
                   SME Internationalisation *165*

Jarmo Nieminen &   9. The Role of Learning in the Evolution of
Jan-Åke Törnroos: Business Networks in Estonia:
                   Four Finnish Case Studies *189*

Paul Houman
Andersen, Per
Blenker, Poul   10. Generic Routes to Subcontractors'
Rind Christensen: Internationalisation *231*

                   *Explaining Foreign Direct Investments
                   and Divestments*

Trond Randøy: 11. Towards a Firm-Based Model of Foreign
                   Direct Investment *257*

Jorma Larimo: 12. Ownership Structures of Finnish Firm's
                   Foreign Subsidiaries in EU Countries *281*

Gabriel R. G. Benito: 13. Why are Foreign Subsidiaries Divested?
                   A Conceptual Framework *309*

                   Part III
                   Managing the International Firm

                   *Managing Inter-Organisational
                   Relationships*

Ingmar Björkman: 14. Towards Explaining Human Resource
                   Management Practises in International Joint
                   Ventures – The Case of Chinese-Western
                   Joint Ventures *337*

D. Deo Sharma &
Carolina   15. Internal Management of Sino-Swedish
Wallström-Pan: Joint Ventures *363*

Lee Davis: 16. Cross-Border Buyer-Supplier
Development Collaborations *391*

Désirée Blankenburg 17. Business Network Connections and the
Holm & Jan Johanson: Atmosphere of International Business
Relationships *411*

Management Control

Rebecca Marschan: 18. Dimensions of Less-Hierarchical
Structures in Multinationals *433*

Cecilia Pahlberg: 19. Cultural Differences and
Problems in HQ-Subsidiary Relationships
in MNCs *451*

Mats Forsgren,
Ulf Holm, 20. Network Infusion in the Multinational
Peter Thilenius: Corporation *475*

The Authors *495*

1. Nordic Contributions to International Business Research

Ingmar Björkman and Mats Forsgren

By comparison with most regions in the world the Nordic countries constitute a homogenous area. They are of about the same size, their history is intertwined and to a large extent their languages are similar. Their economies are also similar. First, they are open economies and therefore depended extensively on the international business environment. In comparison to many other countries in Europe and elsewhere firms have turned towards countries outside the region for business. This apparently reflects the smallness of the region as such, but can probably also be explained by the countries' characteristics and histories. Factors such as the countries' long coastlines, the importance of shipping since prehistoric times, the apprenticeship system, the readiness among industrialists to adopt innovations and technology from other parts of the world and the limited use of tariff protection in politics have all stimulated an internationally oriented business community.

The relative importance of international trade and foreign investment in the countries' economies has also influenced business research among scholars in the Nordic countries. The internationalisation of firms and industries, as well as the strategy and management of the international firm have long been the object of studies among researchers at universities and business schools. Due to the relative similarity between the countries in terms of e.g., industry characteristics, educational system, relationships between the business community and universities/business schools and access to data within firms, international business research in the Nordic countries shows some common characteristics. Thus, to a certain extent we can talk about Nordic research in international business.

The main purpose of this book is to present a picture of the on-going research in the international business field done by Nordic scholars. Although the distinction between international business research and international economics research is far from clear-cut, international business here means theoretical or empirical studies aimed at analysing behaviour or management problems at the firm level (including groups of firms) rather than macro-related aspects, such as trade theory, which are usually covered by the subject of international economics. In this chapter specific characteristics of Nordic research in international business will be discussed. These characteristics can be observed in the way that Nordic researchers tend to look at (1) the international firm as a phenomenon, (2) the driving forces behind internationalisation and (3) management of the international firm. The discussion in this chapter as well as the whole book will be structured along these three areas.

1. Perspectives on the International Firm

Professor Sune Carlson, who established a group for international business research at Uppsala University 30 years ago, stated that it is against human nature to do international business. Ever since then, the international firm as a learning organisation characterised by bounded rationality and limited knowledge has been a characteristic feature of the Nordic scene. This statement reflected the fact that firms which try to export or to invest abroad always do so with an incomplete knowledge about foreign markets and the possible alternatives. Doing business abroad is like making cautious steps into unknown territory rather than a consequence of rational choice based on economic analyses.

This perspective mirrors two fundamental insights. First, there is a difference between business operations made in the home country and those made abroad, and this difference can largely be analysed in terms of the level of knowledge within the firm itself. Borders mean something more than just a legal dimension. Second, and maybe more important for Nordic research in the long run, the concept of the firm as used by the researchers deviated more and more from the one commonly used in main stream economic theory. Inspired by his own empirical research (Carlson, 1951) Sune Carlson had concluded that managers' work in general was much more fragmentary and less rational than was usually assumed and that these conclusions were equally applicable to international business. This picture of the managerial behaviour was later confirmed by organisational researchers (e.g., Mintzberg, 1973; Kurke and Aldrich, 1983) which further underpinned the conviction that any theory of the international firm had to use another concept of the firm than the one normally used in economic theory.

The development of such a theory among Nordic researchers was strongly influenced by the work of Edith Penrose, Richard Cyert and James March (Penrose, 1959; Cyert and March, 1963). Penrose offered a theory of knowledge and change in organisations that could immediately be applied to analyse the prerequisites for international operations. In particular, her discussion of knowledge in an organisation had a profound impact on the assumption that knowledge concerning foreign business can only be acquired through direct experience. Later on, the behavioural theory of the firm, formulated by Cyert and March, became the building block of a theory that could better cope with the empirical observations of managers' work by the Nordic researchers. Their concepts of bounded rationality, uncertainty avoidance, organisational learning, quasi-resolution of conflict and sequential attention to goals were concepts that fitted quite well into such a theory and therefore inspired many researchers. The seminal study of Aharoni (1966) persuasively showed their usefulness in the area of international business research.

The historical influence of Penrose and Cyert & March on thought about organisations in general, and the international firm in particular, largely explains why many Nordic researchers have analysed the internationalisation of a firm as an incremental process, where the manager is a risk avoider rather than a risk taker and the decisions about foreign investments are primarily based on individual knowledge acquired through action. The many contributions in this volume, which deals with the internationalisation process against this theoretical background reflect the inspiration that this concept of the firm still exerts on Nordic researchers (Zander and Zander, Chapter 5; Petersen and Pedersen, Chapter 6; Langhoff, Chapter 7; McGaughey, Welch and Welch, Chapter 8; Nieminen and Törnroos, Chapter 9; Anderson, Blenker and Christensen, Chapter 10).

However, the influence of Cyert and March, goes beyond research on internationalisation. Their discussion of conflict resolution and sequential attention to goals inspired other researchers (e.g., Weick, 1976; Pfeffer 1981; Pfeffer and Salancik, 1978) to apply a loose coupling image on the organisation (Scott, 1981). These theorists proposed that one should view organisations, not as unitary hierarchies or as organic entities, but as a loosely linked coalition of shifting interest groups. It is an

open question why so many Nordic researchers within the field of international business, compared with for instance, American or British researchers, have been inspired by the loose coupling image. A partial answer may be related to the fact that Nordic researchers have been more
inclined to carry out case studies and have had relatively easy access to
data from different levels in the firm. The observations of different
groups and interests have probably been more frequent and less dependent on a common perspective at the top management level. Business
researchers always run the risk of speaking only for top management,
putting across the headquarters' perspective, but perhaps the Nordic researchers have been less affected by that risk than have Anglo-American
researchers.

In any case, the loose coupling image has inclined many Nordic
scholars, explicitly or implicitly, to analyse the international firm as a
heterogenous unit, where the different subsidiaries not only control different sets of resources and play different corporate roles, but also represent different interests and possibilities to exert influence on corporate
strategy. Concepts like heterarchy (Hedlund, 1986) or the political view
of the international firm (Larsson, 1985; Forsgren, 1989) have sometimes been used in conjunction with the loose coupling image. A main
theme behind this research is that the centre-periphery metaphor, so extensively used by researchers within the international business field, has
to be replaced by a multi-centre perspective in the sense that different
units, not only the parent company, play decisive roles in shaping the
strategic behaviour of the whole group.

This way of looking upon the international firm amongst Nordic researchers has certainly been stimulated by the dominating position that
large international firms have come to play in the Swedish economy and,
subsequently those of Finland and Norway (Heum and Ylä-Anttila,
1993). In particular during the recent years, therefore, the large international firm with a highly dispersed resource structure, has often been
the object of study. In these studies, the multi-centre metaphor has
come into play rather than the centre-periphery metaphor.

It is interesting to note that research dealing with strategic and managerial issues in the international firm primarily as an organisational design issue (e.g., Brooke and Remmers, 1970; Stopford and Wells, 1972;
Franko, 1976; Porter, 1986; Egelhoff, 1988; Bartlett and Ghoshal,
1989; Chakravarty and Doz, 1992) has, on the whole, had quite a limited
impact on research issues in the Nordic countries. The view that the

headquarters have the ultimate power to design the organisation according to an overall and uniform strategy, has seldom been a natural element in Nordic researchers' frame of reference. As a consequence, the organisational perspective has been organic rather than instrumental and the research focused on descriptive issues rather than on normative ones.

That the loose coupling image still plays an important role among Nordic researchers is apparent in many of the contributions of this book, especially Chapter 2 (Andersson and Johanson), Chapter 4 (Forsgren), Chapter 18 (Marschan) and Chapter 20 (Forsgren, Holm and Thilenius).

To sum up, Nordic researchers have mostly used a behavioural rather than an instrumental or deterministic perspective of the international firm and its operations. The international firm is considered to be an organisation characterised by bounded rationality, action-based learning processes and a dispersed and complex structure in terms of resources, competence and influence.

Another feature of the Nordic research, especially during later years, is the attempt to formulate a somewhat different market concept than has normally been used in international business research. This is probably a consequence of the dominance of industrial markets in some of the Nordic countries, where specific and long-lasting links between firms, rather than links to more or less anonymous end users, is the rule rather than the exception. This has lead to two important consequences; first, there has been a tendency to analyse the environment of the international firm as a bundle of concrete links with specific counterparts, whether they are called strategic alliances (Lorange and Roos, 1992), buyer-supplier collaborations (Davis, Chapter 16), subcontracting (Anderson, Blenker and Christensen, Chapter 10), joint ventures (Björkman, Chapter 14; Sharma and Wallström-Pan, Chapter 15) or business relationships (Andersson and Johanson, Chapter 2; Blankenburg Holm and Johanson, Chapter 17; Forsgren, Holm and Thilenius, Chapter 20). The conviction that the interplay between the market and the firm cannot be fully understood without an analysis of such links has grown stronger over the years. In some Nordic research, the market surrounding the international firm has become almost as specific and visible in the analysis as the firm's internal structure and links. The environment has got a »face«.

Second, this also means that the operational border between the firm, as a strategic and decision-making body, and the market has become much more blurred. This new market concept, in combination with the loose-coupling image, means not only that the firm's relationships with the market are looked upon as being less »market-like«, but also that the internal relationships are somewhat more »market-like« than is usually assumed in international business research. Apart from its assumption of rationalistic behaviour, this may also explains why the transaction cost theory has had a comparatively little influence on Nordic researchers'choice of tools for analysing the international firm. The idea that internalising can make it possible to turn from no control to full control of a transaction has been difficult to combine with the concepts of the market and the firm. The interdependence and trust of the external relationships can be used to exert control by both parties over specific transactions while the dispersed power structure in a firm circumscribes the management's possibility to fully control internal transactions.

The behaviouristic perspective of the international firm is also in line with the perspective that institutions can deviate from economic efficiency. Contrary to the assumption behind transaction cost theory, a behaviouristic approach means that it is an empirical question whether existing institutions are the most efficient ones or not. This has an important implication for the role of the country in international business research and for the relevance of making comparative studies. From a non-efficiency perspective, it matters what kind of institutions a country has, and hence the home country of the international firm, as well as its subsidiaries' host countries, has a decisive impact on its competitive advantage. Based on such a perspective, Thomsen (Chapter 3) analyses the importance of the difference in corporate governance between USA, Japan and some European countries.

The deviation from the concept of the firm in mainstream economic theory is more or less apparent in most of the contributions in this volume, although it is most apparent in Chapter 2 where Andersson and Johanson present a radically new definition of what an international firm and international business is all about. They argue, in contrast to most studies within for instance the traditional foreign direct investment theory, that production is only one activity among others in a firm and seldom the most important one in terms of competitive advantage. Consequently, there is no reason why, as is usually the case, the location of production should have such a decisive role in defining international business. Based on the market concept discussed above and Austrian economic theory they suggest that business is first of all a question of connecting different actors through exchange relationships and, therefore, a business enterprise becomes international through connecting actors in different countries. Their definition not only stresses trade rather than production as the main business activity, but also the importance of specific exchange relationships in business life.

The market concept applied in conjunction with the loose coupling image can give new insights into the basic advantage of being an international firm. Lately many scholars have proposed that the main competitive advantage of the modern multinational stems from its governance of a global network of units with different capabilities (Dunning 1988; Bartlett and Ghoshal, 1989; Kogut and Zander, 1993). But there is an inherent conflict in developing and transferring capabilities within the international firm, a conflict which is discussed in Chapter 4 (Forsgren).

2. Driving Forces behind Internationalisation

How to explain *why* and in what forms foreign direct investments (FDIs) take place is probably the most popular topic in international business research. The vast majority of researchers attempt to explain FDIs by drawing on economic theories such as transaction cost theory (Hennart, 1982), the internalisation theory (Buckley, 1988), and the eclectic paradigm (Dunning, 1988). However, it is interesting to note that among Nordic scholars the question of *why* FDI is often replaced by the issue of *how* FDI, that is how investments abroad is actually carried out by the firm. There are, of course, some notable exceptions (e.g. Larimo, 1993, Chapter 11; Pedersen 1994; Benito 1995;) but to use mainstream economic theory to investigate why FDIs occurs is, comparatively speaking, quite rare among Nordic scholars. With the exception of Benito's work (Chapter 12), this also concerns FDI disinvestments. Instead, many studies have treated FDI as a process phenomenon, where the main concern has been to understand the underlying forces of the process, rather than why the firm decided to invest abroad in the first place. As was discussed above, the relatively strong influence of Penrose, Cyert and March and others on Nordic scholars' work within the international business field, has probably contributed to this situation. However, in small, open economies like those of the Nordic countries, where foreign operations have long played an important role in business life, the issue of how foreign operations are handled in individual firms, can be expected to take precedence over the question of why firms go abroad. This may also explain the relatively strong interest in the former question, although some scholars have suggested that more research should be conducted on the process leading up to the FDI (Björkman 1989; Larimo, 1995).

Efforts to supplement the mainstream FDI-theory with firm-based models is also apparent in Nordic research. Randöy (Chapter 11) argues that the eclectic paradigm (Dunning, 1988) should be extended by strategic motives like seeking global synergy and new knowledge or reducing uncertainty.

The relative dominance of firm-level studies as well as the process orientation is also reflected in terms of how firm internationalisation is studied. Although a number of Nordic studies have been conducted on large scale samples, several studies have either supplemented this with case studies (e.g. Nordström, 1991; Lindqvist, 1991) or even relied solely on in depth longitudinal data (e.g. Johanson and Vahlne, 1992; Zander and Zander, Chapter 5).

Nordic international business scholars are perhaps best known globally for their research on the internationalisation of the firm (Buckley and Ghauri, 1993:ix). The starting point for this work was a collection of articles published by researchers at the University of Uppsala (Carlson, 1975; Forsgren and Johanson, 1975; Johanson and Wiedersheim-Paul 1975; Johanson and Vahlne 1977), in which they outlined what was later become known as the Uppsala Internationalisation Model. In this model, the internationalisation of a firm is seen as a process in which the firm gradually increases its international involvement. According to the model, the process »evolves in an interplay between the development of knowledge about foreign markets and operations on one hand and an increasing commitment of resources to foreign markets on the other.... A critical assumption (of the model) is that the market knowledge, including perceptions of the market opportunities and problems, is acquired primarily through experience from current business activities in the market. Experiential market knowledge generates business opportunities and is consequently a driving force in the internationalisation process« (Johanson and Vahlne, 1990: 11-12). The model states that incremental commitment manifests itself in terms of the sequence of modes of operations used by the firm in general, as well as in individual markets, and in terms of the sequence of foreign markets entered by the firm. Firms are expected to enter new markets with successively greater psychic distance. The psychic distance between the home country and the focal market is defined in terms of factors like difference in language, culture, and political systems between the two countries, that is, factors which disturb the flow of information between the firm and the market (Langhoff, Chapter 7, Pahlberg, Chapter 19). Loustarinen (1979) later extended the incremental model to include the sequence in which different kinds of products are offered by internationalising firms.

Following initial case studies of Swedish firms carried out by a group of researchers at the University of Uppsala, considerable effort has been made to test the validity of the model empirically, not least in the Nordic countries (for reviews of research outside the Nordic countries, see Young et al, 1989; Johanson and Vahlne, 1990). The sequence of foreign markets entered has been studied in Sweden (Engwall and Wallenstål, 1988; Nordström, 1991; Lindqvist, 1991), Norway (Juul and Walters, 1987; Benito and Gripsrud, 1992), Denmark (Strandskov, 1995) and Finland (Luostarinen, 1979), while the sequence of market entry modes has been analysed by Swedish (e.g. Hedlund and Kverneland, 1985; Ågren, 1990), Danish (Petersen and Pedersen, Ch. 6), and Finnish researchers (Luostarinen, 1979; Björkman and Eklund, 1996). Research has provided considerable, although not undisputed, empirical support for the Uppsala model. It has, for instance, been argued that the boundary assumptions of the model are inadequately specified, and that the model is less valid for very large multinational corporations, firms with extensive international experience, in high-technology sectors, for service industries, and for international operations that are not motivated by market seeking. Much of the criticism as well as efforts at further developing the model have been done by Nordic scholars (e.g. Hedlund and Kverneland, 1985; Welch and Luostarinen, 1988; Johanson and Vahlne, 1990; Andersen, 1993; Petersen and Pedersen, Ch. 6; Langhoff, Ch. 7).

Although the Uppsala Model has occupied a central position in much of the work on corporate internationalisation, alternative or suppliant models and frameworks have also been offered. Scandinavian researchers have occupied a central role in the development of the (industrial) network perspective (e.g. Håkansson, 1982), which has also been utilised to analyse the internationalisation of firms (e.g., Johanson and Mattsson, 1988; Johanson and Vahlne, 1990; 1992; Forsgren and Johanson, 1992). The network perspective draws our attention to the often long-lasting business relationships that exist between firms in industrial markets. Case studies have shown the way in which the development of a company's operations in foreign markets has been influenced by the relationships gradually developed in that particular market (Johanson and Vahlne, 1992).

As Johanson and Mattsson (1988) argued, the internationalisation of a firm means that it develops business relationships in networks in other countries. This can be achieved through (1) the establishment of relationships in country networks that are new to the firm, i.e., through international extension, (2) the development of relationships in those networks, i.e., by penetration, and (3) connecting existing networks in different countries. Existing relationships can be used as bridges to other networks, for instance when a customer invites or even demands that a supplier follows the company abroad (Johanson and Sharma, 1987). Existing personal networks are also likely to facilitate the entrance into new foreign networks (Lindqvist, 1991; McGaughey, Welch, and Welch, Ch. 8; Björkman and Eklund, 1996).

Neither the Uppsala Model nor the network perspective include conventional »economic drivers« in their explanations of internationalisation of firms. As argued earlier in this chapter, while much of international business research has stemmed from an economics perspective, the Uppsala model is based on the behavioural theory of the firm (Cyert and March, 1963), and the network perspective attaches considerable importance to the social and cognitive ties that are formed between actors engaged in business relationships. The latter perspective points to the great difficulties in planning or formulating a strategy for market entry and then in implementing it, and underscores the way in which ongoing interactions between actors shape the network structure: In other words, the perspective stresses on-going interaction rather than strategic decision making (Johanson and Vahlne, 1992). While the traditional foreign market entry literature seeks to describe how firms decide about markets, entry modes and planning the entry (e.g., Root 1982), the network theory focuses the network to entry in terms of important actors and their relative positions (Axelsson and Johanson, 1992, Blankenburg Holm 1995).

3. Managing the International Firm

As was pointed out in Section 1, the concepts of the firm and the market used by many Nordic researchers imply that specific exchange relationships within the firm, as well as externally, play an important role in the analysis. This is also reflected in the contributions which deal more explicitly with managerial aspects. Some of these (Björkman, Chapter 14; Sharma and Wallström-Pan, Chapter 15; Davis, Chapter 16; and Blankenburg Holm and Johanson, Chapter 17) discuss different aspects of external relationships across borders while others (Marschan, Chapter 18; Pahlberg, Chapter 19 and Forsgren, Holm and Thilenius, Chapter 20) also deal with internal relationships. A crucial question here is how the development of an international firm's core capabilities, can be handled in a context that includes external collaborations. From the perspective of transaction cost theory, a collaboration with an external partner, where the firm's core competence is involved, will pose problems because of opportunism, especially if the core competence is based on tacit knowledge. Thus, one conclusion is that firms should avoid such collaborations to minimize transaction costs. But lately there has been increasing attention in the literature to the notion of firms competing primarily on the basis of capabilities rather than low transaction costs and the corresponding notion of collaboration formation for the purpose of the development of a firm's capabilities (Kogut 1988; Hamel 1991). As pointed out by Madhok (1996), this line of argument is theoretically and intellectually rooted in the behavioural and evolutionary theory of the firm. Therefore it has also been a tendency among Nordic researchers to look upon a firm's collaboration with an external counterpart involving its core competence as an opportunity more than as a problem.

At the heart of this issue, though, is the crucial question of whether a firm's core competence can best be understood as an *inhouse* capability (although supported by collaborations with other firms) or if it can best be understood as a resource, inevitably associated with relationships with other firms in the market (although supported by inhouse development activities). Neither research using the resource-based theory (Wernerfeldt, 1984) nor research applying network theory has so far been able to give a satisfactory answer to this question. The different views are reflected in the contributions in this section, for instance those by Davis (Chapter 16) and Forsgren, Holm and Thilenius (Chapter 20).

The emphasis on the firm's specific business relationships among Nordic scholars' recent work has also had an impact on how cultural difference in international business is perceived. As pointed out by Langhoff (Chapter 7), the psychic distance concept was quite underdeveloped in the original versions of the Nordic internationalisation models. Although the concept itself related more to individuals' cognitive thinking, it was primarily used to reflect cultural differences between countries. But on a relationship level, cultural difference can be seen as not only affecting exchange between the parties, but also getting affected by this exchange. It is dependent on the character of the specific relationship rather than on general differences on a country level. Blankenburg-Holm and Johanson's discussion of the atmosphere in international business relationships (Chapter 17) and Pahlberg's analysis of the headquarters-subsidiary relationship (Chapter 19) both reflect this new way of looking upon cultural difference in international business.

4. Current trends

Internationalisation has traditionally been analysed as a question of foreign sales or production abroad. Recently, though, Nordic research has been increasingly devoted to other functional areas. For instance, the internationalisation of R&D has been studied, in particular through analyses of Swedish companies (Håkanson and Nobel, 1993; Zander 1994; Riddersstråle 1996). But there has also been studies of ownership internationalisation (Didner, 1994) and internationalisation of headquarters organisation (Forsgren, Holm and Johanson 1995). There also seems to be a growing interest in portraying the international firm as a social community, that specialises in the creation and internal transfer of knowledge. The international firm arguably does not arise out of failure of markets for the buying and selling of knowledge, but out of the corporation's efficiency as a vehicle for transferring knowledge across borders. Empirical research carried out by Udo Zander has shown that the less codifiable and the harder to teach a new technology is, the more likely that the transfer of this technology will be to a wholly owned subsidiary (Zander, 1991; Kogut and Zander, 1993). The tendency to consider the international firm as a vehicle for transferring knowledge is in line with the change of focus from an analysis of headquarters-subsidiary relationships (e.g. Hedlund, 1980, 1984; Leksell, 1981)to an analysis of the international firm as a heterarchy (Hedlund 1986; Hedlund and Rolander 1990), a multi-centre firm (Forsgren, 1990, Holm, 1994), an interorganisational network (Holm, Johanson and Thilenius, 1995) or as a less-hierarchical organisation

(Marschan, 1996, Chapter 18). The question of to what extent knowledge can be transferred between different units with different capabilities becomes crucial when global efficiency, local responsiveness and corporate-wide learning and action are quintessential for its competitiveness (Hedlund and Ridderstråle, 1994; Sölvell and Bresman, 1995). But behind these issues perhaps even more important questions lie on the distant horizon; what are the underlying factors behind the development of organisational capabilities in the different subsidiaries and to what extent is it possible for headquarters to influence these factors. In that sense, the difficulties of extending a firm's operations to markets outside its home-base, which occupied so much interest among Nordic researchers 20 years ago, has gradually changed to an interest in the difficulties of managing networks of subsidiaries with different resources and environments.

However, several studies of business in the »economies in transition«, such as the post-socialist countries in Europe and the People's Republic of China, have revealed that market entry is often conducted in an incremental way characterised by learning-by-doing. Hence, research on entry into new markets can still benefit from the basic ideas behind the original Uppsala Model. Although one cannot say any longer that it is against the human nature to do business abroad many of these studies clearly indicate that it is still a question of taking cautious steps in an unknown terrain.

References

Aharoni, Y., 1966. *The Foreign Investment Decision Process.* Harvard University, Boston.

Andersen, O., 1993. »On the Internationalization Process of Firms: A Critical Analysis«, *Journal of International Business Studies,* Vol. 24, 209-231.

Axelsson, B. and J. Johanson, 1992. »Foreign Market Entry – the textbook vs. the network view«. In Axelsson, B., Easton, G., (eds.), *Industrial Networks – A New view of Reality.* London: Routledge.

Bartlett, C. A., and S. Ghoshal, 1989. *Managing across Borders. The Transnational Solution,* Harvard Business School Press, Boston.

Benito, G.R.G, 1995. *Studies in the Foreign Direct Investment and Divestment Behaviour of Norwegian Manufacturing Companies.* Bergen: Norwegian School of Economics and Business Administration.

Benito, G.R.G. and G. Gripsrud, 1992. »The Expansion of Foreign Direct Investments: Discrete Rational Location Processes or a Cultural Learning Process?«, *Journal of International Business Studies,* Vol. 23, 461-476.

Björkman, I., 1989. *Foreign Direct Investments – An Empirical Analysis of Decision Making in Seven Finnish firms.* Ekonomi och samhälle 42, Swedish School of Economics, Helsinki.

Björkman, I. and M. Eklund, 1996. »The Sequence of Operational Modes Used by Finnish Investors in Germany«, *Journal of International Marketing,* Vol. 4.

Björkman, I. and S. Kock, 1995. »Social Relationships and Business Networks: the Case of Western Companies in China«, *International Business Review,* Vol. 4, 519-535.

Blankenburg Holm, D., 1995. »A Network Approach to Foreign Market Entry«. In Müller, K. and D. Wilson (eds.), Business Marketing: *An Interaction and Network Perspective.* Boston: Kluwer Academic Publishers.

Brooke, M. and L. Remmers, 1970. *The Strategy of Multinational Enterprise.* London: Longman.

Buckley, P. J., 1988. »The Limits of Explanation: Testing the Internalization Theory of the Multinational Enterprise«, *Journal of International Business Studies,* Vol. 19, 181-194.

Buckley, P. J. and P. N. Ghauri, 1993. »Introduction and overview«, in Buckley, Peter J. and P. N. Ghauri, (eds.) *The Internationalization of the Firm – a Reader.* Academic Press, Harcourt Brace Jovanich, London.

Carlson, S., 1951. *Executive Behaviour: A Study of the Work Load and the Working Methods of Managing Directors.* Stockholm: Strömberg.

Carlson, S., 1975. *How Foreign is Foreign Trade – A Problem in International Business Research.* Uppsala University, Uppsala.

Chakravarty, B. S. and Y. Doz, 1992. Strategy Process Research: Focusing on Corporate Renewal, *Strategic Management Journal,* Vol. 13, pp. 5-14.

Cyert, R. D. and J. G. March, 1963. *The Behavioral Theory of the Firm,* Prentice-Hall, Englewood Cliffs, NJ.

Didner, H., 1992. »Managing Ownership Internationalization«. In Forsgren, M., Johanson, J., *Managing Networks in International Business.* Philadelphia: Gordon and Breach.

Dunning, J. H., 1988. *Explaining International Production,* London: Unwin Hyman.

Dunning, J. H., 1988. »The Eclectic Paradigm of International Production: A Restatement and some Possible Extensions«, *Journal of International Business Studies,* Vol. 19, 1-31.

Egelhoff, W. G., 1988. *Organizing the Multinational Enterprise: An Information Processing View.* Cambridge, MA.: Ballinger.

Engwall, L. and M. Wallenstål, 1988. »Tit for Tat in Small Steps. The internationalization of Swedish banks«, *Scandinavian Journal of Management,* Vol. 4, 147-155.

Forsgren, M., 1989. *Managing the Internationalization Process: The Swedish Case.*London: Routledge.

Forsgren, M., 1990. »Managing the International Multi-Centre Firm: Case Studies from Sweden«. *European Management Journal,* 8, pp. 261-267.

Forsgren, M. and J. Johanson, 1975. *Internationell företagsekonomi.* (International Business Management). Stockholm: Norstedts.

Forsgren, M. and J. Johanson, 1992 (eds.). *Managing Networks in International Business.* Philadelphia: Gordon and Breach.

Forsgren, M., U. Holm and J. Johanson, 1995. » Division Headquarters go Abroad – A Step in the Internationalization of Multinational Corporation«. *Journal of Management Studies,* Vol. 32, Number 4, July.

Franko, L. G., 1976. *The European Multinationals.* London: Harper and Row.

Hamel, G., 1991. »Competition for Competence and Interpartner Learning within International Strategic Alliances«. *Strategic Management Journal,* 12, pp. 83-103.

Hedlund, G., 1980. »The Role of Foreign Subsidiaries in Strategic Decision-making in Swedish Multinational Corporations«, *Strategic Management Journal,* Vol. 1, 23-26.

Hedlund, G., 1984. »Organization-in-between: the Evolution of the Mother-Daugther Structure of Managing Foreign Subsidiaries in Swedish MNCs«, *Journal of International Business Studies,* Vol. 15, 109-123.

Hedlund, G., 1986. »The Hypermodern MNC – A Heterarchy?« *Human Resource Management,* Spring, 25: 9-35.

Hedlund, G. and D. Rolander, 1990. »Action in Heterachies: New Approaches to Managing the MNC«, In C. A. Bartlett, Y. Doz and G. Hedlund, eds. *Managing the Global Firm,* Routledge, London.

Hedlund, G., and P. Åman, 1984. *Managing Relationships with Foreign Subsidiaries,* Sveriges Mekanförbund, Stockholm.

Hedlund, G., and Å. Kverneland, 1985. »Are establishments and growth strategies for foreign markets changing?«, *International Studies of Management and Organization,* Vol. 15, No. 2, 41-59.

Hennart, J.-F., 1991. »The Transaction Cost Theory of the Multinational Enterprise«. In C. N. Pitelis and R. Sugden, eds. *The Nature of the Transnational Firm,* Routledge, London.

Heum, P. and P. Ylä-Antilla, 1993. *Firm Dynamics in a Nordic Perspective. Large Corporations and Industrial Transformation.* Helsinki: Taloustieto Oy.

Holm, U., 1994. *Internationalization of the Second Degree.* Uppsala: Department of Business Studies, Uppsala University.

Holm, U., J. Johanson and P. Thilenius, 1995. »HQ Knowledge of Subsidiary Network Contexts in the MNC«. *International Studies of Management and Organization.* Spring/Summer, Vol. 25, 1-2.

Hoon-Habauer, S., 1994. *Management of Sino-Foreign Joint Ventures,* Lund University Press, Lund.

Håkansson, H., 1982. *International Marketing and Purchasing of Industrial Goods. An Interaction Approach.* John Wiley, Chichester.

Håkanson, L. and R. Nobel, 1993. »Foreign Research and Development in Swedish Multinationals«, *Research Policy,* Vol. 22, 373-396.

Johanson, J. and D. Sharma, 1987. »Technical Consultancy in Internationalization«, *International Marketing Review*, Vol. 4, 20-29.

Johanson, J. and F. Wiedersheim-Paul, 1975. »The Internationalization of the Firm: Four Swedish Cases«, *Journal of Management Studies*, Vol. 12, No. 3, 305-322.

Johanson, J. and J.-E. Vahlne, 1977. »The Internationalization Process of the Firm – A Model of Knowledge Development and Increasing Foreign Market Commitments«, *Journal of International Business Studies*, Vol. 8, Spring/Summer, 23-32.

Johanson, J. and J.-E.Vahlne, 1990. »The Mechanism of Internationalization«, *International Marketing Review*, Vol. 7, No. 4, 11-24.

Johanson, J. and J.-E. Vahlne, 1992. »Management of Foreign Market Entry.«, *Scandinavian International Business Review*, Vol. 1, No. 3, 9-27.

Johanson, J. and L.-G. Mattsson, 1988. »Internationalization in Industrial Systems – A Network Approach«, in N. Hood and J-E. Vahlne, (eds.) *Strategies in Global Competition*. Croom Helm, London.

Juul, M. and P. Walters, 1987. »The internationalization of Norwegian Firms: A Study of the UK Experience«, *Management International Review*, Vol. 27, No. 1, 58-66.

Kogut, B., 1988. »Joint Ventures: Theoretical and Empirical Perspectives«. *Strategic Management Journal*, 9, pp 319-332.

Kogut, B. and U. Zander, 1993. »Knowledge of the Firm and the Evolutionary Theory of the Multinational Corporation«, *Journal of International Business Studies*, Vol. 24, 625-645.

Kurke, L. B. and H. Aldrich, 1983. »Mintzberg was right!: A Replication and Extension of the Nature of Managerial Work«. *Management Science*, Vol. 29, No 8, August

Larimo, J., 1993. *Foreign Direct Investment Behaviour and Performance*. University of Vaasa, Vaasa.

Larimo, J., 1995. »The Foreign Direct Investment Decison Process: Case Studies of Different Types of Decision Processes in Finnish Firms«, *Journal of Business Research*, Vol. 33, 25-55.

Larsson, A., 1985. *Structure and Change. Power and Politics in the Transnational Enterprise*. Acta Universitatis Upsaliensis Studia Oeconomiae Negotiorum, 23, Stockholm: Almquist & Wiksell.

Leksell, L., 1981. Headquarter-Subsidiary Relationships in Multinational Corporations. Institute of International Business, Stockholm School of Economics, Stockholm.

Lindqvist, M., 1991. *Infant Multinationals: The Internationalization of Young, Technology-Based Swedish Firms.* Institute of International Business, Stockholm School of Economics, Stockholm.

Lorange, P. and J. Roos, 1992. *Strategies Alliances. Formation, Implementation and Evolution.* Cambridge, Mass.: Blackwells Publishers.

Luostarinen, R. 1979. *Internationalization of the Firm.* Acta Academiae Oeconomicae Helsingiensis, Helsinki School of Economics, Helsinki.

Madhok, A. 1996. »Cost, Value and Foreign Markt Entry Mode: The Transaction and the Firm«. *Strategic Management Journal.* (Forthcoming).

Mintzberg, H., 1973. *The Nature of Managerial Work.* New York: Harper and Row.

Nieminen, J. and J.-Å. Törnroos,(eds.), forthcoming. *Starting and Developing Business Activities in Eastern Europe: A Learning Perspective.*

Nordström, K., 1991. *The Internationalization Process of the Firm – Searching for New Patterns and Explanations.* Institute of International Business, Stockholm School of Economics, Stockholm.

Penrose, E. T., 1959. *A Theory of the Growth of the Firm* Oxford: Basil Blackwell..

Pedersen, T., 1994. *Danske virksomheders direkte investeringer i udlandet og udenlandske virksomheders direkte investeringer i Danmark* (Danish firms' investments abroad and foreign firms' investments in Denmark). Copenhagen: Copenhagen Business School.

Pfeffer, J., 1981. *Power in Organizations.* Boston, Mass.: Pitman.

Pfeffer, J. and G. Salancik, 1978. *The External Control of Organization. A Resource Dependence Perspective.* New York: Harper & Row.

Porter, M. E., 1986. »Competition in global industries: a conceptual framework«. In M. E. Porter (ed), *Competition in Global Industries.* Boston, Mass.: Harvard Business School Press.

Ridderstråle, J., 1996. *Global Innovation – Managing International Innovation Projects in ABB and Electrolux.* Institute of International Business, Stockholm School of Economics, Stockholm.

Root, F., 1982. *Foreign Market Entry Strategies.* New York: AMACON.

Salmi, A., 1995. *Institutionally Changing Business Networks.* Acta Academiae Oeconomicae Helsingiensis, Helsinki School of Economics, Helsinki.

Scott, W. R., 1981. *Organizations. Rational, Natural, and Open systems.* Englewood Cliffs, N.Y.: Prentice Hall.

Stopford, J. M. and L. T. Wells, 1972. *Managing the Multinational Enterprise*. London: Longman.

Strandskov, J., 1995. *Internationalisering av virksomheder (Internationalization of Firms)*. Copenhagen: Copenhagen Business School.

Sölvell, Ö. and H. Bresman, 1995. »Managing and Organizing the Innovation Process in the Multinational Enterprise. Between Heterarchy and Home-Base«. In Schiattarella, R.(ed) *New Challenges for European and International Business*. Urbino: European International Business Academy.

Weick, C., 1976. »Educational Organizations as Loosely Coupled Systems«. *Administrative Science Quarterly*, 21, pp. 1-19.

Welch, L. S. and R. Luostarinen, R., 1988. »Internationalization: Evolution of a Concept«, Journal of General Management, Vol. 14, No. 2, 34-55.

Young, S., J. Hamill, C. Wheeler and J. R. Davis, 1989. *International Market Entry and Development: Strategies and Management*. Prentice Hall, Englewood Cliffs, NJ.

Zander, I., 1994. *The Tortoise Evolution of the Multinational Corporation – Foreign Technological Activity in Swedish Multinational Firms 1890 – 1990*. Stockholm: IIB, Stockholm School of Economics.

Zander, U., 1991. *Exploiting a Technological Edge – Volontary and Involontary Dissemination of Technology*. Institute of International Business, Stockholm School of Economics, Stockholm.

Ågren, L., 1990. *Swedish Direct Investment in the U.S.* Institute of International Business, Stockholm School of Economics, Stockholm.

Part I

Perspectives
on the International Firm

2. International Business Enterprise

Ulf Andersson and Jan Johanson

1. Introduction

In the modern literature on MNC competitive advantage, interest has moved from competitive advantage as an antecedent to international development to competitive advantage as an outcome of international development. And the MNC strategy literature has, in consequence, changed its focus from how to exploit competitive advantage by international expansion (Caves, 1982; Dunning, 1988) to how to gain competitive advantage through international expansion (Bartlett and Ghoshal, 1989; Ghoshal and Bartlett, 1990 and 1993; Porter, 1986 and 1990). Evidently the two subjects are interrelated. We believe, however, that each of the two main strands of MNC literature – economic theory based and organisation theory based – misses some important aspects of the interrelation. We suspect that this has to do with the ways in which these approaches conceptualise the relation between the MNC and its environment. While the economic theory based literature views the MNC primarily as a production unit operating in a faceless market environment perfectly separated from the MNC, the organisation theory based literature, although explicitly treating the environment of the MNC, does not have a pertinent view of the critical part of the environment, the market. Thus there is need for a discussion of the conceptual base. The purpose of this chapter is to outline a slightly different view of the MNC. We introduce and elaborate the international business enterprise concept focusing on market exchange and business relationships as distinctive features of the multinational firm.

2. The Conceptual Base of the MNC

As a starting point, consider the old operational definition of a multinational firm which is still usually applied, as a firm with at least one production subsidiary abroad (in some studies several production subsidiaries are required) (Caves, 1982). This definition implies that production is the main activity of interest in the firm (Dunning, 1988). Evidently, with such a definition, other kinds of activity or operations than production become insubordinate, or even irrelevant, when considering the competitiveness and the strategy of the multinational. It seems to mean that the ways in which the firm's production is organised around the world is of paramount importance for the competitiveness of a multinational. Either the main concern of the firm is to produce at low cost by utilising the cost advantages of different production environments or to use production conditions in different environments to produce or develop better products. The revenues of the firm are only marginally dependent on other activities.

However, there are several reasons for considering other sources of competitiveness than production. In the modern literature on industrial organisation and on business strategy, R&D is frequently assumed to be a – almost the only – critical source of competitiveness. Much attention is also devoted to R&D in the literature on the multinational (Håkanson and Zander, 1986). Furthermore, marketing is often stated as having considerable impact on the ability of the firm to compete in the market. Sometimes purchasing – or sourcing – is said to have a strong effect on the competitiveness of a firm. Moreover, costs of R&D in many industries are as high as the cost of production and variations in such costs may make significant differences between firms. The same holds for marketing. In addition, the cost of purchased inputs are often higher than production costs. Thus, we have reason to consider the ways in which R&D, marketing and purchasing activities are organised and performed if we want to explain the competitive advantage of firms. In an international context, the global structure of these activities is important if we want to explain the competitiveness of the multinational firm, and, indeed, this is the approach taken in most studies of the multinational firm (Bartlett and Ghoshal, 1989). However, we take this a step further as we believe that we have reason to consider a concept of the firm that explicitly places these activities in focus when discussing competitiveness.

Production, i.e. the transformation of resources into products, can be seen as one extreme source of competitiveness of a firm. It corresponds to the neo-classical definition of the firm, which provides a basis for much of the theoretical underpinning of the concepts characterising the multinational firm (Dunning, 1988). It implies that the acquisition of resources for use in production and the disposal of the products are of interest only to the extent that they have a bearing on production conditions in the firm. They are only important for competitiveness indirectly, through their influence on production. An opposite view would suggest that the competitive advantage of a firm is associated primarily with the acquisition of resources and the sale of the products through market exchange. According to this approach, production is assumed to have an impact on competitiveness only indirectly, by way of exchange. Such a view suggests that we need a firm concept placing attention on exchange, or what we can call the business aspect of the firm's activities. We posit that competitiveness is based on the exchange structure of the firm. Business activity, that is, trading across markets, is the distinctive feature of firms in a market economy.

Against this background we consider the business enterprise concept of the firm, with roots in the Austrian theory (Jacobson, 1992; Kirzner, 1973). Business enterprise, according to Snehota (1990, p.42), is

> »...*a pattern of activities that link together a set of actors and resources with the purpose of exploiting exchange opportunities in a market*«.

Business enterprise is an exchange entity rather than a production entity. We will return to this concept after a discussion of exchange conditions in business markets.

3. Business Relationships

Studies of business markets have demonstrated that exchange in such markets is carried out to a large extent within the framework of long-lasting business relationships (Axelsson and Easton, 1992; Ford, 1990; Håkansson, 1982; Hallén, 1986; Turnbull and Valla, 1986). A basic explanation for the continuity and stability of exchange in business relationships is the initial unfamiliarity of the parties. Through repeated business exchange two partners can gradually learn about each other's needs and capabilities, and thereby, can see possibilities of reducing the cost of exchange and raise their joint productivity through mutual adaptation. The weak interdependence of an initial ordinary market relation is gradually transformed into the strong interdependence of a business relationship in which the parties are tied to and trust each other (Dwyer, Schurr and Oh, 1987; Hallén, Johanson and Seyed-Mohamed, 1991; Ring and Van de Ven, 1992; Zajac and Olsen, 1993). In the following discussion we call the firms involved in business relationships business partners.

In business relationships between two firms, the managers develop and maintain extensive contacts with each other. Such contacts may involve not only marketing and purchasing managers, but also production, R&D, quality and logistic managers, on several levels, who learn about each other's needs, capabilities and ways of dealing with different problems.

In business relationships exchange has a wider scope than mere product exchange. It also includes knowledge development as an important element. This means not only that knowledge exchange takes place and is intertwined with product exchange in business relationships, but it means also that, as a consequence of the recurrent confrontation between producer knowledge and user knowledge in a business relationship, new and unique knowledge is created. Evidently, much of this is of a tacit nature and cannot be transferred to others. Business relationships are critical as means for developing competence, new products and processes as well as for the modification of existing ones (Håkansson, 1989; Laage-Hellman, 1989; Lundvall, 1985). It is, however, important to observe that the knowledge development does not take place in isolation from the product exchange; rather, it should be considered as an aspect of the exchange.

A working business relationship is the result of earlier investment, associated with exchange activities with the business partner. It may take years of costly activities before the partners have demonstrated their willingness and ability sufficiently to each other to be able to reap the benefits of their business relationship. Such a relationship is an important asset, it is a platform for future business transactions and for knowledge development, and it creates knowledge and develops competence that may be of wider significance for the firms' competitive ability. Evidently, business relationships also constitute important structural constraints on the firm's business.

Concerning business relationships some important aspects need commenting on. Although business relationships tend to be long-lasting and can be viewed as structural constraints, they are by no means stable in the sense that they are given once for all. They are the outcome of interaction between the two partners and last as long as both consider it worthwhile continuing the exchange. Thus the relationships only exist because the partners think that it is advantageous to go on doing business with each other, that is as long as they think that the partner has something to offer that is better than what can be expected from doing business with an alternative partner. This, in turn, is dependent on their beliefs about the counterpart's willingness and ability to continue the exchange in the future. Obviously, there is a basic difference between this kind of structural constraint and the kind of structural constraint associated with a production unit. The relationship is fundamentally dependent on the partners, it is more fluid than the production unit as it is a social construction, and it is in a quite different way a matter of interpretation. It cannot be formed through a unilateral decision as it is created and developed through interaction between two parties. Nevertheless, some business relationships are important strategic assets of the firm and when considering the competitiveness of the firm, one should give them their due attention.

As indicated by the discussion, business relationships are multifarious phenomena. They differ with regard to the interdependence – technical, social, cognitive, legal, administrative, etc. – between the partners. Furthermore, they are based on trust and mutual knowledge and they comprise intentions, expectations and interpretations. Consequently, they cannot be understood by those who are not personally involved, and still less can they be controlled.

The impossibility for an outsider to understand business relationships, in combination with the fact that they are the result of the investment of resources in the relationship, gives rise to an important problem: Only the insider has the possibility of judging if the effort spent on a business relationship represents an investment. Thus, the insider can invest much or little in a relationship without any possibility for an outsider to know which.

Moreover, since the business partners are interdependent, there is a power relation between them. They can exercise some, although limited, control over each other. Of course, this control is not limited to the immediate exchange between the business partners: It could just as well concern the business partner's strategies and its relations to others. Thus, the partners in a business relationship are not sovereign units, they are directly tied to each other and indirectly tied to, or embedded in, a wider network of business relationships.

Thus, business relationships are important sources of competitive advantage, they are structural constraints that have to be recognised, maintained and developed in order to remain valuable. They cannot be fathomed by those not involved and they expose the firm to partial control from another firm.

Studies of business markets have shown that a limited number of customers, suppliers and other actors constitute an important base for the firm due to their share of the business of the firm, their significance for its knowledge development or their use as bridgeheads to other firms and markets (Håkansson, 1989; Holm, Johanson and Thilenius, 1995).

4. Business Enterprise

A business enterprise is an entity engaged in business activity. Business is a matter of selling and buying, which concerns the transfer of property rights between different legal units (Snehota, 1990). The business enterprise, unavoidably, is a legal unit, which, within its boundaries, performs activities in order to exploit exchange opportunities. The distinctive feature of business enterprise is exchange rather than production. The importance of production in business enterprise is derived from exchange. What does that mean? It means that, while in received economic theory, the firm, is an entity defined without reference to other firms, business enterprise is an entity that is defined on the basis of its exchange relations with others. In fact, in the extreme, the firm in economic theory exists irrespective of whether it is engaged in market exchange and the business enterprise exists even if it is not engaged in production. By no means does the definition say that business enterprise is not engaged in production. Production activities may very well be extensive, but they are assumed to be performed in order to make the exchange possible.

The discussion of business relationships above indicates that there is reason to expect that business relationships are the critical source of competitiveness because of their importance to both product exchange and knowledge exchange.

Proposition 1: In business enterprise, business relationships are the critical source of competitiveness.

It is our viewpoint that market exchange is a necessary attribute of business enterprise. But, due to the significance of those market exchange relations that evolve to the kind of business relationships discussed earlier, competitiveness is based on business relationships rather than on market exchange per se. Only those exchange relations that develop into business relationships have long-term consequences for the firm. Moreover, the nature of the competitive advantage of an enterprise comes out of the specific way in which its business relationships are connected. In various ways the different relationships of a firm can be connected to each other in the sense that development of one relationship facilitates or hinders the performance in another, or requires the adaptation of activities in yet more relationships (Anderson, Håkansson and Johanson, 1994). Changes in the way business activities are carried out in the relationship with an important customer may require that business activities in relation to other customers are adjusted and that business with suppliers is modified. Product development activities with a certain customer may require that development activities are carried out in conjunction with suppliers and thus may make it possible to offer a new product to other customers. More subtly, the intentions and expectations of one business relationship are interrelated with those in other relationships, as is the interpretations of any one relationship. Thus the competitiveness of a firm may be a result of its ability to connect business relationships.

Proposition 2: The competitiveness of business enterprise is a result of its ability to connect business relationships.

Each business enterprise is based on a unique, connected set of business relationships. With regard to knowledge, we mean, that although each business relationship is unique and provides unique, tacit knowledge, the combined knowledge from a set of business relationships gives the business enterprise its specific competitive ability. Thus, the business enterprise creates new knowledge through market exchange in a set of interrelated business relationships. It is worth observing that this knowledge creation process is not separated from business activities, it is embedded in those activities. It is also worth noting that this process is not only a matter of the firm's activities, it is as much a matter of the activities of the exchange partners. The knowledge creation processes of the partners are co-ordinated by working business relationships and this coordination may very well extend far beyond the horizon of a specific firm. In this way the long-term business relevance is secured.

The business enterprise develops knowledge that is relevant to the needs and capabilities of its most important business partners.

5. *International Business Enterprise*

Against this background we define international business enterprise as a business enterprise connecting business relationships in several countries (Figure 1). This definition does not say anything at all about production abroad or about foreign subsidiaries. From a definitional point of view, international production is irrelevant for the business enterprise.

The definition says that the international business enterprise is engaged in business relationships with business partners abroad. It means that market exchange in international or foreign markets is a necessary, but not sufficient, condition for international business enterprise. To satisfy the requirements the international business enterprise must have the kind of structural constraint associated with business relationships. Without such constraints, there is no reason to assume that the term international means anything specific with regard to the competitiveness of the enterprise. International business enterprise assumes a commit-

Figure 1. The Structure of International Business Enterprises.

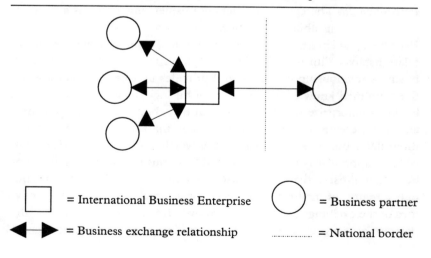

☐ = International Business Enterprise   ◯ = Business partner

◀▶ = Business exchange relationship   ⋯⋯ = National border

ment to exchange abroad and a corresponding commitment by actors abroad to exchange with the business enterprise. Basically, it assumes a history of at least one business relationship abroad and expectations of future exchange in this business relationship abroad.

The definition also suggests that internationalisation of business enterprise is a matter of the degree to which the business enterprise connects business relationships in different countries. Connections can be of various kinds. We can make a distinction between, product connections, on one hand, that is the interdependencies between business relationships due to resource and product exchange among suppliers and customers, and knowledge connections based on knowledge exchange on the other.

Production activities, the transformation of resources into products, can be seen as the main product connection. It connects supplier relationships and customer relationships. There are also product connections among different supplier relationships if they are complementary, or otherwise interrelated. Correspondingly, there are product connections among customer relationships if they are interrelated in some way. Evidently, there are also a number of logistic product connections.

Clearly, the two kinds of connection are closely related. R&D is a kind of knowledge connection; even production may be a knowledge connection since it may combine knowledge gained in several business relationships. There is reason, however, to assume that product and knowledge connections are intertwined. A connection which, from one point of view is seen as a product connection can, from another, be regarded as a knowledge connection. And knowledge from one business relationship may be used in production for another (Anderson, Håkansson and Johanson, 1994).

Connections are not given once and for all. They are created, developed, modified and broken by those who manage them because they consider it to be beneficial for some reason. In fact, the connections evolve when ordinary arms-length transactions become transformed into business relationships in which the partners are aware of each other's specific needs and capabilities. When they learn about these needs and capabilities they may connect them to their own, which, in turn, are based on their business relationships with other partners.

We have reason to consider the scope of connections, that is, the number of connected business relationships and the extent of exchange in the business relationships that are connected. In the extreme case we have all production and R&D concentrated in a single unit connecting all supplier and all customer relationships. But direct connections may also exist between two specific business relationships. Thus, in every business enterprise there is a specific pattern of connections between the business relationships, and in every international business enterprise there is a specific pattern connecting the business relationships in different countries.

The operational connections mentioned above are managed through various organisational arrangements. The typical way of managing connections in international business enterprise is through the subsidiary, which usually manages connections between the business relationships in a certain country market as well as those with other markets (Figure 2a). Other organisational units may manage connections among business relationships in several countries. Still other units manage connections among business relationships concerning a specific product field or knowledge field. Some connections are managed without special formal organisational units, i.e. through bilateral relations between different subsidiaries.

The internationalisation of a business enterprise can increase through the extent to which the business enterprise is engaged in business relationships with actors in different countries and through the extent to which the business enterprise connects those relationships. Moreover, we can speak about multinational business enterprises (Figure 2b) as different enterprises from international business ones: the former being business enterprises comprising business enterprises in several countries without necessarily having connecting relationships. In that sense, it is a more general phenomenon than the international business enterprise.

The multinational business enterprise contains separate business enterprises in different countries, while the international business enterprise does not necessarily have business enterprises in several countries, it may very well be one single business enterprise engaged in international business relationships. But international business enterprises may also comprise a number of business enterprises in different countries that are connected to each other.

This definition of the international business enterprise and the corresponding view of internationalisation implies that production, production activities and production units are seen primarily as means of support to, and as the connections of, the business relationships. In the

Figure 2a. The International   Figure 2b. The Multinational
Business Enterprise.   Business Enterprise.

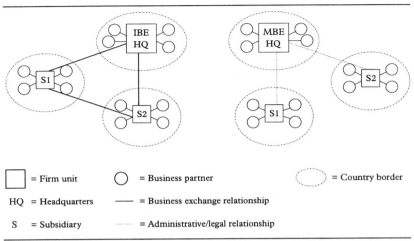

= Firm unit   ◯ = Business partner   ⬭ = Country border

HQ = Headquarters   —— = Business exchange relationship

S = Subsidiary   ⋯⋯ = Administrative/legal relationship

same way, R&D units are considered as supporting and connecting business relationships. Once again, this does not mean that production and R&D are irrelevant, but rather that their relevance is derived from their ability to facilitate business relationship building and utilisation. It means that the relationships with customers and suppliers are lasting, structural constraints that can serve as a starting point when trying to understand the distinctive competitive ability of business enterprise better than production. It is meant to be a contrasting approach to the received view that market exchange mainly has the function of finding an outlet for the products and of getting access to resources.

From an international business point of view, we say that being engaged in business relationships with customers in a certain country market is more constraining than having a production unit in that country. Thus we say that it is easier to serve those customers from another production unit than to establish new business relationships in order to find an outlet for the production. It is easier to replace a production unit by another than to substitute a business relationship for another. Moreover, and perhaps more importantly, we say that with regard to knowledge development, and consequently long term competitiveness, the business relationships are more important than the production units.

Let us illustrate our discussion so far. Our definitions stress the operating characteristics of the firm. An exporting firm is an international business enterprise if it is engaged in working business relationships with foreign customers. It has supplier relationships in the domestic market, and possibly also in foreign markets, and customer relationships in the foreign market and, at a minimum, the relationships are connected through the product and resource flows, and possibly also through feedback of knowledge from the foreign markets. In such a case, internationalisation means that the non-domestic business relationships increase in importance in relation to the domestic ones. They may become more important in terms of value or quantity of business but also in terms of knowledge development. Evidently, the connections can be organised in various ways and we have reason to return to that later on.

As a contrast, consider AGA, the Swedish gas company, which has subsidiaries in a great number of countries. Most of these subsidiaries serve only their home market and use resources supplied in that market. There are no product or resource connections amongst markets and, unless there is exchange of knowledge among the subsidiaries and the parent, AGA is not an international business enterprise, but a multinational one. But if there are knowledge connections between the subsidiaries or between the parent and subsidiaries, it is an international business enterprise and internationalisation in such a firm is primarily a matter of knowledge connections among the subsidiaries. However, the single subsidiaries may very well be business enterprises in the sense that they connect business relationships. The subsidiary can even be an international business enterprise if it connects business relationships across borders (Forsgren, Holm and Johanson, 1992).

As another example, consider SKF, the ball-bearing company. It manufactures different ball bearings in specialised factories in different countries from which all other countries are supplied. It is most definitely an international business enterprise. Resources, products and knowledge flow among the subsidiaries in the different countries. Obviously, there are a number of connections between the different countries and these connections clearly require a complex organisation structure. Thus, SKF is a highly internationalised business enterprise in our terms. Observe, however, that SKF is not highly internationalised because it has big production units in a number of countries, it is highly internationalised because those units are closely connected to each other.

6. Control of International Business Enterprise

In the discussion of business relationships, we stressed that business relationships cannot be understood by those who are not directly involved. Still less can they be controlled by outsiders except in so far as they can be damaged. Thus, headquarters cannot understand what is going on in business relationships unless they participate actively. Nor can they judge if the subsidiary invests suitably in its business relationships or if it reduces their value by making too little effort. As subsidiaries in international business enterprises derive their profits from business relationships, ordinary profitability criteria are meaningless when considering their profitability. This places severe restrictions on the possibility of controlling subsidiaries in the international business enterprise.

In fact we have reason to assume that management of international business enterprise is a struggle for power to influence the future development of the enterprise (Fliegstein 1985, Forsgren 1989, March 1962, Pfeffer 1978). In this process the different units mobilise resources in pursuit of the interests of their own units. Involvement in important business relationships is critical in the struggle since business relationships can be seen as the most important resources in the international business enterprise. Power is therefore derived from control over business relationships (Pfeffer and Salancik 1978).

Proposition 3: In international business enterprises, power is derived from control over important business relationships.

Observe that control over business relationships is not unilateral. To some extent it can be exercised by the business partner. This means that control in international business enterprise, to some extent, emanates from important business partners.

Proposition 3 means that subsidiaries in international business enterprises can exercise control over other units and activities to the extent that they control business relationships that are important for those units. Power may be based on customer relationships, supplier relationships or other relationships in which either product exchange or knowledge exchange is important.

Since the connections among business relationships are the distinctive feature of business enterprise, there is reason to assume that the subsidiaries – or other units – with power based on business relationships use this power to gain control over critical connections (Forsgren, Holm and Johanson, 1995). In that way they are able to develop their exchange and thereby the future development of the international business enterprise.

Proposition 4: In an international business enterprise, units controlling important business relationships use their power to gain control over important connections.

Business relationships with external partners are usually managed by subsidiaries hence they can use this resource to gain influence inside the international business enterprise. Internal relationships, in contrast, are connected to headquarters on both sides, which strengthens headquarters' control over subsidiaries. The combination of internal and external relationships in the international business enterprise contributes to its complex control structure.

7. *Conclusion*

In this chapter, we have introduced and elaborated on the concept of the international business enterprise. By emphasising the business aspect of the firm, i.e., the exchange relationships between the business enterprise and its business partners, quite another appearance of the international firm is forged. In contrast to the received view of the firm, where production and the way it is organised around the world is the key constituent of competitive advantage, we have argued that it is the capability to connect business relationships that creates competitiveness. Production and R&D are seen as means of maintaining and developing business relationships. In addition to the effect on competitive advantage, the lasting relationships are assumed to influence the control structure of international business enterprises. We propose that units in international business enterprises use their control over important business relationships to gain control over important connections. We have related this to the difficulties of controlling business enterprises at a distance. Because of the long-term horizon of the business relationship, it is impossible to know if efforts made today is an investment in the business relationship in the long run.

References

Anderson, J. C., H. Håkansson and J. Johanson, 1994, »Dyadic Business Relationships Within a Business Network Context«, *Journal of Marketing*, Vol. 58, pp. 1 – 15.

Axelsson, B. and G. Easton, 1992, *Industrial Networks: A New View of Reality*, Routledge, London.

Bartlett, C. and S. Ghoshal, 1989, *Managing Across Borders – The Transnational Solution*, Hutchinson Business Books, London.

Caves, R. E., 1982, *Multinational enterprise and economic analysis*, Cambridge University Press, Cambridge.

Dunning, J. H., 1988, *Multinationals, Technology and Competitiveness*, Pergamon Press, Oxford.

Dwyer, F. R., P. H. Schurr and S. Oh, 1987, »Developing Buyer – Seller Relationships« *Journal of Marketing*, Vol. 51, pp. 11 – 27.

Fliegstein, N., 1985, »The spread of the multinational form among large firms, 1919 – 1979«, *American Sociological Review*, 50, June, pp. 377 – 91.

Ford, D., (ed.), 1990, *Understanding Business Markets: Interaction, Relationships and Networks*, Academic Press, San Diego.

Forsgren, M., 1989, *Managing the Internationalization Process: The Swedish Case*, Routledge, London.

Forsgren, M., U. Holm and J. Johanson, 1995, »Internationalization of the Second Degree – The Emergence of European-Based Centres in Swedish Firms, in S. Young, and J. Hamill, (eds.), *Europe and the Multinationals – Issues and Responses for the 1990s*, Edward Elgar, London.

Forsgren, M., U. Holm and J. Johanson, 1995, »Division Headquarters Go Abroad: A Step in the Internationalization of the Multinational Corporation«, *Journal of Management Studies*, 32:4, July.

Ghoshal, S. and C. Bartlett, 1990, The Multinational Corporation as an Interorganizational Network, *Academy of Management Review*, 15 (4), pp. 603 – 25.

Ghoshal, S. and C. Bartlett, 1993, »The Multinational Corporation as an Interorganizational Network«, in S. Ghoshal and D. E. Westney (eds.) *Organization Theory and the Multinational Corporation*, St Martins Press, New York.

Hallén, L., 1986, »A Comparison of Strategic Marketing Approaches«, in Turnbull, P. W. and J.-P. Valla, (eds.), *Strategies for International Industrial Marketing*, pp. 235-264, Croom-Helm, London.

Hallén, L., J. Johanson and N. Seyed-Mohamed, 1991, »Interfirm Adaptation in Business Relationships«, *Journal of Marketing*, Vol. 55, pp. 29-37.

Holm, U., J. Johanson and P. Thilenius, 1995, »Headquarters' Knowledge of Subsidiary Network Contexts in the Multinational Corporation«, *International Studies of Management & Organization*, Vol. 25, Nos. 1-2, pp. 97-120.

Håkansson, H., (ed.), 1982, *International Marketing and Purchasing of Industrial Goods – An Interaction Approach*, Wiley, New York.

Håkansson, H., 1989, *Corporate Technological Behavior: Cooperations and Networks*, Routledge, London.

Håkanson, L. and U. Zander, 1986, *Managing International Research and Development*, Sveriges Mekanförbund, Stockholm.

Jacobson, R., 1992, The Austrian School of Strategy, *Academy of Management Review*, 17 (4), pp. 782-807.

Kirzner, I. M., 1973, *Competition and Entrepreneurship*, The University of Chicago Press, Chicago.

Laage-Hellman, J., 1989, *Technological Development in Industrial Networks*, Acta Universitatis Upsaliensis, Comprehensive Summaries of Uppsala Dissertations, The Faculty of Social Sciences, 16, Almqvist & Wiksell, Stockholm.

Lundvall, B. Å., 1985, *Product Innovation and User-Producer Interaction*, Aalborg University Press, Aalborg, Denmark.

March, J. G., 1962, The Business Firm as a Political Coalition, *Journal of Politics*, 24, pp. 662-678.

Pfeffer, J. and G. R. Salancik, 1978, *The External Control of Organizations: A Resource Dependence Perspective*, Harper & Row, New York.

Pfeffer, J., 1978, »The Micropolitics of Organizations«, in W. M. Marshall and associates (eds.), *Environment and Organizations*, pp. 29-50, Jossey-Bass, San Francisco.

Porter, M. E., 1986, »Competition in Global Industries: a conceptual framework«, in M. E. Porter (ed.), *Competition in Global Industries*, Harvard Business School Press, Boston, Mass.

Porter, M. E., 1990, *The Competitive Advantage of Nations*, The Free Press, New York.

Ring, P. S. and Van de Ven, A. H., 1992, Structuring Cooperative Relationships Between Organizations, *Strategic Management Journal*, 13, pp. 483-498.

Snehota, I., 1990, *Notes on a Theory of Business Enterprise*, Doctoral dissertation, Uppsala University

Turnbull, P. W. and J.-P. Valla, 1986, in P. W. Turnbull and J.-P. Valla, (eds.), *Strategies for International Industrial Marketing*, Croom-Helm, London.

Zajac, E. J. and Olsen, C. P., 1993, From Transaction Cost to Transaction Value Analysis: Implications for the Study of Interorganizational Strategies, *Journal of Management Studies*, Vol. 3 (January), pp. 131-45.

3. Comparative Institutional Advantage:[1]

Assessing the Impact of International Differences in Corporate Governance

Steen Thomsen

1. Introduction

Although the great debate between communism and capitalism may have reached a conclusion, a battle of the systems between different modes of capitalism continues (Walter, 1993; Albert 1991). This implies a »systems competition« in which sets of institutions compete at the global level. In international business studies the »wealth of nations« theme has been restated by Michael Porter's influential contribution (Porter, 1990) and a number of researchers have addressed the importance of institutions for international competitiveness (Kogut, 1993; Casson, 1991a, 1991b; Zysman, 1995; Delorme and Dopfer, 1994).

This chapter argues that the new institutional economics provides a powerful approach to international business research on international competitiveness and the wealth of nations. Contributions by Ronald Coase (1937, 1960, 1972), Oliver Williamson (1975, 1985), Kenneth Arrow (1969, 1974), James Buchanan, Douglas North (1990), Michael Jensen and Eugene Fama (1983a, 1983b), Armen Alchian and Harold Demsetz (1972), Oliver Hart (1995) and others have important implications for assessing the competitiveness of alternative modes of capitalism[2]. Focusing on institutional differences, national and corporate competitiveness can be analysed as a question of comparative institutional advantage: how effective are national and corporate institutions in sav-

---

1. I am grateful to Peter Nedergaard for suggesting the phrase "comparative institutional advantage".
2. A survey of some of the main ideas is given in Millgrom and Roberts (1992).

ing on transaction costs? Lowering transaction rather than production costs is considered the key to productivity and wealth.

At first glance evaluating institutions by their ability to lower transaction costs represents a gross simplification since institutions should ultimately be evaluated on their total wealth creation including the benefits which they allow society to capture net of the total costs of production and exchange. To deal with this problem transaction costs are defined simply as the opportunity costs of institutions (i.e. the »costs of running the economic system«, Arrow 1969). This definition still leaves unresolved a priori how much of the wealth creation differential between nations or companies is attributable to institutional differences and how much can be attributed to other factors like capital and labour supply, natural resource endowments or technology and how much is due to interaction effects. The underlying assumption behind the comparative institutional advantage concept is that institutions and especially interaction effects between institutions and technology explain a large share of the differentials. This approach may be contrasted both with the neoclassical view which places more emphasis on the availability of production factors and with more recent attempts at explaining endogenous technological change (Romer 1987).

2. Institutions and the Competitive Advantage of Nations

In *The Competitive Advantage of Nations* Michael Porter (1990) attempts to explain the causes of the international competitiveness of nations. He measures the competitiveness of nations by a kind of revealed comparative advantage, i.e. »large exports« of certain products supplemented by other measures. He observes that nations' exports are often concentrated on groups of related commodities or industries (»clusters«) and explains these patterns by a broad framework (the »diamond«) encompassing domestic supply and demand conditions, industrial structure and of other factors. No mention is made of institutional differences.

The »diamond« is a very broad framework bordering on the all-encompassing. The validity of such a framework cannot easily be tested, nor can it give unequivocal policy guidelines. In contrast, a theory of national competitiveness should arguably give rise to at least one refutable hypothesis. To the extent that the Porter project does contain meaningful (refutable) hypotheses, it seems to be the continued insistence on the importance of domestic conditions to international competitiveness: the importance of national factor conditions, the qualitative nature of the domestic market, domestic related and supporting industries and domestic rivalry. If the word domestic is left out or replaced by »national and international«, these hypotheses reduce to a complete truism: international competitiveness depends on international supply and demand. Or even worse: international competitiveness depends on the international conditions of competition.

Therefore the nation effect is crucial to Porter's argument. But why should national conditions be so important? Why cannot international conditions equally well stimulate national competitive advantage? This question is not addressed in Porter's study. For instance, factor conditions broadly defined may be influenced by foreign technology and other imports. The qualitative nature of foreign markets may exert a strong demand-pull effect on the national economy. National producers may rely on an international network of related and supporting industries. International rivalry could substitute for rivalry among domestic producers.

One answer is to focus on the definition of a nation. What is a nation? What makes nations different? Under the institutional approach nation states can be conceived as sets of institutions and institutional efficiency may be seen as the primary determinant of comparative advantage.

Of course, as is well known in international economics, trade patterns do not necessarily reflect revealed national comparative advantage. And as noted by Adam Smith and others, the interesting question is not really the trade, but rather the wealth of nations. If, for instance, a particular industry in one nation enjoys privileged access to low cost factor inputs, this may lead to artificially high production and exports of particular products, but this does not necessarily reflect national competitive advantage. This is trivial if the industry is subsidised by the government – in that case every dollar of exports financed by the taxpayers may well deduct from national wealth. It may also be true, however, if national factor conditions are payed less than their opportunity costs and could have been used more efficiently if exported as raw materials to other nations. In short, more (exporting) in the Porter sense is not necessarily better.

Comparative institutional efficiency can explain why nations with apparent factor advantages such as abundance of raw materials or educated labour do not necessarily reap the benefits, as seems to have been the case in Eastern European and many developing countries. Institutional advantage may furthermore explain why some countries without initial factor advantages manage to develop them over time (e.g. Japan's car and electronics industry).

Institutions are defined as socially created »rules of the game«, which govern a country's economic activities – e.g. laws or organisational forms. Of primary interest are the allocation of economic activities between the private sector and government, between markets and hierarchies within the private sector as well as between formal institutions and informal mechanisms like customs, culture and ethical standards.

Apart from efficiency considerations, institutional differences may also lead to different national price and quantity distortions (North 1990) which will of course influence international trade patterns. For instance, different forms of capitalism may have different implications for the costs of capital and labour, corporate objectives etc.

Historically, economic growth has often taken place in virtuous circles in which spill overs between sectors or between buyers and sellers have lead to mutually reinforcing product development and productivity growth. Porter recognises the dynamic interaction between the diamond factors and that »as this mutual reinforcement proceeds, the cause and effect of individual determinants become blurred« (Porter 1990, p. 132). Clearly, there are important feedback effects between e.g. supply and demand conditions. In contrast, institutions change slowly in response to economic conditions (the short term feedback effects are small so they can be considered as exogenous variables). Institutional analysis therefore provides a good starting point for causal explanations of the international competitiveness of nations.

At present economics has no unified theory of institutions. At least four different perspectives coexist according to their analytical focus and their conclusions about economic efficiency (figure 1). Economic theories may be focused on markets and prices only or include a broader theory of non-market institutions. They also differ by their views on efficiency – i.e. to what extent the outcomes of market and political processes are socially optimal.

Figure 1. Economic perspectives on institutions

	Efficiency	Inefficiency
Markets	Efficient markets	Market failure
Institutions	Efficient institutions	Institutional failure

Efficient markets. The logic of the efficient markets perspective is familiar to economists since it is deeply ingrained in neoclassical microeconomics. Markets are assumed to be efficient (a broadened version of the efficient markets hypothesis in financial economics). Prices and quantities adjust quickly to optimal market clearing equilibria. Information is quickly disseminated so prices reflect all available information – i.e. prices reflect true marginal costs. Abstracting from (small) transaction costs, markets are complete. The obvious implication is to use the market mechanism as much as possible: deregulate and open up capital markets, remove non-standard institutions, barriers to entry and other impediments to the market. Encourage competition. Reduce or regulate monopoly. Such recommendations are very much what has been suggested by policy proposals on the harmonisation of European capital markets.

The market failure perspective, which is embodied in welfare economics, assumes the existence of market failures created by returns to scale, externalities, asymmetric information etc. The obvious policy implication is government intervention.

Efficient institutions. Another brand of economics aims explicitly the comparative analysis of institutions (e.g. Fama and Jensen, 1983; Williamson, 1975, 1985). Here, transaction costs provide a rationale for non-market institutions. But the standard assumption is that in a free enterprise economy, a combination of rational choice and evolutionary pressures will tend to select an efficient mix of markets and non-market institutions (the efficient institutions hypothesis). The policy implications tend to be laissez-faire, e.g. to leave room for alternative non-market institutions: economic agents should be free to write the contracts and create the institutions that they wish to.

Institutional failure. If the prevailing institutions (market or non-market, private or government) are sometimes inefficient, this provides a rationale for government intervention. However, institutional failure can also imply government failure or the failure of non-market institutions, which calls for more, not less market governance.

The lack of agreement on the proper content of a new institutional economics may seem to be an obstacle to application in international business studies or international economics. But this chapter argues that a theory of comparative institutional advantage must rely on an »institutional failures framework«.

The argument is simple. First, if all nations adopt efficient institutions, institutions cancel out as a parameter of international competition among nations. Instead, as in neoclassical economics, the analysis of comparative advantage can be accomplished without reference to the institutional set up. Secondly, by the same argument market failure will only matter as long as they are not all corrected by the same kind of public intervention in all nations. If market failures go uncorrected in some countries, but not in others this is an instance of (non-market) institutional failure. All in all, therefore, only the »institutional failure« view can generate an interesting theory of the international competitiveness of nations. This still leaves room for the usual political viewpoints: one being that political or private non-market failures generate too little market governance in the economy, the other being that political failures imply too little intervention.

A theory of comparative institutional advantage, therefore, needs to contain both a theory of efficient institutions (to make interesting recommendations) and a theory of institutional failure (to explain why the efficient institutions have not already been adopted).

Neoclassical economics more or less explicitly assumes that national economies operate at the production possibility frontier. Applied to institutions, this means that countries will adopt the most efficient set of institutions at their disposal. In many circumstances (some of which are specified as standard conditions for efficiency in general equilibrium theory) markets will do. Relaxing these assumptions, government intervention has traditionally been explained by market failures – e.g. externalities and transaction costs (see Shepherd 1989). However, more recent theory (public choice) makes clear that there can also be political failure in which case government intervention may occur as a response to interest group pressures (e.g. to salvage failing firms or industries, to protect vested interests etc.). Public choice theory offers a much more sophisticated view of government intervention than the naive »nirvana economics« in which the government acts impeccably to correct market inefficiencies. It provides a theory which can explain why political intervention is sometimes inefficient.

This concept of political failure can be generalised to include non-market failures in the private sector as well. For instance, agency problems can be a source of inefficient decisions in both private and government companies. It is not unreasonable so assume, for instance, that inefficient managers will generally oppose changes which may damage their own position. Secondly, inertia and other path dependencies may generate an institutional stability that may not correspond to a changed environment. Evolutionary theory (e.g. Nelson and Winther, 1982) predicts that institutional misfits may survive for extended periods of time in environments characterised by loose selection mechanisms (e.g. a low intensity of competition).

Allowing for inefficiencies raises the possibility that nations may differ with respect to institutional efficiency: i.e. that economic activities in some nations may be conducted at smaller (transaction) costs which will give them a comparative advantage in the international marketplace. The concept of endogenous inefficiency therefore provide a crucial first assumption in developing a theory of »comparative institutional advantage«. Paraphrasing Roe (1994), the neoclassical model explains institutions as arising from economies of scale, risk aversion and individual self interest. But if the neoclassical model were universal, it would predict that nations with similar economies would have similar institutional structures. There is a best way to make steel and presumably there is a best way to organise large steel firms. But, on the contrary, international differences in institutional structure suggest that there is more than one way to deal with economic problems. And, the differences suggest that differing histories, cultures and paths of economic development better explain the differing structures than neoclassical economics.

3. Corporate Governance as Modes of Capitalism

This section applies the institutional approach to the recently very popular topic of corporate governance.

The institutional view traces the origins of corporate governance back to comparative ownership institutions, the idea being that if capitalism is defined by private ownership, modes of capitalism can be characterised by alternative private ownership institutions. A classical example well known in the field of comparative economic systems is market-based (Anglo-American) vs financial (e.g. German) capitalism. In market-based systems, share markets play a dominant role as regulators of company behaviour, whereas financial intermediaries (banks) appear much more prominently in financial modes. Market-based systems tend to be atomistic with many buyers and sellers as well as many securities traded which implies obvious advantages in terms of liquidity and risk efficiency (low capital costs). Financial modes of capitalism, on the other hand, tend to be more concentrated with concentrations of share ownership in banks and financial institutions – which should in theory mean more monitoring and greater incentive efficiency (closer alignment of managerial actions with owner preferences).

To illustrate, Table 1 (taken from Pedersen and Thomsen, 1995) compares ownership of the 100 largest industrial corporations in the USA, Japan and Europe.

Table 1. Types of ownership of the 100 largest companies in USA, Europe and Japan

Ownership	USA	Europe	Japan
Dispersed ownership	90	36	40
Dominant ownership	7	33	57
Family owned	3	13	2
Government owned	0	18	1
Total	100	100	100

Sources: Pedersen and Thomsen (1995).

The table demonstrates that dispersed ownership (defined as the largest owner holding less than 20% of the voting rights) is the rule in the US but much less common (although not insignificant) in Europe and Japan. Dominant minority ownership (defined as the largest owner holding between 20 and 50% of the votes or alternatively as Keiretsu affiliation) is predominant in Japan. In Europe, a significant share of the largest industrial companies are majority owned by either individuals/families or governments. These differences primarily reflect the operation of different corporate governance models. The U.S. system can be characterised as market based since the markets for corporate control play an important role in the corporate governance of US companies and since these market resemble the perfect markets in neoclassical microeconomics: many buyers and sellers, transparency, liquidity etc. On the other hand, the Japanese model depends on cross-ownership within corporate groups (Roe, 1994), which may under certain circumstances improve the incentives for information sharing and transaction specific investment (Kester 1992).

Further analysis finds little evidence of a distinct European governance model, but rather a set of highly differentiated national systems (Pedersen and Thomsen 1995). The UK system is market based with high degrees of ownership dispersion. Like the Japanese model the German system tends to rely on dominant minority ownership, but ownership concentration tends to be larger, and bank ownership tends to be more important. Government ownership of industry plays a significant role in France, Sweden, Austria and Italy. Subsidiaries of multinational companies predominate in Belgium. Personal and/or cooperative ownership is important in many of the smaller countries like Denmark, the Netherlands and Norway. Whether this pluralism is a liability or an asset for the global competitiveness of European companies is a fundamental question for corporate strategies as well a for industrial policy at the national and EU level.

The answers given to this question depend critically on the underlying theory of institutions. Figure 2 applies the institutional typology developed in section 2 to the corporate governance discussion.

Figure 2. Institutional perspectives on European corporate governance

	Efficiency	Inefficiency
Markets	**Efficient markets:** Establish stock market efficiency by increasing market size, transparency and homogeneity. Adopt the Anglo-American model. Abolish dual class shares and majority ownership of public companies, merge stock exchanges, internationalise and diversify portfolios, standardise accounting and privatise.	**Market failure:** Scale Economies and market power create big companies with agency problems which must be regulated (in the interest of the small shareholder and society). Adopt laws on information disclosure etc. to defend minority shareholders.
Institutions	**Efficient institutions:** Existing institutions are efficient so let them be, but deregulate and privatise. Malfunctions are caused by government intervention. Privatise and end differential tax treatment.	**Institutional failure:** Establish the optimal degree of intervention. Enable competition between institutions (e.g. one and twotier boards. Government and private ownership).

Under the efficient markets perspective share markets are supposed to function well at small transaction costs. For instance, share markets are supposed to value shares correctly or at least make no systematic errors in the valuation. Share prices will therefore correctly represent the risk-adjusted value of companies and market transactions of ownership (like mergers and acquisitions) will be efficient in allocating ownership to its highest and socially most productive value in use. This trust in the market mechanism has been the underlying logic behind the European integration process, e.g. the internal market. The same view was adopted in the Booz-Allen report which recommended opening up European share markets to promote industrial restructuring.

An alternative viewpoint is to allow competition between institutions. An implication of the efficient institutions hypothesis is that the ownership structures observed in a free enterprise economy will tend to be efficient even though they do not necessarily imply open markets. For example; if there are significant costs of transacting in unfettered markets for corporate control, it may under some circumstances pay off to circumvent the markets by restricted ownership, anti-takeover amendments, conglomerate ownership, Keiretsu structures etc. According to the efficient institutions hypothesis such non-standard ownership institutions will under some circumstances be more effective than the classic joint stock company. The obvious policy implication is to end government restrictions and let the individual private agents decide on the institutions they want.

The market failure approach regards failures in the stock market as a rationale for government intervention: protection of minority shareholders, measures to improve the social accountability of companies (ethics, industrial relations, the environment), and measures to abolish hostile takeovers. Strangely, this is the view which underlies the highly regulated US corporate governance model which has set high standards for information disclosure and limited the influence of banks and financial investors to protect small shareholders. A different version is the traditional French preference for government intervention in strategic industries, although government ownership is not currently fashionable.

The institutional failure approach is to recognise that both private and government agents make mistakes and that an optimal mix of intervention should be found. A possible solution is to recognise the importance of asymmetric information, i.e. to advocate only general intervention which does not require the political decision makers to have too much information about the economy. This means that policy makers should concentrate on institutions rather than specific activities.

Since, under the institutional failure perspective, it is not clear what kind of corporate governance model is optimal, Figure 3 and table 2 compare the performance of US, European and Japanese companies on some relevant performance dimensions.

Figure 3 compares OECD estimates of the return on capital in the business sector in the US, Japan and OECD Europe. The estimates are based on national accounts and as such subject to national differences in accounting methods. The measure calculates gross operating surplus (value added net of labour costs) and divides by a measure of the capital stock at replacement costs (which makes the capital returns more accurate than many accounting measures). Unfortunately the housing stock is included both in the profit measure (imputed services) and in the capital stock measure. The OECD estimates that the measures therefore tend to overestimate capital returns by an average of 3 % points.

Figure 3. Return on capital (%).

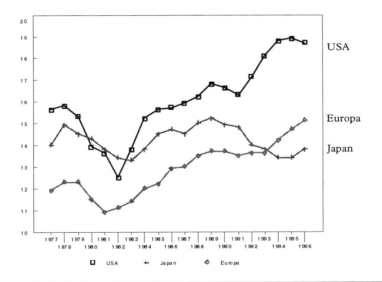

Source: OECD Economic Outlook 1994.

Nevertheless, abstracting from uncertainties about the general level, it would appear that US companies have consistently had higher rates of return their European and Japanese competitors. Note also that profitability in the US appears to have increased substantially since the mid 80s, while it remained at roughly the same level in Europa. At the same time important US industries like electronics and cars appear to have regained competitiveness vis-a-vis Japan and the rest of the world. Part of the reason may have been increasingly active markets for corporate control in the US (Jensen 1989). This raises the provocative question of whether the US corporate governance model has proved to be more efficient and adaptive in the business climate of the 1990s.

In answering this question, higher profit rates should not be taken as an unqualified measure of success. They could also indicate high costs of capital or accounting differences. Blaine (1994) compares the profitability of US, German and Japanese companies and finds no significant differences after controlling for accounting principles.

Furthermore, other performance measures neeed to be considered.

Table 2 presents relative market shares of the largest corporations in selected industries.

It appears that US companies have lost relative market share over the

Table 2. The share of US, Japanese and European companies of total turnover of the world's 200 largest non-financial companies 1986 and 1992.

Industry	1986			1992		
	USA	Europe	Japan	USA	Europe	Japan
Oil	48,5%	33,6%	5,4%	40,7%	35,9%	9,2%
Metal	18,3%	39,4%	36,9%	4,1%	40,5%	47,0%
Chemicals	41,5%	43,2%	6,6%	34,4%	44,0%	9,7%
Electronics	26,7%	22,8%	34,7%	14,8%	23,7%	41,4%
Computer	83,6%	5,1%	11,2%	78,7%	0	21,3%
Cars	42,5%	27,5%	26,2%	33,1%	34,1%	31,1%
Aerospace	91,3%	8,7%	0	69,6%	24,7%	5,7%
Food	58,4%	26,7%	2,8%	51,5%	30,6%	8,6%
All industries	44,1%	31,5%	15,8%	34,0%	34,5%	21,7%

Source: EU: Panorama of European Industries, 1994, p. 77-82.

Adopted from Thomsen and Pedersen (1995b).

six year period in all manufacturing industries. While there may be a number of reasons for this apart from corporate governance (e.g. the decline of the dollar), there is no indication that US companies are outcompeting their Japanese and European competitors in the global market place. Doubts have been raised of whether the quantitative and profitseeking investment policies adopted by US companies have lead to myopia and too much profittaking whereas soft investments have been neglected. But doubts have also been raised about the efficiency of the Japanese system during the recent recession, especially about the value of close ties between financial institutions and industry during a financial crisis. Similar doubts have surfaced in Germany and France. The battle of the systems remains undecided, which makes it unclear what model EU policy makers and companies should aim for.

In addition, there are other reasons to avoid policy activism. By nature institutions are supposed to be long term, structural constraints. Institutional policy may therefore be something of a contradiction in terms. It may be better to think of »institutional reforms«. Policies are alternative courses of action open to a government. Institutions are long term rules of the economic game. If institutions are frequently changed by government decree, they cease to have this long term property and create uncertainty instead of reducing it which is one of the principal rationales for establishing them in the first place. It seems more correct to distinguish between institutional reforms which happen only rarely and government policies which are changed every once in a while. In most countries this difference is highlighted by the existence of a constitution – a law that defines the basic principles by which the country is run. Constitutions are only rarely changed and it usually takes a qualified majority to do so. Consequently policies are always subject to institutional constraints.

Furthermore, institutions are almost invariably tied to culture and ideology. While it is possible to think of several institutional reforms which will affect ownership patterns, (e.g. abolishing dual class shares in Europe or US restrictions on institutional ownership), such initiatives are likely to be opposed for a number of non-economic reasons. In Europe, for instance, dual share schemes and the Keiretsu structure in Japan are also seen as a protection against foreign takeovers. And the US restrictions on institutional ownership appear to be rooted in a cultural resentment of big business and big finance.

4. Conclusion and Research Perspectives

This chapter has proposed a institutional approach to international business studies on the wealth of nations. To further develop this ap-proach it seems necessary to develop and test more specific models of the impact of institutions on the competitiveness and wealth of compa-nies or nations. One possible avenue is to test the »efficient markets« per-spective. Do nations that rely on neoclassical markets do better? Or in terms of ownership: is dispersed ownership associated with better per-formance in terms of profitability, growth or international market share. Given the plurality of institutions actually observed it is very unlikely (and very much against the spirit of the new institutional economics) that one and just one set of institutions will be optimal for all nations un-der all circumstances. It is much more likely that institutions will have to be judged according to their fit with the national and international environment.

In principle, therefore, the research agenda proposed by the institu-tional view is a very broad one: to document the range of institutions that different nations use for certain activities, to asses the fit between institutions and activities as a function of the environment, to test the predicted fit against the actual performance of nations or companies and to give policy and strategic advice on institutional reform where the benefits of institutional change are expected to outweigh the presumably high costs of adjustment.

The range of institutions that can be studied under this approach is large: International comparisons of ownership and board structure, managerial compensation systems, the influence of banks and other credit institutions on corporate decision making, the organisation of la-bour markets as a determinant of labour costs and productivity etc plus of course the organisation of the business sector itself in terms of: differ-ences in aggregate concentration as an indicator of hierarchy, vertical in-tegration and distribution system as a determinant of marketing costs etc. Many of these issues have already been examined, but fewer studies have attempted to relate their finding to international competitiveness and fewer still have made use of transaction cost analysis.

References

Arrow, Kenneth J., 1969. »The Organization of Economic Activity« published in K. J. Arrow, 1983. *General Equilibrium.* Collected Papers. Volume 2, Basil Blackwell.

Aoki, M., Gustafsson, B. and Williamson, O., 1990. *The Firm as a Nexus of Treaties,* Sage Publishers, London.

Bhide, Amar, 1994. »Efficient Markets, Deficient Governance«, *Harvard Business Review,* November-December.

Blaine, Michael, 1994. »Comparing the Profitability of Firms in Germany, Japan and the United States«, *Management International Review,* Vol. 34, No. 2, p. 125-148.

Buchanan, J. M., 1991. *The Economics and the Ethics of Constitutional Order,* University of Michigan Pres, An Arbour.

Casson, Mark, ed. 1991a. *Global research strategy and international competitiveness,* Economic and Social Research Council Competitiveness Series, Cambridge and Oxford: Blackwell.

Casson, Mark, 1991b. *The economics of business culture: Game theory, transaction costs, and economic performance,.* Oxford, Oxford University Press, Clarendon Press.

Charkham, J. P., 1994. *Keeping Good Company – A Study of Corporate Governance in Five Countries.* Clarendon Press, Oxford.

Coase, R. H., 1937. »The Nature of the Firm«, *Economica,* Vol. 4.

Coase, R. H., 1960. »The Problem of Social Cost«, *The Journal of Law and Economics,* Vol. III, October.

Coase, R. H., 1972. »Industrial Organization: A Proposal for Research«, in V. R. Fuchs (ed.). »*Policy Issues and Research opportunitiesin Industrial Organization*«, New York, National Bureau of Economic Research.

Delorme, R. and K. Dopfer, (Eds.), 1994. *The Political Economy of Diversity: Evolutionary Perspectives on Economic Order and Disorder.* European Association for Evolutionary Political Economy Series. Aldershot, U.K.: Elgar;

Fama, E. F. and M. C. Jensen, 1983. »Separation of Ownership and Control«. *Journal of Law and Economics,* Vol XXVI, june, pp. 301-325.

Fama, E. F. and M. C. Jensen, 1983. »Agency Problems and Residual Claims«. *Journal of Law and Economics* Vol. XXVI, june, pp. 327-349.

Holmstrøm B. and J. Tirole, 1989. »The Theory of the Firm«, Schmalensee and Willig (Eds.). *Handbook of Industrial Organization*, Volume I, Elsevier Science Publishers, B.V.

Jensen, M., 1989. »Eclipse of the Public Corporation«. *Harvard Business Review*, September-October.

Kester, W. Carl, 1992. »Industrial Groups as Systems of Contractual Governance«, *Oxford Review of Economic Policy*, Vol. 8, no. 3.

Kogut, B., 1993. *Country competitiveness: Technology and the organizing of work*, Oxford; Oxford University Press.

Milgrom, P. and J. Roberts, 1992. *Economics, Organization and Management*. Prentice-Hall International.

Nelson, R. and Sidney Winther, 1982. »*An Evolutionary Theory of Economic Change*«, Harvard, Belknap Press.

North, D. C., 1990. *Institutions, Institutional Change and Economic Performance*. Cambridge University Press, Cambridge.

Pedersen, T. and S. Thomsen, 1996. »European Models of Corporate Governance«, INT *Working Paper* no 4, Papers and Proceedings, European International Business Academy annual meeting, Urbino, december.

Porter, M. E., 1990. *The Competitive Advantage of Nations*, Free Press.

Porter, M. E., 1992a. »Capital Choices: Changing the Way America Invests in Industry«. *US Council of Competitiveness.*

Porter, Michael E., 1992b. »Capital Disadvantage: America's Failing Capital Investment System«, *Harvard Business Review*, September-October.

Prentice, D. D. and P. R. J. Holland, (Eds.), 1993. *Contemporary Issues in Corporate Governance*. Clarendon Press, Oxford.

Prowse, S., 1995. »Corporate Governance in an International Perspective: A Survey of Corporate Control Mechanisms Among Large Firms in the U.S., U.K., Japan and Germany«, *Financial Markets, Institutions and Instruments* Vol. 4, no. 1 february.

Putterman, L., 1993. »Ownership and the Nature of the Firm«. *Journal of Comparative Economics*, 17, pp. 243-263.

Roe, M. J., 1991. »A Political Theory of Corporate Finance«. *Columbia Law Review* 10. Roe, M. J., 1994. Some Differences in Corporate Governance in Germany, Japan and America., Baum, T., Buxbaum, T. and Hope K. J.

Rydkvist, L. »Dual Class Shares«, *Oxford Review of Economic Policy* Vol. 8 no.3.

Schneider-Lenee', Ellen, 1992. »Corporate Control in Germany«, *Oxford Review of Economic Policy*, Vol. 8, no. 3.

Stiglitz, J. E., »Credit Markets and the Control of Capital«, *Journal of Money, Credit and Banking*, Vol. 17 no. 2.

Stonehill, A. and K. B. Dullum, 1990. »Corporate Wealth Maximization, Takeovers and the Market for Corporate Control«. *Nationaløkonomisk Tidsskrift*, Copenhagen.

Thomsen, S. and T. Pedersen, 1994. European Ownership Structures: The 100 Largest Companies in 6 European Nations, *Proceedings of the 20th Annual Conference of the European International Business Association*, december 13-15th.

Thomsen, S. and T. Pedersen, 1995. »Nationality and Ownership Structure«, *Management International Review*, forthcoming.

Thomsen, S. and T. Pedersen, 1995. »Perspektiver for europæisk virksomhedsstyring« (»Perspectives for European Corporate Governance«), Paper presented to the Federation of Industries EU conference May.

Turnbull, Shann, 1994. »Competitiveness and Corporate Governance«, *Corporate Governance*, Vol. 2, No. 2 April.

Walter, Ingo, 1993. »The Battle of the Systems: Control of Enterprises and the Global Economy«. Institut für Weltwirtschaft and der Universität Kiel, *Kieler Vorträge Neue Folge*, no. 132.

Williamson, O. E., 1985. *The Economic Institutions of Capitalism*. Free Press.

Zysman, John. »National Roots of a »Global Economy«, *Revue-d'Economie-Industrielle*, 71, 1st Trimester, pp. 107-21.

4. The Advantage Paradox of the Multinational Corporation

Mats Forsgren

1. Introduction

An MNC's long-run survival and growth depends on its ability to develop new products and new methods of organisation. In a geographically spread organisation, competitive advantage rests upon its ability to transfer the innovations developed in one subsidiary to the rest of the organisation (Kogut and Zander, 1994). But what are the conditions for innovation in the first place? And what are the possibilities of transferring the innovation from one subsidiary to another, or to the organisation as a whole? This will be dealt with in this chapter. In the first section the preconditions are discussed for an multinational corporation (MNC) to reach a higher degree of competitiveness through innovation than domestic firms. In the following sections some empirical facts are presented about international development projects and knowledge transfer in the MNC. The chapter concludes with a brief summary.

2. The Location of R&D Activities in the MNC

As long as internationalisation of the first degree (Forsgren et al., 1992) was the dominating trend and object of study, the location of innovation activities in the MNC was of minor concern. It was implicitly assumed that the centre, the parent company, was carrying out the innovation of new products and processes and the subsidiaries were then exploiting this innovation in the local markets. This is the usual way to look upon the MNC – as an organisation which successively expands its activities out from the centre and into more and more peripheral countries. Internationalisation starts with exports, advances into production abroad and eventually ends up with extensive internationalisation of the innovation activities. Along with these forms of internationalisation, geographical spreading can also be observed in other functions such as corporate finance, procurement and location of management.

Several studies concerning the location of R&D indicate that the fraction of R&D carried out beyond the home country has been increasing and is now rather extensive in some firms. For instance, the proportion of the Swedish ball-bearing producer, SKF's, US patents of foreign origin has been about 70 per cent since the beginning of 70s. The corresponding figures during the period 1986-90 for Esselte (office equipment), ESAB (welding equipment), Electrolux, (household appliances), AGA (gas applications), Perstorp (chemical products) vary between 40 and 90 per cent. The average share of U.S patents of foreign origin among 29 of Sweden's most internationalised manufacturing firms has increased from 8 per cent in 1970 to over 40 per cent in 1990. (Zander 1994).

According to another study, large Belgian and Dutch firms today perform more of their technological activity outside the home country than inside it and in British, Canadian and Swiss firms the foreign share of R&D activities ranged from between 30 to 40 per cent (Granstrand et.al., 1992). In an investigation of development projects in some Swedish MNCs, it was found that on average 60 per cent were international ventures, that is ventures also involving the foreign subsidiaries as project members. The corresponding figure ten years ago was estimated to be about 40 per cent (Ridderstråle and Hedlund, 1994).

The increasing share of foreign R&D has various explanations which can be accounted for in different ways depending on the type of internationalisation. A basic difference is whether internationalisation has been brought about through organic growth or through acquisition. The former involves a gradual transformation from parent-dependent affiliates that implement innovations developed in the home-base to fully fledged subsidiaries where adaptation of products and processes to meet the demand of local customers becomes more important. Such adaptations may also lead to R&D activities in these subsidiaries. The other route to internationalisation, through the acquisition of foreign firms, means that some of these new subsidiaries' operations will include development activities, which will form part of the MNC's R&D, and thus automatically increase the proportion of foreign R&D in the company. Sometimes the subsidiary's R&D activities can be a strong factor behind the acquisition. Irrespective of the route to internationalisation, and the increase in the proportion of R&D activities abroad, we can conclude that the further the company has developed into a second degree internationalisation (Forsgren ibid.), the higher the probability that the R&D activities in the company will be, to a large extent, geographically spread in the organisation and partially controlled by different subsidiaries. The development of new products and processes, which will form part of the company's core competence in the future, is no longer carried out entirely in the centre, nor is it controlled totally by headquarters.

This is actually one important part of the competitive edge of a multinational firm. By having different assets in different industrial and commercial contexts, a firm's ability to capture new ideas about products and processes increases. It has sometimes been argued that this is an important driving force for internationalisation (Cantwell, 1991). In this perspective foreign direct investment allows the firm to enhance its technological process by operating in a different, but complementary technological environment than its home base (Yamin, 1995). Dissimilar business environments enrich the innovative capacity of MNCs thus improving their competitive advantage vis-à-vis firms with a more concentrated asset structure (De Meyer, 1992; Pearce and Singh, 1992; Nohria et al., 1994).

The geographical distribution of innovative activities does not mean that all subsidiaries in an MNC have the same capacity to innovate. Some researchers have proposed that the subsidiary manager can have an important impact on the decision about where in the MNC the innovation activities will be carried out (Birkinshaw and Hood, 1995). Nohria et al. have suggested that the location is dependent on structural characteristics such as the subsidiaries' internal organisation, the control system used by the parent company, the degree of centrality in the MNCs inter-subsidiary network and the subsidiary's business context (Nohria ibid.).

3. Transfer of Knowledge within the MNC

If the geographical spread of the assets is the first part of the MNC's competitive advantage, the second, and vital, part is the company's ability to transfer innovations from one part of the organisation to another. This can be seen as the main advantage of a firm comprising a variety of assets held together under one structure, compared to a set of independently operating units. The capability of creating *and* the ability to communicate knowledge is very much what organising is all about, and the better these two functions are performed the greater the competitive strength of the company. For instance, it is obvious that the transfer of manufacturing capabilities within an organisation by communication should be faster than the transfer of the same capabilities through imitation by independent organisations (Kogut and Zander, 1995).

So, here we have the two legs on which the competitive strength of a multinational firm stands; the capability of creating new knowledge and the ability to transfer this knowledge between countries and subsidiaries. We have already said that the first capability is dependent on the distribution of operations among countries and different business contexts. The variation in the environments provides an advantage because it increases the possibility of tapping new knowledge wherever it emerges. The second capability has more to do with the organisational and communicative skill of the multinational firm. By transferring innovation created in one subsidiary to others in the group, the innovation can be used on a larger scale and the profit from it can be multiplied. Thus, transferring knowledge from one subsidiary to another is crucial for the competitive strength of the whole MNC.

But this way to identifying the competitive advantage of the MNC also introduces a paradox. The greater the variation in the different subsidiaries' business contexts, the higher the prospects for creating new knowledge somewhere within the MNC. But the greater the variation in the business contexts, the more difficult it will be to exploit this new knowledge on a more general basis. The reason for this is quite obvious if we consider the MNC as an interorganisational network (Ghoshal and Bartlett, 1990; Andersson and Forsgren, 1995). In such an MNC, a subsidiary's environment is, first of all, its set of direct exchange relationships with other counterparts along with indirect exchange relationships which are connected to the direct relationships. The subsidiary's embeddedness in such a set is dependent on the attributes of the exchanges in terms of activity interdependence and adaptation between the subsidiary and other actors. The stronger the specific activity interdependence between the subunit and other actors, the more all will be inclined to develop close relationships rather than conducting business through arm-length negotiations. Inversely, two actors who are engaged in a close relationship will tend to strengthen their specific interdependence over time to raise the joint productivity of their activities. We can assume that the closer a subsidiary's relationships with specific counterparts, the higher the degree of embeddedness, because close relationships are more difficult to replace. The subsidiary's »root system« is deep. It follows from the discussion above that the more lucid the counterparts are to the subsidiary, the more the subsidiary's behaviour and activities are likely to be influenced by them. The more dependent the subsidiary is on its counterparts and the more adapted it is to its counterparts, the more embedded it is. If, in their turn, these counterparts are dependent on and adapted to the subsidiary, this is likely to strengthen the subsidiary's embeddedness because interdependence is more prone to produce long-term relationships.

In the network MNC the relationships with customers, suppliers, competitors, government agencies etc, are more or less unique from the subsidiary's point of view, regardless of whether they are local or international. Much of what we call knowledge development is actually the result of problem solving in the course of daily transactions within these relationships. The development work is carried out because activities performed by one actor have to be continuously adapted to the needs of others in the network, and vice versa (Håkansson, 1989). Thus, the development is performed by producers and users of the technology and, to a major extent, is characterised by interaction between them. An action by one company encounters different reactions from closely related actors so development of products and processes within a single subsidiary is formed through its interaction with its counterparts in the business network (Håkansson, 1994). For instance, when applications for gas are developed in a subsidiary belonging to AGA, the Swedish gas producer, this is done in close co-operation with a specific customer who needs this application in an industrial process. The development is linked to that relationship and is very much situation-specific rather than general.

The argument can be further illustrated by Ericsson, the Swedish telecommunication company. It has a well-known product, the AXE-system, which is sold in many countries all over the world. The cost of research and development linked to the AXE-system is enormous. It is therefore of the utmost importance for Ericsson to co-ordinate the different subsidiaries to avoid the duplication of investments in R&D and to obtain large scale economy in production and development. The ability to integrate is assumed to be one of the most critical competitive forces among the main competitors in the telecommunication industry. But the driving forces behind product development are, to a large extent, local. Specific customers demand special adaptations of the AXE-system which sometimes result in more or less customised R&D-activities at the subsidiary level. From the subsidiary's standpoint there can be a very good reason to start such an activity, especially if the counterpart is a large customer (as telephone companies usually are). From the perspective of the Ericsson group, though, it is important whether or not the expected results of such an investment have a wider application to the group as a whole.

4. Impediments to Knowledge Transfer within the MNC

There are at least two conclusions we can draw from this perspective of the development process. The first one is that the greater the difference between the subsidiaries' business networks in terms of the actors' needs and capabilities, the more difficult it is to use knowledge developed in one subsidiary in another subsidiary's context. This is so because the solutions on the subsidiary level are, to a large extent, customer, supplier or even competitor specific. They are dependent on the activities these actors and the subsidiary perform and the resources they use. The variation between the different subsidiaries' networks within the MNC, which can be seen as an advantage for the advancement of knowledge, will turn into a disadvantage when the MNC wants to transform this knowledge into a more general competitive strength for the whole group.

But the second, and maybe more problematic conclusion, is that there is often lack of incentive for the subsidiary to participate in knowledge transfer within the group. On a general level, this follows from the subsidiaries representing different interests in the group. In the network MNC, a main interest of the subsidiary is to fulfil and develop the role in its business network. To a large extent its behaviour is shaped by the relationships it has with important business counterparts. To the extent that the subsidiaries belong to different networks, the incentive to be a »giver« of new knowledge within the MNC or, for that matter, to search for innovations among the sister units, is limited. The development work, as well as the communication of the results from this work, is primarily relevant for the counterparts in the subsidiary's network. The sister units will only benefit from these activities if they belong to the network.

In the Ericsson case, the managers of Ericsson Telecom, one of the business areas within the Ericsson Group, strive to increase the proportion of resources invested in so called standard development at the subsidiary level. Standard development means the development of specific applications of the AXE-system that are suitable for all or many of the countries Ericsson operates in. Thus it excludes the development of existing or new applications for a local customer or group of customers which, within Ericsson Telecom, is known as market development. The objective of Ericsson Telecom's top manager is for a larger part of the proposals initiated at the subsidiary level as market development to be allocated to standard development. (Karlsson and Olsson, 1993).

But that seemed to be difficult to accomplish. One obvious reason is the way the research and development in Ericsson Telecom was organised. Different proposals from local subsidiaries were transmitted to a specific central unit which operated as a link between the central R&D unit and the subsidiaries. If a proposal was defined as a request for standard development, it was sent to the central unit for R&D for further processing and for a decision to be made about, if and where, in the organisation the proposed standard development should be carried out. If it was described as a demand for market development, it was transmitted back to the local subsidiary for execution.

This organisation was considered to be too time-consuming, especially from the subsidiaries' point of view. For standard applications, too much time elapsed from the time of the customer's request to the start of the development. The subsidiaries were therefore inclined to define proposals as market development instead of standard development in order to speed up the process. In part because of this, different applications, which could have been integrated into one standard application, were developed for different markets instead.

Ericsson Telecom tried to support the standard development process by change of organisation. The process at the central level for handling standard development was shortened by combining decision making and handling in one and the same unit. Further, in the new organisation, the central and local units of standard development and market development were placed within the same organisational body to facilitate communication and integration between these two activities.

This change did not have any profound impact on the proportion of standard development in the subsidiaries (Karlsson and Olsson 1993). One reason for this is probably that the conflict between the two types of development processes is too fundamental to be solved by a change in the formal organisation. It is rooted in different interests at the subsidiary and business area level, interests that are conditioned by the network context of the two levels. At the subsidiary level, the relationships with local customers, suppliers and other counterparts constitute important parts of the business context. These relationships are not only crucial for the subsidiaries' operation and survival, but also for the subsidiaries' formulation of what is important for development of new applications. This explains the tendency, at the local level, to give higher priority to local needs than to corporate or business area needs irrespective of the type of organisation, especially if external relationships dominate over corporate ones (which often is the case).

At the level of Ericsson Telecom the network context is different. It includes relationships with the corporate level, other divisions and relationships with other subsidiaries in Ericsson Telecom. In general this is a context more receptive to standard development than to development suitable for specific local customers.

The influence from the two contexts produces different results depending on the resource configuration in the company. For historical and other reasons, the resources for development in Ericsson are spread to several units, some of which are at the central level and some others at the subsidiary level. This gives the subsidiary context a direct influence on resources used for development which increases the difficulty of integrating R&D and supporting standard development projects at the subsidiary level. The difficulties of transferring knowledge gained in one part of the organisation to other parts will probably be further aggravated by the not-invented-here syndrome (Allen, 1977) and the widespread use of profit-centre control. Several studies seem to indicate that such control devices often have a negative impact on co-operative behaviour between units, including the transfer of knowledge.

We can conclude that there are different factors that improve the innovative capacity of the subsidiaries in the MNC. Some of these factors are internal, for instance the »organic« character of the subsidiary, and some are external, for instance the control system used by the parent headquarters, the subsidiary's degree of centrality in the MNC and the business context of the subsidiary. Inspired by the growing body of literature that confirms that development activities in a company are shaped to a considerable extent by the relationships with important counterparts in the business network (Axelsson and Easton 1992; Håkansson,1989; Laage-Hellman, 1989; Lundgren, 1994) we have emphasised the latter more than any other factor. According to this, differences between subsidiaries, in terms of innovation-demanding relationships will explain a lot of observed differences, not only in the capacity to innovate, but also in the type of development activities at the subsidiary level.

We can also conclude that the factors that improve innovation in the MNC will not automatically improve the *transfer* of new knowledge between different units. For instance, even if successful socialisation of the subsidiaries can reduce the barriers of knowledge transfer, empirical research indicates that socialisation can have a negative impact on innovation because it reduces differentiation and »outside the box« thinking (Nohria et al. 1994). Our main point here is that a subsidiary's specific relationships with customers, suppliers and other counterparts, along with the demands that they make, are positive and important factors for innovation activities in that subsidiary, but retarding factors for the giving and receiving of knowledge vis-à-vis other subsidiaries. This is the inherent paradox of the network MNC.

5. Knowledge Integration in some Swedish MNCs

The notion that the competitive MNC should be highly integrated in terms of knowledge transfer between the different units has been discussed much more than the question of whether transfer of knowledge really exists within the MNC and, if so, to what extent. The empirical evidence for knowledge transfer seem to be limited. In the investigation of development projects in 12 Swedish MNCs mentioned above, it was confirmed that the motives for initiating the projects were very much related to the need for market knowledge, personal characteristics and co-operation with suppliers and customers that was not to be found in the home country (Ridderstråle and Hedlund, 1994). This supports the view that the variation that arises when having subsidiaries in different countries is one of the main advantages of the MNC. One conclusion from the investigation is that greater variety of knowledge bases and perspectives in international development projects seem to trigger increased creativity. The involvement of more than one party also increases the chances of gaining internal acceptance of new products.

But it was also found that the transfer of knowledge between units was difficult to accomplish during some phases of the projects. One reason for this was the physical distance between the projects. Another, of perhaps even greater importance, was the problem of communication between different functions, for instance production and marketing. To some extent these problems were also related to different interests connected to different units. The interfunctional problems seemed to be intensified by the fact that the functions of the MNC had different location patterns. Among the projects R&D was found to be relatively concentrated and marketing relatively dispersed, with manufacturing somewhere inbetween. As a consequence, the functions', and therefore also the subsidiaries', perspectives and interests differed. The marketing units wanted to adapt the products to meet local needs, whereas R&D and manufacturing units were more interested in standardisation on a world-wide basis (Ridderstråle and Hedlund op. cit.).

In an investigation of a number of the largest and best known Swedish companies, representing the pulp and paper industry, industrial supplies, industrial equipment and engineering, the form and extent of knowledge transfer between the single subsidiary and the rest of the MNC has been estimated (Andersson and Forsgren, 1994). This investigation included 11 international divisions in which the proportion of employees abroad varied between 22 and 97 per cent. Five of the divisions belong to companies that are listed among the 100 largest MNCs in the world. All together 59 subsidiaries, mainly located in Europe, were investigated. In general these subsidiaries represent the largest and most important subsidiaries in the division according to the divisional headquarters.

From the perspective of the subsidiary under study, knowledge integration can be considered in terms of the importance of the division for the subsidiary's knowledge about new products and production processes, *or* the subsidiary's importance for the division's corresponding knowledge, *or* both. The greater the importance, the more knowledge transfer we would expect, and therefore the larger the knowledge integration in the division. This way of considering knowledge integration between a specific subsidiary and the rest of the MNC has much in common with Gupta and Govindarajan's distinction between subsidiaries as Integrated Players, Global Innovators, Implementers and Local Innovators (Gupta and Govindarajan, 1994).

Knowledge integration has been mapped by using the respondents' estimations of the importance of product and production development, and separating the different subsidiaries according to Gupta and Govindarajan's classification. The data are based on interviews with three different managers from each subsidiary and the divisional headquarters, and the degree of importance in each case was constructed as an additive index where the respondents have been asked to rank the importance from very low to very high on a five-point scale. An Integrated Player would then be a subsidiary which is important for the rest of the division's R&D to a high or very high degree at the same time as the division being important for its development to a high or very high degree. A Global Innovator is important for the rest of the division to a high or very high degree, while for the Implementer, the division is important to a high or very high degree. Finally, the Local Innovator is not important for the development in rest of the division, nor is the development in the rest of the division important for it.

In Table 1 the subsidiaries are classified according to these definitions.

Table 1. Subsidiaries classified as Local Innovators, Implementers, Global Innovators and Integrated Player with respect to Product Development and Production Development.

	Product Development		Production development	
	No	%	No	%
Local Innovator	21	35	37	63
Implementer	25	42	11	19
Global Innovator	7	12	4	6
Integrated Player	6	11	7	12
Total	59	100	59	100

Source: Andersson and Forsgren, 1994.

Table 1 shows that all four types are represented among the 59 subsidiaries. It also indicates that the subsidiaries with substantive transfer of knowledge to and from sister units in the division are not very common. Only 23 per cent of the subsidiaries are either Global Innovators or Integrated Players with respect to product development, while the corresponding figure for production development is 18 per cent. A majority of the units seem to function either as »islands« in the division, or simply as a receiver of knowledge.

The classification of the subsidiaries into the four types for each division is shown in Tables 2 and 3.

Table 2. Classification of the subsidiaries into Local Players, Implementers, Global Innovators and Integrated Players for each division with respect to Product development.

	Local Innovator	Implementer	Global Innovator	Integrated Player
Division A, 10sub	6	3	1	
Division B, 4 sub		2		2
Division C, 4 sub	1	1	1	1
Division D, 6 sub	5		1	
Division E, 8 sub	1	5		2
Division F, 6 sub		2	2	2
Division G, 4 sub	3		1	
Division H, 4 sub	1	3		
Division I, 4 sub	3		1	
Division J, 3 sub	1	2		
Division K, 6 sub	5		1	
Total	21	25		6

Source: Andersson and Forsgren, 1994.

It is evident from Tables 2 and 3 that all divisions contain subsidiaries with different roles, even though Local Innovator and Implementer seem to be the most common ones. The majority of the divisions have at least one subsidiary functioning as a Global Innovator, but there are only four divisions with at least one Integrated Player for product development and production development respectively. The difference between the divisions is considerable. For instance, Division F, with four of the six subsidiaries being either Global Innovators or Integrated Players, and with no Local Innovators, can be considered highly integrated. This division produces and sells relays on a global scale. Two of its subsidiaries are specialised in production while four subsidiaries function as so called engineering firms, which means that they sell and install relays in different power systems. This situation calls for a high degree of co-operation between the subsidiaries. In contrast, Divisions H and J contain only Local Innovators and Implementers, which indicates that the knowledge transfer is rather low in these divisions. Division H is a

Table 3. Classification of the subsidiaries into Local Innovators, Implementers, Global Innovators and Integrated Players for each division with
respect to Production development.

	Local Innovator	Implementer	Global Innovator	Integrated player
Division A, 10 sub	6	2	1	1
Division B, 4 sub	4			
Division C, 4 sub	3	1		
Division D, 6 sub	6			
Division E, 8 sub	4	3		1
Division F, 6 sub		2	1	3
Division G, 4 sub	3		1	
Division H, 4 sub	2	2		
Division I, 4 sub	3		1	
Division J, 3 sub	3			
Division K, 6 sub	3	1		2
Total	**37**	**11**	**4**	**7**

Source: Andersson and Forsgren 1994

machine tool supplier with operations in the world market, but with a
mixture of rather autonomous local production companies and sales
subsidiaries. Division J is a gas manufacturer with the subsidiaries functioning as suppliers of different gas applications for the local market,
and with no purchase or sales relationships between the different subsidiaries.

To sum up, we can draw three main conclusions from Tables 2 and
3. First, it is common that the subsidiaries have different roles in the
process of knowledge transfer. Second, there are large differences between the divisions in terms of the degree of integration of the development of new products and production processes. Third, it seems to be
the exception rather than the rule that there is an intensive flow of
knowledge about products and production processes between units in
the division.

Perhaps the third conclusion illustrates the complexity of striving for
global competitiveness in an MNC. First, transferring knowledge about

new products and production processes between different units is quite another matter from developing the same knowledge somewhere in the organisation. Secondly, there is an inherent contradiction between the innovative capacity of a subsidiary and its propensity to transfer the results from that capacity to other corporate units. Innovative capacity is dependent on the intensity of the interactions with counterparts in the subsidiary's business network. But the higher the intensity, the more context specific the innovations will be, and thus the less appropriate it will be to use them in other contexts. The subsidiary's incentive to participate in internal knowledge transfer will also probably be low in this case.

6. *Summary*

The main theme in this chapter has been the link between the competitive advantage of the MNC and its ability to develop new products, processes and methods of organisation, and its capability to transfer knowledge about innovations within the MNC. It has been argued that the variation in the business environments in the different subsidiaries improves its development capability vis-à-vis firms with a more concentrated asset structure. The variety of environments is an advantage in itself because it increases the possibility of tapping knowledge wherever it emerges. Several studies also indicate that the development activities in the MNC today are often spread among the different units.

But competitive advantage also requires that the innovations created in one subsidiary can be transferred to other subsidiaries in the group in such a way that the innovation can be exploited on a larger scale and the profit from it be multiplied. Otherwise the competitiveness of the MNC as an entity would not exceed that of the independent units. Thus the transfer of knowledge from one subsidiary to another is crucial for the competitive strength of the MNC as a whole.

But this is the paradox of the MNC's competitive advantage. The greater the variety in the environments of the different subsidiaries, the greater the prospects for creating new knowledge somewhere within the MNC but the greater the difficulty there will be in exploiting the knowledge gained on a larger scale. The main reason for this is that development activities are closely linked to business relationships. Every subsidiary has its unique network of relationships. Development is carried out because activities performed by one actor have to be continuously adapted to the needs of others in the network and vice versa. From this we can draw two conclusions. First, the greater the difference between the subsidiaries' business networks the more difficulty there will be in applying the knowledge, originally developed through one subsidiary's specific relationship, in another subsidiary. Second, there is often a lack of incentive for the subsidiaries to participate in knowledge transfer within the MNC. On a general level, this follows from the subsidiaries representing different interests in the group. The subsidiary's primary interest is to fulfil and develop its role in its business network rather than in the corporate system. This unwillingness to participate in knowledge transfer can also be aggravated by the use of profit-centre derived control systems.

Finally, the chapter presented some empirical notions about the existence of knowledge transfer in MNCs. An investigation of international development projects in twelve Swedish MNCs seems to support the view that the competitive advantage of these firms contains a paradox. First, it was found that the motivation behind these projects was the possibility of access to a greater variety of resources and knowledge, including relationships with different customers and suppliers. But secondly, it was found that knowledge transfer within these projects was obstructed by communication problems, and differences in perspectives and interests between the participating units.

The empirical evidence of knowledge transfer within the MNC is limited. In an investigation of eleven, highly internationalised divisions in Swedish MNCs, the form and extent of knowledge transfer between the single subsidiary and the rest of the MNC was mapped. One main conclusion from this investigation was that the highly complex structure, in terms of flow of knowledge about new products and production processes between units in the division, seemed to be rather an exception than a rule. This could indicate the complexity and difficulty of the battle for global competitiveness in the MNC.

References

Allen, T. J., 1977, *Managing the Flow of Technology*. MIT Press, Cambridge, Mass.

Andersson, U. and M. Forsgren, 1994, *The Degree of Integration in some Swedish MNCs*. Working Paper 1994/4, Department of Business Studies, Uppsala University.

Andersson, U. and M. Forsgren, 1995, Using Networks to Determine Multinational Parental Control of Subsidiaries. In Paliwoda, S. and J.K. Ryans Jr, (eds) *International Marketing Reader*, Routledge.

Axelsson, B. and G. Easton, 1992, *Industrial Networks – A new View of Reality*. Routledge, London.

Birkinshaw, J. and N. Hood, 1995, An Empirical Study of Development Processes in Foreign Owned Subsidiaries in Canada and Scotland. In Schiattarella, R. (ed) New Challenges for European and International Business. European International Business Academy, Urbino.

Cantwell, J., 1991, A Survey of Theories of International Production. In Pitelis, S. and R. Sugden (eds), *The Nature of the Transnational Firm*. Routledge, London.

Forsgren, M., U. Holm and J. Johanson, Internationalization of the Second Degree. In Young. S., J. and Hamill (eds), *Europe and the Multinationals*. Edward Elgar, Aldershot.

Ghoshal S. and C. Bartlett, 1990, MNC as an Interorganizational Network. *Academy of Management Review*, 15(3): 603-625.

Granstrand, O., L. Håkansson and S. Sjölander, 1992, *Technology Management and International Business*. John Wiley & Sons, London.

Gupta, A. K. and V. Govindarajan, 1994, Organizing for Knowledge Flows within MNCs. *International Business Review*. Vol 3. No. 4 pp. 443-457.

Håkansson, H., 1989, *Corporate Technological Behaviour*. Routledge, London.

Håkansson , H., 1993, Networks as a Mechanism to Develop Resources. In Beije, P., J., Groenewegen and O. Nuys (eds), *Networking in Dutch Industries*. Garant, Apeldoorn.

Karlson, T. and Å. Olsson, 1993, *Integration och koordination av produktutveckling i ett internationellt företag: en fallstudie* (Integration and Coordination of Product Development in an International Company: a Case Study). Department of Business Studies, Uppsala University, Uppsala.

Kogut, B. and U. Zander, 1993, Knowledge of the Firm and the Evolution Theory of the Multinational Corporation. *Journal of International Business Studies.*

Laage-Hellman, J., 1989, *Technological Development in Industrial Netorks.* Acta Universitatis Upsaliensis, Uppsala.

Lundgren, A., 1994, *Technical Innovation and Industrial Evolution.* Routledge, London.

De Meyer, A., 1992, Management of International R&D Operations. In Granstrand, O., L. , L. Håkansson and S. Sjölander, *Technology Management and International Business.* John Wiley & Sons, Chichester.

Pearce, R. D. and S. Singh, 1992, Internationalisation of Research and Development among the World's Leading Enterprises: Survey Analysis of Organisation and Motivation. In Granstrand, O.L., L. Håkansson and Sjölander, S., *Technology Management and International Business.* John Wiley & Sons, Chichester.

Ridderstråle, J. and G. Hedlund, 1994, *International Development Projects – characteristics, communication patterns, problems and performance.* Institute of International Business Studies, Stochholm School of Economics, Stockholm.

Yamin, M., 1995, Determinants of Reverse Transfer: The Experience of UK Multinationals. In Schiattarella, R. (ed) *New Challenges for European and International Business* European International Business Academy. Urbino.

Zander, I., 1994, *The Tortoise Evolution of the Multinational Corporation – Foreign Technological Activity in Swedish Multinational Firms 1890 – 1990.* Institute of International Business, Stockholm School of Economics, Stockholm.

Part II

Driving Forces
Behind Internationalisation

5. The Oscillating Multinational Firm – Alfa Laval in the Period 1890-1990 [3]

Ivo Zander and Udo Zander

Although several schools of thought have proposed explanations to the existence and development of the multinational corporation, a significant stream of research has come to embrace what might be called the received view of the internationalisation process. It emphasises the firm's initial dependence on technological advantages created at home, making it possible to overcome the disadvantages associated with carrying out business activities in foreign markets (Dunning, 1977, 1988a, 1988b). Over time, an increasing proportion of all activities is expected to become located outside the country of origin, starting with sales, service and manufacturing and eventually extending into research and development (as indicated by Håkanson, 1981; Cantwell, 1992, 1995; Håkanson and Nobel, 1993; Dunning, 1994).

In the established multinational corporation, with long-time experience in international markets and well-developed organisational structures and management routines, activities in many locations may turn into an advantage 'per se'. This development has been addressed in the context of sequential advantages from multinationality (Kogut, 1983, 1990; Dunning, 1993), in which the integration and coordination of functional activities across country borders figure prominently. Recently, the question of how advanced multinationals can achieve advantages from the integration and coordination of geographically dispersed technological capabilities has become an important part of international business literature (Ghoshal and Bartlett, 1988; Bartlett and Ghoshal,

3. Financial support from the Swedish Council for Research in the Humanities and Social Sciences (HSFR) and the Expert Group on Regional and Urban Studies (ERU) is gratefully acknowledged. The authors would also like to thank Professor John Cantwell and the research group at the University of Reading for the original data collection.

1989; Hedlund and Rolander, 1990; Hedlund and Ridderstråle, 1995; Ridderstråle, 1996).

The underlying and often implicit logic of the received view of the internationalisation process includes determined sequences with regard to the functional activities that are established in foreign countries, the modes of foreign expansion, and the markets that are approached (the origins are found in Johanson and Wiedershiem-Paul, 1975; Johanson and Vahlne, 1977, 1990)[4]. It also involves expectations about an *incremental* and *irreversible* internationalisation process out of *one single country*, leading the firm towards higher degrees of commitment to foreign markets and factors of production[5]. An extrapolation of the process suggests a final stage of internationalisation where the multinational firm operates a well-dispersed set of activities and assumes the advantages of being able to integrate and coordinate operations across borders to reach customers worldwide. It sells, manufactures and conducts research and development in potentially all countries of the world.

The purpose of the present chapter is to critically assess some of the underlying logic and implicit assumptions of the received view of the internationalisation process. It illustrates the evolution of foreign technological activity in Alfa Laval AB, a multinational firm of Swedish origin with long-time experience in international operations. The analysis extends over the period 1890-1990, and shows an early, rapid and substantial increase in technological activity in the U.S. subsidiary. It also provides evidence on reversibility in the internationalisation of technological activity, as illustrated by the oscillation of the overall foreign share of technological activity and recurrent shifts in the location of technological capabilities related to the important separator technology. The expectation about internationalisation out of one single country is challenged by observations that important technologies which first emerged in the U.S. and German units were subsequently shifted to units located in Sweden. The picture is further complicated by the simultaneous internationalisa-

---

4. Rapid internationalization processes have been observed by other researchers (Hedlund & Kverneland, 1983; Lindqvist, 1991), who attribute this development to convergence among industrialized nations, increasing knowledge about international business and foreign markets, or increasing international competition requiring more rapid moves into foreign markets.
5. The term 'incremental' should not be confused with what established theory calls 'sequential'. In the context of this chapter, incremental means slow or gradual and does not relate to the order in which functions are internationalized or markets are approached.

tion and de-internationalisation of technological activity related to various technologies at the time of the second world war.

The concluding discussion addresses the evolutionary determinism in the received view of the internationalisation process, including what is seen as a natural and incremental drift towards higher and more 'advanced' levels of internationalisation. It is suggested that the continuous struggle to in a profitable way sustain technological development, use factors of production, and sell to customers is the engine that drives the geographical location and re-location of various activities performed by the firm. It is also proposed that the use of the firm as the starting point for an analysis of the internationalisation process produces results that are often too aggregate to be useful, and that studies carried out on the technology or product level will lead to an improved understanding of the phenomenon.

1. Methodology

The chapter is based on a longitudinal analysis of technological activity in Alfa Laval AB, which was originally founded as Separator AB in 1883. The main part of the empirical investigation is based on Alfa Laval's U.S. patenting over the period 1890-1990, which is employed as an indicator of technological activity (a full account of the data collection is provided in Zander, 1994). The number of patents might not necessarily be in direct proportion to the amount of resources or people involved in the inventive effort, although there is an underlying assumption that a large output in terms of patenting also reflects the existence of relatively substantial technological capabilities. The patenting data are complemented by information from secondary sources (Wohlert, 1982; Gårdlund and Fritz, 1983; Åman, 1996), illustrating the general development of both foreign operations and technological activity.

The pros and cons of using U.S. patents as an indicator of technological activity are well covered in the literature (see e.g. Schmookler, 1950, 1966; Basberg, 1987; Pavitt, 1988). One essential advantage of using patents granted in the United States is that the patent records reveal the nationality of the inventor rather than the nationality of ownership of the research unit. Assuming that inventors are typically based in research units in their home country, it is therefore possible to identify where the research and development underlying the invention was carried out[6]. Thus, for every patent it is known if it originated in e.g. Sweden, France, Germany, Italy, the United States, or any other country. This is an important advantage because patenting policies (e.g. aimed at registering patents under the name of the parent firm) might otherwise distort the correct distribution of home and foreign developed technologies.

A second advantage of using U.S. patenting data is that the attractiveness of the U.S. market encourages patenting of inventions that are believed to be of significant commercial importance. It is therefore likely that the U.S. patenting data reflect high-quality inventions that have been transformed into innovations to a relatively large extent. It has also been shown that Swedish firms in general find the U.S. market highly attractive although difficult to break into (Ågren, 1990), which should have encouraged systematic patenting in this particular market. This is particularly the case with Alfa Laval, for which the U.S. market appears to have been of significant importance already before the turn of the century (see below).

In order to make longitudinal comparisons of Alfa Laval's patenting activity, a historical examination identified name changes and also changes in ownership through mergers and acquisitions[7]. The data also include the patenting by first-order, majority-owned subsidiaries, both Swedish and foreign, for the periods during which they belonged to the parent company (Appendix 1)[8]. Overall, reliability is likely to have improved over the measured time period, in particular because of improved coverage of the publications that were used in the consolidation work. However, it can be assumed that patenting in itself provides a good indicator of Alfa Laval's technological activity, as the importance of patents in international competition appears to have been recognised from very early on (Wohlert, 1982).

The identified patent records reveal the technological classes and sub-classes to which individual patents have been assigned. The defini-

6. This assumption receives some support from comparisons between studies based on patenting data and R&D expenditure, in which figures for the overall foreign share of technological activity among Swedish multinational firms in the 1980s are very similar (Zander, 1994; Håkanson, 1981; Håkanson & Nobel, 1993).
7. This search involved a number of publications, in particular 'Svenska Aktiebolag – Handbok för Affärsvärlden' for the years 1946-1977.
8. These subsidiaries were identified through an extensive and systematic search into the history of Alfa Laval, the most important sources of information being 'Svenska Aktiebolag – Handbok för Affärsvärlden', 'Koncernregistret- KCR' and 'Who Own Whom – Continental Europe'.

tion of individual technologies employed in this chapter follows the classification used by the U.S. Patent Office, which makes a distinction between some 600 classes of technology, of which currently some 400 are in use. The chosen level of aggregation makes it possible to distinguish between rather narrowly defined technological capabilities and their related technological output, and allows for a meaningful analysis of changes in technological activity over time (for example, a distinction is made between 'electrical resistors' and 'electrical connectors'). Also, the level of aggregation provides information about technologies which could be used together to create final products or complex systems (for example, 'pipes and tubular conduits', 'pumps', 'valves and valve actuation', and 'liquid purification or separation' might be used in the production of 'chemistry compounds' of different kinds).

2. Alfa Laval – The Technological Foundation

The establishment and international growth of Alfa Laval was very much based on its separator technology. One of the founders, Gustaf de Laval, was experimenting with cream separators as early as in 1877, and together with other private interests formed the company Oscar Lamm J:r in 1878[9]. Having carried out much of the early development work, the company was restructured and renamed AB Separator in 1883. The name Alfa Laval was not adopted until 1963, but will be used throughout the following sections for practical reasons.

When Alfa Laval introduced its first cream separator in 1879, it was lagging behind competing firms from Germany and Denmark[10]. The technological lead of German and Danish manufacturers appears to

9. The first satisfactory separator design was based on a de Laval patent from 1878, and engineered in cooperation with O. Lamm in 1879.
10. The German inventor W. Lefeldt had constructed the first commercially used cream separator in 1877, but other German patents dated back to 1858 and 1864. The first Danish patents on cream separators, associated with H. Jensen, appeared in 1873. However, the most important patent was granted to Nielsen & Petersen in 1878, and was subsequently acquired by the firm Burmeister & Wain (Burmeister & Wain was a shipyard, but possessed the necessary welding and manufacturing skills to produce the separators). The first U.S. patents were based on British technology (separating liquid from paint and other substances), and were granted to D.M. Weston in 1868. In addition, both German and Danish patents had been registered in the United States before Alfa Laval made its first U.S. patent applications. In fact, Alfa Laval was unable to receive patents on the separation idea itself, but had to rely on patents on specific technical solutions. The firm also experienced problems when entering the French market, because of the risks of patent infringements (the first French patents dated back to 1874, but had apparently not been actively commercialized).

have been closely linked to relatively early market demand and penetration of the separator technology (Wohlert, 1982)[11]. While cream separators had already been installed and tested in several German and Danish diaries, the substitute ice method, which was particularly suited for the Nordic climate, delayed the introduction of new separation techniques in Sweden[12]. This required frequent travelling to Europe to stay in touch with new technological developments and to establish contacts with early customers.

Although many of the technological impulses in terms of basic designs initially came from Germany and Denmark, development work at Alfa Laval was very much associated with Swedish engineers, customers, research institutions, and component manufacturers. Practical tests were performed on Swedish farms, which often passed on their experiences and technological improvements to Alfa Laval, and more scientifically based tests were performed by research institutions at the Swedish agricultural schools in Alnarp and Ultuna[13]. Also, critical parts such as the bowl and other components were manufactured by Swedish firms, such as Gundbergska Fabriken and Ludwigsbergs Mekaniska Verkstad[14]. As the development work continued in Sweden, technological impulses were still being acquired from Germany and Denmark. One

11. Early demand was found among large farms and cooperatives, and focused on large-sized separators. In 1893, there were about 700 co-operative dairies in Denmark, compared to only 322 in Sweden in 1895. Also, educational as well as research institutes were established earlier in Denmark (1876, 1883 respectively) and Germany (1876, 1876) than in Sweden (1883, 1898).
12. It seems that Alfa Laval's relatively late entry into the separator business was compensated by its in some aspects more advanced technology. In particular, the Alfa Laval machines were characterized by high-speed rotation and small-sized bowls, requiring durable components and power transmission (a critical component was the belt for power transmission), and also accurate balancing of the bowls. While a direct comparison of competing machines is difficult, the first Alfa Laval separators seem to have enjoyed an advantage in terms of smaller size, easier handling, lower energy consumption, and in that they could not explode during separation.
13. Tests at Alnarp started in 1879. Technological tests were also carried out at Hamra Gård, a company-owned farm that was acquired in 1894.
14. The Gundbergska factory was initially rented by Alfa Laval and acquired in 1887. It manufactured the bowl, which was cast in one piece, as opposed to the welded design used by other competitors. This improved durability, which was essential in the Alfa Laval design. Ludwigsbergs manufactured various separator parts and also stands and supports. Other early suppliers of components were Bolinders Mekaniska Verkstads AB, Surahammars Bruks AB, and Bultfabriken i Hallstahammar. Alfa Laval later moved much of its production to Olofströms Bruk, which was acquired in 1884 (the name of this unit was changed to Svenska Stålpressningsaktiebolaget Olofström in 1887). Over the following ten years, Alfa Laval internalized most of the production of separators, including raw materials and sub-components.

particular vehicle for the dissemination of new technological advancements were the trade fairs that were regularly staged throughout Europe. Also, some foreign research institutions were employed in testing the Alfa Laval machines, as management realised that positive evaluations were critical for acceptance in the local markets.

A significant event, which manifested the importance of foreign technological advancements, was Alfa Laval's acquisition of the Alfa patent for hand separators from the German inventor von Bechtolsheim in 1888 (the patent was initially granted in 1883, and acquired in direct competition with the Danish competitor Burmeister and Wain)[15]. The new Alfa separator was launched in the following year and proved a great commercial success, opening up the segment of smaller separators used by individual farms. By and large, it was the Alfa patent and the hand separator which established Alfa Laval's position as one of the leading firms in the industry.

3. Early Shifts in the Location of Technological Activity: Separators, Milking Machines and Plate Heat Exchangers

Throughout the decades before the second world war, established customer groups such as dairies and farms were instrumental in guiding the development of new technology in Alfa Laval. Consequently, the firm developed new applications around the separator technology and only engaged in cautious diversification into technologies related to the separator business[16]. Significant development work was associated with milking machines from the 1920s, and with plate heat exchanger technology from the 1930s and onward.

Separators: Early cream separator technology required steam or horse power, and hand separators for small producers and farms did not ap-

15. Alfa Laval also acquired a patent by the Belgian competitor Mélotte in 1895 (although it was never commercially exploited), and several U.S. patents (in 1898 and 1901/1902). The link-blade patent acquired in 1901/1902 was an alternative to the alfa-plates of the Alfa patent. This technology was developed by AB Rotator, a wholly-owned subsidiary of Alfa Laval, to be used as a blocking brand in the low-price segment.
16. The only other major product group, churning machines, accounted for not more than 5 per cent of total sales in 1914. In part, the reluctance to engage in unrelated diversification has been explained by several unsuccessful diversification efforts around the turn of the century, involving steam turbines and casein production (Gårdlund & Fritz, 1983).

pear until the late 1880s[17]. The Alfa patent proved very important for consolidating Alfa Laval's position in the industry, as the hand separator came to account for 97 per cent of Alfa Laval's separator sales or about 70 per cent of total sales in 1913. It remained the single most important product line in the separator industry until the second world war. Gradually, Alfa Laval developed interests in other separation applications, particularly in the food processing and chemical areas. Industrial separators such as yeast separators were developed in the 1890s (the first patent dates to 1895), followed by the development of slurry separators used in sugar production in the early 1900s[18]. However, the development of industrial separators was sluggish, and they did not achieve a significant breakthrough until after the second world war (industrial separators accounted for 9 per cent of Alfa Laval's total sales in 1923, and 13 per cent in 1928)[19]. Trials with separation of lubricants and mineral oils also started in the 1890s, supported by the establishment of a research laboratory in 1893. Research on separators for cleaning lubricant oils in the mechanical engineering field resulted in one major group of machines.

Improved technological capabilities were important for the expansion of international sales. Having established several foreign agents in the late 1870s (Denmark, Germany, France, Great Britain, and the United States), Alfa Laval established its first foreign subsidiary, the De Laval Separator Co., in New York in 1885. The United States very rapidly became the most important market in terms of separator sales. Early production was carried out in cooperation with Sharples, a sub-supplier from 1883 until the late 1880s and also a future competitor, which however seems to have lacked much of the required design and production skills[20]. For this reason, the cooperation initially involved the transfer of Swedish designs, blueprints and qualified personnel. Large-scale man-

---

17. The first de Laval patent on hand separators appeared in 1885/1886. Also, household separators became available just after the turn of the century.
18. The slurry separators were associated with 34 Alfa Laval patents granted in the period 1902-1906 (these patents were related to development work by the Ljungström brothers). Development was discontinued in 1910, but started again in 1922, this time in the context of separating mineral oils.
19. Yeast separators did not account for more than 4 per cent of Alfa Laval's sales in the early 1910s. New fields of application, emerging in the 1920s and 1930s, were rubber latex, olive oil, wool (separating lanolin), and wine. In the late 1950s, Alfa Laval was to develop processes like Centrifish (continuous production of fish oil), Centriflow (production of edible fat), and Shortmix (production of vegetable oil).
20. Local production was promoted by custom duties amounting to 45 per cent of the sales price.

ufacturing in the United States started in Alfa Laval's Poughkeepsie plant in 1892-93.

In spite of extensive separator know-how in Alfa Laval's Swedish units, it appears that the U.S. subsidiary already at the turn of the century had taken over a substantial part of the development work (Figure 1). For example, a patent by Berrigan in 1899 provided an important technological advancement when the Alfa patent expired at the turn of the century[21]. One particular application that was pioneered by the U.S. subsidiary was industrial separators, in particular for marine purposes (marine separators achieved their breakthrough after the first world war as a result of increased prices for lubricant oils and the expansion of the U.S. Navy). Also, the U.S. operations came to include development and manufacturing of turbine separators and steam turbines. The U.S. subsidiary became very profitable, and contributed significantly to Alfa Laval's profits from an early stage. Between 1895 and 1914, it supplied 46 million SEK in profits, which was roughly equal to shareholder dividends paid by Alfa Laval between 1897 and 1914 (Wohlert, 1982, p. 136).

Milking machines: Having assumed a significant role in the development of separators, the U.S. subsidiary also became actively involved in the milking machine business. Trials with milking machines had started

Figure 1. Imperforate bowls and centrifugal separators, number of U.S. patents of Swedish and U.S. origin, 1890-1990

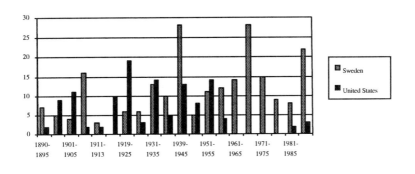

21. Berrigan had been working on the development of slurry separators in the Swedish unit before the turn of the century.

in Sweden in 1895 (in AB Laktator, founded by de Laval), but were discontinued in 1912[22]. The technological breakthrough in milking machines was instead to take place in the U.S. subsidiary, which had produced a promising design for the U.S. market in 1917 (Figure 2)[23]. It was followed by a machine developed by N.J. Daysh in 1920. In the following year, the Swedish parent company acquired the rights to sell the new milking machines in all markets outside the United States, establishing a new subsidiary, AB Separators Mjölkningsmaskin, to carry out the international introduction. Also, in 1922, Alfa Laval set up manufacturing operations in Sweden. Although demand for milking machines developed rather slowly in the 1920s (the most important markets were the United States, Sweden, and the United Kingdom), milking machines had come to represent 16 per cent of the U.S. subsidiary's total sales in 1928.

As milking machine sales became more important, it appears that the development work started shifting to Sweden and the European markets in what could be characterised as a 'reverse' internationalisation pro-

Figure 2. Animal husbandry, number of U.S. patents of Swedish and U.S. origin, 1890-1990.

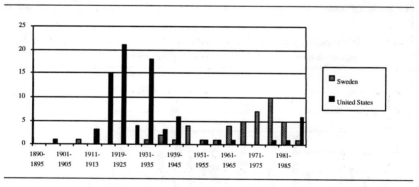

22. Several unsuccessful experiments were carried out between 1905 and 1910, involving a design by the Ljungström brothers (developed in 1902), the Scotch Lawrence-Kennedy machine (introduced in the 1890s), machines developed by Dalén (1909) and a new de Laval design introduced in 1911.
23. In the United States, large animal populations required rationalization of milking routines. Milking machines had come to account for 13 per cent of total sales of the U.S. subsidiary in 1926.

cess. The U.S. unit kept a technological lead until the 1940s, reflected by the introduction of stainless steel models in 1948 and further incremental improvements in 1949. Since then, however, most of the new improvements appear to have been made in Sweden (Gårdlund and Fritz, 1983, pp. 180-181)[24], which is also well-reflected in the number of patents of U.S. and Swedish origin.

Plate heat exchangers: A similar 'reverse' internationalisation process, combined with a rapid shift in the geographical location of technological activity, also took place in plate heat exchangers. Alfa Laval's first plate heat exchanger was introduced by the German subsidiary Bergedorfer Eisenwerke in 1931, saving energy and improving quality in the process of pasteurising milk[25]. For a few years, critical development work was carried out in the German subsidiary, which introduced a series of improvements to the original design[26]. With emerging political threats associated with the upcoming war, production and development of the plate heat exchangers was moved to Lund in Sweden in 1938, where it has since remained[27]. The first Swedish products in the field of plate heat exchangers appeared in 1940, and the technology subsequently spread into other industrial applications in the 1950s, including food processing and pulp production[28]. Servicing and repair (termed regasketing) would later require knowledge in related technologies, such as deep freezing, ultrasonic cleaning of plates in fluid, searching for cracks using fluorescent light and the vulcanisation of new gaskets.

Other technologies: In the period before the second world war, Alfa Laval also became engaged in steam turbines, heating and cooling equip-

---

24. The most important Swedish competitor, AB Manus (which had incorporated Uppsala Separator), was acquired in 1963.
25. In Germany, Alfa Laval established the first manufacturing operations in 1902 (Berlin) and 1907 (Hamburg), in the latter case acquiring Bergedorfer Eisenwerke. The Bergedorfer unit rapidly became one of the most important foreign units, perhaps more in terms of sales than in terms of profits. In addition to various separators, the acquisition of Bergedorfer introduced complementary products such as dairy equipment (constituting 59 per cent of sales in 1912) and margarine machines. Throughout most of the period before the second world war, Bergedorfer was to remain a comparatively diversified unit. It became involved in cooling equipment before the second world war, and maintained production of textile machinery until the early 1970s.
26. The first designs were developed by P. Hytte and J. Risberg, who were to follow the technology when it was subsequently moved to Sweden.
27. The plate heat exchanger technology was transferred to Rudelius & Boklund, which had been incorporated as part of the acquired firm Baltic (1918).
28. Rosenblads Patenter, a firm with a strong position in the pulp segment, was acquired in 1962.

ment, and emulsion equipment. Measuring equipment, used for measuring the fat content in milk, became another business area. Pumps of own design were introduced in 1897. Other products included more distantly related separators and dairy equipment. Agricultural machines and equipment were introduced for a short period in the 1910s. Transport cans, compression moulded articles, and household products, but also products like torpedo components and grenades, were incorporated through the acquisition of foreign and Swedish suppliers[29]. While the Swedish units accounted for most of the technological activity until about 1910, the U.S. subsidiary at that time came to dominate technological activity in the great majority of all technologies. From a technological point of view, Alfa Laval was a U.S. rather than Swedish firm throughout much of its infancy (Figure 3).

Figure 3. Number of technologies dominated by U.S. patents originating in Sweden and abroad, 1890-1938[30]

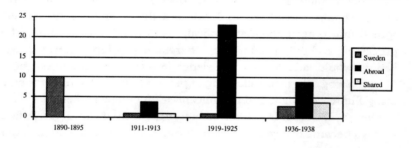

Note: Dominated implies that 75 per cent or more of the number of patents originated in either Sweden or abroad.

4. Shifts in the Location of Technological Activity to Swedish Units in the Postwar Period

In the two decades following the second world war, Alfa Laval by and large remained within the fields of cream separation, milking machines,

29. The Swedish units were Olofström (acquired in 1884) and Eskilstuna (1908).
30. The U.S. subsidiary accounted for almost all patents of foreign origin until the second world war. It lost its predominance among the foreign units as a supplier of new technology in the 1960s and 1970s, but re-established its leading position in the late 1980s. Overall, the Swedish and U.S. units accounted for 80 per cent or more of total patenting throughout the postwar period.

preheating and pasteurising milk, pumping the liquids[31], and measuring dairy product quality. Growth was generated by the milking machines, industrial separators, and the plate heat exchangers, whereas hand separators lost much of their importance. While some diversification efforts were undertaken in the 1940s and 1950s (involving household products, washing machines, and lawn mowers), the 1960s were mainly characterised by a concentration on the traditional technologies[32].

An interesting observation is that the geographical location of technological activity shifted from foreign subsidiaries to Sweden in several important classes of technology starting at about the time of the second world war. This did not only involve increased technological activity in Swedish units, but also a simultaneous reduction in technological effort in the foreign units. With the shifting of technological capabilities the Swedish units re-assumed the main responsibility for separators (mainly larger units for dairy and chemical industries, and also marine separators), and also took over the responsibility for milking machines and plate heat exchangers. In effect, the process of shifting the location of technological activity from foreign subsidiaries to Swedish units included several other areas, such as fluid handling, mineral oils, processes and products, and process disinfecting, deodorising, preserving or sterilising chemical apparatus (see Zander, 1994). By the 1970s, Sweden had again assumed a dominant role in the development of the majority of all technologies (Figure 4).

While technological activity was shifted from the United States to the Swedish units throughout a range of technologies about the time of the second world war, there is also evidence that technological knowledge in some cases started spreading from Sweden into other European countries. A slight increase in patenting activity in the United Kingdom

31. Zander & Ingeström was acquired in 1969. It had started off in steam turbines and later moved into pumps and fluid handling.
32. In a few instances, Alfa Laval had also become involved in rather unrelated technologies. One case of unrelated diversification was associated with an acquired firm, Svenska Stålpressningsaktiebolaget Olofström (formerly Olofströms Bruk). This unit, primarily because of spare capacity, started producing car bodies for the Swedish car and truck manufacturer Volvo in the late 1920s. As it grew with the expansion of the car industry, it was eventually acquired by Volvo in 1969. Other unrelated technologies had been introduced by some of the foreign subsidiaries. For example, Bergedorfer had introduced manufacturing of textile machines in 1949, which was not discontinued until the early 1970s.

Figure 4. Number of technologies dominated by U.S. patents originating in Sweden and abroad, 1946-1975

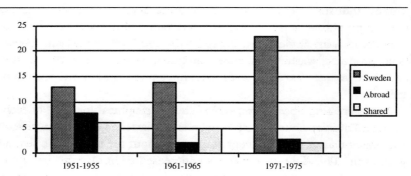

Note: Dominated implies that 75 per cent or more of the number of patents originated in either Sweden or abroad.

could be explained by the transfer of blueprints of both industrial separators and milking machines which was conducted just before the war[33]. This type of technology transfer was typically the result of nationalistic policies and wartime restrictions on trade, and thus transformed sales subsidiaries into units with manufacturing and later research and development capabilities. Similar technology transfers had been made to the Italian unit, which started the manufacturing of separators in 1936, and later became a center for developing olive oil separators within Alfa Laval[34].

5. Re-Internationalisation through Technological Diversification

As demand for separators, milking machines, and plate heat exchangers stagnated in the 1960s, efforts were made to build systems around

33. The U.K. unit had become majority owned in 1923, and named De Laval Chadburn (later re-named Alfa Laval Co. Ltd.). It became Alfa Laval's second center for developing industrial and marine separators in 1926 (the first had been established in the United States).
34. The first Italian agent (M. Sordi) had been established in 1911.

these components[35]. Some of these systems combined components for a specified customer need, while others took the form of complete turn-key dairies and food processing plants. In both cases, an increasing number of technologies were drawn together to sustain sales among the established customer groups. The development of very large dairy systems of a turn-key nature started in the 1950s, with two complete diaries delivered to Egypt (Cairo) and India (New Delhi) as important landmarks. The increasing involvement in what was called the Agri business, formally established as a separate division in 1963, resulted in the design of milking stalls, computer-controlled feeding systems, as well as a wide range of products and consumables (e.g. detergents).

A more substantial broadening of Alfa Laval's technological portfolio started in the 1970s and became particularly pronounced in the late 1980s, when a series of major acquisitions were made to diversify out of the traditional but mature businesses[36]. As some of the acquisitions involved foreign firms, this simultaneously led to an increase in the overall share of technological activity carried out outside the Swedish units (Figure 5).

The acquisition of Stal Refrigeration in 1973 increased Alfa Laval's presence in the field of refrigeration equipment. In 1974, Alfa Laval began to develop electronic systems control for food processing lines, and expanded this area by acquiring the Swedish firm SattControl in 1986. Precision measuring, dosing, analysing and mixing equipment for food processing were added through the acquisition of the German firm Bran+Lübbe (1981) and the U.S. firm Technicon (1987). The field of flow equipment, including advanced plumbing and piping, was developed through a series of acquisitions towards the mid-1980s (including TriClover in the United States and Saunders in the United Kingdom). Several acquisitions of manufacturers of convenience food equipment followed, and during the 1980s Alfa Laval also became involved in biotechnology (primarily through minority stakes in the U.S. firm Genentech and the acquisition of the Swiss firm Che-

---

35. Alfa Laval's move into complete dairy systems has a historical parallel. In the early days, competitors supplying complete dairy machinery and systems had an advantage in selling the separators. Being able to sell separators as parts of larger systems was one factor underlying the acquisition of the German firm Bergedorfer Eisenwerke.
36. Between 1985 and 1989, Alfa Laval acquired 22 companies with combined sales of approximately 4 billion SEK.

Figure 5. Number of technologies dominated by U.S. patents originating in Sweden and abroad, 1976-1990

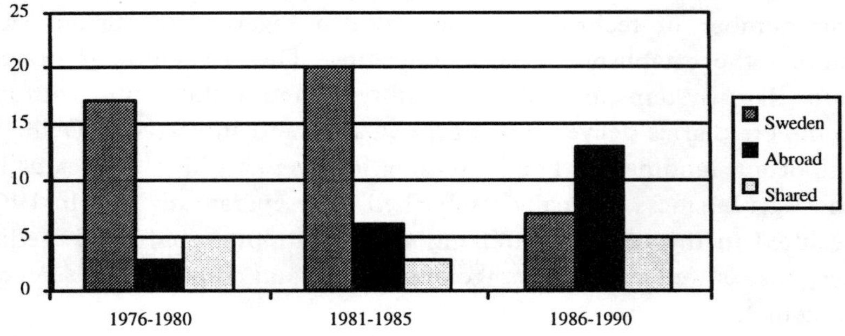

Note: Dominated implies that 75 per cent or more of the number of patents originated in either Sweden or abroad.

map in 1986). Positions in this field were eventually divested, although Chemap was restructured and retained. Ewos was acquired in 1979 and maintained until 1987. For part of this time, it was assigned responsibility for a separate business area, namely animal health and nutrition.

As several foreign production centres developed, there were also deliberate attempts to create "centres of excellence" in various foreign units[37]. The U.K. subsidiary concentrated on marine separators (which were later discontinued) and milking machinery, while the French subsidiary concentrated on production systems for wine and cheese. The Italian subsidiary, which had started production of local types of separators in the 1930s, was given responsibility for the development, production and export of olive oil separators. Titan, a Danish firm which was acquired in 1969, became the center for decanter centrifuges, which was complemented with an additional center through the acquisition of the U.S. firm Sharples (1988)[38]. Bran+Lübbe became the center for

37. In some cases, decisions to create centers of excellence had been taken quite early on. In the 1920s, one of the appointed centers for the development of marine separators was the De Laval Chadburn company in the United Kingdom.
38. As shown above, Sharples and Alfa Laval's U.S. subsidiary had cooperated in the 1880s, but since 1887 Sharples had carried out independent operations and developed the decanter technology.

dosing and analysing after the acquisition in 1981, while centres for pumping technology were established in Denmark, the United States, and the United Kingdom. The center for fermentation processes was located in Switzerland (Chemap), and the greater parts of fast food equipment operations were located in the United States.

6. Discussion

The evolution of foreign technological activity in Alfa Laval contains several elements which are not in line with the logic and implicit assumptions of the received view of the internationalisation process. The first element relates to the early, rapid and substantial shift of technological activity to the U.S. subsidiary, the subsequent oscillation of the overall foreign share of technological activity, as well as the recurrent shifts in the location of technological capabilities related to the separator technology. This development goes against the assumptions about incremental and irreversible internationalisation of the firm. The second element relates to the observation that technologies which first emerged in the U.S. and German units were subsequently shifted entirely to units located in Sweden. This development questions the assumption about internationalisation out of one single country. Indeed, the Alfa Laval case illustrates how design and manufacturing technology was transferred from Sweden to some European units at the same time as technological activity was generally being shifted back to the Swedish units.

The Alfa Laval case also questions the use of the terminology 'internationalisation of the firm', in particular in the context of multi-technology or multi-product companies. If the entire firm is studied by recording the sequence of established operations in foreign countries, data will represent an aggregate of several internationalisation processes, viz. one for each type of technology or product the firm represents. Consequently, the large and diversified firm is likely to display several patterns of internationalisation that differ at the technology or product level. If the various processes follow a logic of their own, the use of the firm as the basic unit of analysis produces results that in many cases are too composite to be useful (Zander, 1991)[39].

39. Zander (1991) provides an illustration of how four major innovations of the ABB group show vastly different patterns as to location and the conditions under which the final products have been manufactured outside Sweden.

6.1 The oscillating multinational firm

With separator demand picking up only slowly in Sweden, foreign sales became important for Alfa Laval from very early on. Foreign sales already in the first year of operation accounted for 50 per cent of the total, and had increased to 80 per cent by 1883. The three most important early markets were the United States, Germany, and Denmark[40]. With early foreign establishments and a majority of sales in foreign markets, it is not surprising that Alfa Laval would become involved in foreign technological activity from early on. What is surprising is that the firm's foreign technological activity became dominant at such an early stage. The U.S. subsidiary already in the period 1911-1913 dominated technological activity in more than 50 per cent of all technologies. This figure had reached more than 90 per cent around the time of the first world war (Figure 6). In effect, a majority of all technologies represented by Alfa Laval were dominated by technological activity in the U.S. subsidiary from 1910 and until the second world war.

It is reasonable to assume that the U.S. subsidiary had a relatively high propensity to patent in its home market, making the importance of U.S. technological activity appear greater than it actually was. At the same time, the Swedish units of Alfa Laval had shown that they were accustomed to patenting in the U.S. market before local operations were established (collaboration with local patenting agencies and consultants was extensive when Alfa Laval first entered the U.S. market). Although the foreign share of technological activity is probably inflated before the second world war, the substantial share of patenting by the U.S. subsidiary is unlikely to be explained by patenting propensity alone.

The early and rapid shift in technological activity to the U.S. subsidiary might be explained by the search for early customers (sales activities were set up where there were large populations of cows and early de-

---

40. In the period 1911-1913, Sweden accounted for 11 per cent of total sales, and foreign sales were concentrated to continental Europe and the United Kingdom (65 per cent of total sales), other countries including the United States (20 per cent), and the Scandinavian countries (4 per cent). The period after the second world war did not bring about any substantial changes in terms of the distribution and share of foreign sales. The European Communities, the Scandinavian countries, and the United States continued to account for the majority of total sales. During the 1960s, the share of Swedish sales had increased to about 35 per cent, mostly as a result of the expansion of the Olofström unit (which was later sold). Typically, however, foreign sales accounted for more than 80 per cent of the total, and approached the 90 per cent mark in the late 1980s.

Figure 6. The share of Alfa Laval's technologies dominated by U.S. patents originating outside Sweden, 1890-1990

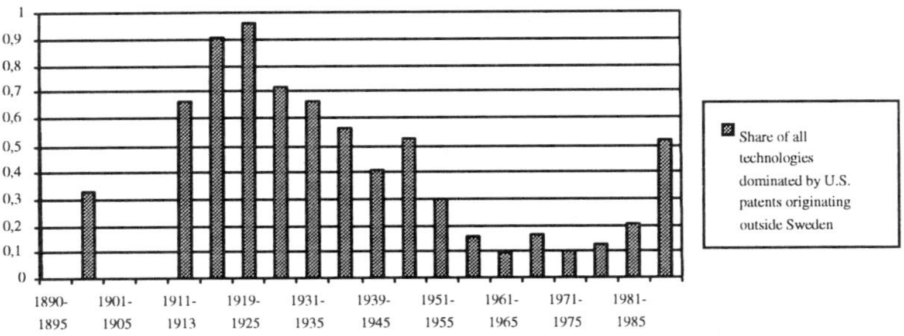

Note: Dominated implies that 75 per cent or more of the number of patents originated outside Sweden.

mand for the separation technology), an initial transfer of manufacturing knowledge from Sweden, and the subsequent exchange of technical information between the Swedish and U.S. units[41]. The U.S. subsidiary rapidly appears to have developed an environment conducive to innovation, as it took over not only a substantial part of the development of separators but also came to dominate technological activity throughout a range of other technologies. In particular, the important milking machine technology was pioneered in the 1920s, probably as a response to large and sophisticated demand among the U.S. customers.

While the U.S. subsidiary took on a dominant role in a majority of all technologies from about 1910, the overall foreign share of technological activity subsequently displayed a distinct pattern of oscillation. There are indications that responsibility for the separator and other technologies was shifted back to the Swedish units at about the time of the second world war. This development did not only involve increased technological activity in Swedish units, but also a simultaneous reduction in technological effort in the foreign units. Foreign units and in particular the U.S. subsidiary maintained a dominant share of technological activity in slightly more than 50 per cent of all technologies in the period

41. The U.S. subsidiary developed particular skills in manufacturing and materials, and is also known to have been involved in knowledge exchange concerning the design of separator bowls (Wohlert, 1982).

1946-1950, but the foreign share gradually declined to reach a level of just below 10 per cent in the period 1971-1975.

One answer to the shift of technological activity to Swedish units could be that the U.S. subsidiary for various reasons lost its development power, and that other units had to take over the responsibility for technological development. Sales had been down in the U.S. subsidiary in the 1920s and 1930s, and this might have reduced the propensity to invest further in research and development. It is also possible that the location of technological activity shifted from the United States to the Swedish units because of the turmoil created by the second world war, although this suggestion is not entirely in line with the outward transfer of technology which was effectuated to some European units just before the outbreak of the war.

Another suggestion would be that headquarters did not feel comfortable with having lost control over important technological capabilities, especially as the strong-headed management group in the United States for extended periods prevented cooperation on technological development[42]. As long as the U.S. subsidiary supplied a dominant share of profits, headquarters in Sweden might have found it inadvisable or politically impossible to interfere with local operations. However, as sales in the U.S. subsidiary were down in the 1920s and 1930s, and mistrust became an important aspect of headquarter-subsidiary relationships, headquarters might have felt that it was the right time to re-gain control over some of the most important technologies. The re-centralisation process may have been supported by the inclusion of Alfa Laval in the Wallenberg-sphere of interest and the assignment of Jacob Wallenberg to the board of directors in the 1930s. The Wallenberg group was actively involved in management and the restructuring of Swedish industry, which could have resulted in tighter control and a related re-centralisation of important functions in Alfa Laval.

As a related note, there is also the question of why the location of technological activity was shifted to Sweden rather than to other units in the international network of subsidiaries. It is reasonable to assume that development responsibility would be transferred to units with major financial and technological resources, but in the case of the milking

42. As the U.S. operations grew, there appears to have been very little exchange of information between headquarters and the U.S. subsidiary, and headquarter managers were at times not welcome at the U.S. subsidiary (Gårdlund and Fritz, 1983).

machine the Swedish units had notably failed in their development efforts. The United Kingdom would have been a better choice, as it had
proved profitable during much of the postwar period and was also capable of handling the milking machine technology. Possibly, the choice of
location indicates the existence of ethnocentricity which at the time in-
terfered with technological considerations.

Although the Swedish units had re-assumed a dominant role in the
development of separators and also taken over the main responsibility
for a majority of all technologies in the 1970s, the foreign share of technological activity started increasing again in the following two decades.
This development probably reflects Alfa Laval's attempts to sustain
growth by moving into new technologies in the late 1980s, in particular
by means of foreign acquisitions. In the period 1986-1990, the overall
foreign share of technological activity had risen again, reaching almost
40 per cent. The most likely scenario is that foreign acquisitions were
followed by the maintaining of local technological skills and the desig-
nation of development responsibility to the foreign units. It is also likely
that some of the new technologies were accidentally unrelated to existing businesses but kept for the time being.

6.2 'Reverse' internationalisation

The reverse internationalisation of technological activity related to milking machines and plate heat exchangers is particularly interesting under
the assumption of an internationalisation process starting out of one single country. The shift of technological activity related to the milking machine could be part of the overall trend of reduced technological activity
in the U.S. subsidiary in the postwar period. In plate heat exchangers,
uncertainty about the viability of operations in wartime Germany is likely to have initiated the rapid transfer of technological knowledge to the
Swedish units. In both cases, the shift might be interpreted as concern
about the ability to sustain growth through a continuous supply of new
and upgraded products to established customers.

Of course, reverse internationalisation is only relevant in a strict interpretation of established theory of the internationalisation process,
which emphasises the importance of one single country as the starting
point of all internationalisation efforts. If viewed from the perspective of
the foreign units that came up with the original technologies, the shift
of technological activity to Swedish units can be seen a traditional out-

ward drift of technology as it matures. Yet, the rapidity of change in the case of the plate heat exchangers and the significance of the shift in both technologies are not in line with expectations about incremental internationalisation processes. Also, even if the United States and Germany were regarded as 'home countries' the shift of technological activity to the small and in the case of the milking machine distant Swedish market appears odd in the light of established internationalisation theory.

While it is difficult to determine why the milking machine and plate heat exchanger technologies were shifted to Sweden, concerns about the ability to supply products to established customers appear to have been an important factor in the decision to transfer design and manufacturing technology to the U.K. and Italian units before the outbreak of the second world war. These manufacturing capabilities apparently developed into the capacity to produce new and upgraded products in later stages, as both units developed into centres of excellence in selected technologies in the 1980s. It is interesting to note that the transfer of design and manufacturing technology to the U.K. and Italian units took place at the same time as a major part of the technological activity in the U.S. subsidiary was shifted to the Swedish units. At about the time of the second world war, Alfa Laval was thus engaged in parallel processes of internationalisation and de-internationalisation of technological activity.

7. *Summary and Conclusions*

The evolution of technological activity in Alfa Laval over the past century casts some doubt on the underlying logic and implicit assumptions of the received view of the internationalisation process. Specifically, the empirical observations contradict the assumptions about an incremental and irreversible internationalisation process out of one single country, and complicate the identification of the 'home country' of the multinational firm. The chapter has only touched upon some possible explanations to the rapid and recurrent shifts in geographical location of technological activity. However, the observed patterns might be interpreted in the context of a firm with an overall ambition to sustain technological development and long-term growth. We find it fruitful to view the continuous struggle to profitably sustain technological development, use factors of production, and sell to customers as the engine that drives the geographical location and re-location of various activities performed by the firm.

This view emphasises how the need to sustain technological development in combination with changing demand conditions will not necessarily allow the firm to follow a predetermined and symmetrical pattern of internationalisation. It also emphasises the stochastic elements which are part of the development and internationalisation of the firm. The evolutionary determinism in international business literature downplays the possibility of setbacks or random events in firm histories, such as the re-introduction of trade barriers, shifts in the location of customer demand, changes in relative factor prices, or the creation or loss of local technological capabilities. These setbacks have been emphasised in the re-formulation of classic evolutionary theory, in which the gradual development towards increasingly advanced and 'higher' forms of life is questioned.

The empirical observations also highlight the problem of analysing the internationalisation process at the firm level, in particular in the context of multi-technology or multi-product firms. Indeed, when analysing the aggregate of many processes related to the exploitation of technology within the legal shell of the firm, there is a distinct risk that some of the driving forces cannot be detected or understood. By focusing on the evolution of individual technologies and products, the present study could provide a step towards a better understanding of firm growth across national borders.

References

Bartlett, C.A. and S. Ghoshal, 1989. *Managing Across Borders: The Transnational Solution.* Boston, MA: Harvard Business School Press.

Basberg, B.L., 1987. »Patents and the Measurement of Technological Change: A Survey of the Literature«, *Research Policy,* Vol. 16, 131-141.

Cantwell, J., 1992. »The Internationalisation of Technological Activity and its Implications for Competitiveness«, in O. Granstrand, L. Håkanson and S. Sjölander, (eds.). *Technology Management and International Business – Internationalization of R&D and Technology.* Chichester: John Wiley and Sons.

Cantwell, J., 1995. »The Globalization of Technology: What Remains of the Product Cycle Model?«, *Cambridge Journal of Economics,* Vol. 19, 155-174.

Dunning, J.H., 1977. »Trade, Location of Economic Activity and the MNE: A Search for an Eclectic Approach«, in B. Ohlin, P.-O. Hesselborn and P.M. Wijkman,(eds.). *The International Allocation of Economic Activity.* London: MacMillan Press.

Dunning, J.H., 1988a. *Multinationals, Technology and Competitiveness.* London: Unwin Hyman.

Dunning, J.H., 1988b. *Explaining International Production.* London: Unwin Hyman.

Dunning, J.H., 1993. *Multinational Enterprises and the Global Economy.* Addison-Wesley Publishing Company.

Dunning, J.H., 1994. »Multinational Enterprises and the Globalization of Innovatory Capacity«, *Research Policy,* Vol. 23, 67-88.

Ghoshal, S. and C.A. Bartlett, 1988. »Innovation Processes in Multinational Corporations«, in M.L. Tushman and W.L. Moore, (eds.). *Readings in the Management of Innovation* (2nd ed.). Ballinger Publishing Company.

Gårdlund, T. and M. Fritz, 1983. *Ett världsföretag växer fram – Alfa-Laval 100 år,* Del 1 och 2.

Hedlund, G. and Å. Kverneland, 1983. »Are Entry Strategies for Foreign Market Entry Changing? The Case of Swedish Investments in Japan«, in P.J. Buckley and P. Ghauri, (eds.) (1993). *The Internationalization of the Firm – A Reader.* Academic Press.

Hedlund, G. and J. Ridderstråle, 1995. »International Development Projects – Key to Competitiveness, Impossible, or Mismanaged?«, *International Studies of Management and Organization*, Spring-summer, Vol. 25 (1-2), 158-184.

Hedlund, G. and D. Rolander, 1990. »Action in Heterarchies: New Approaches to Managing the MNC«, in C.A. Bartlett, Y. Doz and G. Hedlund, (eds.). *Managing the Global Firm*. Routledge.

Håkanson, L., 1981. »Organization and Evolution of Foreign R&D in Swedish Multinationals«, *Geografiska Annaler*, Vol. 63B, 47-56.

Håkanson, L. and R. Nobel, 1993. »Foreign Research and Development in Swedish Multinationals«, *Research Policy*, Vol. 22, 373-396.

Johanson, J. and J.-E. Vahlne, 1977. »The Internationalization Process of the Firm – A Model of Knowledge Development and Increasing Foreign Market Commitments«, *Journal of International Business Studies*, Vol. 8 (1), 23-32.

Johanson, J. and J.-E. Vahlne, 1990. »The Mechanism of Internationalization«, *International Marketing Review*, Vol. 7 (4), 11-24.

Johanson, J. and F. Wiedersheim-Paul, 1975. »The Internationalization of the Firm – Four Swedish Cases«, *Journal of Management Studies*, October, 305-322.

Kogut, B., 1983. »Foreign Direct Investment as a Sequential Process«, in C.P. Kindleberger and D. Audretsch, (eds.). *The Multinational Corporation in the 1980s*. Cambridge, MA: MIT Press.

Kogut, B., 1990. »International Sequential Advantages and Network Flexibility«, in C.A. Bartlett, Y. Doz and G. Hedlund, (eds.). *Managing the Global Firm*. Routledge.

Lindqvist, M., 1991. *Infant Multinationals – The Internationalization of Young, Technology-Based Swedish Firms*. Published doctoral dissertation, Stockholm, Institute of International Business.

Pavitt, K., 1998. »Uses and Abuses of Patent Statistics«, in A.F.J. van Raan, (ed.). *Handbook of Quantitative Studies of Science and Technology*. Elsevier Science Publishers, North-Holland.

Ridderstråle, J., 1996, forthcoming. *Global Innovation – Managing International Innovation Projects in ABB and Electrolux*. Doctoral dissertation, Stockholm: Institute of International Business.

Schmookler, J., 1950. »The Interpretation of Patent Statistics«, *Journal of the Patent Office Society*, Vol. 32 (2), 123-146.

Schmookler, J., 1966. *Inventions and Economic Growth*. Cambridge, MA: Harvard University Press.

Wohlert, K., 1982. *Framväxten av svenska multinationella företag – en fall-studie mot bakgrund av direktinvesteringsteorin Alfa-Laval och separatorindustrin 1876-1914.* Uppsala: Almqvist and Wiksell.

Zander, I., 1994. *The Tortoise Evolution of the Multinational Corporation – Foreign Technological Activity in Swedish Multinational Firms 1890-1990.* Published doctoral dissertation, Stockholm: Institute of International Business.

Zander, U., 1991, *Exploiting A Technological Edge – Voluntary and Involuntary Dissemination of Technology.* Published doctoral dissertation, Stockholm: Institute of International Business.

Ågren, L., 1990. *Swedish Direct Investments in the U.S.* Published doctoral dissertation, Stockholm: Institute of International Business.

Åman, P., 1996, forthcoming. *The Making of a Cross-Border Firm – Transformation of International Management in Alfa-Laval AB.* Doctoral dissertation, Linköping University.

Appendix 1

Consolidated affiliates of Alfa Laval AB

Name of Unit	Year of Majority Ownership
Alfa Laval AB	
AB Separator	
AB Profila	1976-
AB Separator Nobel	
AB Zander & Ingeström	1969-
Alfa Laval Agrar GmbH	1977-
Alfa Laval Agri Inc.	1988-
Alfa Laval Agri Scandinavia A/S	1987-
Alfa Laval Cheddar Systems Limited	1979-
Alfa Laval Company Limited	1977-
Alfa Laval Inc.	1982-
Alfa Laval Marine and Power Engineering AB	1984-
Alfa Laval N.V.	1977-
Alfa Laval Pty Ltd.	1977-
Alfa Laval SA	1977-
Alfa Laval Separation AB	1984-
Alfa Laval Separation A/S	1980-
Alfa Laval Stalltechnik GmbH	1977-
Alfa Laval Thermal AB	1986-
Bran + Lubbe	1981-
Chemap AG	1986-
De Lavalco Co. Ltd. (Canada)	
De Laval Separator Co.	
Ewos AB	1978-1987
Formax Inc.	1989-
Hedemora AB	1990-
IMO-Industri AB	1969-1979
Jönköpings Mekaniska Werkstad AB	1969-1981
Koltek Oy	1990-
Lavrids Knudsen Maskinefabrik A/S	1979-
O.G. Hoyer A/S	1977-
Rosenblad Corporation (of Canada Ltd.)	1977-
Stal Refrigeration AB	1973-1976
Tagland (NZ) Ltd.	1990-
Tebel Machinefabrieken B.V.	1990-

Note: Total number of U.S. patents 1890-1990: 1,220.

6. Twenty Years After – Support and Critique of the Uppsala Internationalisation Model[43]

Bent Petersen and Torben Pedersen

1. Introduction – the two Levels of the Uppsala Model

Twenty years have passed since a research team from the Institute of Business Studies at the University of Uppsala published some seminal articles on the internationalisation process of firms (Carlson, 1975; Forsgren and Johanson, 1975; Johanson and Wiedersheim-Paul, 1975; Johanson and Vahlne, 1977). The subsequent debate, criticism and vigorous testing bear witness to the inspiration and influence of those articles, which together constitute the Uppsala Internationalisation model. The two basic assertions of the model are that 1) the internationalisation of firms should be seen as a process, and 2) the process will precipitate a manifest pattern of incremental commitment to foreign markets. Few, if any, have contested that the internationalisation of firms is associated with a process (if not in other ways, then as a cognitive process taking place in the minds of the decision-makers), whereas quite a few scholars have questioned the pattern of incremental commitment as a general rule.

The controversial part of the Uppsala model – the assertion that firms in general will display a pattern of incremental international commitment – comprises two levels: a theoretical and an operational level (Andersen, 1993). The latter, operational level was the first to be introduced (Johanson and Wiedersheim-Paul, 1975; Forsgren and Johanson, 1975): Based on in-depth, retrospective observations of four Swedish multinational firms, the revealed patterns of international operations were seen as reflecting incremental behaviour. Two years after the predominantly descriptive and inductive 1975-study, Johanson and Vahlne

---

43. The authors like to thank Mats Forsgren for his comments on a draft version of the paper. However, the responsibility for remaining errors and misinterpretations lies solely with the authors.

(1977) addressed the »Why«-question, and offered an explanation for the incremental behaviour in respect of internationalisation. By pure deduction, the theoretical level of the Uppsala model was introduced. A brief outline of the main elements of the theoretical and operational levels follows.

1.1 The theoretical level of the model

At the theoretical (deductive) level, the model tells us that time-consuming accumulation of foreign market knowledge will result in a pattern of incremental commitment to foreign markets. Let us briefly recapitulate the explanation provided for the incremental behaviour of firms. We will do this by quoting Johanson and Vahlne in their articles from 1977 and 1990, respectively:

> *In the [Internationalisation] model, it is assumed that the firm strives to increase its long-term profit, which is assumed to be equivalent to growth... The firm is also striving to keep risk-taking at a low level. These strivings are assumed to characterise decision-making on all levels of the firm.* (1977:36)

> *A critical assumption [of the Internationalisation model] is that market knowledge, including perceptions of market opportunities and problems, is acquired primarily through experience from current business activities in the market. Experiential market knowledge generates business opportunities and is consequently a driving force in the internationalisation process. But experimental knowledge is also assumed to be the primary way of reducing market uncertainty. Thus, in a specific country, the firm can be expected to make stronger resource commitments [...] as it gains experience from current activities in the market.* (1990:12)

1.2 The operational level of the model

At the operational (inductive) level, the model states that incremental commitment is observable through the formation of establishment chains (in the individual foreign market) and in the geographical sequence of foreign country markets (entered by the individual firm) with successively greater psychic distance.

Perhaps with the exception of the very large companies, the internationalisation of firms should be seen as an incremental process, i.e. a gradually deepening involvement in contrast to a one-off, discrete operation. The gradually deepening involvement manifests itself in two dimensions: a geographical dimension and an entry mode dimension, see Figure 1.[44]

It was asserted that the incremental or gradual internationalisation manifests itself geographically, by saying that, as a general rule, firms will enter countries successively in accordance to their resemblance to (psychic distance to) the home country. In addition, the foreign operation modes of a firm were supposed to make up a chain of establishments, reflecting an increasing commitment. The establishment chain most commonly observed by the Swedish research team involved five links in the chain (Forsgren and Johanson, 1975): 1) Sporadic export; 2) export via foreign intermediary (sales agency, distributor); 3) export via sales subsidiary; 4) a mix of export and FDI in the form of a subsidiary with assembly activities; and, 5) a fully-fledged production subsidiary. Figure 1 depicts this establishment chain.

Figure 1. The establishment chain most commonly observed by Swedish economists in the 1970s (Forsgren and Johanson, 1975).

Market \ Mode	Sporadic export	Foreign intermediary	Sales subsidiary	Assembly production	Production subsidiary
A					
B					
C					
.					
.					
.					

44. Later on, other Nordic scholars (Loustarinen, 1979; Hörnell and Vahlne, 1982) have added a third dimension to the incremental approach, namely an evolution in terms of the product offered. The observation was that the offering to foreign markets began with goods; thereafter, services, systems and know-how were added on a sequential basis until a complete problem-solving package was on offer.

2. Testing the Uppsala Model on the Theoretical Level

The theoretical part of the Uppsala Internationalisation model is a purely deductive construction. Very few empirically based investigations of the theoretical part have emerged since 1977. To our knowledge only two empirical studies have addressed the theoretical part of the Internationalisation model directly. Sullivan and Bauerschmidt (1990) did not find any support for the incremental process hypothesis, and neither did Millington and Bayliss (1990) in their empirical testing.

Other scholars (Benito and Gripsrud, 1992; Bonaccorsi and Dalli, 1992; Ali and Camp, 1993; Pedersen, 1994) have tested the Internationalisation model indirectly. In accordance with Johanson and Vahlne (1990)[45], it is assumed that the Internationalisation model will apply primarily to small and medium-sized firms. To the extent that large, diversified firms – all other things being equal – will be less risk averse to foreign market resource commitments than small firms, leap-frogging behaviour will also be more frequent.[46] However, the studies did not find the expected correlation between company size and cumulative behaviour: compared with a population of large firms, the propensity to leap-frogging (in contrast to the formation of establishment chains) was not particularly low among small and medium-sized firms.

In addition to the (sparse) challenges to the Uppsala Internationalisation model by studies based on empirical data, some criticism has been adduced from a deductive, theoretical point of view. Thus, Hirsch and Meshulach (1991:2) have noticed a »near absence of conventional economic drivers« in the model. In the same vein, Andersen (1993) argues that:

> »[The model] *seems to lean on assumptions about the firm's behaviour that dominated the literature in the 1960s ... while later theories ... to a higher degree incorporate the influence of the mar-*

---

45. »*When firms have large resources the consequences of commitments are small. Thus* big firms *or firms with surplus resources can be expected to make larger internationalisation steps.*« Johanson and Vahlne, 1990:12, our emphasis.
46. It is somewhat uncertain in which way the size and risk preference of a company are associated. Furthermore, company size may affect internationalization behaviour in other ways than via risk preference variation. As an example, resource constraints are less likely to restrict the internationalization behaviour of a very large company, whereas it is conceivable that a small firm occasionally will be precluded from making otherwise profitable foreign direct investments, cf., subsection 2.2.

ket side and regard the decision-maker as strategically more conscious« (1993:219).

Presumably, the originators of the Internationalisation model will make reference to the view that the model is partial, and will welcome *supplementary* explanations to the incremental behaviour of firms.[47] In this spirit we will submit three supplementary (rather than *alternative*) explanations for the incremental behaviour of firms in terms of servicing modes (establishment chains). These explanations are supplementary to the »conventional« explanation of incremental commitments as a result of experimental knowledge acquired over a period of time.

2.1 Export sales growth

Basic microeconomic theory tells us that a middleman (*in casu* a foreign intermediary) because of his accrued scope economies will be more cost effective in marketing and distribution than a producer (*in casu* an exporting firm). But as the sales of the individual product line reach a certain volume, the producer may reap scale economies. The producer integrates the marketing and distribution function into his organisation when scale economies exceed the scope economies of the middleman. Among others, Horst (1974) and Buckley and Casson (1985) have applied this microeconomic reasoning in the context of foreign market servicing modes. In their model of the optimal timing of an FDI it is favourable in terms of total costs to enter the foreign market via an intermediary and then, later on, to switch to a subsidiary. In the case where it becomes advantageous to locate production in the foreign market, a licence arrangement may appear as the most cost-effective servicing mode (bridging the intermediary mode and the FDI mode).

47. In the first of their two articles about the internationalization process Johanson and Vahlne (1977:32-33) emphasized the explanatory limitations of the model: »*Because we, for the time being, disregard the decision style of the decision-maker himself, and, to a certain extent, the specific properties of the various decision situations, our model has only limited predictive value*«. As noted before, the 1990-article included reservations as well. One of the originators of the Internationalization Model, Jan-Erik Vahlne, has pointed to the need for other explanations of firms' incremental internationalization than experiential learning (Nordström & Vahlne, 1988).

2.2 Accumulation of financial and management resources

In the realms of industrial organisation Michael Porter lists an array of entry barriers (Porter, 1980), one of which is large capital requirements. The argumentation can easily be transferred to the entry into a foreign market (instead of the entry into an industry) where the set-up costs of a subsidiary may exceed the financial capacity of a small or medium-sized firm. It is here assumed that the (venture) capital market is imperfect in the sense that no external financing of risky international ventures is open to the exporting firm. The exporting firm has to resort to internal accumulation of financial resources, and meanwhile, the servicing of the foreign market is left to low-investment modes such as an intermediary.

2.3 Increased global competition

As an effect of the ongoing liberalisation of trade and integration of national economies in general, companies experience increasing global competition. An imperative of the trend of increasing global competition is a continuous reassessment of the firm's foreign market servicing mode. It is argued that, all else being equal, increased competition will induce a deeper involvement by the entrant firms (see, as an example of this argument, Kim and Hwang, 1992). More specifically, the escalation of competition in a foreign market exposes the insufficiencies of the marketing mix as it is conducted by a local sales agency: more control of – and commitment to – the marketing policy is needed, and only a wholly-owned subsidiary can fulfil this need.

It is, however, an argument with a twist: other things being equal, increased competition will also heighten the risk of retaliation. Deeper involvement of a competitor in the home market may trigger retaliation in other export markets or the domestic market of the exporting firm (Sölvell, 1987). Accordingly, low-commitment servicing modes, such as local agencies or licensees, will be an appropriate option in this situation from an overall (concern-wise) point of view.

2.4 Empirical evidence of Danish MNCs

In a cross-sectional mail survey (see Box) the managers of Danish multinational companies were asked to rank the possible explanations of incremental entry mode behaviour.

Facts about cross sectional survey carried out in Denmark

The data were gathered through a mail survey comprising all Danish companies operating foreign subsidiaries. The companies were identified by studying the annual reports of all Danish companies reporting a 1993/94-turnover of more than DKK 40,000,000 (equivalent to approximately US $ 7,000,000). The population comprised 610 companies operating foreign subsidiaries of various kinds: sales-, service-, or production subsidiaries. The reason for choosing this population is that these companies operate a subsidiary in at least one foreign market. So, the companies have made a substantial resource commitment to at least one foreign market. After having carried out two time-separated test interviews the initial mailing was made in the beginning of February 1995. The questionnaires were mailed personally to the CEO. Most questionnaires were completed by CEOs or other top executives. A reminder was mailed two months after the initial mailing. Upon this follow-up procedure the number of replies reached 212, corresponding to a 35 per cent response rate. For various reasons (e.g., limited foreign operations) a number of returned questionnaires were inadequate. After excluding incomplete questionnaires, a total of 165 replies – making up a net response rate of 27 per cent – were usable for data processing. Reflecting a considerable variation the average company size (1994) of the sample is 803 employees providing turnover of DKK 872,000,000 (US $ 145,000,000). Almost one half of the personnel is employed outside Denmark and three quarters of the average company turnover originate from overseas activities.

The managers were asked to rank reasons for the observed *incremental* entry mode behaviour of their companies.[48] The resulting ranking is shown in *Table 1*. The Uppsala explanation of acquisition of knowledge about the foreign market is ranked second. The respondents attach greater importance to basic economic drivers (i.e. scale economies). Considerations about global competition are ranked on a par with expe-

48. Thus, companies undertaking leap-frogging behaviour were not included in this part of the questionnaire.

riential learning, whereas concerns about managerial and financial constraints are ranked below.

Table 1. Explanations of incremental entry mode behaviour as ranked by
Danish managers

Explanation of incremental entry mode behaviour	% of firms ranking the explanation as important
Increase of sales volume in the foreign markets	53%
Acquisition of knowledge about foreign markets	30%
Intensification of global competition	28%
Accumulation of financial resources	15%

An additional problem with the Uppsala Internationalisation model is
that it postulates a linear relation between market knowledge and market commitment. However, research by Erramilli (1991) on US service
companies has shown that this relationship is not straightforward. Erramilli found the relationship between the desire for market commitment (control) and market experience to be U-shaped. A manager with
little international experience will understate the obstacles of doing
business in the foreign market. Therefore, he will have a relatively high
desire for control of foreign operations. In as much as most of the subsequent actual experiences based on these presumptions are likely to be
unpleasant ones, a manager with a limited amount of experience is
likely to overstate barriers on foreign markets; lastly, additional experience is likely to restore the manager's confidence in his ability to overcome the barriers and increase the desire for commitment to the foreign market.

Keeping Erramilli's observation in mind, we cannot conclude that
more market knowledge, *ceteris paribus*, will make the decision-maker
more inclined to commit resources (increase control). Presumably, the
accumulation of market knowledge *does* have a bearing on the level of
foreign market commitment, but in both positive and negative ways depending on the decision-maker's level of informational sophistication in
the first place.

3. Testing the Uppsala Model on the Operational Level

While empirical studies on the theoretical level of the Uppsala internationalisation model are scarce, a disproportionately large number of studies have been made with the aim of testing the Uppsala model at the operational level.

The individual theory testing should take due regard of the specific set of boundary assumptions and constraints which delimit the application of the particular theory (Andersen, 1993:217). The scholars of the Uppsala research team have been vague about the boundary assumptions of their model; indications, rather than explicit specification of the assumptions have been given. Nevertheless, we find that it is reasonable to assert at least one boundary assumption of the Uppsala model: the model is primarily applicable to operations motivated in *market seeking*.

It appears implicitly from Johanson and Wiedersheim-Paul's empirical 1975-study that the dominant, or sole, motive of internationalisation is market seeking. If other motives, such as resource- or technology-seeking, were dominant, internationalisation via sporadic export, agents and sales subsidiaries would be meaningless. Accordingly, one should accept the market seeking motive as a boundary assumption of the Uppsala model.

A great deal of the empirical studies claimed to be testing the Uppsala model on the operational level (for an overview see Larimo, 1987) take production subsidiaries as their unit of analysis. On the face of it, this seems to be a good idea: in general, production subsidiaries represent the ultimate resource commitment to a foreign market in as much as they constitute large and mainly irreversible investments. Thus, the attendant market risk of production subsidiaries is accordingly high. Predictably, a risk averse entrant firm would have a strong preference for a gradual expansion in order to get a first-hand impression of the particular foreign market. Put differently: the larger the foreign investment, the more likely is a gradual entry mode behaviour (or, the *less* likely is leap-frogging behaviour).

On second thoughts, though, only including production subsidiaries would bias the parent firm population in the direction of above-average size firms. All else being equal, the parent company of a randomly chosen production subsidiary is likely to be bigger than the parent company of a randomly chosen sales subsidiary. However, the average production subsidiary assets *relative* to the average parent firm assets may not necessarily exceed the average sales subsidiary assets *relative* to the average parent firm assets. In other words, it is uncertain if production subsidiaries in general constitutes a larger market risk than do sales subsidiaries when the size of the parent firm is taken into consideration.

What seems certain, however, is that the market seeking motive is not as prevalent in relation to production subsidiaries as is it in relation to sales subsidiaries. As a consequence, those studies taking production subsidiaries as their unit of analysis generally pay too little regard to the boundary assumption of the model, which is the market seeking motive.

Presumably, a great deal of the empirical studies claimed to be testing the Uppsala model on the operational level, will be excluded if we subscribe to the boundary assumption screening criterion of the market seeking motive. In the following pages we will account for the ramifications more specifically, i.e. in respect to tests of establishment chains and geographical sequence.

3.1 Testing the establishment chain postulate

A number of empirical studies have suggested leap-frogging as the general rule of resource commitment to the individual foreign market. In doing so, the studies have questioned the Uppsala model postulates. However, these suggestions may be misplaced for three reasons:

1) the studies include international operations not motivated by market seeking,
2) leap-frogging is too broadly defined,
3) the studies do not take into account that *the individual* entry mode may reveal gradual expansion over a period of time.

Re 1) – the studies include international operations not motivated by market seeking:
a simple Chi-square test applied to our sample of establishments of Danish companies reveals that the propensity towards leapfrogging is significantly higher among those establishments motivated by resource seeking or global competition, instead of market seeking, see *Table 2.* Among the establishments motivated by market-seeking, only one third practices leap-frogging against more than two-thirds of the establishments with other motives. This difference is statistically significant on a $p<0.001$ level. It goes without saying that an internationalisation pro-

cess induced by sourcing motives (e.g. access to cheap labor) will exceed sales-oriented entry modes such as foreign sales agencies and sales subsidiaries.

Table 2. Relationship between motives and leap-frogging propensity

Pattern of commitment	Motive	
	Market-seeking	Resource-seeking or Global competition
Gradual	71 (67%)	17 (30%)
Leap-frogging	35 (33%)	40 (70%)
Total	106 (100%)	57 (100%)

Chi-square= 20.601 (p < 0.001)

Re 2) – leap-frogging is defined too broadly:
the Uppsala research team was rather rigid about what pattern would emerge from a gradually increasing involvement in the individual foreign market. The team outlined the above-mentioned establishment chain as the predominant way incremental behaviour would be implemented. However, other »establishment chains« are indeed conceivable. Welch and Luostarinen (1988) have comprehensively surveyed the literature on the process of internationalisation and argue that there is a wide range of potential paths any firm might take in internationalisation. Looking at their Internationalisation model in retrospect, Johanson and Vahlne (1990) accept that the model is too deterministic in its prediction of sequences.

Results from our track records of the most recent foreign establishments undertaken by Danish companies[49] may illustrate how the incidence of leap-frogging will diminish if other establishment chain sequences are considered.

Among the Danish firms included in this part of the study (N=162) the incidence of discrete internationalisation (»leap-frogging«) spans from every fourth to every second observation unit. The high estimate

49. The figures originate from the earlier-mentioned 1995-survey of Danish multinational companies, cf., *Box* in subsection 2.4.

of leap-frogging (51.2%) appears when we apply the original Uppsala (residue) definition of leap-frogging: an incremental entry mode pattern/strategy is associated with the establishment chain indicated in Figure 1, i.e. foreign intermediaries (agents or distributors) precede the establishment of subsidiaries. Other modes of previous activity – such as domestically based intermediary and own, home-based salesforce – are not considered to qualify for the term »systematic export activity«.

It appears from *Table 3* that, in particular, a home-based salesforce is a widely used pre-subsidiary entry mode (22.2%) among the Danish companies. »Pure« leap-frogging behaviour in the form of the establishment of subsidiaries with no preceding, systematic activity (but perhaps some sporadic sales activity – see the above-mentioned) makes up one quarter of the observations (25.9%); but with the addition of subsidiaries preceded by home-based salesforces (22.2%) and domestically based intermediaries (3.1%), this Uppsala-defined leap-frogging behaviour is observed in every second Danish company. Conversely, subsidiaries preceded by foreign sales agencies or distributors makes up the other half (48.8%).

Hence, gradually deepening involvement in terms of foreign market servicing modes can take other forms than the five-link establishment chain indicated by Forsgren and Johanson (1975). Firms may undertake a sequential build-up of foreign commitment by intensifying the sales effort carried out by home-based sales people (in this way omitting externalisation of marketing activities). Or some firms may commence foreign market servicing by setting up licence arrangements, later on making joint ventures with the licensees, and eventually establishing production subsidiaries. Surely, one can envisage additional manifestations of gradually deepening involvement; and these additional forms of establishment chains with equal right call for our attention.

Re 3) – the studies ignore that the individual *entry mode may reveal gradual expansion:*
furthermore, the individual institutional mode may in itself display an increasing involvement over a period of time:

> »*Understanding of the [internationalisation] process probably requires a more detailed case-by-case analysis, and a move away from simplistic pattern measures, from which wide-ranging infer-*

Table 3 Establishment patterns of Danish companies

PURE LEAP-FROGGING:	N	%
No systematic activity subsidiary	42	25.9
UPPSALA-DEFINED LEAP-FROGGING:		
No systematic activity subsidiary	42	25.9
Home-based salesforce subsidiary	36	22.2
Home-based intermediary subsidiary	5	3.1
Σ	83	51.2
UPPSALA-DEFINED ESTABLISHMENT CHAINS:		
Foreign sales agency subsidiary	25	15.5
Foreign distributor subsidiary	54	33.3
Σ	79	48.8
Total	**162**	**100.0**

ences about process are sometimes drawn. As it is, the categories of agent and sales subsidiary are relatively broad, making a wide range of feasible variation in types of operation within them.«
(Benito and Welch, 1994:12, our emphasis)

The quotation from Benito and Welch (1994) refers to the foreign market servicing modes of agents and sales subsidiaries, but the argumentation can apply to other modes as well. As an example, one may think of a production subsidiary which expands from very modest manufacturing activity (e.g. repair service and assembly activities) to a fully-fledged production plant. Actually, these production subsidiary sequences are explicitly indicated in the original establishment chain of Forsgren and Johanson (1975), but seldom operationalised in empirical studies.

3.2 Testing the geographical sequence (psychic distance) postulate

Several empirical studies have found that the observed firms in general did not enter foreign market in accordance with successively increasing psychic distance as predicted by the Uppsala model. However, these discrepancies with the operational level of the Uppsala model may be erroneous for two reasons :

1) the studies include international operations not motivated in market seeking,
2) the studies are based on psychic distance indices reflecting a national aggregate, instead of gauging psychic distance specifically for the individual firm or decision-maker.

Re 1) – the studies include international operations not motivated in market seeking:
again, the inclusion of other than market seeking motives tends to bias the empirical studies away from the Uppsala prediction of geographical sequence.

> »*One would expect [Scandinavian] firms that move abroad in search of cheap labor not to move to other Nordic countries, where labor costs are similar, but to move to Southern Europe or Asia. Similarly, investments that are undertaken to obtain natural resources must be distinguished from those whose purpose is to exploit intangibles. The choice of countries for firms seeking natural resources is limited by their uneven geographic distribution.*«
> (Hagen and Hennart, 1995:9)

Compared with sales subsidiaries production establishments are, in general, more likely to be motivated by other motives than market seeking. Studies based on observations of production subsidiaries are accordingly biased towards sourcing motives and strategic motives not covered by the Uppsala model. Thus, it has been indicated that the Uppsala model primarily explains export activities, and to a lesser extent involvement in overseas *production*. As an example, when Johanson and Wiedersheim-Paul (1975) outlined the establishment chain they noticed that:

»*The production establishments are influenced by different forces; on one hand, by psychic distance, on the other, by factors such as, e.g. tariffs, non-tariff barriers and transport costs. As a result it is hard to observe any correlation between psychic distance and production establishments*« (1975:18).

Besides, only a few observations of production subsidiaries are included in the 1975-study: the great majority of observations are agents and sales subsidiaries.

Re 2) – the studies are based on psychic distance indices reflecting a national aggregate:
most studies testing the geographical sequence predicted by the Uppsala model are using psychic distance measures reflecting a national aggregate, such as the Kogut-Singh index (Kogut and Singh, 1988). However, the observation of companies not complying with the geographical sequences defined on the basis of nationally derived psychic distance indices does not exclude that, after all, psychic distance factors do determine the country market selection. In principle, all deviations from a certain psychic distance pattern can be explained by special circumstances on the part of the observed company.

As an example, the managing director of an exporting firm may have spent several years in the Far East, and accordingly perceives little psychic distance in this market. In order to capture these particularities, the researcher should replace the very aggregated psychic distance indices with firm- or individual-specific information: how does the respondent export manager rank foreign countries in terms of psychic distance?

Admittedly, the gathering of such data requires more effort from the researcher, but is difficult to see how the potentially serious reliability problems in existing studies are otherwise to be eliminated.

4. Conclusion

On the theoretical level, the Uppsala Internationalisation model remains empirically unchallenged, and the fundamental idea of incremental internationalisation seems quite robust. However, it seems difficult to justify why accumulation of market knowledge should be the sole explanation of incremental entry mode behaviour. Competing explanations of gradually increasing commitment are available, which with equal right, can claim a pivotal role. Furthermore, the prescribed linear interrelationship between market knowledge and market commitment is questionable. Alternative, more complex interplays (such as U-curved functions) are possible.

Although numerous empirical studies have refuted or questioned the model in respect to its operational level, they have done so without taking due regard to the limitations of the model. Thus, a boundary assumption of the model is its delimitation to international expansion motivated by market seeking. On the other hand, we advocate that the very restrictive premises regarding the establishment chain should be slackened. Other establishment chains than the one submitted by the Uppsala research team are indeed conceivable and, accordingly, one should not reject gradualism because firms do not behave as prescribed by the »Uppsala establishment chain«.

Hence, twenty years after the emerge of the Uppsala Internationalisation model, many empirical studies and a lot of theoretical development still remain to be done.

References

Ali, A.J. and R.C. Camp, 1993. »The Relevance of Firm Size and International Business Experience to Market Entry Strategies«, *Journal of Global Marketing*, Vol. 6, No. 4, 91-108.

Andersen, Otto, 1993. »On the internationalization process of firms: a critical analysis«, *Journal of International Business Studies«*, Vol. 24, No. 2, 209-231.

Benito, G.R.G. and G. Gripsrud, 1992. »The Expansion of Foreign Direct Investments: Discrete Rational Location Choices or a Cultural Learning Process?«, *Journal of International Business Studies*, Vol. 23, No. 3, 461-476.

Benito, G.R.G. and L.S. Welch, 1994. »Foreign Market Servicing: Beyond Choice of Entry Mode«, *Journal of International Marketing*, Vol. 2, No. 2, 7-27.

Bonaccorsi, A. and D. Dalli, 1992. »Internationalization process and entry channels: evidence from small Italian exporters«, in Cantwell, (ed.). *Proceedings of the 18th Annual EIBA Conference*, University of Reading, 509-526.

Buckley, P.J., G.D. Newbould and J. Thurwell, 1978. *Going International: The Experience of Smaller Firms Overseas*. Macmillan, London.

Buckley, P. and M. Casson, 1985. *The Economic Theory of the Multinational Enterprise.* Macmillan, London.

Carlson, Sune, 1975. »How Foreign is Foreign Trade?«, *Acta Universitatis Uppsaliensis,* Studiae Oeconomiae Negotiorum 11, Uppsala.

Erramilli, K., 1991. »The experience factor in foreign market entry behavior of service firms, *Journal of International Business Studies,* Vol. 22, No. 3, 479-501.

Forsgren, M. and J. Johanson, 1975. *Internationell företagsekonomi.* Norstedts, Stockholm.

Hagen, J.M. and J.-F. Hennart, 1995. »Foreign production: The weak link in tests of the Internationalization Process Model«. *Competitive paper* presented at the AIB-meeting 1995 in Seoul, Korea.

Hirsch S. and A. Meshulach, 1991. »Towards a Unified Theory of Internationalization,« in Vestergaard, (ed.). *Proceedings of the 17th Annual EIBA Conference: An Enlarged Europe in the Global Economy (Volume 1),* Copenhagen Business School, 577-602.

Hornell, E. and J.-E. Vahlne, 1982. The Changing Structure of Swedish Multinational Companies, *Working Paper* 1982, No. 12, CIBS, University of Uppsala.

Horst, T.O., 1974. »The theory of the firm«, in J.H. Dunning, (ed.). *Economic Analysis and the Multinational Enterprise.* Allen and Unwin, London, 31-46.

Johanson, J. and J.-E. Vahlne, 1977. »The Internationalisation Process of the Firm – A Model of Knowledge Development and Increasing Market Commitment«, *Journal of International Busienss Studies,* Vol. 8, No.2, 23-32.

Johanson, J. and J.-E. Vahlne, 1990. »The Mechanism of Internationalisation«, *International Marketing Review,* Vol. 7, No. 4, 11-24.

Johanson, J. and F. Wiedersheim-Paul, 1975. »The Internationalization of the firm – Four Swedish cases«, *Journal of Management Studies,* Vol. 12, No. 3, 305-322.

Kim, W.C. and P. Hwang, 1992. »Global Strategy and Multinationals' Entry Mode Choice«, *Journal of International Business Studies,* Vol. 23, No 1, 29-53.

Kogut, B. and H. Singh, 1988. »The Effect of National Culture on the Choice of Entry Mode«, *Journal of International Business Studies,* Vol. 19, No. 3, 411-32.

Larimo, Jorma, 1987. »The foreign direct investment decision process. An empirical study of the foreign direct decision behavior of Finnish firms«, *Research Paper* No. 124, Proceedings of the University of Vaasa.

Luostarinen, Reijo, 1979. *The Internationalization of the Firm.* Acta Academic Oeconomicae Helsingiensis, Helsinki.

Millington, A.I. and B.T. Bayliss, 1990. »The Process of Internationalisation: UK Companies in the EC«, *Management International Review,* Vol. 30, No. 2, 151-161.

Nordström, K.A., 1991. *The Internationalization Process of the Firm: Searching for New Patterns and Explanations.* Doctoral dissertation, IIB, Stockholm School of Economics, Stockholm.

Nordström, K.A. and Vahlne, J.-E., 1985. »The Impact of Global Competition on the Process of Internationalization«, *Working Paper* presented at the Annual Meeting of SMS, Barcelona 1985. Stockholm: Institute of International Business.

Pedersen, Torben, 1994. *Danske virksomheders direkte investeringer i udlandet og udenlandske virksomheders investeringer i Danmark.* Ph.D.-thesis (in Danish with an English summary). Copenhagen Business School. Samfundslitteratur, København.

Porter, M.E., 1980. *Competitive strategy.* Free Press, New York.

Sullivan, D. and A. Bauerschmidt, 1990. »Incremental Internationalization: A Test of Johanson and Vahlne's Thesis«, *Management International Review,* Vol. 30, No. 1, 19-30.

Sölvell, örjan, 1987. *Entry Barriers and Foreign Penetration.* Doctoral dissertation. Stockholm School of Economics.

Welch, L. and R. Luostarinen, 1988. »Internationalization: Evolution of a Concept«, *Journal of General Management,* Vol. 14, No. 2, 34-55.

7. The Influence of Cultural Differences on Internationalisation Processes of Firms

An Introduction to a Semiotic and Intercultural Perspective [50]

Tine Langhoff

1. Introduction

In particular, international business research deals with the behaviour of multinational or transnational companies. A part of the research, usually denoted International Business Research, forms a distinct area, however, as it deals with internationalisation from a dynamic perspective. Within this area researchers have analysed firms' internationalisation processes, i.e., the way firms internationalise from their first contact with markets abroad until they become multinational companies. As a result, the research also deals with some aspects of small and medium-sized companies' international behaviour.

Research in internationalisation processes includes several studies conducted within the framework of the so-called Stage-Theory (Bilkey and Tessar, 1977; Cavusgil, 1980; Czinkota, 1982; Johanson and Wiedersheim-Paul, 1975; Johansen and Vahlne, 1977; Reid, 1981). In particular, the researchers have focused on the relationship between the so-called psychic distance and firms' market choice as well as their choice of operation forms (e.g., agents or own subsidiaries). The framework has been heavily criticised for being too simplistic and deterministic (e.g., Hedlund and Kverneland, 1985; Turnbull, 1987; Sullivan and Bauerschmidt, 1990; Andersen, 1993). Nobody has, however, analysed the concept of psychic distance in details.

50. The author thanks professor Tage Koed Madsen, Department of Marketing, Odense University for very valuable comments and suggestions.

The concept of psychic distance has been defined as »factors preventing or disturbing the flow of information between firm and market« (Johanson and Wiedersheim-Paul, 1975; Hörnell, Vahlne and Wiedersheim-Paul, 1973). The way the concept is described, it is supposed to be a kind of cultural variable. The assumption is that cultural differences create a distance between a firm and its markets (markets defined by national borders), which in turn influences the firm's internationalisation process.

After an introduction to the Stage-Theory, the concept of psychic distance will be analysed in detail below. It will be argued that the concept is poorly defined and measured. A review shows that other methods used for estimating a psychic or cultural distance between nations are problematic as well. This implies that the measurements do not capture the significance of cultural differences on firms' internationalisation processes.

As an alternative to the psychic distance concept, the chapter will introduce an established cultural approach, used in the field of anthropology. The approach is based on semiotics which has been successfully applied to international marketing and consumer behaviour. In semiotics, cultural differences are analysed as communication barriers. Cultural barriers exist because the firm and its markets »are living« in different meaning systems. These different meaning systems may create cultural heterogeneity across a firm's markets, depending on meanings assigned to the firm's products and marketing concepts by the users. Accordingly, firms are influenced by cultural differences in different ways. However, we do not know how cultural heterogeneity influences firms' processes of internationalisation.

It is suggested that we have to deal with cultural heterogeneity *and* the firm's ability to handle this heterogeneity if cultural influences on internationalisation processes are to be established. It is the firm's ability to internationalise in cross cultural contexts that determines how culture influences its internationalisation process. Accordingly, the chapter introduces an intercultural approach which focuses on a firm's ability to interact with foreign cultural contexts. This ability is conceptualised as a firm's intercultural competence.

The concept of intercultural competence is a contribution to the field, because it deals with cultural aspects based on an established cultural approach. So far the framework of the Stage-Theory has been based on a cognitive approach. In doing so, the research assumes that there is a linear relationship between the knowledge and the behaviour of the firm. According to the field of psychology, however, this may not be the case. The intercultural approach may be a useful contribution to future research, because it focuses on how firms interact with foreign cultural contexts instead of what they know about these contexts.

2. The Framework of the Stage-Theory

The internationalisation process literature has its roots in two pioneering articles written by Swedish researchers (Johanson and Wiedersheim-Paul, 1975; Johanson and Vahlne, 1977), where they describe firms' international development processes as a series of stages. The following introduction will concentrate on these Swedish studies because they form the first, and hence most quoted model, conducted within the framework of the Stage-Theory. The model is usually referred to as the Swedish Internationalisation Model (Johanson and Vahlne, 1977).

Inspired by Cyert and March (1963) and Penrose (1959), the model describes the internationalisation process as slow, sequential and gradual, since it represents the firm's gradual establishment in, integration of, and knowledge about foreign markets. A firm's internationalisation starts when the domestic market is close to saturation and it seeks new alternatives. Abroad the firm is confronted by considerably more uncertainty, however, and consequently the model assumes that it seeks alternatives that resemble the present ones as much as possible. The uncertainty will encourage the firm to first exploit those opportunities where the degree of »foreignness« is least. Only later, alternatives with a higher degree of foreignness are exploited when the perceived uncertainty is reduced due to an increasing experience with international operations.

The degree of foreignness alludes to the fact that a lack of knowledge about local business methods, patterns of consumption, etc. creates uncertainty. Activities undertaken outside the firm's home base are perceived as more uncertain than similar activities carried out at home, even where the physical (geographical) distance is the same. This degree of foreignness between a firm and its markets is conceptualised as »psychic distance«.

A fundamental characteristic of the model is that it is the individual decision maker's cognitive perceptions of a firm's capabilities and the perceived opportunities and problems associated with the markets, which explain corporate behaviour. It is therefore expected that decisions to begin operations in a foreign market partly depend on already acquired experiences within the firm and partly on the relation of the new venture to the firm's present business activities. In doing so, the model is operating on the cognitive level.

According to Johanson and Vahlne (1977, 1990), the model explains two patterns of firms' international behaviour: Firstly, the psychic distance between the home market and the host countries explains the timing and location of the establishments to the effect that the markets first served are those to which the psychic distance is smallest. Secondly, the psychic distance explains or at least influences the number of markets served, the absolute amount of commitment, and the degree of commitment to each market at any given point of time (see also Johanson and Wiedersheim-Paul, 1975).

At the time the model was published, it was considered as pioneering due to a new approach applied to international business research. Later, the model has been heavily criticised, mainly because of its simplicity and determinism, but also because of the changing behaviour of international oriented firms. Today, the internationalisation processes of firms are much more heterogeneous than they were decades ago. Nobody has considered the psychic distance concept, however. Other international business researchers have suggested different cultural concepts and methods but, as it is discussed further below, their research questions are different.

3. Psychic Distance Analysed

The concept of psychic distance (for a review of the Swedish research on the concept see Nordström and Vahlne; 1992) is a kind of cultural concept which deals with a distance between a firm and its markets (see the definition above), i.e., the firm and its markets are units of analysis. This psychic distance is caused by *individual* decision-makers' perceived uncertainty of the present and future characteristics of different markets as a result of a perceived degree of foreignness (Johanson and Vahlne, 1977). The purpose is, however, to use the concept as an independent variable in order to explain *firms'* internationalisation. Accordingly, the psychic distance concept is applied to the firm level as unit of analysis, not the individual level.

A psychic distance is not, however, an objective factor that exists between a firm and its markets. This means that the distance cannot be seen as an independent variable which influences all firms in the same way. It is a distance that exists in the minds of individuals and the perceived distance depends on the way these individuals see the world – the individual perception of reality. As such, the term »psychic« refers to something in the mind of each individual.

As a result, it is a critical concept for business researchers to adopt when examine a firm as the unit of analysis. The concept does not refer to an objective concept or measurement of a cultural distance which may influence *corporate behaviour*. Hence, the psychic distance may not capture the influence of cultural differences on *firms'* internationalisation processes. The question is whether the concept is supposed to capture the influence of cultural differences in general, i.e., is the psychic distance the same as cultural distance?

It is not possible to uncover the precise semantic meaning of psychic distance because the researchers (Johanson and Wiedersheim-Paul, 1975; Hörnell, Vahlne and Wiedersheim-Paul, 1973; Johanson and Vahlne, 1977) are vague in their descriptions. The factors, supposed to »prevent or disturb the flow of information«, are only emphasised as examples, such as: »Differences in language, culture, political systems, level of education, level of development etc.« (cf. Johanson and Wiedersheim-Paul, 1975). It seems reasonable to believe, however, that a cultural concept is attained because it is supposed to capture a perceived degree of foreignness – a foreignness that may be caused by cultural differences. Further, other researchers interpret psychic distance as cultural distance (see e.g., Carlson, 1975; Kogut and Singh, 1988; Nordström, 1991; Nordström and Vahlne, 1992). Accordingly, it may be justified that psychic distance refers to the effect of cultural differences on firms' internationalisation processes.

There are several problems with this concept and hence the Swedish Internationalisation Model. First of all, the model assumes that all firms at a given stage of internationalisation are influenced by cultural differences in the same direction and by the same intensity. This implies that firms are only influenced by cultural differences (or psychic distance) as long as they are in the beginning of their internationalisation process, i.e., they have not penetrated the entire world market. It is not justified, however, that multinational companies as opposed to smaller companies are not influenced by cultural differences in all aspects of their international behaviour.

Secondly, it has been shown that it may be problematic to use the country as the unit of analysis when dealing with psychic or cultural distances. Madsen (1990, p. 20) concluded from his research on cultural biases of Danish sales people acting in foreign cultures: »Interestingly, the study indicates that the effect of cultural biases may be most important when exporting to culturally close markets. The reason may be that management as well as export sales people are more concerned with the large and obvious cultural differences.« This implies that neither an actual cultural distance (as an »objective« measurement of the distance between two countries) nor a perceived cultural distance (as a »subjective« measurement of the distance between two countries) thus seem to be the most relevant units of analysis in investigating the impact of culture on international marketing management. What really matters in a relationship between individuals from different cultures is the gap between actual and expected behaviour of the sales person and of the buyer.

An introduction of a semiotic concept of culture implies that Madsen's conclusion may be applied to firms' relationships with its markets as well (i.e., the firm and its markets are units of analysis). This is the subject of a later section. In the following, the concept will be analysed more in details.

The problems of the psychic distance concept become evident when the definition and the methodology are analysed. The missing description of the concept's exact meaning implies that there is no consistency between the definition of the psychic distance and the conclusion of the Swedish model. Johanson and Vahlne (1977) conclude that the internationalisation process is driven by experiential knowledge (learned by experience) as opposed to the so-called objective knowledge (taught knowledge). In the literature published in Swedish (Hörnell, Vahlne and Wiedersheim-Paul, 1973; see especially Carlson, 1975) it is argued, however, that information is data which may be collected from books, statistics etc., i.e., objective knowledge. According to the definition of psychic distance, psychic distance exists because of factors preventing or disturbing the flow of information (i.e., objective knowledge). This means that either the internationalisation process is not driven by experiential knowledge, or it is not influenced by psychic distance. This is not, however, in accordance with the conclusion of the model.

Secondly, the Swedish researchers do not discuss in details how the concept is to be operationalised. It seems that there is a poor connection between the definition of the concept and the method used for estimating a psychic distance between a single country (Sweden) and 15 other countries in the world. Their estimate is based on »hard« as well as »soft« data. The »hard« data originates from statistical macro information (e.g., level of development and education in different countries) while the »soft« data is based on subjective estimates. The researchers then identify the most significant variables (multiple regression analysis) which are: (1) the level of development of the foreign country in question; (2) the difference in level of development between the home and the foreign country; (3) the level of education; (4) business language; (5) cultural distance; (6) everyday language; and (7) existing relationships between the home and the foreign country. At last, the results are adapted according to export managers' experience. In order to give an impression of the final results, the list of countries, defined by the psychic distance from Sweden, is shown in Figure 1 below.

The construction and use of this list seem very problematic. It is a very unusual construction as the Swedish researchers are trying to make an – subjectively adjusted – objective list of countries. It is not clear how they achieve the dependent variable used in the multiple regression analysis. Secondly, they do not discuss the problems of using macro information. They assume without any arguments that there is a linear relationship between (1) macro information, where a country is unit of analysis; (2) individual perceptions of a distance, i.e., that individual is unit of analysis; and (3) firms international behaviour, i.e., the firm is unit of analysis. They do not at all discuss whether the statistical variables used are independent of one another. This is rather suggestive because Loustarinen (1989) in a comparable study reduced the variables from nine to one due to multicollinearity in the data.

Figure 1. Psychic Distance From Sweden to Other Countries

Denmark	1	Switzerland	9
Norway	2	Canada	10
Finland	3	Austria	11
W. Germany	4	France	12
Great Britain	5	Italy	13
Netherlands	6	Spain	14
Belgium	7	Portugal	15
USA	8		

Source: Adapted from Nordström and Vahlne, 1992.

As a result, the concept of psychic distance is estimated by an unusual method and is based on an arbitrary definition. There is no clear connection between definition and method[51].

4. Other Estimates of a Cultural or Psychic Distance

In the field of international business and export behaviour, research has used four different methods for estimating cultural differences.

Müller and Köglmayr (1986) have used cognitive-mapping for uncovering *individuals'* subjectively perceived images of a psychic distance between nations. This is an interesting method for this particular study as their unit of analysis is individual decision-makers, not firms. The way the cognitive-mapping has been used has, however, some drawbacks. First of all, they try to control the measurement for a geographical (objective) distance between countries in order to achieve the »real« psychic distance. They do not achieve this goal because they are controlling for one of those factors which the subjective image may be composed of. Hence, a person's subjective image may be composed of impressions originating from many different sources – geographical distance may be just one of them. This may be the reason why the researchers find the estimate systematically biased. Secondly, the measurement attempts standardisation, using a neighbouring country as reference stimuli. As a result, the measurement cannot be use for cross national/cultural comparisons, because the reference stimuli are not the same across countries (i.e., the perceived distance between home and a neighbouring country is not the same in different countries). This implies that the measurement can only be used for comparisons between decision-makers in the same country.

The three other methods are used in studies where the firm is the unit of analysis. In this respect, they are different from the first one mentioned.

---

51. The critique of the Swedish research concerns the measurement and results of the psychic distance. It is not a critique of Swedish international business research in general. Other Swedish researchers (see e.g., Hallén & Wiedersheim-Paul, 1979; Sandström, 1992) have discussed the influence of a cultural distance on business relationships, i.e., according to a network approach. They are focusing on the influence of cultural differences on buyer-seller relationships, i.e. the cultural distance is individualised. The newer Swedish research is not, however, based on an established anthropological approach to culture, it is more descriptive in nature.

Nordström (1991) replicated the original Swedish study by focusing on internationalisation processes of Swedish firms. However, Nordström estimates psychic distance in a different way: A psychic distance between Sweden and several nations in the world is estimated based on an average of individual perceptions. The estimate seems more in accordance with accepted methods, even with a weak representativity in the study. It is questionable in international business research, however, because it assumes a linear relationship between individuals' perceptions of a distance and the influence of this distance on the behaviour of the entire firm. As pointed out earlier, the behaviour of a person and the behaviour of the entire firm is not always in accordance with a single person's knowledge.

Several other studies (Kogut and Singh, 1988; Shane, 1992; Benito and Gripsrud, 1992; Nordström and Vahlne, 1992) have based their estimates of a cultural distance between nations using the same method. Beside Nordström and Vahlne (1992), these studies are not complete replications of the Swedish study as they focus on special aspects of firms' international behaviour, not the entire internationalisation process. The estimates of the cultural distance are based on a method developed by Kogut and Singh (1988, p. 422): »Using Hofstede's (1984) indices a composite index is formed based on the deviation along each of the four cultural dimensions (i.e., power distance, uncertainty avoidance, masculinity/femininity, and individualism) of each country from the United States rating. The deviations are then corrected for differences in the variances of each dimension and then arithmetically averaged.«

The use of this method seems very problematic. Hofstede's dimensions uncover four fundamental dimensions of national cultural differences as they are expressed in an organisational setting. For researchers, subscribed to the so-called ETIC approach (as opposed to the EMIC approach mentioned below), the dimensions may be considered as ostensibly universal as this approach is primarily concerned with identifying universals (see e.g., Sekaran, 1983; Usunier, 1993). Each of the dimensions covers *different* cross cultural aspects of management (the main purpose of the study). They are supposed to reveal different universal dimensions of the cultural relativity of management theories. As a result all the dimensions may be used separately or in combination, but they may not be averaged. This means that each of the dimensions may be applied to a study like Kogut and Singh (1988), because it is analysing the influence of culture on the choice of entry mode (i.e, the choice of greenfield investment, joint venture or acquisition), and this choice may be influenced by cultural differences in management principles. Hofstede's dimensions and the results of the studies mentioned above cannot, however, be used to criticise the Swedish model, even though they all do so. Hofstede's results concerns cross-cultural differences in people's relationships with one another when they act as employees, i.e., intra-organisational relationships across nations. They do not explain cultural differences in general, for instance cross cultural differences in consumer behaviour.

The Swedish model focuses on cultural differences between a firm and its markets (see the definition of the concept). In a very simple way the model tries to take the cultural characteristics of a firm's markets into account. These characteristics must also include cultural variations in the behaviour of a firm's customers because it may influence its internationalisation process (it influences the potential market of a firm's products for instance, see also below). Identification of universal dimensions applied to cross cultural variations in firms' relationships with their markets is not, however, the research question in the studies examined as their measurement of culture is based on cross cultural variations in intra-organisational relationships.

The last method identified is developed by Klein and Roth (1990, p. 33-34): »Perceptions of the foreign market relative to Canada were elicited, using 7-point scales ranging from »very similar« to »very different«. Five aspects of psychic distance were assessed: (i) language of the country; (ii) accepted business practices; (iii) economic environment; (iv) legal system; and (v) communications infrastructure.« The reason for doing so is that the measure is based on the theoretical definition of the psychic distance concept. However, as pointed out in the last section, these five aspects are not a part of the theoretical definition. They are partly included in the seven significant variables, resulting from the multiple regression analysis. Accordingly, the method by Klein and Roth may be criticised in the same way as the original Swedish construct

As a result of the methodological problems, this chapter introduces a theoretical approach to culture. The purpose is to achieve a more comprehensive and richer understanding of firms' internationalisation processes in foreign cultural contexts.

International business researchers have not discussed the potential problems of using »culture« as an independent variable. Cultural researchers who subscribe to the so-called EMIC approach point out that culture cannot be treated as an independent variable due to the nature of culture itself (see Sekaran, 1983). This implies that it is not possible to identify any causal relationships because no universal dimension will meaningfully describe the cross cultural variations. Culture defines people's reality – people's relationship to and perception of reality. As a result, the EMIC approach holds that behaviour, attitudes, values etc. are expressed in a unique way in each culture, i.e., what is meaningful is defined by each culture.

This means that universal dimensions do not cover all relevant aspects of cultural differences, especially not when the research question is so complex (i.e., the influence of culture on firms' internationalisation processes and on their relationships with their markets). The author will focus on developing a conceptual framework rather than a ready-made method to measure cultural differences, simply because the results of such studies are problematic.

5. A Semiotic Approach to Cultural Analysis

By their very nature cultural analyses are extremely difficult to carry out because there exists no ready-made conceptual approach to analyse culture. Furthermore, there is no single defined concept which completely and perfectly covers both culture's contents and its effects on and importance for human beings since the signs which different societies collectively call »culture« merely reflect these societies' (and each single author's) cultural universe. In other words: »There is far from being agreement on how to define 'culture', and even less on how it can be studied. No scientific discipline offers a complete culture-analytical approach« (Askegaard, Gertsen and Madsen; 1991, pp. 111-12). Accordingly, the perspective chosen for a study can always be discussed. The perspective in this chapter is an established approach in the field of anthropology which originates from semiotics. This approach has been successfully applied to international marketing and consumer research and, as we shall see, it may contribute successfully to the field of internationalisation research as well.

It is very difficult to compare different cultures because behaviour, phenomena, values, ideas, constructs, artifacts, etc. may have different meanings across cultures. For instance, the meaning of the concept »individual« is different in different parts of the world. As a result, Hofstede's (1984) dimension Individualism/Collectivism may not be considered as universal because people do not share the same meaning (comprehension) of this dimension. This implies that cultural analysis which focuses on culture as consisting of many different »variables« (e.g., values, artifacts, constructs, behaviour) do not capture the nature of culture itself. The significance of culture on human life cannot be explained and understand by reducing cultural studies to these variables.

Common to all cultures, however, is the assignment of meaning, i.e., humans' creation of meaning of the world, which is analysed by semiotics. A semiotic perspective on culture implies that culture is seen as a network of significations (Geertz, 1973); a network which defines reality as it represents itself to people. Human beings use and need culture as a »mechanism« to organise a coherent meaning of the world around themselves and they do so by developing and applying symbols. The organisation of intellectual fellowship in human societies takes place primarily through communication as a means of establishing meaningful coherences which integrate individuals into a shared identity. Geertz (1973) shows that cultural barriers mainly become visible as communication barriers due to the fact that man is a symbol-creating being.

According to reception theory, this assignment of meaning occurs at the individual level. This means that even though two persons may come from the same culture, they cannot be perfectly sure that their communication and behaviour (i.e., symbolic meanings) are interpreted correctly. However, in every culture people use some general patterns or codes in the assignment of meaning which makes it easier for them to interpret each other's behaviour. In a way, the codes of a given culture delimit the range of conceivable possibilities regarding the meaning assigned to a given sign (Christensen, 1993). This means that culture helps people to understand the behaviour or communication of others. People do not interpret communication in an absolutely predetermined way.

Relating the semiotic perspective to the results of the Swedish research implies that cross national comparisons are not interesting in themselves, because the »factors preventing or disturbing the flow of information« may have different meanings in different cultures. To Geertz it is neither possible nor relevant to identify causal relationships. What is central is to *understand* the behaviour, the artifact, the values etc. in the cultural context which they form a part of.

Secondly, the semiotic perspective questions whether it is possible to identify the significance of cultural differences on firms' internationalisation processes without reference to a specific firm and to the firm's specific markets/segments. Using nations and firms in general as units of analysis are not in accordance with a meaning perspective. This is the subject of the next section.

6. Implications for Internationalisation Research

International marketing has focused on consumers' buying behaviour, using a semiotic perspective. A pioneering result is that people communicate something about themselves when they act as consumers: »Consumers buy the meaning that they find in products for the purpose of cultural identification« (Usunier, 1993, p. 206; see also Levy, 1959). This point has been expressed by Myers and Myers (1992) as »you cannot not communicate« and »everything is communication«. Conceptualising everything as communication implies that there are many more symbols than those used in our language. Meaning is to be found in many other situations than just verbal communication situations. Bouchet (1991, p. 5) describes consumption as a way of communicating: »Individuals and groups use consumption to communicate something about the way they organise the world into a hierarchy of values. Meaning is to be found in any human relationship from the reading of poetry to the buying of bread.«

These results from consumer behaviour have very important implications for internationalisation research. They show that different firms may be influenced by culture in different ways depending on the specific cross cultural meanings of their supply (in a very broad sense, e.g., products, marketing concepts, services). The cultural assignment of meaning happens both in the consumer markets and in the industrial markets due to the fact that employees also organise the world (i.e., defines the firm, market, competition, and potential consumers by applying symbols (see Weick, 1979; Christensen 1993).

Based on Geertz' (1973) semiotic concept of culture, the world of complex meaning patterns is also a part of the firm's reality when internationalising. A cultural difference between a firm and its market exists, because the firm and market »are living« in different meaning systems, i.e., a cultural barrier is first and foremost a communication barrier (e.g., Geertz, 1973; Askegaard et al., 1991).

Some firms operate in culturally very heterogeneous markets compared to others whose markets are more homogeneous in a cultural sense. The cultural heterogeneity of a firm's international markets depends on the meaning patterns assigned by potential users of the firm's supply. Firms are influenced by cultural differences as their product and marketing concepts are being related to the user's cultural meaning systems (e.g., Buhl, 1993). The concepts have symbolic meanings which are related to the overall meaning systems of the users in the cultural contexts where they are living. As a result some firms are faced with a high degree of cultural heterogeneity because the cultural meanings of their products and marketing concepts vary significantly across markets (or segments, depending on how they are defined). Other firms are luckier because the cultural meanings are rather similar across markets.

Some authors (e.g., Levitt, 1983) have argued that the world has become more globalised and that consumers' behaviour, preferences and taste tend to homogenise. However, little empirical evidence have been found for the world-wide homogenisation of the preferences of the consumer. The discussions for and against the worlds homogenisation is characterised by many anecdotes, myths and examples. Usunier (1991, 1993) discusses this in details and concludes that the competition tends to be globalised but consumers' preferences and behaviour do not. The cultural variation still remains quite significant even for so-called globalised brands: »Consumers always 'construct' the identity of brands, even for 'global products', and they do so on a local culture and identity base« (Usunier, 1993, p. 174). This implies that firms may be confronted and influenced by cultural heterogeneity even though the products sold world-wide are identical because it may influence the necessary marketing concepts and marketing communication.

These results show that the cultural diversity may differ across firms, independent of their experiential knowledge. This is not recognised by the Swedish Internationalisation Model. From the semiotic approach it follows that the cultural diversity of the firm's export markets can only be established based on each single firm's supply. This means that a »psychic« or cultural distance between the firm and its markets can only be established based on which firm we are talking about.

A second implication, related to the first noted, is that the markets or segments of a firm are not, or only on very rare occasions, defined by national borders, e.g., the US-market. Markets are first and foremost defined by a homogeneity of meaning patterns among a certain group of product users. This means that markets may exist across nations. In fact, the concept of a national culture may seem dangerous in many respects, because it sums up a complex and multiform reality. As a result, cultural boundaries are not following national boundaries (Usunier, 1993).

It may be concluded that the Swedish Internationalisation Model does not explain cultural influences on firms' internationalisation processes. The psychic distance concept is a questionable concept based on an arbitrary definition and an unusual empirical method. The distance concept is an analytical abstraction but it is necessary to enrich the concept and/or the entire approach because the distance concept blur important aspects of the analysed behaviour. The Swedish Internationalisation Model cannot explain how cultural diversity of export markets may influence firms' internationalisation patterns. These patterns can be described in several dimensions (cf. Strandskov, 1987). However, the Swedish Internationalisation Model does not even explain how the psychic distance and cultural differences in general influence the: (1) products exported; (2) markets served; and (3) operations forms used by a firm (i.e., three dimensions often used to describe firms' internationalisation patterns). Beside this, it does not deal with cultural influence on the interrelationships between these three dimensions. Consequently, the analytical abstraction of psychic distance is not able to grasp important aspects of firms' internationalisation processes.

7. An Intercultural Approach to Internationalisation Processes

The intercultural approach deals with firms' interaction with their markets from a cultural perspective. It is suggested that cultural heterogeneity can be analysed from a competence-based point of view, i.e., firms' ability to internationalise in a cultural heterogeneous world is a part of their competence development (see the resource-based point of view; e.g., Wernerfelt, 1984). In doing so, the influence of cultural differences on firms' internationalisation processes is analysed from a interactionist/ behavioural point of view. It is a firm's ability to handle cultural heterogeneity across its culturally defined segments and its ability to interact with these segments that determines how the cultural dimension influences its internationalisation process. Hence, it will be argued that is not the firm's knowledge about cultural differences in itself that determines this process (as asserted by the Swedish Internationalisation Model).

According to Graham and Adler (1989), an intercultural approach differs from a cross-cultural approach. In a cross-cultural approach one compares two or more groups of people belonging to particular cultures, i.e., the study is comparative in nature, whereas in an intercultural approach one is analysing the encounter between people belonging to different cultures. This means that in an intercultural approach the analysis includes the totally new relationships which arise as a result of the interaction. The interactionist perspective is also important when analysing firms' relationships with their markets because a firm may be confronted with new cultural meaning systems during its internationalisation process. The cultural heterogeneity may change as a result of a firm's own strategic changes which in turn influence the firm's further internationalisation process. For instance, the cultural heterogeneity may change as a result of the firm's product developments. Hence, the influence of cultural differences on the firm is – at least to some extent – influenced by its own strategic decisions. This implies that we may get a better understanding of cultural influences on internationalisation processes when it is analysed from an intercultural perspective.

The effect of cultural heterogeneity on the firm as a whole has, as yet, not aroused much interest in the internationalisation literature as well as in international business research in general. Research has largely been centred on organisational and managerial aspects – including the demands made on managers working in an intercultural environment. Interest has therefore focused on individuals as units of analysis. What is interesting is the extent to which the results of this research can contribute to an understanding of how firms as a whole can deal with cultural heterogeneity in their process of internationalisation.

Gertsen (1990) has focused on the »internationalisation process of the individual« when she studied expatriates living in foreign cultural contexts, i.e., people who have reached a »late stage« in their personal internationalisation process. For that purpose she introduces the concept of intercultural competence. The concept emphasises the individual's ability to communicate successfully in a foreign culture, i.e., the ability to understand the correct symbolic meaning of »the sign« in its cultural context, thereby enabling the individual to adopt the proper communicative behaviour. Hence, the internationalisation process of the individual is analysed from an intercultural perspective.

Gertsen defines intercultural competence as »an ability to function in other cultures«. Although an overall theoretical framework for the concept does not exist, Gertsen identifies three interdependent dimensions of intercultural competence: (1) the affective dimension which implies an acceptance and understanding of other cultures. Attitudes are of special importance here and so are the characteristics of the native personality; (2) the cognitive dimension which deals with the way the person thinks about and the knowledge (s)he possesses about foreign cultures, and (3) the communicative/behavioural dimension which is the most important dimension because affective and cognitive competences need to be expressed in the communicative behaviour.

This definition implicitly implies that cultural differences are of neither a static nor objective size. The necessary qualities of the intercultural person are changeable, or dynamic, since both attitudes and knowledge develop and change continuously in the different cultural contexts in which a person finds himself/herself (i.e., the person interacts with the different cultural contexts). It can therefore be said that the ability to function in a foreign cultural context is a lifetime learning process.

These dimensions of communicative ability, open attitudes and adequate knowledge, represent a useful extension of the internationalisation model of Johanson and Vahlne (1977). They may lead to a better understanding of the necessary conditions for the international development of – first of all – the individual or the employee and, secondly, in an altered form the entire firm. These dimensions emphasise that knowledge does not necessarily ensure a proper behaviour.

In the light of these findings, the challenge is to create an approach which focuses on the intercultural competence of the entire firm as a way of understanding its interaction with different cultural contexts. The significance of cultural differences on firms' internationalisation may be analysed by focusing on how firms function in and interact with different cultural contexts as well. This raises a number of questions: How do firms develop and exploit the ability to handle different meaning patterns across different markets and target segments? How do they create the ability to innovate according to the different meaning systems of target markets?

Consequently, a firm's ability to operate in culturally heterogeneous contexts may be seen as a source to its distinctive competences of which it may gain advantages vis-a-vis competitors. This means that cultural differences between a firm and its markets can be an opportunity, not only a treat, for the further international development of the firm.

8. The Intercultural Competence of the Firm

Following Gertsen's focus on the behavioural abilities of an individual when he/she interacts with different cultural contexts, it is important to understand and deal with the analogous behavioural abilities of a firm in its interaction which these contexts. In this respect, what really matters for the firm's internationalisation process to continue and to develop successively is its improved ability to carry out its international operations in the cultural contexts where it finds itself, given financial, technological, and human resource constraints.

A concept of a firm's intercultural competence is also based on its ability to function in intercultural contexts. As an analogy to the individual's intercultural competence, the firm must be able to communicate with its target markets/segments. Following the semiotic approach this implies that the firm's supply (e.g., product and marketing concepts) harmonises with the cultural meaning systems of the target segments. This means that an ability to handle cultural heterogeneity and to harmonise the symbolic meaning of the firm's supply with that of the target markets' is an ability to interact with the market.

A firm's international operations are, however, not of a static nature. When the firm penetrates several cultural contexts as it internationalises, the cultural meanings systems of its environment may change. That is the same as saying that a firm's definition or understanding of its surroundings are changing. Furthermore, the competitive forces, the necessary technology, consumption patterns and the specific cultural contexts it deals with are not static. The cultural context may change, for instance, as a result of so-called cultural borrowing between cultures (Usunier, 1993). Consequently, a concept of the firm's intercultural competence must include its persistent ability to interact with its target and potential segments. This means that the firm's ability to identify and exploit new opportunities in foreign cultural environments is a part of its intercultural competence.

As a result the concept of a firm's intercultural competence can basically be seen as a dynamic concept and it is defined as the ability to identify and exploit those commercial opportunities in foreign cultural context that both create long lasting competitive advantages and make the firm able to interact with its cultural surroundings. Following the interaction perspective described above, this implies that a firm's intercultural competence is based on three different but related dimensions, (1) an ability to *handle* cultural heterogeneity across different markets or segments (2) an ability to *harmonise* its product and marketing concepts with the symbolic meaning which target segments in different cultures assign them (i.e., it can communicate with target segments) and, (3) an ability to *identify and exploit* new opportunities in foreign cultural contexts in anticipation of long lasting competitive advantages.

The first part of the definition stresses the importance of the fact that the firm either employs, or can draw on, persons who have both sufficiently open attitudes and sufficient knowledge of foreign cultures to enable them to: 1) recognise that cultural differences affect the firm's commercial options; and 2) to identify these in light of the firm's core competence/resources. This does not necessarily imply, however, that the firm's employees must be able to understand these opportunities in the special cultural context in which they exist. The firm's employees may not be so interculturally competent in Gertsen's (1990) sense of the concept. Unlike employees who are posted abroad, it is not absolutely necessary for a firm's employees to cope both professionally and socially in foreign cultures or to be able to understand the opportunities in a culturally correct sense, i.e., understand the right cultural meaning of opportunities. This must be seen in relation to the last part of the definition, which emphasises the firm's ability to exploit market opportunities. From a resource and network point of view (e.g., Wernerfelt, 1984; Barney, 1991; Håkansson, 1982; Hägg and Johanson, 1982) the definition, therefore, includes that the firm can acquire those resources which it does not possess itself. Hamel (1991) deals with different kinds of collaborations and stresses that collaborations represent an important source to knowledge or competence development. The exploitation of opportunities can thus be conditional upon access to »supplementary competences« from, or the development of »joint competences« with, foreign partners (Christensen, 1988) who can deal with the cultural heterogeneity of the firm's target segments on the firm's behalf.

The above raises a number of questions: First, how does the firm deal with cultural heterogeneity, given the fact that an understanding of a product's meaning in different cultural contexts can demand enormous human resources? Secondly, how can the firm acquire and utilise knowledge strategically as to exploit commercial opportunities in changeable and culturally heterogenous and different environments, and, in addition, how does it acquire the ability to influence and adapt itself to these? The answers relate to the cross cultural dimension of firms internationalisation and are the challenge for future research in the field of internationalisation processes.

A pilot study conducted in the food processing industry (Langhoff; 1994a, 1994b) is based on the intercultural approach to firms' internationalisation processes introduced in this chapter. The cultural heterogeneity can be expected to be of significant importance to food companies because food consumption, to a large extent, is culturally determinated (see, e.g. Fishler, 1988; Usunier, 1993). The study shows that external partners play a crucial role when firms are confronted with culturally heterogeneous markets. In many situations these external partners (e.g. agents, large industrial customers, supermarket chains and the like) deal with the cultural heterogeneity of the firm's target segments on the firm's behalf. They are not only important in the marketing of the firm's present products to different cultural contexts. They are first and foremost important in product development processes where the necessary cultural information is mediated through the so-called »flying prototypes« (see also Kristensen, 1992a, 1992b). From a more dynamic point of view this implies that external partners are crucial for the firm's persistent ability to exploit new commercial opportunities in changeable and culturally heterogenous and different environments.

A case will illustrate this point. A firm produces and exports one main product and several complementary products which are used by both retail customers, and catering and industrial customers for further processing. The main product is made in more than a hundred different variants. It is the most internationalised company within its distinct field. The market for the firm's main product is characterised by the fact that, traditionally, it has only been used and known in Europe. As a result competition is concentrated on the European market. Competitors have, however, until now been mainly home-market oriented. The way the product is used in the different markets varies widely. This is partly due to the decisive role which food traditions play in both the retail market and the professional market (i.e., professional users of the product) and partly because the skills of professional users vary widely from country to country and segment to segment. In spite of the special conditions, the firm has succeeded in exporting to markets outside Europe, especially to areas with many European emigrants or with many international hotels. The market conditions have led the firm to build up an extensive network of sales distributors. The firm has a very close relationship with its distributors. Constantly, they work together to develop and improve an already comprehensive cookery book system which the firm offers to both retail and professional customers. The cookery book system is designed to cater for the traditions and educational level of each individual market. The firm also employs consultants, who hold courses and educate potential users. In addition, the firm often develops special products for industrial customers, and is also heavily engaged in the development of convenience products, since these are expected to be a continuing source of growth in the years ahead. Convenience products are developed partly by the firm itself and partly in collaboration with its distributors.

Due to a wide-ranging development of products and ideas in each individual market, the firm's transaction-specific investments (Williamson, 1979) are, from a qualitative point of view, fairly extensive. Following a transaction cost perspective, this would indicate that the firm may internalise (own distribution network and own subsidiaries) depending on the level of uncertainty and frequency. The firm's expansion strategy would not have been possible without the assistance of its distributors, however, since they have provided the necessary cultural information. Despite the complicated international situation the firm has gained access to information that is »sticky« in nature (cf. von Hippel, 1991), and which is difficult to separate from the cultural context of which it is part. In order to internalise, it has been necessary to incorporate an element of cultural insight because of the cultural heterogeneity of its markets. Hence, the distributor solution may have been the most cost-minimising because the firm has used its limited resources to develop and consolidate its core competence which best fits its culturally heterogeneous markets for the time being.

The case illustrates that culturally heterogeneous markets may lead to other internationalisation strategies than those recommended by Johanson and Vahlne (1977). These researchers operate from the assumption that high international involvement (in terms of number of markets served) and high international commitment (in terms of resources committed to international operations, e.g., in subsidiaries) indicates a high degree of internationalisation. This may not, however, be the case as the firm may be able to interact with foreign cultural contexts, i.e. to have a high international and intercultural orientation, without committing themselves to many geographically defined markets and without operating through subsidiaries on each of these markets. The firm may have a high international and intercultural orientation if it able to interact closely with the cultural contexts in parts of the world market. Consequently, it is able to innovate and market products even though the use and meaning of these products are very different and hence are closely bound to different cultural contexts and traditions around the world.

As a result of the approach developed in this chapter figure 2 illustrates the concept of intercultural competence.

Figure 2. Intercultural competence as the firm's interaction with its defined markets.

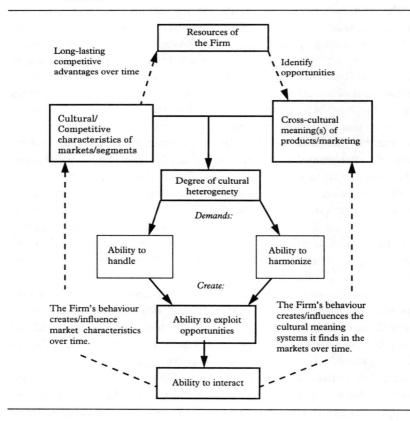

The figure demands a short explanation: The upper part of the figure shows that opportunities are identified based on the firm's resources. The existence of real opportunities depends on whether they fit the cross-cultural meaning systems of products and marketing concepts the users may demand.

Based on the opportunities the firm may gain long lasting competitive advantages depending of what happens in the lower part of the figure: The cultural characteristics og the market, including the potential different meaning system(s) of the firm's products and marketing concepts may create a cultural heterogeneity which demands the firm's ability to handle this heterogeneity and to harmonise its product and marketing concepts. If it is able to do so, it is able to exploit opportunities. The exploitation of opportunities implies that the firm over time may interact with the market because its behaviour may change the cross-cultural meaning systems of the markets and the competitive and cultural characteristics of these markets in a later period. This is due to the fact that the firm and its competitors are themselves actors in the market. Hence, they have earlier exploited products and marketing concepts which influence their opportunities now and their exploitation now may influence the cultural and competitive characteristics in the future. Further, the firm's interaction with the market may influence its long lasting competitive advantages as well as its future resources. The circle is reestablished and it shows the dynamic characteristics of the concept of intercultural competence.

9. Conclusion and Directions for Future Research

The chapter has introduced the research of internationalisation processes where the concept of psychic distance plays an important role. The concept forms the main way of dealing with the significance of cultural differences on firms' internationalisation processes. It is not appropriate, however, as it in its commonly used form leads to confusion rather than solving the problems related to the understanding of a firm's behaviour in cross cultural contexts. The concept itself relates more to individual cognitive thinking that to the behaviour of the entire firm. The problems are intensified by an arbitrary definition of the concept. Furthermore, the methodology used in the study is very unusual as the authors seek an – subjectively adjusted – objective list of countries. It seems that there is no consistency between the definition of the concept and the methods used.

The chapter includes an analysis of studies within the field of international business research and export behaviour which have used other methods for estimating cultural differences. Several problems with these methods are identified. The major problem is that the methods used either are not built on accepted anthropological theories or they build on the research by Hofstede (1984) which cannot be applied to this kind of research. The studies take for granted that »culture« can be treated as an independent variable (i.e., the ETIC approach as opposed to the so-called EMIC approach) even though the search for cultural universals applied to their research questions are not major concern of the studies.

As a result of the problems with the existing methods the chapter introduces a conceptual framework which is based on an established anthropological approach to culture (semiotics) where cultural barriers are seen as communication barriers. A semiotic perspective on culture is based on the EMIC school of thought which focuses on understanding the meaning systems in different cultural contexts.

It is shown that firms are influenced by cultural differences in different ways. A complex world of meaning systems is a part of firms' reality when internationalising due to an assigned cultural meaning of consumption. This implies that some firms are faced with a high degree of cultural heterogeneity while the markets of other firms are more homogeneous in a cultural sense.

The effect of cultural heterogeneity on firms internationalisation processes has, as yet, not aroused any interest in the field. Therefore, the chapter introduces an intercultural approach which focuses on the interaction between firm and market, i.e., the analysis is centred on firms ability to behave in and interact with different cultural contexts as this contexts changes through their internationalisation processes.

The intercultural approach is a contribution to the field because it operates on the behavioural as well as interactionist level (i.e., focuses on the behaviour of the firm and market) as opposed to the existing models which are operating on a cognitive level (i.e, focus on knowledge of the firm). In doing so, the approach builds on recognised research where expatriates living in foreign cultures have been studied. Central to this research is the concept of intercultural competence. In the chapter the concept of intercultural competence is applied to the firm as the unit of analysis in an adapted form.

The firm's intercultural competence is based on three different but related dimensions: (1) an ability to *handle* cultural heterogeneity across different markets or segments (2) an ability to *harmonize* its products and marketing with the symbolic meaning which target segments in different cultures assign them (i.e., it can communicate with target segments) and, (3) an ability to *identify* and exploit new opportunities in foreign cultural contexts in anticipation of long lasting competitive advantages.

Using an intercultural approach including the concept of intercultural competence may be fruitful in future research. We may analyse how cultural heterogeneity on firms export markets influences their process of internationalisation, e.g. in terms of the three dimensions often used to describe (some aspects of) firms' internationalisation patterns: Products exported, markets served and operation forms used. Especially, this kind of research may uncover some interrelationships between these dimensions.

The chapter shortly mentions a pilot study conducted in the food processing industry where the intercultural approach has been used. It seems that external partners play a crucial role when firms are confronted with culturally heterogeneous markets, especially when it comes to product development processes (i.e., the future opportunities – the dynamic aspects of their internationalisation). Collaboration makes it possible for firms to interact with foreign cultural contexts, i.e., to have a high international and intercultural orientation, without committing themselves to many geographically defined markets and without operating through subsidiaries on every of these markets. Instead they may be broadly defined on the product dimension due to the cultural heterogeneity. From a more dynamic point of view this implies that external partners are crucial for the firm's persistent ability to be interculturally competent. This is a contribution to the field as the significance of collaboration is not included in research on internationalisation processes (i.e., the dynamic development of firm's). It is only included in research on entry mode decisions which is static in nature.

It is important to note that the study is only a pilot study and as such it is only identifying some indications. It is not possible to make any generalisations. The question is whether this is possible at all! It is necessary to recognise that cultural studies must be based on accepted cultural approaches – also when studying internationalisation processes. This implies that the nature of culture must be taken into account. Each culture is unique as it is defining the reality as it represents itself for a group of people. Firms internationalise in a world characterised by the fact that different meaning systems do exist. As a result we cannot understand the significance of cultural differences without reference to the specific cultural context the firm and its markets are living in, i.e., without reference to the cultural meanings of the firm's supply in different cultural contexts.

Accordingly, it is impossible, or at least extremely difficult, to identify the influence of cultural differences on firms' internationalisation processes in general, i.e., it is not possible to identity causal relationships. We can only contribute to firms' internationalisation processes by analysing how they can become interculturally competent and this is very important due to the fact that the world is characterised by different cultural meaning systems. In doing so, cultural differences between firm and market may be an opportunity, not only a treat, for the international development of firms. Through this kind of research we may be able to identify some strategies that seem more applicable than others in different situations. In some situations it may be fruitful for a firm to follow a standardised or globalised strategy, i.e., a strategy where the firm's product and marketing concepts appeal to homogeneous meaning systems in the world market across different cultures. In other situations it may be better for the firm to follow an intercultural marketing strategy. Such a choice will among other things depend on the resources and competences of the firm, the competitive forces and the cultural differences across different markets/segments. An intercultural approach to firms' internationalisation processes could be a useful step for future research in this kind of studies.

References

Andersen, O., 1993. On the Internationalization Processes of Firms: A Critical Analysis, *Journal of International Business Studies*, Vol. 24, No. 2, 209-231.

Askegaard, S., M.C. Gertsen and T.K. Madsen, 1991. Danske kultur-barrierers betydning for virksomhederne, *Ledelse & Erhvervsøkonomi*, Vol. 55, No. 3, 111-122 (in Danish).

Barney, J. B., 1991. Firm Resources and Sustained Competitive Advantage, *Journal of Management*, Vol. 17, No. 1, 99-120.

Benito, G.R.G. and G. Gripsrud, 1992. The Expansion of Foreign Direct Investments: Discrete Rationel Location Choices or a Cultural Learning Process?, *Journal of International Business Studies*, Vol. 23, No. 3, 461-476.

Bilkey, W. J and G. Tesar, 1977. The Export Behavior of Smaller Wisconsin Manufacturing Firms, *Journal of International Business Studies*, Vol. 8, Spring/Summer, 93-98.

Bouchet, D., 1991. Advertising as a Specific Form for Communication, in Larsen, H. H., D. G. Mick and C. Alsted (eds.), *Marketing and Semiotics. Selected Papers from the Copenhagen Symposium*, 31-51, Copenhagen: Handelshøjskolens Forlag.

Buhl, C., 1993. Produktsemiotik, *Ledelse & Erhvervsøkonomi*, Vol 57, No. 3, 165-173 (in Danish).

Carlson, C., 1975. *How Foreign is Foreign Trade – A problem in International Business Research*, Uppsala: Acta Universitatis Uppsaliansis.

Cavusgil, T.S., 1980. On the Internationalization Process of Firms, *European Research*, Vol. 8, 273-281.

Christensen, L. T., 1993. *Marketing som organisering og kommunikation*, Odense: Odense University Press, (in Danish).

Christensen, P. R., 1988. Industriel fleksibilitet og lokalisering i et netværksperspektiv, in Møller, K. (red.), *Virksomheder i netværk I*, 55-80, Roskilde: Forlaget Planlægning og Samfundsøkonomi, (in Danish).

Cyert, R. M. and J. G. March, 1963. *A Behavioral Theory of the Firm*, Englewood Cliffs, New Jersey: Prentice-Hall.

Czinkota, M. R., 1982. *Export Development Strategies. US Promotion Policies*, New York: Praeger Publishers.

Fishler, C., 1988. Food, Self and Identity, *Social Science Information*, Vol. 27, No. 2, 275-292.

Geertz, C., 1973. *The Interpretation of Cultures*, London: Hutchinson.

Gertsen, M.C., 1990. *Fjernt fra Danmark*, Copenhagen: Nyt Nordisk Forlag Arnold Busck, (in Danish).

Graham J.L. and N. J. Adler, 1989. Cross-Cultural Interaction: The International Comparison Fallacy?, *Journal of International Business Studies*, Vol. 20, No. 3, 515-537.

Hallén, L. and F. Wiedersheim-Paul, 1979. »Psychic Distance and Buyer-Seller Interaction«, *Organisasjon, marked og samfunn*, Vol. 16, No. 5, pp. 308-324.

Hamel, G., 1991. Competition for Competence and Inter-Partner Learning Within International Strategic Alliances, *Strategic Management Journal*, Vol. 12, Special Issue Summer, 83-103.

Hedlund G. and Å. Kverneland, 1985. Are Strategies for Foreign Markets Changing?, *International Studies of Management and Organization*, Vol. 15, No. 2, 41-59.

Hippel, E. von, 1991. The impact of Sticky Data on Innovation and Problem-Solving. *Working Paper #3147-90-BPS*, Sloan School of Management, Massachusetts Institute of Technology, Cambridge, Mass, October.

Hofstede, G., 1984. *Culture's Consequences*, abridged edition, California: Sage Publications.

Hörnell, E., J-E. Vahlne and F. Wiedersheim-Paul, 1982. *Export och utlandsetableringer*, Stockholm: Almqvist and Wiksell, (in Swedish).

Hägg, I. and J. Johanson (eds.), 1982. *Företag i Netverk*, Stockholm: Norstedts forlag (in Swedish).

Håkansson, H., 1982. *International Marketing and Purchasing of Industrial Goods*, New York: Wiley and Sons.

Johanson, J. and J-E. Vahlne, 1977. The Internationalization Process of the Firm, *Journal of International Business Studies*, Vol. 8, Spring/Summer, 23-32.

Johanson, J. and J-E. Vahlne, 1990. The Mechanism of Internationalization, *International Management Review*, Vol. 7, No. 4, 11-24.

Johanson, J. and F. Wiedersheim-Paul, 1975. The Internationalization of the Firm – Four Swedish Cases, *Journal of Management Studies*, Vol. 12, No. 3, 305-322.

Klein, S. and V. Roth, 1990. The Effects of Experience and Psychic Distance Reconsidered, *International Marketing Review*, Vol. 7, No. 5, 26-38.

Kogut, B. and H. Singh, 1988. The Effect of National Culture on the Choice of Entry Mode, *Journal of International Business Studies*, Vol 19, No. 3, 411-432.

Kristensen, P. S., 1992a. Flying Prototypes: Production Departments' Direct Interaction with External Customers, *International Journal of Operations and Production Management*, Vol. 12, No. 2, 195-211.

Kristensen, P. S., 1992b. Product Development Strategy in the Danish Agricultural Complex: Global Interaction with Clusters of Marketing Excellence, *Journal of International Food and Agribusiness Marketing*, Vol 4, No. 3, 107-118.

Langhoff, T. N., 1994a. Cultural Influences on the Internationalization Process of the Firm, *Working Papers in Marketing*, No.1/January.

Langhoff, T. N., 1994b. The Internationalization of the Firm in an Intercultural Perspective -With Case Studies From the Food Processing Industry, *MAPP Working Paper*, No. 15/January.

Levitt, T., 1983. The Globalization of Markets, *Harvard Business Review*, Vol. 61 (May/June), 92-102.

Levy, S.J., 1959. Symbols for Sales, *Harvard Business Review*, Vol. 37, 117-124.

Loustarinen, R., 1989. *The Internationalization of the Firm*, (3. edition), Helsinki: Helsinki School of Economics.

Madsen, T.K., 1990. Cultural Biases of Danish Salespeople Acting in Foreign Cultures, *Working Papers from Department of Marketing*, Odense University, No. 1.

Myers, G.E. and M.T. Myers, 1992. *The Dynamics of Human Communication: A Laboratory Approach*, 6. edition, New York: McGraw-Hill.

Müller S. and H-G Köglmayr, 1986. Die psyshiche Distanz zu Auslandsmärkten, *Schmalenbachs Zeitshrift für betriebwirtschaftliche Forschung*, Vol. 38, No. 9, 788-804.

Nordström, K. A., 1991. *The Internationalization Process of the Firm: Searching for New Patterns and Explanations*, Stockholm: IIB, Stockholm School of Economics.

Nordström, K. A. and J-E Vahlne, 1992. Is the Globe Shrinking? Psychic Distance and the Establishment of Swedish Sales Subsidiaries During the Last 100 Years, *Working Paper from IIB*, Stockholm School of Economics.

Penrose, E., 1959. *The Theory of the Growth of the Firm*, London: Basil Blackwell.

Reid, S., 1981. The Decision-Maker and Export Entry and Expansion, *Journal of International Business Studies*, Vol 12, Fall, 101-112.

Sandström, M., 1992. The Culture Influence on International Buniness Relationships. In Forsgren, M and J. Johanson (eds.), *Managing Networks in Internaitonal Business*. Phipadelphia: Gordon and Breach, pp. 47-60.

Sekaran, U., 1983. Methodological and Theoretical Issues and Advancements in Cross-Cultural Research, *Journal of International Business Studies*, Vol. 14, No. 2.

Shane, S. A., 1992. The Effect of Cultural Differences in Perceptions of Transaction Costs on National Differences in the Preference for Licensing, *Management International Review*, Vol 32, No. 4, 295-311.

Strandskov, J., 1987. *Virksomhedens internationalisering. Teorier om processer og udviklingsforløb*, Copenhagen: Nyt Nordisk Forlag Arnold Busck (in Danish).

Sullivan, D. and A. Bauerschmidt, 1990. Incremental Internationalization: A Test of Johanson and Vahlne's Thesis, *Management International Review*, Vol. 30, No. 1, 19-30.

Turnbull, P.W., 1987. A Challenge to the Stage Theory of the Internationalization Process, In Rossen, P. and S.D. Reid (eds.), *Managing Export Entry and Expansion*, 21-40, New York: Praeger.

Usunier, J-C., 1991. The 'European Consumer': Globalizer or Globalized?, in Rugman, A. and A. Verbeke (eds.), *Research in Global Strategic Management*, Vol. 2, 57-78, Greenwich, CT: JAI Press.

Usunier, J-C., 1993. *International Marketing. A Cultural Approach*, New York: Prentice-Hall.

Wernerfelt, B., 1984. A Resource-based View of the Firm, *Strategic Management Journal*, Vol. 5.

Weick, K. E., 1979. *The Social Psychology of Organizing*, Reading, Mass: Addison-Wesley.

Williamson, O. E., 1979. Transaction-cost Economics: The Governance of Contractual Relations, *The Journal of Law and Economics*, Vol. 22, October, 233-261.

8. Managerial Influences and SME Internationalisation

Sara McGaughey, Denice Welch and Lawrence Welch

Introduction

During the last two decades, there has been growing research emphasis on the internationalisation of small and medium-sized enterprises (SMEs) (Luostarinen, Korhonen, Jokinen and Pelkonen, 1994; Mulhern, 1995). Much of this research reveals that SME internationalisation patterns appear to follow the evolutionary model identified in earlier Nordic studies, although there is evidence of some companies moving more rapidly, even directly, into exporting (Johanson and Vahlne, 1977; Luostarinen, 1979; Welch and Luostarinen, 1988; McKinsey, 1993). A variety of studies in different countries have clarified many of the factors which have an impact on why and how companies start and expand international operations (Bilkey and Tesar, 1977; Wiedersheim-Paul, Olson and Welch, 1978; Yaprak, 1985; Axinn, 1988; Bonaccorsi, 1992). However, the character of the process and the way in which influences operate through time have yet to be fully explored (Benito and Welch, 1994). In addition, the role and impact of personal factors connected with key decision-makers, such as personal networks, while identified in early research on internationalisation, have received surprisingly little coverage in subsequent studies (Welch and Wiedersheim-Paul, 1980; Bonaccorsi, 1992; Björkman and Eklund, 1996). For example, although there has been a burgeoning body of literature on networks in general (see Ford, 1990), relatively scant attention has been given to their impact on the process of SME internationalisation. One such aspect is the role of personal networks in triggering initial export inquiries or orders: while research has shown they are potentially important (Dept. of Foreign Affairs and Trade, 1995), there has been limited investigation of the operation of this factor.

To some extent, the growing interest in SME internationalisation reflects their importance in most economies (Mulhern, 1995; Dept. of

Foreign Affairs and Trade, 1995). SMEs typically contribute more to employment growth than larger organisations, and appear to be increasingly involved in international operations (Luostarinen, Korhonen, Jokinen and Pelkonen, 1994; Davis, 1995). However, small firms appear to experience significant problems and high failure rates in the process of internationalisation (Rosson and Reid, 1987; Welch, 1992). Inevitably, there has been government concern to improve performance in this area.

The purpose of this chapter, therefore, is to explore the managerial influences on SME internationalisation, through a longitudinal study of a small asparagus exporting firm (referred to here as OzGreen[52]) over its full life cycle: from the initial impetus to establish the organisation in 1980 to its demise in 1989 when it was subsumed into a larger organisation. Studies of internationalisation so far have tended to utilise cross-sectional, questionnaire approaches. For example, in a review of 35 empirical studies of barriers to exporting, Leonidou (1995) found that three-quarters of the studies used mail surveys as the method of data collection, and all but one study was of a one-time nature – the only exception being a study in which data was collected at two different points in time, using different samples. While such approaches have provided a broad picture of internationalisation factors, quantitative studies have limited ability to expose the nuances of these factors' operation through time – that is, to capture the process perspective (Strandskov, 1993; Macharzina and Engelhard, 1991).

Key influences on OzGreen's internationalisation, particularly the role of the key decision-makers, and personal networks, are identified from the case data. A conceptual model is presented as an organising framework to illustrate and discuss these key influences. As the issue of how to promote internationalisation by SMEs remains of considerable concern to governments, policy implications arising from the analysis of OzGreen are discussed, and areas for future research suggested.

1. Methodology

A qualitative case study was considered the appropriate research method to explore the role of managerial influences in the SME internation-

---

52. The names of the company and interviewees have been disguised in order to respect confidentiality.

alisation process, given that such an approach allowed investigation of the phenomenon within its real-life context (Yin, 1994). Because the case company, OzGreen, had completed its life cycle, it was possible to take a holistic, longitudinal view of the phenomenon under investigation: the process of internationalisation. As well, the single case approach allowed an in-depth examination of managerial influences throughout the SME's life. OzGreen was selected as, following the logic of purposeful sampling, it appeared *a priori* to represent a critical case: one »that can make a point dramatically, or [is] for some reason, particularly important in the scheme of things« (Patton, 1987:54). The case was instrumental, as argued by Stake (1994:237): »examined to provide insight into an issue or refinement of theory«. Thus, the case examination allowed both confirmation and extension of existing knowledge on the process of internationalisation (Patton, 1987; Yin, 1994).

Data were collected through semi-structured interviews (tape recorded) with two key actors: Mr. Ajin, the former Managing Director of OzGreen (1987-1989), and Mr. Cole, the former Marketing Manager (1986-1987). Mr. Cole had met one of the founders of OzGreen in 1981 in Japan while working for the Australian Trade Commission (Austrade), the trade promotion arm of the Australian Government. Austrade played a key marketing role in the start-up phase for OzGreen in Japan. Mr. Cole left OzGreen in 1987 for the large Australian company which used some of OzGreen's product for canning purposes, and was to eventually take over OzGreen in 1989. A semi-structured interview (tape recorded) was also conducted with Mr. Daye, who was a member of OzGreen's board from 1983 to 1987. Telephone interviews were conducted with the two founders, Mr. Oz and Mr. Green.

The interview data was dependent on the hindsight and memory of the interviewees. Some inaccuracies may have resulted given the fact that perceptions change over time and memories fade. This limitation in the methodology was minimised through a process of data triangulation (Miles and Huberman, 1994) involving interviews with multiple actors. Documentation on OzGreen also formed an important part of the triangulation, and was obtained from: Austrade and agricultural industry material, promotional and government produced documentaries, publicly available company brochures, newspaper and business magazine reports, and financial press analyses. In addition, it was considered that the period of reflection and distance from involvement only possible through the elapse of time was critical to obtaining a depth of information concerning the factors affecting the »rise and fall« of OzGreen's international operations. Content analysis of the interview data and documentation were based on the case narrative, and themes and patterns which emerged were explored using analyst-constructed typologies.

2. The Case of Oz Green

2.1 The founding of OzGreen

In early 1980, OzGreen was founded by two semi-retired Australian businessmen, Mr. Oz and Mr. Green. This was prompted by a visit to Japan by Mr. Green who recognised a previously unidentified need for the supply to Japan of quality, out-of-season asparagus during the months of September to December. They effectively pioneered the export of asparagus to Japan from Australia, during these months. The company was established specifically for exporting, a somewhat rare beginning in that the majority of exporting firms tend to be established with the domestic market in mind.

For example, in a recent study of 310 manufacturing SMEs in Australia it was found that 75-80% had operated in the domestic market for an average of 27 years before initial export operations (McKinsey, 1993).

The export culture of OzGreen was strong at the outset. Mr. Oz had experience in international food broking and his knowledge of export processes predisposed him to respond more readily to the market opportunity in Japan. Mr. Green provided expertise in agriculture, especially asparagus:

> *My father was the pioneer of a special asparagus plant that came from the US. We had an asparagus farm so you see I came home from school onto the asparagus farm. I had asparagus in my veins from my very early life.*

Being a third generation farmer, he had extensive contacts in the industry which assisted OzGreen in gaining access to fresh, high quality produce supplies.

An important feature of the case company was that the founders were able to start operations with a minuscule investment of no more than AUD1,000.

Mr. Green recalled:

> *It would be more accurate to say that we started it from a zero capital base. Well, we might have put in 500 dollars each. But the shipments were paid for by letters of credit, so we could pay our rent and the growers each week.*

This meant that OzGreen was in a somewhat unique position: it started operations without debt, and its cash flow position was positive from the outset (Buttery and Shadur, 1991). Fresh asparagus was purchased from growers so the founders did not face the high risks associated with crop failure due to poor weather (Wardlaw, 1992). Overall, the expertise and previous experience of both the founders was instrumental in their ability to recognise an opportunity, and successfully implement their export strategy through OzGreen without undertaking any formal strategic planning.

2.2 Japanese operations

From 1980 to 1984, OzGreen's core operation was the export of high quality asparagus to Japan, sourced from local Australian farmers. Shipment from Australia to Japan was by air. As one of its quality objectives, OzGreen aimed to have the asparagus harvested and on the plane within 48 hours, and usually 24. This helped ensure freshness upon arrival in Japan, and freight was therefore a critical aspect of OzGreen's operations. In this respect, as the level of exports grew, OzGreen received favourable treatment from the airlines, as the subsequent Managing Director (Mr. Ajin) related:

> *[OzGreen] got good treatment from the airlines, and this was critical to their success. As a large shipper of fresh produce, on occasions [OzGreen] obtained space at the expense of smaller shippers of asparagus.*

Relationships with distributors were vital for OzGreen in ensuring that the product not only reached the end user but did so in the unspoilt state required by the market. Personal selling to and the building of relationships with the Japanese distributors was the major form of promotion in Japan during the early period of OzGreen's operations. Generally, OzGreen used one main distributor in each of Tokyo and Osaka, as well as some smaller ones from time to time. Assistance in finding these was obtained from Austrade's Japan Office at minimal financial cost to OzGreen.

Being a luxury item in a country with high spending capacity, asparagus was able to be sold in Japan at a price which yielded high margins. As well, OzGreen tended to trade in the Yen which was rising in value – both of these aspects assisting profitability of the company.

Not surprisingly, the initial success of OzGreen's Japanese campaign drew competitive responses, especially as its success was highly publicised. Within a short period of time, OzGreen's market pioneer advantages were being challenged by the entry of Australian and New Zealand competitors.

Over the first four years of operation, OzGreen's market share of Australian and New Zealand asparagus in Japan dropped from 80% to less than 40%, although it remained the dominant supplier from September to December.

As a direct response to this emerging competition, OzGreen sought to strengthen customer satisfaction through enhanced emphasis on product quality and service. For example, by establishing freight systems that were more efficient than those of their competitors, OzGreen was able to convert what was generally viewed as a disadvantage in fresh produce export – namely perishability – into a major competitive advantage. Through the success of strategies such as this, OzGreen was able to maintain its high prices, and annual turnover grew from AUD50,000 to approximately AUD four million over the first six years of operation.

2.3 Backward integration

The increased attention to quality and service prompted greater concern about control over the production and supply of asparagus. Volume of supply was important to consistently meet commitments to OzGreen's distributors in Japan, and to ensure continued favourable treatment from the airlines.

Mr. Oz relates:

> *We were by this stage starting to ship enough that it was completely
> in the hands of the growers whether or not we were able to get what
> we wanted. So we bought our own land. Actually, the land we ini-
> tially bought was from [Mr. Green's] family.*

As a result, in 1984, OzGreen began processing its own asparagus. At
the same time, the company increased its coolroom capacity, designed an elaborate, mechanised packing shed, and employed six permanent staff. This involved a significant investment for the company
necessitating outside financing through a share issue and bank loans.
The founders held 60% of the shares, selling 40% through a unit
trust.

Through these steps, OzGreen became fully integrated, from the
preparation of the land for planting through to shipment, although it
still drew on other suppliers to meet market demand. Of course, its risk
level increased as it was more exposed to crop failure, and debt had been
acquired in order to finance its expanded asset base. Although a unit
trust was issued in 1984, two million Australian dollars of the equity in-
jection was not channelled back into OzGreen.

2.4 New markets

Following the development of its own productive capacity, the company
was able to generate large volumes of asparagus. However, only 35% of
produce harvested met with the Japanese requirement for long, thin asparagus, the supply of which was part of OzGreen's quality objective.
This meant considerable excess capacity which was available for other
markets. Conveniently, European consumers valued thicker asparagus,
which also had a longer shelf life and could therefore withstand the
greater freight times to Europe. The opportunities in Europe were
known to the founders through frequent visits there and entry was facilitated through a network of distributors known to Mr. Oz.

The North American market was also accessed although it presented
difficulties. Margins were tighter as North American consumers were
less responsive to Japanese-type product features. Competition also was
more severe with New Zealand suppliers already active. Occasional

shipments were also made to Hong Kong and Singapore but these smaller markets were never seriously developed because of their inability to absorb sufficient quantities. A small quantity of non-export quality asparagus was sold to an Australian company for canning.

2.5 New shareholders and management change

In 1987, OzGreen undertook a second sale of shares in the business (just prior to the stock market crash), thereby reducing the founders' equity level so that they and the shareholders from the 1984 share issue retained only a 25% share of OzGreen. The new shareholders were a large Australian organisation with 50% equity, and two partners (Mr. Ajin and Mr. Bunt) held the remaining 25%. One of the latter (Mr. Ajin) was appointed as Managing Director. Mr. Ajin brought with him a background of extensive international financial experience (including Japan).

The new management instituted wide-ranging changes in the approach to operations, particularly in Japan and North America. It became apparent that the profitability of OzGreen was under considerable stress as a result of increased competition in Japan, difficulties in supplying the European market due to limited airline space, and the high debt repayments which were exacerbated by the sharp rise in interest rates around this time (share sales had, once again, not been used for debt reduction).

The new investors in OzGreen had been led to believe that the company had an established trading practice out of the United States. Although seven, unsupervised shipments had been made from the US to Japan, there was no ongoing arrangement. It was decided to significantly upgrade the US operation through exports from the US to Japan and Europe. This enabled OzGreen to exploit its expertise in the logistics and marketing of fresh produce internationally, and capitalise on its brand name. This strategy had the added advantage of sourcing from growers rather than investing in productive capacity in the US, which minimised risk. Only a small number of staff were hired to perform both office duties and quality control checks, and in general, overheads were kept to a minimum.

These operations proved highly profitable, with turnover out of California in the first year matching that of the Australian operation. Due to its success, diversification opportunities emerged – for example, OzGreen's US entity was able to export Californian cherries immediately following the asparagus season as a result of being offered space by the airlines. Mr. Ajin played a major role in this expansion, spending long periods personally overseeing the US operation.

Given that US asparagus was now being sold in Japan under OzGreen's name, endeavours undertaken to improve the Japanese market situation were crucial to both the Australian and US businesses. The new management faced some problems with OzGreen's Japanese market relationships as a result of the business style of Mr. Oz who had been the principal actor in terms of Japanese activities. Mr. Ajin commented that soon after becoming Managing Director, he visited Japan but found that:

Because of [Mr. Oz's] aggressive trading nature, none of the customers wanted to talk to me. In my first trip to Japan, I had to sit for two hours to see our major customer ... [OzGreen] had a bad reputation in Japan.

A similar comment was made by the former Marketing Manager (Mr. Cole):

[Mr. Oz] had done the dirty on every vegetable importer in Japan, and nobody wanted to know us.

In trying to renew relationships with distributors, Mr. Ajin faced a challenging situation:

[Mr. Oz] had insulted [these distributors] to the extent that I had to call six times to get a meeting, and it wasn't until after the third meeting that we actually started talking. That was nine attempts!

He added that it would have been difficult to accomplish even this without using his own contacts in Japan. Mr. Ajin was able to draw on these contacts in adding new distributors. His prior experience in Japan had also given him an appreciation of the Japanese way of doing business and the importance of relationships.

Mr. Ajin commented:

> *Because of my past experience in Japan, I had some contacts. For example, I went into the office of [merchant bank] and got my old secretary to make some appointments in Japanese. She was able to use Japanese and Japanese courtesy.*

These contacts were also invaluable in developing U.S. operations, as explained by Mr. Ajin:

> *[Mr.Bunt] and I had contacts in the banking and legal industry worldwide...so we could be introduced to people and airlines, and not walk in cold off the street. This helped a great deal.*

A Japanese-speaking person was employed in the Melbourne office to enhance customer service and relations in Japan. As well, Mr. Ajin made regular visits to Japan. Due to such moves, and the more sensitive handling of Japanese relations, OzGreen was able to expand its distributor base from three to ten, and was no longer so reliant on their major distributor, whose share of the business reduced from 65% to 35%.

In addition quality was enhanced by switching the packaging. Mr. Oz had developed a heavily-waxed fibreboard carton which was superior to that used by most domestic competitors at the time. However, once supplies of US asparagus began arriving in 1986 in wooden cartons, Japanese distributors began to suggest that OzGreen switch to these as the produce was found to arrive in better condition using the wooden cartons.

The company was slow to respond, as Mr. Ajin explained:

> *For four years the major customer in Japan had wanted [OzGreen] to ship asparagus in wooden boxes, the same as from the States. He had told everyone at [OzGreen], but it was not done. [Mr. Oz] kept promoting the box as great.*

When OzGreen commenced shipment to Japan from the US operation, it did so in wooden boxes and unbundled. The new management was able to learn from their experiences in the US and eventually employed the same techniques out of Australia. This move cut costs as well as improving quality – resulting in increased sales.

2.6 Decision to sell

Through a combination of events, both internal and external, OzGreen's owners decided to sell the business in 1989. The European market for asparagus from Australia had peaked in 1988. By 1989 the Japanese market for out-of-season asparagus had begun to reach saturation point. The loss of a government subsidy in 1987 particularly affected freight costs to Europe, making it more difficult to match competitors. More importantly, the high level of debt at a time of increasing interest rates made it difficult for OzGreen to achieve profitability: at this time, it was only just breaking even after interest costs. As Mr. Ajin commented:

> *But again, our decision to sell was motivated by the fact that we were too highly geared, the risk factors involved in reducing our debt over the following three or four years were so high that we should accept the [takeover] offer.*

The financial situation also inhibited possible diversification moves as a way of countering the threats to its export markets for fresh asparagus. The heavy demands on the Managing Director in maintaining the profitable US business as well as time spent in Japan, and OzGreen's inability to finance additional support staff, contributed to the decision to sell the company. It was sold to the Australian company which had been purchasing some of OzGreen's product for canning, for AUD 2 million (plus responsibility for OzGreen's debt of AUD 5.8 million).

As a postscript, the acquiring company lost the US operations when the US personnel began their own company, taking with them key growers and freight forwarders. Unable to profitably incorporate OzGreen's former operations into its own, the remnants of OzGreen were sold in 1991 at a loss. The company no longer exists.

3. SME Internationalisation Influences

Through analysis of the life cycle of OzGreen, it was possible to identify the various influences on the process of internationalisation. The experience of OzGreen illustrates the impact of many of the factors shown in previous research on SME internationalisation, particularly the key role of the decision-maker/s in both initiating and driving the process, and that therefore the background, attitudes and knowledge of the decision-maker(s) were of critical importance (Welch and Wiedersheim-Paul, 1980). However, analysis of the case data also indicated that an important aspect of this role was the personal networks which the decision-maker(s) was able to activate. The influences in this case are shown in Figure 1.

Figure 1. SME Internationalization Influences.

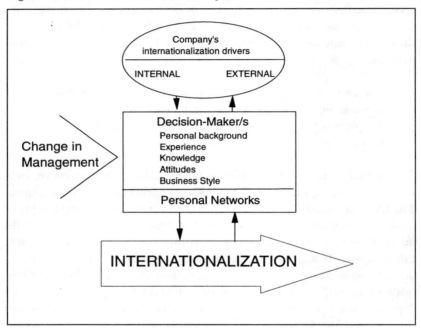

3.1 The role of the Key Decision-Maker/s

As opposed to large firms, where management is often separate from the owners, the experience and personal characteristics of small firm owners have been shown to have significant impact on firm performance (Stuart and Abetti, 1990; Dyke, Fischer, and Reuber, 1992). It is evident from the case company data that personal factors, and the networks key individuals brought to bear on the company's international activities, were critical in the content and direction of OzGreen's internationalisation. Thus, in Figure 1, the key decision-maker/s are given a central place: both as a direct input and as a filter to the wide range of internal and external influences on the company's internationalisation process. As well, the entrance of new top management is included in Figure 1 as, inevitably, a change in the key decision-maker/s at any stage has the capacity to affect the course of internationalisation.

As previously mentioned, OzGreen was founded by two entrepreneurs whose combination of business experience and contacts enabled them to take up an opportunity that might otherwise have seemed a high risk venture. Previous involvement in the food industry, agriculture and exporting, as well as contacts with asparagus farmers (including relatives and neighbours) contributed to the feasibility of the venture from their perspective. No formalised market analysis or evaluation of alternatives was conducted, but as the new Managing Director, Mr. Ajin, commented: »They had one essential ingredient. They chose a product they knew«.

The two founders were nevertheless careful to limit their financial exposure, despite their confidence in the venture. At the same time, being in a position to keep their personal financial commitments at such a low level encouraged the initiation and continuation of export operations. By 1984, when faced with the increased competition in Japan, and the perceived need to achieve greater control over the production and supply of fresh asparagus, the founders were prepared to invest in production and storage facilities thereby increasing the financial commitment of the company. However, Mr. Oz and Mr. Green were able to achieve this without incurring personal debt. In fact, through a sale of company shares, they were able to obtain an immediate personal return from the business, whereas OzGreen incurred debt through external loans. While committed to the Japanese market objective and to achieving success for the company in general, as evidenced by the moves made to counter the competition and steps into other foreign markets, they were clearly at pains to separate their personal financial position and that of the company's to the extent that it was feasible. In some respects, it might be argued that this personal concern ultimately put the company under considerable financial pressure and affected its internationalisation capacity. The second sale of company shares in 1987 enabled the founders to financially remove themselves even further from the business. This left OzGreen with a large debt overhang that became a major issue when the financial environment changed and interest rates began to rise.

Because of the immediate market success and the publicity generated when the company received national Export Awards, the founders enjoyed the wider returns that came from OzGreen's international activities. Undoubtedly, this fed continuing commitment to internationalisation but, at the same time, acted as a 'blind spot' when the Japanese market and its requirements changed. For example, with the shift in preference to unbundled fresh asparagus in wooden cartons, the founders were slow to respond to the clear signals from the marketplace. This appears to have caused some damage to OzGreen's reputation in Japan.

As the Managing Director found:

> *The perception of [OzGreen] in Japan was that it was all show
> .... But a product like asparagus sells on quality and price not on
> colour of carton, which will not be seen by retail customers anyway.*

Such behaviour is not unusual. Lant, Milliken and Batra (1992) note that managers who design strategies, in particular, may overlook or ignore information that signals the current inappropriateness of their strategies.

Thus, the founders' combined attributes (confidence, knowledge, relevant industry background, and networks) explained much of the initial success of OzGreen, and the ability to operate in such a low risk fashion. These same personal characteristics, however, were not necessarily of advantage in the longer term. In fact, case data indicate that the personal goals of the founders ultimately led to OzGreen being exposed to considerable financial risk.

Change in Management
Mr. Oz and Mr. Green withdrew from direct management of the company with the second sale of shares in 1987. Mr. Ajin brought a different background of experience, knowledge, attitudes and business style and had different ideas regarding OzGreen's internationalisation path. Research by Björkman and Eklund (1996) indicates that management change may facilitate 'leapfrogging' in internationalisation, an important ingredient being the incoming manager's foreign market knowledge and networks. A change in top-level management is frequently associated with change in strategy (Lant, Milliken, and Batra, 1992). Doz and Prahalad (1988) concluded from their study of MNEs, that the appoint-

ment of a new key executive, bringing a different vision, was an essential condition for successful strategic redirection.

An important element in this case was Mr. Ajin's strong personal commitment: »it was the lure of small business«. The personal financial commitment of the new shareholders also contributed to a concern for the viability of OzGreen. The company was now highly geared compared to its financial structure prior to the second sale of shares. The financial situation constrained Mr. Ajin's ability to make the type of far-reaching strategic changes that he might otherwise have enacted.

As mentioned earlier, Mr. Ajin was able to retrieve OzGreen's reputation in Japan and to substantially develop the company's US operations as an exporter of fresh produce into Europe and Japan. To this extent, one could argue that what Mr. Ajin did was not so much strategic redirection as bringing to bear a clearer conception of OzGreen's core capabilities as being a broker with skills in the logistics and marketing of fresh produce internationally, and how they might be used to better develop existing activities. This transfer of capabilities was accomplished with considerable success in the US.

It should be stressed at this point that Mr. Ajin played a key role in the implementation of his strategies for both Japan and the US. He personally dealt with distributor relations in Japan and spent long periods in the US overseeing the development of US activities. This meant that he was absent from the Australian base for five months per year for periods of up to six weeks at a time. From 1987, Mr. Ajin was also Chairman of the Australian Asparagus Council, in which position he initiated a number of promotional campaigns for the industry in Japan and Australia.

3.2 Personal networks

Through the life of OzGreen, personal networks were an important component of the influence the key decision-makers exerted on the direction and activities of the company. Much of the ability of the company to initiate and carry through international operations resided in the decision-makers' personal networks. This importance is shown in Figure 1 as part of the attributes of the decision-maker/s.

Mr. Green had extensive contacts in the farming industry, as was mentioned earlier. Through this farming network, OzGreen was able to circumvent the established alliances between Australian growers and wholesalers or processors which typically form a barrier to new entrants (Wardlaw, 1992). This network, based on family relationships and long standing friendships, helped to provide assurance of supply in an industry where loyalty can be somewhat transient in the face of variable weather and market conditions. As Mr. Ajin explained:

> *This was important in the agricultural industry because farmers can be fickle because [sic] they recognise there may be a drought next year and have to maximise profit now, even if it means breaking a gentleman's agreement.*

The founders also activated connections within the farming community in the United States to assist in their experimental sourcing of export shipments to Japan.

In penetrating the Japanese market, the lack of personal networks meant that the founders were forced to rely on the Australian Trade Commission's office in Japan. Mr. Oz commented:

> *[Austrade's Japanese employee] really knew his way around and provided us with a lot of basic information ... [In Japan] you need somebody who is going to analyse the information for you, to tell you what's what ... If we wanted some research done, they'd [Austrade] do it for you. And they didn't charge.*

In general, it appeared that personal relationships were never effectively developed, even with their major distributor in Tokyo. European market penetration was, however, assisted through the personal contacts of Mr. Oz, as noted previously.

The OzGreen case provides an illustration of the way in which a change in top management inevitably brings with it a change in personal networks, with potentially significant flow-on implications for a company's international operations (Björkman and Eklund, 1996; Marschan, Welch and Welch, 1996). This was particularly evident in Japan where Mr. Ajin had maintained his own preceding networks. He activated these in recovering OzGreen's poor reputation among Japanese asparagus importers and distributors, and extended the networks to consolidate the company's Japanese market position. Mr. Ajin and his partner, Mr. Bunt, were also able to use their contacts in the United States to provide OzGreen with influential introductions to the airlines, which helped the company obtain freight space at reasonable prices.

3.3 Internationalisation drivers

Figure 1 shows the inter-relationship between the company's internationalisation drivers (both internal and external) and the decision-maker/s. As suggested in earlier work, the meaning and significance of the various drivers depends on their interpretation by the decision-maker/s (Wiedersheim-Paul, Olson and Welch, 1978; Cavusgil, 1984). Internal drivers are seen as factors which both influence and are influenced by internationalisation, including such aspects as the company's resources (finance, staffing, technology, etc.), international networks, knowledge about foreign markets, skills in foreign operations, etc. They represent the foundation of the company's ability and preparedness to develop international operations (Johanson and Vahlne, 1977; Welch and Welch, 1993). External drivers are essentially factors outside the direct control of the company, such as government policy, that encourage and/or inhibit international activities. Given the size and nature of the company, the internal drivers in OzGreen's case primarily emanated from the decision-makers.

Internal and external drivers, of course, frequently interact. For example, the Japanese preference for thin asparagus led to excess capacity within OzGreen once it had developed its own production facilities. Excess production capacity has been shown in a number of exporting studies to be a potentially important factor in pushing companies to seek new market outlets (Welch and Wiedersheim-Paul, 1980). The associated build-up in debt resulting from increased investment became an additional driving force in pushing the company to seek alternative markets from 1984 onwards. Further, external pressure came to bear as stronger competition emerged in the Japanese market from other Australian and also New Zealand suppliers. This accentuated the perceived need to develop other markets.

The nature of the industry was such that OzGreen was particularly susceptible to external events. As Mr. Ajin remarks:

> *Fresh produce is a difficult business because you are reliant on weather, freight, and currency – all of which are out of your control.*

Reliance on air freight meant that OzGreen was vulnerable to the vagaries of this form of transport and the policies of the airlines out of Australia. For example, in 1989, the airlines imposed significant fines for a failure to keep a freight booking. If hail occurred in the week between when the booking was made and harvest, OzGreen was faced with a fine as well as crop loss. When the Australian government withdrew its freight subsidy in 1987, costs rose the following year from AUD 1.20 to AUD 1.80 per kilogram, thus having a significant impact on profitability, and its ability to compete – particularly in Europe. The loss of the freight subsidy came at a time when the company was facing severe competition in Europe from Chilean suppliers. There was also the perennial problem of obtaining space on the airlines during busy periods such as the lead-up to Christmas. Combined with internal resource constraints, these market servicing difficulties convinced OzGreen management that the company should withdraw from European operations.

4. Conclusion

The case of OzGreen seems to run counter to the typical pattern of internationalisation revealed in much of the research, where firms tend to develop initially in the domestic market, take incremental steps into international operations, and move to culturally familiar and/or geographically close markets (Johanson and Vahlne, 1977; Benito and Welch, 1994). Instead, OzGreen was established as a company in order to exploit an export market opportunity. Not only that, but the market concerned (Japan) is geographically distant from Australia, and its culture is often perceived as a barrier to market penetration (Namiki, 1989). Upon closer examination, though, it was a more typical example of export development, because of the way the founders were able to lower risk and experiment with exporting, while retaining minimal personal financial involvement (Welch and Wiedersheim-Paul, 1980). The founders' backgrounds predisposed them to recognise the Japanese market opportunity and gave them the confidence to act upon it (Wiedersheim-Paul et al, 1978:49).

The relationship web they were able to readily access at the outset further reduced the perceived risk of the venture, and was a source of critical knowledge. SMEs tend not to bring to the export start situation such a widespread set of ready-made, relevant networks (Ford, 1990; Johanson and Vahlne, 1990), although a recent Australian study found that personal contacts were an export precipitating factor for 30 per cent of small firms (Dept. of Foreign Affairs and Trade, 1995). The OzGreen case, however, demonstrates that while personal networks may assist initial entry, continued internationalisation inevitably requires network maintenance and extension. OzGreen's problems with its Japanese networks at the time of the management change in 1987 highlight this point. Networks not only require the allocation of resources and managerial attention, but they are also susceptible to the exit and entry of key players. Had Mr. Ajin not had his own networks in Japan, then his ability to recover OzGreen's position would have been rather more difficult. Likewise, Mr. Ajin's contacts facilitated US market penetration in a way that was not feasible for the two founders.

From the case analysis, it could be argued that the role of networks parallels that of knowledge, as identified in early Nordic studies of internationalisation. Like knowledge, networks act to constrain and support the internationalisation process over time. They are developed by current international activities but, at the same time, require commitment decisions (Johanson and Wiedersheim-Paul, 1975; Johanson and Vahlne, 1977; and 1990). In small firms, such developments tend to be principally associated with the key decision-maker/s (Wiedersheim-Paul, Olson, and Welch, 1978). OzGreen's internationalisation activity was conducted first by its founders, and then by the new Managing Director, Mr. Ajin, who brought a different set of networks, style of doing business, knowledge of international business and foreign markets and range of skills, thereby changing the capacity of the company for international operations. Inevitably, as the founders moved to the sidelines, some of the past knowledge and skills foundation was lost. The new managing director had no experience in the industry, coming from a financial background in one of Australia's largest multinational companies at the time. As Mr. Ajin admitted:

> *Fresh produce trading is very much cut and thrust. There are not many gentlemen. I was used to the well-mannered Japanese in merchant banking. It didn't prepare me to be there as a small Australian businessman ... It took me 12 months to learn the fresh produce business.*

Further, the OzGreen case demonstrates the way in which knowledge and networks are connected: much of the knowledge that the founders required at the outset was accessed through their networks. Of course, with such small companies, the inter-connection of these factors is facilitated by the prominent role of the owner/manager in the development of international operations.

4.1 Future research

The case presented in this chapter demonstrates the critical role of personal factors in initiating and driving the internationalisation process of an SME. The impact of the decision-maker/s' characteristics (background, knowledge, skills, etc) and personal networks revealed in the analysis of OzGreen are not new: these were factors emphasised in the early Nordic research in this area. However, as they have received surprisingly little attention subsequently, it could be argued that considerable room for conceptual development remains. As Johanson and Vahlne (1990:22) in a review of their own work concluded: »Although the internationalisation process has captured the interest of many researchers, there have only been a few attempts at developing the concept«. Nevertheless, the OzGreen case revealed possible avenues for extending understanding of the process, for example, the role of personal networks over time, and the impact of managerial change.

While OzGreen was selected as a critical case, there is clearly need for much more extensive in-depth, case study research which would allow cross-case comparison. There is also a need for the longitudinal methodological approach to be extended, as a way of deepening understanding of the dynamic influences that drive internationalisation (Benito and Welch, 1994). The OzGreen case provides, in a limited way, an indication of the rich potential in this direction. The use of the participant-observer technique may be appropriate, given the subtlety and intangibility of many of the forces involved (Patton, 1987).

4.2 Policy implications

If the role of personal factors is accepted as being critical in the internationalisation of SMEs, it raises significant problems for the effective operation of government-supported export promotion schemes. In considering the case of OzGreen, it is in fact difficult to see where an outside agency could have had an impact on the way the company engineered its export entry. At a broader level though, OzGreen illustrates how difficult it is for outsiders to understand each company's situation when so much of its potential for exporting, and its needs, are tied up with individuals in ways which are not necessarily readily accessible – particularly beforehand. Even the individuals themselves may not be aware of the range of knowledge, skills and networks they possess which could be valuable in an exporting venture. Many of these assets are relatively intangible, and are therefore difficult to communicate to outsiders. As a result, the question of who to support with promotional funds, and in what ways, becomes difficult for promotional agencies with limited funds. The resource base in more tangible areas, such as finance, remains an important part of the evaluation process, but may need to be placed alongside less tangible aspects. Given the demands for accountability of such support schemes, intangible considerations are always much more difficult to justify.

While it is more difficult to take account of personal factors in judging companies deserving of support, a more systematic approach to their inclusion might assist in having personal factors taken more seriously by all concerned. Given the lack of formal market research before their move into the Japanese market, the founders of OzGreen would have been hard pressed to sell a case for support on conventional 'hard' criteria. A systematic listing of their capacity for Japanese market operations using 'softer' criteria such as their background knowledge and Australian networks was nevertheless feasible. When developing support activities, there is a case for focusing on the personal development of key players in SMEs in ways which are conducive to international operations. It may also be appropriate, in some situations, for priority to be given to the hiring of key people rather than specific foreign marketing campaigns.

The issue remains problematic though, raising questions such as the extent of vetting of individuals and how much personal material they should be expected to be forthcoming with, including sensitive personal networks (Marschan, Welch and Welch, 1996).

References

Axinn, Catherine N, 1988. »Export Performance: Do Managerial Perceptions Make a Difference?«, *International Marketing Review*, Vol.5,
No.2, 61-71.

Benito, Gabriel R.G. and Lawrence S. Welch, 1994. »Foreign Market
Servicing: Beyond Choice of Entry Mode«, *Journal of International
Marketing*, Vol.2, No.2, 7-27.

Bilkey, Warren J. and George Tesar, 1977. »The Export Behavior of
Smaller-sized Wisconsin Firms«, *Journal of International Business
Studies*, Vol.8, No.1, 93-98.

Björkman, Ingmar and Michael Eklund, 1996. »The Sequence of Operational Modes Used by Finnish Investors in Germany«, *Journal of International Marketing*, forthcoming.

Bonaccorsi, Andrea, 1992. »On the Relationship Between Firm Size
and Export Intensity«, *Journal of International Business Studies*,
Vol.23, No.4, 605-635.

Buttery, E. Alan and Mark A. Shadur, 1991. »Understanding Corporate
Collapse«, *Management Decision*, Vol.29, No.5, 38-45.

Cavusgil, S. Tamer, 1984. »Organizational Characteristics Associated
with Export Activity«, *Journal of Management Studies*, Vol. 21, No.1,
3-22.

Davis, Brent, 1995, »Globalisation – Who's at it?« *Globalisation: Issues for
Australia.* Commission Paper No.5, Papers and Proceedings from an
Economic Planning Advisory Committee seminar. Canberra. Sep-
tember, 191-200.

Department of Foreign Affairs and Trade, 1995. *Winning Enterprises.*
Australian Government Publishing Service, Canberra.

Doz, Yves L. and C.K Prahalad, 1988. »A Process Model of Strategic
Redirection in Large Complex Firms: The Case of Multinational
Corporations«. In A., editor, *The Management of Strategic Change.* Ba-
sil Blackwell, Oxford.

Dyke, Lorraine, Eileen M. Fischer and A. Rebecca Reuber, 1992. »An
Inter-industry Examination of the Impact of Owner Experience on
Firm Performance«, *Journal of Small Business Management* Vol.30,
No.4, 72-87.

Ford, I. David, editor. 1990. *Understanding Business Markets: Interaction,
Relationships, Networks*, Academic Press, London.

Johanson, Jan and Jan-Erik Vahlne, 1977. »The Internationalization Process of the Firm – A Model of Knowledge Development and Increasing Foreign Market Commitment«, *Journal of International Business Studies*, Vol.8. No.1, 23-32.

Johanson, Jan and Jan-Erik Vahlne, 1990. »The Mechanism of Internationalisation«, *International Marketing Review*, Vol.7, No.4, 11-24.

Johanson, Jan and Finn Wiedersheim-Paul, 1975. »The Internationalization of the Firm – Four Swedish Cases«, *Journal of Management Studies*, Vol.12, No.3, 305-322.

Luostarinen, Reijo, 1979. *The Internationalization of the Firm*, Acta Academia Oeconomica Helsingiensis, Helsinki.

Lant, Theresa F, Frances Milliken and Bipin Batra, 1992. »The Role of Managerial Learning and Interpretation in Strategic Persistence and Reorientation: An Empirical Exploration«, *Strategic Management Journal*, Vol.13, No.8, 585-608.

Leonidou, Leonidas C, 1995. »Empirical Research on Export Barriers: Review, Assessment, and Synthesis«, *Journal of International Marketing*, Vol.3, No.1, 29-43.

Loustarinen, R.K., H. Korhonen, J. Jokinen and T. Pelkonen, 1994. *Globalisation of Economic Activities and Small and Medium-sized Enterprises Development*, Helsinki School of Economics, Helsinki.

Macharzina, Klaus, and Johan Engelhard, 1991. »Paradigm Shift in International Business Research: From Partist and Eclectic Approaches to the GAINS Paradigm«, *Management International Review*, Vol.31 (special issue), 23-43.

Marschan, Rebecca, Denice Welch and Lawrence Welch, 1996. Control in less-hierarchical multinationals: The role of personal networks and informal communication. *International Business Review*, Vol.5, No.2, forthcoming.

McKinsey and Company. 1993. *Emerging Exporters*, Australian Manufacturing Council, Canberra.

Miles, Matthew and Michael Huberman. 1994. *Qualitative Data Analysis: An Expanded Sourcebook*, 2nd edition, Sage, Thousand Oaks, California.

Mulhern, Alan, 1995. »The SME Sector in Europe: A Broad Perspective«, *Journal of Small Business Management*, Vol.33, No.3, 83-87.

Namika, Nobuaki, 1989. »Japanese Trade Barriers: Perceptions of Small Business Exporters«, *Advanced Management Journal*, Vol.54, No.1, 37-41.

Patton, Michael Q, 1987. *How to Use Qualitative Methods in Evaluation*, Sage, Newbury Park.

Rosson, Philip J. and Stan D. Reid, (eds.), 1987. *Managing Export Entry and Expansion*. Praeger, New York.

Stake, Robert E, 1994. »Case Studies«, in N.K. Denzin and Y.S. Lincoln, (eds.). *Handbook of Qualitative Research*. Sage, Thousand Oaks.

Strandskov, Jesper, 1993. »Towards a New Approach for Studying the Internationalisation Process of Firms«, in P.J. Buckley and P. Ghauri, (eds.). *The Internationalisation of the Firm: A Reader*, Academic Press, London.

Stuart, Robert W. and Pier A. Abetti, 1990. »Impact of Entrepreneurial and Management Experience on Early Performance«, *Journal of Business Venturing*, Vol.5, No.3, 151-162.

Wardlaw, Brenda, (ed.), 1992. »Food – Fresh and Produced Vegetables«. *S & P – Australian Ratings Industry Profile*, F05: June.

Welch, Lawrence and Reijo Luostarinen, 1988. »Internationalization: Evolution of a Concept«, *Journal of General Management*, Vol.14, No.2, 34-55.

Welch, Denice and Lawrence Welch, 1993. »Strategic Management and The Internationalization Process«, in Vitor C. Simoes, (ed.). *International Business and Europe After 1992*, Proceedings of the 19th EIBA Conference, Lisbon, December 12-14, 363-380.

Welch, Lawrence and Finn Wiedersheim-Paul, 1980. »Initial Exports – A Marketing Failure?«, *Journal of Management Studies*, Vol.17, No.3, 333-344.

Wiedersheim-Paul, Finn, Hans C. Olson and Lawrence S. Welch, »Pre-Export Activity: The First Step in Internationalization«, *Journal of International Business Studies*, Vol.9, No.1, 47-58.

Yaprak, Attila, 1985. »An Empirical Study of the Differences Between Small Exporting and Non-exporting U.S. Firms«, *International Marketing Review*, Vol.2, No.2, 72-83.

Yin, Robert K, 1994. *Case Study Research*, second edition, Sage, Thousand Oaks, California.

9. The Role of Learning in the Evolution of Business Networks in Estonia: Four Finnish Case Studies[53]

Jarmo Nieminen and Jan-Åke Törnross

1. Introduction

The birth of the New Eastern Europe has given rise to new business opportunities for foreign firms attempting to capitalise on the potential of these markets. As the institutions forcing market economy and the needed infrastructure remain undeveloped, along with political and economic turbulence, it is suggested that a totally different approach to establishing and developing business relationships is needed, especially when compared to trade with market economies.

Understanding business development and business-to-business marketing, interactive mechanisms have, in many cases, replaced discrete transactions as the unit of analysis of industrial markets. The role of combining heterogeneous resources with actors and activities form the base for the network approach to business markets (Håkansson and Johanson 1985, Thorelli 1986, Webster 1992, Hunt 1994). East European markets form a specific case for networking and the formation of business with partners in the shifting stage of the transitionary »postcommunist« era. We therefore use the network paradigm as a base for understanding the logic of business development.

In new and turbulent markets organisational learning can be regarded as a prerequisite for building successful business relationships as learning emphasises the constant improvement of both individual and

53. The authors would like to express their gratitude to the Foundation of Economic Research in Finland for the economic support of this study. The case companies – Hartwall, Paulig, Valio and Raision Margariini – have also shown very positive attitude towards the research. We thank also the interviewed managers for their time and flexibility in taking part in our research. The first draft of the paper was presented in the 10th IMP Conference in Groningen, The Netherlands and we are grateful for all useful comments to the first version of the paper. Finally, we want to thank Ms. Lilian Grahn for checking the English.

collective competencies to meet internal and external demands. Resource dependency and investments into relationships also need adaptive mechanisms and change processes for the mutual fit of the involved business partners (Aldrich 1971, Argyris 1977, Hallén et. al. 1994, Pfeffer and Salancik 1978, Ring and Van de Ven 1994). The IOR-theory and the network theory outline the formation of actor bonds as a result of investments in relationships (Blankenburg and Johanson 1993, Hunt 1994, Usunier 1993). A theoretical model is built on network development in Eastern European markets using learning, commitment and adaptation as core concepts.

This chapter focuses on the evolution of industrial networks between Finnish and Estonian enterprises. Development of industrial undertakings by Finnish food production firms in Estonia is presented in the empirical section. The great market potential for foreign goods has often been cited as being one of the major motives for Western firms to enter East European markets. In the food industry market prospects are seen as especially attractive as in many East European countries there is a shortage in the supply of high quality foodstuffs.

The basic *objective of the study is to understand and explain how business relationships between Finnish and Estonian firms have been initiated, developed and evolved from the entry to the present stage* (April 1994) *and what is the role of learning and adaptation in this development process.* The role of learning is highlighted in terms of 1) factors developing learning, 2) forms of learning, and 3) outcomes of learning in business development.

Consequently, a historical and processual approach is adopted to analyse the results (Cp. Pettigrew 1987, 1992, Van de Ven 1992;). It is believed that in the present volatile environment longitudinal studies are needed in order to highlight the critical elements of 1) the development of relationships, 2) the interaction process and 3) network dynamics and change.

2. *Theoretical Framework*

When looking at business development of industrial firms in new markets, one is faced with a multitude of environmental factors affecting business relationships. In international marketing textbooks the external environment is seen as an uncontrollable part of the environment into which the firm markets its products and services. This environment is also a part of the investment climate, and risks, opportunities and threats are, in a classical sense, aspects to be taken into consideration when entering foreign markets (see for example Bradley 1991, Cateora 1990, Keegan 1989).

Even more restrictive are the notions of markets using the macro-economic paradigm in the classical theory of foreign trade by e.g. Ricardo, Heckscher-Ohlin or Samuelson. Other approaches to understanding business development include e.g. strategic alliances (e.g. Parke 1991) and strategic groups (e.g. McGee and Thomas 1988), the 'eclectic approach' (Dunning 1981, 1988) or the political-economic imperative explaining the direction of foreign trade and investments. In business-to-business marketing these approaches are of limited value. In order to understand the new relationship and network reality of today new theoretical insights are mostly derived from inter-organisational theory and the network approach in business marketing.

The IOR-theory aims to understand how and why inter-organisational relationships evolve (in this case marketing relationships in business-to-business marketing) (Aldrich 1971, 1977; Pfeffer and Salancik 1978; Ring and Van de Ven 1994; Van de Ven 1976). These studies reflect the need to look at multi-firm relationships and the need for using mutual resources and blending of these resources. This fact also creates certain power structures and dependencies between involved firms. Inter-organisational business transactions has also been put forth by Williamson in his transaction cost approach (1975, 1985).

Networks can be used as a way to look at business processes more freely and holistically. We can identify the existence of networks by looking at different aspects of developments in business-to-business contexts (spatio-geographical development, economic aspects, inter-organisational perspectives, social and cultural factors, as well as political perspectives and markets). These factors that affect business development can be understood in the form of networks changing fluidly in time and space through human interaction and communication. For example, in understanding internationalisation Johanson and Mattson (1988) showed hypothetically how network logic can be used as a base for understanding the incremental development of firms' activities across borders.

Definitions of networks, and analysis of different kinds of networks already exist in business literature (Cook and Emerson 1978; Easton, 1992; Ford 1990; Hägg and Johanson 1982; Thorelli 1986; Webster

1992; Håkansson and Snehota 1995). The many different views of the network concept also pose a problem. Network existence and changes can often be grasped only in specific contexts.

Highly neglected are the geographical – or spatial – perspectives playing a part in business development, in the process of internationalisation in general and also in marketing (place, distribution, location, segmentation of markets and so on) (See Dunning 1979; Porter 1990; Törnroos 1991). The role of information networks and the physical infrastructure are other spatially related dimensions inherently needed for establishing efficient international contacts in business. New spaces for economic activities today can be found, for example, in Central and Eastern Europe, the Pacific Rim and China. These new spaces are opening up due to political shifts and the need for modernisation, transition and shifts in global production and trade (see e.g. Dicken 1992; Naisbitt 1995)

This chapter puts forth a processual method for examining Finnish firms' market entry and business development in the newly formed Baltic markets (see also the methodological discussion below). Networks are examined only in a limited sense. This includes the development of business networks in particular, but also considers and analyses the firms' responses to surrounding political, social and infrastructural situation and change. The article focuses on the evolution of Finnish-Estonian business using three main elements of industrial networks and change. These are; (i) learning, (ii) commitment and adaptation, and, (iii) the process of change.

2.1 The Network and Learning Process

Network dynamics cannot be understood without the core concept of learning. Learning is defined here as a cognitive change based on the actors' ability to perceive the world in a new way (Argyris 1977; Garvin 1993; Dodgson 1993). Thus, learning indicates the possibility to behave in a new way in handling situations and problems as a result of this new insight. This understanding of learning implies enactment in a specific context as a prerequisite for learning to take place. Change in behaviour again needs commitment and adaptation. Garvin (1993, 79-80) puts forth that the concept of organisational learning has been studied for a long time but the concept seems to be elusive as considerable disagreement remains about the content of this concept. The definitions have certain aspects in common, for example, that learning is a dynamic phenomenon, a process that unfolds over time, and that a link to previous knowledge is made and thus new insights can be derived (cp. Garvin 1993, 80).

Other important factors in learning are experiences of the partners, creativity and the continuum between individuals and the interacting organisations. In this sense the network concept of »actors«, as both individuals and organisations, connecting activities and resources becomes interesting. Individuals are the carriers of learning and play the role of gatekeepers, processors and communicators of knowledge and learning. In fact, organisations are able to learn through individuals who can identify conflicting aspects between their experiences and their beliefs. These new perspectives can be transferred to the organisation through the communication mechanisms. The new insight passed or filtered through past experiences and combined with new understanding creates in some cases a need for commitment and action (see e.g. Hunt and Morgan 1994). In the case of inter-organisational business and turbulent markets commitment and action create, in turn, a need for mutual adaptation processes to take place when dealing with inter-organisational business matters. This, again forms new environmental conditions and together with other environmental changes creates a new learning »loop«. This notion can be compared with the single- and double-loop (individual and organisational) learning processes as described by Argyris (1977, 1982) and Kim (1993).

According to Simon (1991, 125) organisations learn only in two ways; (i) by the learning of its members, or (ii) by hiring new members who have knowledge the organisation didn't previously have. In some cases the role of being able to absorb knowledge possessed by a counterpart becomes also a crucial issue when dealing with learning. Some firms are prone to learn faster than others and this role of tracing the know-how and transforming it to the own organisation becomes a key issue in explaining the success of some corporations. Also the role of culture, communicative skills as well as being able to transfer technology and marketing skills are core questions.

Business networks are formed as a result of the combination of resources accomplished through the actors' activities (Håkansson 1987, 1989). This triangular view of network dynamics and the view of networks as investments in relationships and creation of actor bonds between partners in the network is therefore seen also as a learning process (see fig. 1). The importance of the learning dimension in business development is therefore stressed. In order to develop business networks, learning can be seen as the outcome of previous commitments, undertakings and business.

Learning is never static. It is an ongoing process of change in (often) many actors' behaviour and learning (cp. Dodgson 1993; Kim 1993). This is based on the notion that change is always a part of networks. Changes occur as a result of internal or external pressures affecting networks and its activities. This can be the result of internal network characteristics such as division of labour, or the new insights gained through co-operation within networks. In the case of Eastern Europe, for example, the new Eastern partners can learn how to use Western technology and Western business practices (Warner 1994). The Western partner, on the other hand, learns how to deal with their Eastern business partners and how to conduct business in these markets, its cultural characteristics and economic and social realities and so on.

2.2 The Network and Commitment

For learning to be transformed to adaptation a commitment has to be created – a will and decision to activate adaptive behaviour and/or to realise other investments. Commitment is a core concept in understanding relationships and networks. Definition of commitment is related to the state of being devoted or dedicated to something. This general definition can be connected to specific investments of resources for achieving specific goals for example to maintain a position in the new East-European markets. Resource commitment means how the firm devotes human and monetary resources to Estonia in order to be able to start business operations in this new emerging market. Commitment is a quite elusive concept in that sense that you can treat it from diverse perspectives. It is related to other partners, it is also processual and changes gradually over time. Commitment is also based on trust and mutuality between network actors. It is furthermore bound to individuals as well as organisations. Commitment means to tie oneself resourcewise for a certain period of time for specific purposes. In this chapter we use the concept of resource commitment and analyse our cases from this perspective (see also Hovi 1995, pp. 45-46). In order for commitment to have desirable outcomes we think individual commitment is in many cases decisive. In the model constructed below commitment is an integrated part of the networking process together with learning and adaptation (see fig. 1.)

Figure 1. Relationships between learning, commitment and adaptation in the evolution of business networks.

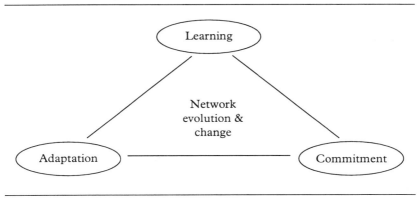

2.3 The Network and Adaptation

Adaptation can be seen as the outcome of learning processes and adaptation consequently shapes new learning processes. Adaptation means to »fit into« other actors' production systems, technology and markets, and indeed, even to certain cultural and social settings (Hallén, Johanson and Seyed-Mohamed 1992). Perspectives about networks affect the adaptation process and how to solve adaptation needs. Some perspectives are, for example, to look at nets as; (i) a focal network, (ii) a focal dyad – network or (iii) the whole networks' perspective (limited to the core actors business network) (Halinen and Törnroos 1995). Adaptation also means, in our mind, the formation of new mutual assets. In fact it is a prerequisite for new assets to be created. If the parties do not adapt successfully the new resources may never become a reality. Created through the combination of heterogeneous resources adaptation is crucial for networks to be successful and to be formed in a dynamic way. The adaptation process means ongoing change. It is learning-based as well as action-based on the part of the participants. Hallén et.al. (1992) state that adaptation is also a learning-based process, altered by power-relations between partners and a change process in itself.

Core aspects of the adaptation process in networks are the ability and the willingness to adapt and recognising the possibilities available by adaptation. In East-West business the role of adaptation is crucial. There is still a lot to be learned about the East, including Estonia. In the Finnish case the physical and cultural closeness, as well as the Finnish experience in Eastern business can explain the success of mutual adaptation.

2.4 The Network as a Process

In management literature, Van de Ven (1992) defines a process to denote three different things: (i) a logic that explains a causal relationship between independent and dependent variables, (ii) a category of concepts or variables that refers to actions of individuals or organisations, and (iii) a sequence of events that describes how things change over time. We shall not go into details here with these three notions except to paraphrase Van de Ven in saying that the last of these is the least understood, but in his mind the most important and valuable. This definition; »..takes a historical perspective and focuses on the sequences of incidents, activities, and stages that unfold over the duration of a central subject's existence« (op. cit. p. 170).

In order to examine networks as processes we need to look at the actors' views of the actual activities, adaptation and learning taking place in entering into Estonia. This process is mutual or reciprocal in its nature. It is altered and affected by the power relations that exist between the partners doing business.

Processes can only be understood from a temporal perspective. In the startup phase where the links between business partners are formed, the process begins by reviewing the history of the counterparts, which frames the initial learning phase and the development of »mental space« between business partners. The role of the transition and change in the East-European economies and the disparities between business partners forms the underlying context for the development of networks in business.

In East-West business the gaps in technology, infrastructure, political systems, levels of economic development and systems, marketing skills and consumer and industrial markets, different tastes, preferences and purchasing power tremendously affect most processes in this specific situation (Kraljic 1990). The stage of this transition process in a specific point of time forms the environment in the business development. In the present situation this environment is in a turbulent stage of change and creates a need for quick adaptation and learning processes in networks.

To sum up, evolution of business networks is seen here as an ongoing change process consisting of three interrelated concepts. In case the business manager perceives a mismatch between the environment and its own activities, learning creates a need for commitment, in order for the adaptation mechanism to come into play. Commitment therefore means the activation of learning in the form of necessary decisions. From adaptation to new forms of learning a new circle is formed which can explain some of the core features of networks in business. Consequently commitment is a prerequisite for adaptation mechanisms to come into play.

Real-life activities are based on the need to act in order to take advantage of learning and adjust to new circumstances and needs and/or gaining new insights about the business environment. Action is a part of adaptation in networks, but it cannot be activated without commitment, i.e. the knowledge of a certain need for action. Actions are the »dynamo« for networks to change and start adaptation processes.

2.5 The Study Context

Up to now the main interest in East-West business activities, and research has been directed to Central Eastern Europe or to Russia. From the Nordic, and especially from the Finnish firms' perspective the geographically close Baltic countries are of special interest. Estonia has been the most successful of the countries of the former Soviet Union in overcoming the difficulties of transition and has by 1994-95 reached economic growth figures higher than in majority of the countries in Eastern Europe. Finnish firms have especially developed their business relations with Estonian companies. The main reasons for the increased interest can be stated as 1) long historical ties, 2) short geographical distance, and 3) cultural proximity and a similar language. In addition, it seems that many Finnish firms are using Estonia as a gateway when developing their business activities to Russia (see Kojo and Köngäs 1995).

The Estonian food industry and markets represent the industrial context for the present study. The latest developments in Estonia's food industry create a challenge for Finnish producers, because the opening of the markets also attracts other foreign producers. Finnish food industry firms – although representing low mobility of production- have been very active in these markets mainly because of two factors: 1) Estonia offers new and close markets for increasingly saturated domestic markets, and 2) the liberalisation of imports as a result of Finland's EU-membership created the need for companies to prepare to increased competition in the domestic market by internationalising and this way getting a more competitive position for possible entrant.

The Estonian food industry has been in crisis since gaining independence from the former Soviet Union. Reasons for this development are numerous. The monetary reform lowered purchasing power, decreased deliveries of cheap feed and raw materials, and also substantially cut down the level of energy received from Russia. In addition, the privatisation of state-owned farms has been slow. Furthermore, the local producers have not been successful in competing with Western producers in providing high-quality delicacies for local consumers. Consequently, Estonia's food supply is very dependent on imports and on the interest of foreign firms to restructure this industry.

In Estonia's transition process the acceptance of the need to change and the adoption of new values, habits, attitudes and actions through learning is of crucial importance when analysing the development of business relationships. This learning process is likely to take a long time, which may create tensions in the establishment and maintenance of business relationships. However, this paper puts forth that foreign businesses can act as important change-agents in this learning process through their activities in Eastern Europe. On the other hand, foreign firms are also confronted by the need to learn and adapt, when entering new and unfamiliar markets.

As a result of the transition, several environmental changes have taken place, which have had some fundamental effects on business life. In Table 1 we have identified some of the major changes that the food industry sector has undergone from the planned to a transition economy. All the presented factors indicate increasing dynamics in business relations as a result of the decreased importance of government interference coupled with the increased importance of direct contacts to customers, suppliers and other actors in the market. This development gives an interesting background for studying business relations from a network perspective, highlighting the importance of organisational learning and adaptation for both partners.

Table 1. Identification of key changes in the Estonian food industry during the transition period. (adapted from Nieminen 1994).

Change factor	Planned economy	Transition economy
Networks	Contacts to government intermediaries	Direct contacts with business actors
Trading partners	Few large government organisations	Many small private firms
Size of deliveries	Large	Small
Quality of relationship	Bureaucratic; high-skilled	Entrepreneurial; diverse
Entry modes	Indirect export	Direct export
	Industrial cooperation	Foreign Direct Investment
Level of competition	Low	Moderate; increasing
Ownership patterns	Government ownership	Private, collective ownership
Market structure	Monopolistic; domestic-driven;	Free market; import-driven; increasing brand recognition
	basic food products	
		Large number of private retailers;
Distribution	Government monopolies; undeveloped wholesale system	hard currency shops; hotels

3. Research Methodology

Learning, adaptation and commitment as building blocks for business networks in Estonia is traced through the case studies of four firms. Thus a multiple case analysis is performed. The case study approach is seen as an appropriate approach in the following situations (see e.g. Yin 1984, Eisenhardt 1988, Miles and Huberman 1984, Seymour 1993, Ghauri et.al. 1994):

1. When the area of study is new and a deeper insight into different factors affecting relationships can be seen
2. When the researcher is looking for new hypothesis or theories
3. When the aim is to give a deeper understanding of a specific context, firm(s) or aspects of e.g. marketing phenomena
4. When processes and dynamic phenomena are studied and longitudinal data are needed

5. When the researcher needs to be in close contact with the research
object(s) and when data is of a qualitative nature.

To trace network development a multiple case study method was used.
The study is based on a qualitative analysis of primary data collected
through personal interviews and interpretation of the collected and
computer-processed narrative data by a reduction of these narratives
in a formalised way (Miles and Huberman 1984; Tesch 1990). The
multiple cases are thereafter compared and analysed in order to find
out certain phases, development stages and/or critical events which
have been found through constant comparison between the data and
theoretical constructs (Glaser and Strauss 1967; Glaser 1987). In this
sense the study is »grounded« in the data. The multiple cases also outline the contextual factors that influence learning, commitment and
adaptation.

All the cases are taken from the food-industry (Paulig [Coffee], Valio
[Fish fingers, Hartwall [Brewing], and Raision Margariini [human fats]
(see closer in the empirical section). Three of these – Hartwall, Paulig,
and Valio – are concerned with direct production investments in Estonia. Raisio Margariini has so far only been active since 1992 with only
exports. The data was mostly collected in March-April 1994. Given the
rapidly changing and turbulent environment in Estonia, the data was
collected in a three week period to reflect the opinions and attitudes of
the four companies in the same frame of time. Historical data and secondary written materials where also obtained from the firms.

The structure of research and data analysis aims at an understanding
of the process of change since entry through deriving data from the
datamass related to the entry decision, present stage of operation and
future prospects. In this sense the study tries to capture the basic logic
of the process. This would ideally be done through participatory research which was, unfortunately, not possible in this study. Temporally
the youngest cases date back only four-five years since initiation of the
first business negotiations, which makes the validity of the research rea-
sonably fair.

The data was collected through personal interviews in the case companies. The narratives were then transformed into data-narratives. One
individual per company was interviewed, and he was the manager responsible for the operations in the countries studied. First some preliminary questions were tested and then modified and improved to be used

as the set of questions in the case studies. The managers interviewed were given the same questions to answer. After the data was collected it was divided to fit either the model outlining learning, commitment and adaptation or added to the processual data describing what had been learnt through business transactions and networks and how this occurred.

Supplementary data were collected in the form of case histories, company records, statistics, articles in the economic press, Annual Reports and the like. These provided some important background data. After writing the preliminary case histories, the transcripts were sent back to the managers for them to check and add some feedback.

The research method can be criticised on many grounds, for example on its validity, reliability and possibility to generalize. However, at present the case study approach offers good possibilities to learn about specific problems instead of generalising. The case study approach also reveals the uniqueness of each entry process and network evolution and can reveal the core concepts of learning and adaptation in more depth than many other available approaches.

4. Case Descriptions

The cases are presented by first studying the process of development from the starting point to the present situation and finally by outlining the future prospects of Estonian business from the perspective of Finnish firms.

Case 1: Hartwall Ltd

Hartwall is the market leader in sales and production of beer and soft drinks in Finland. The combine consists of five business units with a total turnover of 1600 million FIM. The company has 2385 employees. Hartwall's internationalisation has mainly been based on exports of beer with the brand name 'Lapin Kulta'. Estonia was their first foreign direct investment project and the case is discussed below in more detail. Hartwall has a joint venture, Baltic Beverages Holding Ltd (BBH) with Procordia Beverages (Sweden). BBH's acquisition of Estonia's leading brewery Saku õlletehas is outlined here. In addition to Saku, BBH has acquired two other breweries, Alusdaritava Aldaris in Latvia in 1992 and Baltika in St. Petersburg in 1993.

Market Entry Decision

The idea to enter the Estonian market came in the Fall of 1989 after the political revolutions in Eastern Europe, which resulted in the opening of the markets. Saturated home markets created a threat, which made the firm look for new markets abroad. Another strong motivating factor for Hartwall to invest in Estonia was that if they had a strong market share in Estonia, this would strengthen their position in their domestic market. A threat posed by the European common market forced Hartwall to strengthen its brands in order to protect its strong market position. Estonia is seen on the corporate level as Hartwall's extended home market, and it was crucial to enter Estonia before their main foreign competitors.

Hartwall started the Estonian operations by using small experimental export deliveries in order to assess the new markets. It was soon realised that Hartwall needed to establish a market presence in order to utilise the market potential. The corporate managers decided that the best way to proceed was to get a partner and acquire a local brewery. Hartwall had previously worked together with a Swedish company, Procordia Beverages Ab (PB), in product and production development cooperation, selling the other's products in their domestic markets. The cooperation had been regarded as fruitful by both companies and both had an interest in more intensive cooperation. Estonia was seen as their major challenge, and if the cooperation was successful, joint activities could be extended to cover the whole Baltic Sea region. Each company regarded their own resources as too small – even though both were market leaders in their domestic markets – to enter the market on their own. The companies decided to put their resources together and set up a joint venture if they could find a suitable partner in Estonia.

The Baltic Beverages Holding Ltd. (BBH), a joint venture between Hartwall and Procordia Beverages Ab, was created in 1991, with the goal of locating prospective breweries in the Baltic States and Russia. After negotiations with several breweries in Estonia, BBH finally chose Saku ölletehas, the market leader in the Estonian brewery industry for acquisition and bought a 60% stake in the company. BBH wanted to acquire a company that had the basic infrastructure to set up a brewery operation which was big enough to be competitive. The acquisition has proven to be a good solution, and BBH has used this same concept when entering other countries in the region. BBH bought a 60% stake in Latvia's leading brewery Alusdaritava Aldaris in 1992, and St. Petersburg's leading brewery Baltika in 1993.

Market Potential and Growth

Hartwall's managers emphasise that they did not have great expectations in the short run for the Baltic market, as these markets were seen as quite small, being hindered by the low purchasing power of consumers. From the beginning, they wanted to be a part of the development process in this industrial branch and by being active in this way, to acquire a steady market position. The investment was based on the premise that quick returns on invested capital were not expected. Thus, market growth was anticipated to take place only in the long run.

The expectations of the company were much lower than the actual potential for their products proved to be. The whole industry has undergone fundamental changes as a result of improved product quality and economic changes. It took two years to build distribution channels, and to make the improved brand known and accepted by local consumers. They have improved the quality of their own brand Saku (previously produced by their Estonian partner) considerably and after improving their market position Hartwall has been able to increase their direct sales from Finland with other brands as well. During the partnership Saku's market share has risen from 42% to 55% within two years. Saku Reval Luxus, a high quality import beer, is produced in Finland and imported by BBH to Estonia. This brand is also a market leader in its own class. In fact, Saku is at present the most profitable business unit of Hartwall.

During the past few years the demand for beer has decreased throughout the Baltic states because of weakening purchasing power, high inflation and general poor economic conditions. However, since early 1993 there has been a dramatic increase in the sales of both Saku and Hartwall's own brands exported directly from Finland.

Competition

The level of competition was quite low before the market entry. Hartwall foresaw that the company first able to penetrate the market would have a strong position in the future. Other factors that increase the competitiveness of Hartwall are a logistical advantage (near location), strong brand names and local support from the beginning. The acquisition of a local brand has proved to be successful and its improved quality has increased BBH's market position in comparison to its major foreign competitors.

Competition has increased considerably since the market entry. At present all the major European breweries are operating in the market.

The general trend at the moment seems to follow the example of BBH: Western breweries are trying to improve the quality of the local brands together with local manufacturers.

Risks and Problems
The major problems faced by Hartwall were mainly related to human resources management. Poor infrastructure also created problems. The factory had to be reconstructed because it was technically in poor condition. Patience and determination were needed to overcome these problems. Hartwall has committed itself to the decision of gaining a position in the market and is prepared to overcome the obstacles that may appear.

Political and environmental risks have significantly decreased. The major problems perceived by Hartwall at the moment are related to import tariffs, taxation and to the acquisition of raw materials. Another concern is the poor economic situation in Estonia, which has resulted in low purchasing power. This creates a problem of adapting the brewery industry to local economic conditions, because sales are extremely dependent on the level of the local purchasing power. However, it is believed that once Hartwall is an insider in the market and thus a part of the local brewery culture, that they can better influence demand. Problem-solving procedures have been influenced by the experience gained from the company in Estonia.

Political Imperative
The rapid market entry was greatly influenced by the fact that BBH negotiated the contract directly with the Estonian authorities, and not with the Soviet authorities in Moscow like many other companies. Having a good relationship with the political decision-makers was regarded as extremely important in the entry phase, as the government is a minority partner in the acquired Estonian company. BBH had even one Estonian minister on the board of directors. In general, Estonia's independence was seen as a factor in decreasing political turbulence.

Although the Estonian partner was a government-owned enterprise, Hartwall has met with some political problems. It has been difficult to convince the political decision-makers of the benefits of what Hartwall is doing. Trust building has been of crucial importance in this matter and it has been increased by convincing the local population that Hartwall wants to take part in the development of the local industry. At the beginning the local population thought that they were being taken advantage of by the foreign partners. It has been difficult to convince them how much both Hartwall and Procordia Beverages have invested in the venture in terms of capital, time, money and other resources in order to get the production on its feet. This has resulted in numerous conversations between the partners.

Business Relations

Unlike the other cases presented in this study, Hartwall has to deal with two different partners, PB and Saku. Relations with PB are based on long-term cooperation, trust and joint objectives in the Baltic region. Thus, no major problems have occurred in these relations. When dealing with their local counterparts Hartwall wants to emphasise the importance of patience and understanding when establishing and developing business contacts. They have decided not to act arrogantly towards their partners in a way that carries the sentiments »We know how this thing« should be handled, and you don't know anything about this«. Local partners have to be respected as equals and a positive attitude taken towards communication. »They have their own culture and traditions, which must not be criticised. The poor economic situation is not their fault. We want to be a part of the society's development process in local terms«, stated one of Hartwall's executives.

In the beginning many new contacts were initiated in order to find the most appropriate partner. Hartwall did not know at the beginning whether their brewery project would succeed. The development of business relationships was initially regarded as difficult. The relics of the Soviet impact on individual behaviour was very strong and it was hard to make the local employees think with a Western business mentality. The interviewed export manager used the term »work culture« to indicate differences in attitudes towards hard work.

Despite the problems related to establishing business relations with local partners, they have been eager to learn and they have learned surprisingly quickly. It was emphasised that at present Hartwall trusts its partners 100 percent. Mutual trust has developed only after 3-4 years of intensive communication, cooperation and education. They expect from their counterparts a commitment equal to their own. However, much work is needed yet to increase production efficiency.

BBH has allowed Saku's top management great flexibility, and this has been important in dealing with the rapidly changing environment.

The general managers in all subsidiaries are local, and thus they are ready to react quickly to changes in the environment.

Resource Commitment

Hartwall has invested more in internal resources for the project than they anticipated at the outset. In addition to the acquisition of Saku, both Hartwall and PB have been forced to use much of their own personnel in the target country. Saku was in poor condition when it was acquired, and practically everything had to be rebuilt. Of the foreign partners, it is Hartwall which has invested heavily in the improvement of the production machinery. Hartwall has also invested about 20-25 million FIM annually in BBH, and the investments are expected to be at the same level during the next few years. Although their breweries are profitable, they cannot invest too much of their capital for production development.

Case 2: Paulig Ltd.

Paulig Ltd. is one of the major combines in the Finnish food industry. The basic areas of business are coffee and spices. Coffee is the combine's major product with 60% of the total turnover and Paulig is a clear market leader in this field in Finland. Paulig's turnover was 925 million FIM in 1993 and it employed 697 people.

Although Paulig is a newcomer to Eastern Europe it has had a marketing affiliate in Tallinn, Estonia in 1938-42. The relationship had to be terminated in 1942 because of the war. Some of the brands they are selling today were present in the market already then. This case will outline the development process of A/S Paulig Baltic, a roastery, Paulig's greenfield investment in Estonia. In addition to the production unit in Estonia, Paulig has a marketing unit in St. Petersburg.

Market Entry Decision

Interest in the Estonian market rose in the summer of 1991. Estonia, the other Baltic countries, St. Petersburg and Poland were regarded as »interesting markets« for industrial operations. The main motive for market entry to Estonia was the market potential for coffee. At the time of the market entry there were great difficulties with foodstuff supplies, and these supply difficulties were the main triggering signal for entry. In addition, cultural and geographical proximity favoured Estonia as opposed to other near-border countries. In the long run, location-specific advantages were also considered significant. After the completion of the Via Baltica route Paulig would have better access to the other Baltic countries, Russia and Poland.

Before the market entry decision Paulig had bought production equipment from a Swedish roastery that had stopped operations. This suited Paulig's purposes in Estonia well as the production lines were not as automated as in Paulig's own production process. In the fall 1991 Paulig looked for a potential factory in which to start production, however, they did not find anything suitable, and they decided to build a new factory.

After the registration of the company, Paulig began thorough market research in Estonia. They sent one representative to do field work and look for potential customers in Tallinn. They were especially interested in shops, restaurants and hotels. They collected information from approximately 500 different distributors. In further decisions, the results of this survey were decisive.

The second investigation aimed at finding out what kind of coffee the local population wanted. Paulig arranged several consumer tests in hotels and restaurants of seven cities. The potential local consumers tasted different types of coffee and the most popular ones were chosen for production.

The third investigation was done by a consulting firm, which tested local consumer behaviour. They found out in what kind of circumstances Estonians usually drink coffee, and how much they spend on it. At that time there was no secondary information available. After these investigations the construction of the plant was started.

Competition
At the time of market entry there were already approximately 50 different coffee brands on the market from several West European countries. However, there was no local production and the local demand was fully satisfied by imports. Paulig's brands were exported by several dealers and they kept the price at a very high level. When Paulig began the construction of its own plant, it also started to export its own brands to Estonia. They lowered the price by 40 % and the coffee was an instant success. Paulig was also able to utilise its advertisements on Finnish television, because Tallinn receives Finnish TV broadcasts. Thus, local consumers recognised the company immediately. Sales accelerated dra-

matically after Estonia received its own currency in the summer of 1992.

Paulig has also created a local brand, Olümpia coffee. Estonians now have a strong national identity and Paulig capitalised on this by sponsoring Estonia's Olympic team for the Lillehammer Winter Olympics in 1994. Based on a contract with the Olympic Committee of Estonia, a certain percentage of the sales of Olümpia coffee was donated to the Estonian Olympic team; altogether it amounted to 40% of the team's total budget. After the Olympics in February 1994 both parties wanted to continue this cooperation until the next Olympics in 1998. Paulig has made a similar arrangement with Latvia and Lithuania.

Another factor which improves Paulig's competitive position in the market is that the local citizens regard Paulig's brands as local – because they are produced in Estonia – and seem to favour these against competing brands. Another survey carried out in September 1993 about consumer knowledge of different brands in the market showed that Paulig's brands were ranked as the four best known. Thus far Paulig has exceeded its sales budget by over 50% and has been able to keep expenditures down.

Competition has increased as competitors have noticed Paulig's success. However, Paulig's market share is at the moment 25-30%. One of the major threats is the illegal imports of coffee, and unlicensed importers do not pay customs duties or turnover tax. In the long run, Paulig feels that their competitive position will remain strong because of their »local« image. Local consumers have a strong loyalty to Estonian high quality brands. High quality coffee remains the cornerstone of Paulig's operations.

Risks and Problems
Paulig perceived that the commercial risks were low as they did not invest more than they could afford to lose. Although the economic and political conditions were poor at the time of market entry, no major problems were encountered because Paulig was the first to enter this kind of business, and thus received special advantages from the Estonian government.

The major problem in the operation was the underdeveloped wholesale system. It started to develop in the spring of 1993 and now Paulig has seven wholesalers. Additional problems included bureaucracy at a later stage and the lack of business legislation. Poor import control has also been a problem and it is estimated that only about 30% of coffee comes into the country legally.

Local water proved to be different from that in Finland which meant that those coffee brands Paulig produced in Finland would lose much of their quality due to the hardness of the local water. Thus, the coffee needed to be darker than in Finland. Furthermore, the price of imported coffee would have been too high because in the production of some brands up to 16 different sorts of coffee are used. The investigations made by Paulig showed that the local coffee contained at the highest 25% coffee, the rest consisting of grain or something else. In some cases the local coffee did not contain any coffee at all.

In addition to the core product adaptation, Paulig has also adapted the packages to local circumstances. Paulig's coffee imported from Finland is sold in smaller packages so that local consumers can afford to buy it and the package texts have been translated to Estonian, along with instructions on how to make good coffee. Paulig made the product adaptation as a good service gesture to their customers and also to prevent their products from being exported back to Finland by »jobbers«.

Political Imperative
During the entry phase the most important relations were those connected to the Estonian government. The president of Estonia realised that the country needed foreign firms to restructure the economy and wanted Paulig to be a good example for other foreign companies. Coffee was also perceived as a potential export product for the country. At that time there were already quite many joint ventures with foreign companies (mainly Finnish and Swedish firms), but only a few had built totally new production facilities. Thus, the government committed itself to the project and all permissions were received quickly. The local authorities were also interested in the case and helped Paulig in all possible ways. They realised that a new factory would bring jobs to the region. Relations to the local authorities have developed over time in a way that even family relations have been established between some executives of Paulig and the local authorities. Paulig found a site for the plant in Saue, about 20 kilometres away from Tallinn and the local authorities donated the site to Paulig in the spring of 1992. Paulig built a new residence for the family who had lived on the site for many years and received the site quickly with no complications.

Marketing Channels and Distribution
Before the establishment of A/S Paulig, Paulig's brands were exported
by several dealers to Estonia. However, they kept the price at a very high
level and sales were quite low. When Paulig started the construction of
its own plant, Paulig also started to export its own brands to Estonia. At
the beginning the retailers bought the coffee straight from the factory,
but it became a problem as they had to pay for the goods in cash. The
situation has improved significantly since the development of a wholesale system. In Latvia and Lithuania, Paulig relies on local importers.

Business Relations
Paulig's policy in business relations has always been based on the estab-
lishment of good personal relationships. At the beginning, the Estonian
Chamber of Commerce and Industry was a very important contact.
They gave valuable market knowledge to Paulig's personnel. Hiring an
Estonian as the general manager also proved to be successful.

Paulig has continuously been in contact with several other Finnish
businesses having committed operations in the Estonian market. Paulig
is a member of the Pro Baltica Forum, a business forum of more than
50 big Finnish, German and Baltic companies. The association works as
a link between companies and the government decision-makers in the
Baltic states.

At the beginning the biggest problem in business relations was communication. Their local partners did not have any business experience
and the main problem was to make them understand Western business
practices. Establishing relationships has required most of all patience
and understanding. A Paulig executive emphasised the ability to listen
to the locals and to understand their problems. »It would have been a
mistake to tell them straight away that they were wrong. I usually said
that OK, we can consider your propositions, but we can also try together
one of my own ideas. This way they learned to trust us and they noticed
that they were not being fooled.«

Resource Commitment
After the market entry decision was made Paulig decided not to invest
in the project more than they could afford to with their own capital. By
making the investment with no external financing Paulig was able to
minimise the financial risk related to the operation.

Besides financial resources, Paulig has also used a lot of their own personnel from Finland especially during the construction period. At present most of the business is managed by Estonians after intensive training by Paulig.

Case 3: Valio Ltd.

Valio Ltd. is a company owned by 54 Finnish cooperative dairies. It was established in 1905 to take care of butter exports to England. At present it manufactures and markets milk, dairy products and other foods in Finland and abroad. Valio, its subsidiaries and the cooperative dairies form the Valio Group. Milk is supplied to the Group by 32 000 producers, and the Group processes 90 per cent of the milk in Finland. The Group employs an average of 3 000 people, 450 of them abroad. Originally founded to handle butter exports on behalf of countryside dairies, Valio has, over the decades, expanded the range of its export products to cover more than 500 different items from very basic dairy products to more sophisticated specialities.

Valio is an increasingly international dairy company and is among the 20 biggest Finnish exporting companies with exports to about 135 countries, of which 70 are on a regular basis. Total exports are approximately FIM 1,4 billion annually, and total sales of FIM 7,3 billion in 1993. The firm has 8 foreign subsidiaries, one joint venture and 2 sales representatives abroad. Eastern Europe, especially Russia and the former Soviet Union, Belgium and the USA are major target markets of Valio's products. This case describes the initiation and market development of Esva, a manufacturing joint venture, which produces and markets fish fingers. Valio's has a 48% minority stake in the venture.

Market Entry Decision
Valio has been engaged in trade with the former Soviet Union for about 40 years, and the Soviet Union remained Valio's biggest foreign buyer of butter and milk powder for decades. The collapse of Soviet trade in 1991-92 was extremely difficult for the firm as they had relied too heavily on this market. However, since the birth of the new independent nations, Valio's market position has gone back to the level where it had been before the collapse. Russia is regarded as the firm's major market area in Eastern Europe. Their main export products are butter and milk powder. In general, a wide product range is available in the transborder areas because of the short distance from Finland.

The idea for the formation of a joint venture came from the Soviet side. In fact, they insisted Valio enter into a joint venture, or they threatened to cancel their butter orders from the company. This would have been disastrous for Valio because of overproduction of butter in Finland, which, however, had been decreasing during the previous years.

The negotiations began in 1988 with the intention of starting either milk or juice production in Estonia. The quality of milk in Estonia was very poor and the idea of starting milk production was abandoned. Juice production was likewise disregarded as a feasible option. Valio had experience in frozen food production and they finally decided to invest in a factory to produce fish fingers. The Soviet partner was supposed to contribute fish, and Tallinn was regarded as suitable for this purpose: it was located on the coast of the Gulf of Finland, it was geographically close to Finland and cultural and language problems were easier to handle than e.g. in the other Soviet republics. Tallinn was located close enough to Finland that Valio could guarantee the quality of the production and the final products. The plant Esva was completed in 1990.

Market Potential and Growth

The plan was to sell approximately 30% of the production to Western markets in order to earn hard currency and thus finance the investments made for setting up the venture. The production aimed at export markets was to be based on white-fleshed fish, which was regarded as a good raw material by western customers. The other 70% of the production was supposed to consist of a cheaper raw material – a darker fish to be sold in the Baltic states and Russia. Valio decided that the majority of the production had to be targeted to Western countries in order to facilitate quick returns on investment and to be able to pay back the loans that were needed for the investment. However, market potential outside of Estonia was significantly overestimated.

Esva's access to Western markets other than Finland has been quite limited. Instead they have been able to penetrate Polish, Czech and Romanian markets, where they can take advantage of the product's low price. In Finland Valio has a market share of 30%. Exports to Russia are increasing rapidly. Thus, market prospects are seen as promising.

Competition

At the beginning Valio aimed to export a majority of its production outside of Estonia in order to earn hard currency. Because of poor product image and difficulties in building distribution channels Valio has increased its commitment in local markets. At present the main competitors in the food industry come from Finland, Sweden, Denmark, Italy, and in some product categories, the USA. Especially in dairy production foreign firms seem to be hesitant as the threat of a sharp increase in the price of milk is prevailing.

Risks and Problems
The main problems related to the JV creation were in fact mistakes made in the planning stage of the JV and problems related to partner relations. The business idea was too production-oriented, and the main idea was that they should only secure the obtaining of raw materials, and that the business should have something to do with the food industry, Valio's main competence area. They also made an assumption that the products could be sold to world markets, although Valio had no experience in marketing fish fingers abroad. They had no customers and no distribution channels, which further increased the problems.

The European markets had already been saturated and the image of the products were poor because of the negative perception of products produced in Estonia. Consequently, they had to invite every potential buyer to the factory and convince them of the quality of the production. In terms of production quality the factory is assumed to be one of the most modern in Europe.

Another problem occurred in raw material supplies. The Soviet partner had convinced them that they could supply the fish Valio needed. The first problems occurred when Estonia gained back its independence: they did not have any international fishing rights as these rights belonged to the Soviet Union. At that time Estonia had bigger concerns than taking care of its fishing rights. The fish they were able to supply was grey instead of white. Customers in Esva's main market areas did not like the colour of the flesh. Soon afterwards, the partner could not supply anymore fish. Finally Esva was forced to import its fish from other countries, mainly from Argentina and Poland using hard currency. This was also fatal because they had calculated that all the raw materials could have been bought in rubles and the final products sold in hard currency. Thus, they lost their low cost advantage over their major competitors. As the products did not meet the qualifications of customers, they had to sell the products at a much lower price than anticipated. Additionally, the distribution networks did not function well enough. As a consequence of these problems, Esva finally went to bankrupt in 1993. Since the bankruptcy, Esva has been able to continue production and today the company is operating profitably.

Esva has also encountered problems with local organisation. The old hierarchy in management decision-making seems to still prevail. The older managers have achieved their position through previous achievements and usually have low commitment to the firm's decision-making. Thus, Esva is more willing at the moment to hire young managers, which are eager to learn new management techniques, are devoted to their work and want to succeed in what they are doing.

Political Imperative

The most important political imperative has been the independence of Estonia, which resulted in confusion over Estonia's fishing rights. This had a direct effect on the raw material supplies to Esva. At times there were shortages of fuel for the fishing boats. This lack in supply of essential commodities reveals how business operations are affected by the political and economic environments.

Originally, an Estonian fishing association Estrybrom had 52% ownership in the joint venture. In order to improve the acquisition of better quality raw material, 35% of the equity was sold to an All-Union fishing association Sovrybflot in 1991. At this point Valio still owned 48% of the venture. Hopes for getting better raw material soon proved to be vain and even bigger problems developed with the Russian partner, especially in management issues. Soon after, the Soviet partner ceased to exist as a result of the break-up of the Soviet Union.

At the moment Esva has strong trust in the local government and political risks are thus regarded as minimal. It is believed that the local political decision-makers understand the importance of foreign firms in the restructuring of the economy.

Business Relations

Relations to agricultural officials and production organisations have been important during the whole existence of Esva. Long-term personal contacts have been established. In order to develop its image, Valio has annually, at no cost, educated Estonian students in their own Dairy School in Hämeenlinna, Finland. Relations to political decision-makers have been important because it was considered difficult to set up food production without local participation. Market information is collected mainly through Valio's own personnel in Tallinn.

At the beginning Valio had only one partner, a government-owned Estonian fishing group Estrybrom. Shortly afterwards a Soviet All-Union fishing group Sovrybflot joined Esva in order to improve the raw material supply. Their contribution was low from the beginning as they could not improve the raw material supply.

Good personal contacts with the Estonian managers working at Esva are seen as critically important. Maintenance of good relationships has, for example, resulted in joint leisure trips to Lapland.

Resource Commitment
During the past five years Valio has invested in Esva about 80 million FIM (including the guarantees paid to the bank). Valio has also invested in management education. After the bankruptcy Valio has decided to invest in advertising in order to improve the company image and to get a wider awareness of the company and its products both in Estonia and Russia. This aggressive policy is also a way to prepare for the future. They are also investing in the education of local retailer sales personnel.

Valio had partly guaranteed the loans for Esva and as it went bankrupt, Valio had to pay a debt of 65 million FIM. The Estonian partner had approximately the same amount of guarantees, but it was unable to pay its debts. Thus, the Estonian partner still owes the bank the debt, which complicates matters for the company.

Case 4: Raisio Margariini Oy

Raisio Margariini is a firm producing consumer margarine for human consumption. It is one of the largest actors in this market in Finland. It is a part of the Raision Group which specialises in producing different food-products. Its main international activities are export activities, which are fairly new.

Market Entry Decision
In 1992, Raision Margariini [RM] decided to move the headquarters of its export operations from Finland to Germany. At that time exports of margarine to the Eastern bloc (Russia and the Baltic countries) were few.

The first contacts to Estonia were sought in 1992. Mr. Jonsson of

RM, the interviewee, was at that time responsible for the firm's exports. At the beginning he made several trips and took part in many seminars in Estonia. These first visits did not produce any direct business. The decisive moment for the take-off was after the summer 1992 when Estonia introduced its own currency. Many so called »jobbers« appeared and requested products from the West. This kind of small business did not interest RM. They wanted larger contracts and were looking for buyers wanting a minimum order of a full container of butter (and/or margarine). The business was started in August 1992, and has reached a relatively stable level quite quickly in the first half of 1993.

Estonia is considered to be a home-market area for Raisio. For this reason RM has kept a percentage of their exports readily available for this market, despite the fact that the export markets of Russia and Poland are huge in comparison to Estonia.

Estonia's geographical proximity to Finland is an important factor. Due to the population concentration in the area around the capital Tallinn, the products of Raisio are familiar to many Estonians through Finnish television advertisements. As expected, the Estonians initiated contacts with RM, and thus began RM export operations.

Market Potential and Growth

The company knows the potential of the market both in relation to the population and it's income level. The company did not set up strict objectives concerning sales volumes in this specific market. In relative terms, if they consider Estonia as being a home-market, the country altogether would, in fact, constitute the second largest market-area after Helsinki, according to the population figures.

The company has a fat index that indicates how much fat is used for human consumption in a given market and the accumulation of this kind of data is a complex process.

RM has had and still continues to have close relations to the margarine factory in the Estonian capital of Tallinn. The local figures of consumption and markets were based on the Estonian firms' own business experience. Official regional or national statistics on these matters did not exist.

Possibilities for further market development still exist. Estonia can be regarded as a virgin »standing forest«, full of exploitation possibilities, according to Mr. Jonsson. Everything is still in the hands of the company itself in taking the opportunity to exploit these possibilities. RM's strategy from the start has been brand-name marketing in Estonia which has proven successful for the company.

Competition
Right from the start the competition in these new markets was strong. RM started exporting to Estonia by selling the product »Voimix« (a soft high quality margarine to be spread on bread). At the beginning RM could not take advantage of the »pull« from the market. The smaller quantities were ordered from some other suppliers.

The most important competitors were (and still are) the Swedish margarine producers, and most European brands are also on the market. Another competitor from Finland is Unilever, which exports an international brand produced in Finland.

The competitors (Swedish, Danish, Norwegian and other European producers and Unilever in Finland) have used another strategy. They have tried to produce low-quality products and compete on price. According to Mr. Jonsson there are important differences between the margarine products.

The competitive situation is developing all the time. According to the company manager the competition has closely followed the following stages of development:

1. Unorganised private business in a new unstructured »wild« market
2. Currency-based trade
3. Privatisation stage of currency-based firms and wholesale functions have emerged
4. Organised wholesale structure for food products

The competition at present is strong. Many producers use the slogans, names and advertisements closely related to the ones used by RM in marketing its margarine »Voimix«, which has a strong position on the market. The legislation is still undeveloped and therefore RM has little legal recourse. The slogans were used when competitors sold minarin (at least 40% fat content) instead of margarine (at least 60% fat content). This would be unacceptable and illegal, for example, in Finland.

Risks and Problems
The risks were eliminated from the start. The fact that business started with cash against delivery of products enabled RM to eliminate some of

the risks. This prepayment arrangement worked until the autumn of 1993 when a wholesaler structure was taking new steps forward. The foreign sellers have shifted to payment periods of 25-30 days. RM has to adapt to this situation, meaning that they have to take credit risks. Guarantees are almost impossible to get from an Estonian business partner and there are still problems with banks in Estonia.

Except for the monetary risks and problems with guarantees RM has not faced any other forms of risks. RM has not yet experienced any contact with Estonia's criminal element. Up to the present, RM has had only positive experiences in the Estonian market.

Political Imperative

Raisio Margarine has developed relationships with the highest political leaders in Estonia. The managers of the company have been involved in discussions with these political leaders. According to the company manager these discussions have not had any impact whatsoever on company operations in this specific market. There was an objective to build up a contact network from the outset, but the real network, important for exports, was formed from contacts other than political. The discussions with political leaders was aimed at possible establishments in Estonia of direct investments or joint ventures. According to the informant, nothing new has emerged politically since the initial talks.

Marketing Channels and Distribution

The operation involves close cooperation with the local dealer, which is also the local buyer. This indicates that the country does not yet have a national dealer system, seller system or marketing organisation.

Today Estonian business is done using the ex-works clausule, meaning that the Estonian partner picks up the goods from Finland. The dealer structure and channels of distribution at present face a rapid change, as already indicated. The wholesaler network, to a large extent, is now being developed using foreign capital and under foreign ownership. The Finnish wholesalers are on the fringe of this new development. For example the Finnish firm KESKO (the biggest wholesaler chain in Finland) will during the spring 1994 open its own wholesaling outlet in Tallinn. As larger and more efficient chains enter the market, more demands are being put on deliveries. Before the market in Estonia was demand driven. The day when distributors become active sellers in the market is not too far away.

Business Relations

RM has established business contacts only with serious business partners in the market. The first intense phase of »wild« contacts was at the
startup, and after this phase more serious relationships were established.
The development of business relationships is much more straightforward on the East-European markets than in the West.

Local firms claiming to be experts in marketing, selling and advertising made contacts with RM at this first stage. They told RM that they
were specialists in this field. It was then revealed that they had no experience in these areas at all.

Returning to the role of wholesalers on the market, one can say that
the triggering function in RM's entry was held by, to a certain extent,
the renewed trading houses of the former Eastern trade. The Raisio
Group had contacts to the old Soviet-Estonia. The country became independent but the old trading structure was able to continue its operations. This was especially the case concerning food products. The trading houses first contacted the newly formed wholesalers. Many of the
former margarine business people now are in charge of the banking
business in Estonia (after reaping huge profits from early market prices
of consumer foodstuffs, including margarine).

The first intense phase of contacts has now been stabilised and contacts with the largest wholesaler of food products on the market have
been made. The structure of business development is now in the hands
of those business people who have decided that the food business is their
main target, and the old method of »scrambled merchandising« is disap-
pearing.

Resource Commitment

The single most important resource commitment has been the 10 mill.
FIM investment in RM's new factory in Finland. In total the investments have been much larger. Some of the investments are so called
»forced investments« because of the needed larger quantities of fat products.

Employment figures have also increased. The investment into an export organisation is another internal investment which was built up a
few years ago. Today Raisio Margariini has in food production four employees tied to export activities.

5. Discussion

This study has analysed the business development processes of Finnish food industry firms in Estonia from the viewpoint of learning in networks. The process itself, commitment and adaptation are other theoretical constructs that are closely related to learning, and will also be discussed below. The most striking evidence we can derive from our study is the extreme dynamics of the business networks in Eastern Europe and the environment they are embedded in. Consequently, the ability of foreign firms to learn from their business networks and environments are extremely important success factors in these changing markets.

5.1 Learning

There are certain aspects of learning we would like to discuss in more detail. Firstly, and most importantly, learning is not a single process outcome that can be analysed separately from adaptation. The results provide us with clear evidence that *learning and adaptation are interdependent:* learning needs prior actions (adaptation) and adaptation is the outcome of a perceived need for change in the cognitive level (learning) of business managers. The concept of learning is especially important for business development in Eastern Europe as it is considered to reduce the uncertainty related to these presently turbulent markets.

Secondly, the results also indicate that *learning is a gradual process,* in which the foreign firms step by step increase their understanding of the surrounding reality. In fast changing markets learning is a continuous process, emphasising the benefits a firm can get through an early market entry. As learning takes time, it must be considered as an investment to company assets: by increasing the knowledge of the functioning of the networks and external environment a firm can reduce uncertainty related to its market operations. Consequently, the benefits of learning can be capitalised only in the long run, suggesting the need for long-term market involvement.

Factors facilitating learning
A fundamental question in learning is *why are some firms more capable to learn than others?* Based on our results, this depends on a number of reasons. Successful learning in business networks is strongly influenced by

the ability of the Western partner to interpret the cultural and managerial differences of the East European network actors. In business networks partners are involved in a process of exchange of ideas, thoughts and behavioural patterns, which in turn are culturally bound. The results seem to indicate very strongly that flexibility and understanding of the partner differences, equality and sensitivity in network relations are vital when establishing and developing business relations. This tacit knowledge becomes an internalised company asset in the long run.

We identified three different types of learning in our cases: experimental, network and mutual learning. *Experimental learning* seemed to be characteristic for the market entry stage. It was based on direct market experience, which resulted in behavioural change prior to cognitive change. Thus, the firms tested certain behavioural patterns prior to understanding what the suitable behaviour would look like. Certain actions were taken »...because this just seemed the best way to proceed.« The firm needs feedback from its altered actions. Whether the feedback is positive or negative the firm changes its behaviour until it finds a satisfactory match/fit with its partner and the environment. Repetition of the action is necessary to achieve this match, which in turn lengthens the process.

This kind of behaviour suggests low initial market involvement and increasing resource commitments only after the firm has gained more experience and knowledge of local conditions. The more experimental nature of learning can be explained in two ways. Some of the companies were among the first to penetrate the markets in their own fields. Another explanatory factor is that the experiences gained from other markets are not directly applicable to the present markets of Eastern Europe.

Network (or relationship) learning is another type of learning that proved to be relevant in our study. The basic premise in network learning is that foreign firms learn from their partner, customer, supplier and from other network actors in the market. These actors in the market provide foreign firms with primary information of the market changes and their impact to business. A prerequisite for successful learning to take place seems to be the ability of foreign managers to understand and respect their Estonian partner's areas of competence. Time for understanding the logic of the local market environment can be substantially reduced by utilising local network actors. In FDI operations the use of local managers seems to be a crucial asset. Our results show that the learning opportunities associated with Estonian network actors were not usually tangible, visible knowledge, but rather related to more complex tacit knowledge, for example, different management routines and philosophy. The more attention is paid to the establishment of good personal relationships – even to politicians and local authorities – the better are the possibilities for learning.

Reciprocity in learning was also emphasised in several cases, i.e. to be efficient, learning has to be two-sided. *Mutual learning* is especially important in undertakings where Western managers must interact with local management teams. Understanding of the mutuality in learning is relevant: if the partner/customer needs and expectations are not understood, the project is bound to fail. The results indicate that the Estonian partners' motives and ability to absorb skills from their Finnish partners succeeded usually better than anticipated.

It is believed that organisations providing an intensive interaction between both Eastern and Western management teams (cases Hartwall and Valio) provide a successful context for learning. They provide the firms with access to the embedded knowledge of the other organisation. This access creates the potential for firms to internalise partner skills and capabilities – not just to access them. The Eastern partner can provide the Western firm e.g. with market knowledge, access to raw materials, distribution channels etc. The Western partner provides the Eastern firm with new technology, financial capital, access to local networks etc. In joint ventures and acquisitions partners' resource complementarity and differences are the building blocks for learning. Thus, the partners must develop a shared understanding among each other as to how to proceed with the venture.

Pure export operations (as in the case of RM) do not give the same possibilities for learning as in FDI operations because the firm is operating in the market from the outside. In export operations network building to local resellers, personal visits to the market and secondary market information seem to act as building blocks for learning.

Learning takes place to a major extent on the individual level. This suggests that firms have to hire specialists for their management teams working in the region. Learning effects are internalised into the management team, but the results did not give us enough evidence on the integration of individual learning to the organisational level.

Paradoxically, we found that »unlearning« is equally important for firms as learning. This concerns both parties of the business relationship. Many Estonian managers are still burdened by the legacy of the planned economy era, emphasising characteristics that are not suitable for the present, more dynamic relationship, and environmental demands: 1) the lack of initiative and responsibility, 2) changed role of management in general, and 3) the old hierarchical organisation structures still hinder both vertical and horizontal communication. Local managers must unlearn this kind of behaviour in order to meet the challenges of today.

Also Western managers that have experience of doing business during the planned economy era, must unlearn the past and be more receptive to the demands of the new context of business relationships that are based on intensive interaction with the product end-user. Thus, unlearning of the old behavioural patterns is important in the new era of East-West business, and also a part of the learning process itself.

Outcomes of learning
In organisation theory learning is often related to company success. It is evident that the outcomes of learning are also positive in the context of East-West business in terms of increased productivity, improved understanding of the behaviour of the market, and improved working climate between the partners. Furthermore, and perhaps most importantly, it facilitates the constant improvement of firms' competence to meet the internal and external environmental demands. Although learning is emphasised and encouraged is business relationships, it does not necessarily result in financial success. The case of Valio clearly showed that although the firm learns, radical changes in the external environment may be too complicated for the venture to survive.

5.2 Commitment

Commitment is argued to have at least two different dimensions: 1) individual, and 2) organisational. On the individual level it is a question of a person's dedication to accept change and act in a new way. Organisational commitment relates to the different resources the company has to invest in order to adapt to the relationship or the market environment. From this viewpoint, commitment is an integral part of the learning process and it has to take place in order to facilitate adaptation.

In our case studies individual commitment appeared in all the business relationships studied. It was mainly related to problem-solving: when the relationship did not work in an anticipated way, the managers had to make a commitment to change their own behaviour and this way try to affect their partner's behaviour to gain harmony.

The firms' investments in resources to develop the business relationship have been made in very different ways: new technology, capital, management know-how, start-up training, and education on different levels of the Estonian counterpart's organisation. In fact, organisational commitment can be seen as a dynamic, continuous process, in which the firm increase their resources in the venture. Generally, the investments were smaller in the initial stages (with the exception of Valio) and increased after the Finnish partner had gained more experience of the external environment and partner relations, and was thus able to reduce the perceived uncertainty. This confirms that learning is a continuous process, in which both commitment and adaptation are necessary parts.

5.3 Adaptation

Analysing adaptation was much easier than analysing learning because adaptation is more visible than learning and thus easier to be traced. The results revealed that adaptation is a continuous process that is needed when coping with the turbulent environment. As discussed above, the results reveal a strong interdependence between learning and adaptation. Whereas learning is basically related to the changes in the state of knowledge, adaptation is based on action outcomes. As the company's knowledge of the market, economic and political environment etc. increases, it will change its behaviour to meet with the demands of the surrounding environment.

Firstly, the temporal dimension in adaptation was highlighted. One important way to adapt was the overcoming of the different 'mental maps' of the Estonian counterparts. Due to the disparity in technology between the Finnish and the Estonian partners, both technological and product adaptation was needed.

Secondly, adoption of a »local« image is expected to be important especially in the long run when self-sufficiency in food supplies becomes more pronounced than at present. Paulig and Hartwall emphasised their interest in being a part of the development of their industry in Estonia and both have created local high quality brand names. Consumer attitudes are influenced by strong nationalistic feelings. Although products that are produced in the market have a strong local image, there seems to be difficulties in selling them abroad because of this local image. Thus, country images matter only locally as they seem to have more negative effects in exporting, either to the Western market economies or to other countries in Eastern Europe.

Thirdly, trust-building seems to be a critical factor facilitating adaptation. The managers of the case companies have found it extremely difficult to convince the local managers/authorities of the benefits of cooperation. In spite of the big investments by Finnish companies, the local actors felt that they were being exploited. Time and training schemes are also crucial when adapting to business networks in Estonia. The relics of the Soviet impact in business decision-making is still prevailing, which demands understanding, patience and sensitivity in business networks. The needs and expectations of the local actors should not be neglected, instead they should be respected and encouraged to change.

Fourthly, the adaptation capability of foreign firms is based on organisational flexibility. Because of the constant changes, the firms must be prepared to react quickly. In FDI operations this has been solved in building an organisation headed by local managers.

Despite the foreign firm's willingness to learn and adapt, changes in the external environment may be so dramatic that the consequences may be fatal to the foreign company. This became evident in the case of Valio as its partner »disappeared« as a result of the collapse of the Soviet Union. It seems that especially pioneering ventures have met with more radical changes than those who have entered the market after the independence of Estonia. Since Estonia gained back its independence, the environment has become more stable.

Finally the link between learning and adaptation is emphasised. If firms are not capable of learning – that is, interpret and understand the meaning of internal and external signals – they also cannot adapt successfully, and instead just adjust their activities randomly. In the latter case, any successful experiences of the business are purely accidental.

As the final conclusion we want to stress that learning and adaptation are both ongoing, mutual processes of the actors involved in a business network. Further information is needed to examine the factors that facilitate or inhibit learning and adaptation in starting and developing business networks between West and East European companies.

References

Aldrich, H., 1971. »Organizational Boundaries and Interorganizational Conflict«, *Human Relations*, Vol. 24, 279-293.

Aldrich H., 1976. »Resource, Dependence and Inter-organizational Relations«, *Administration and Society*, Vol. 7, 419-453.

Argyris, Chris and Donald Schön, 1978. *Organizational Learning*. Addison Wesley, Reading, Mass.

Argyris, Chris, 1982. *Reasoning, Learning and Action*. Jossey-Bass, San Francisco.

Blankenburg, Desirée and Jan Johanson, 1993. »Managing Network Connections in International Business«, *Scandinavian International Business Review*, Vol. 1, No. 1, 5-19.

Bradley, Frank, 1991. *International Marketing Strategy*. Prentice Hall, Cambridge.

Buckley, Peter and Pervez Ghauri (eds.), 1993. *The Economics of Change in East and Central Europe*. The Academic Press, London.

Cateora, Philip, 1990. *International Marketing*. Seventh Edition, Irwin, Boston.

De Wit A. – Johanson M. – Monami E. – Seyed-Mohamed N.,1993. »Scanditronix« Business in Saint Petersburg«. Uppsala University, Department of Business Studies, Working Paper 1993/2.

Cook, K.S. and R.M. Emerson, 1978. »Power, Equity and Commitment in Excange Networks«, *American Sociological Review*, Vol. 43, 721-739.

Dicken, Peter, 1992. *The Global Shift: The Internationalization of Economic Activity*. Second Edition, Paul Chapman Publ. London.

Dodgson, Mark, 1993. »Organizational Learning: A Review of Some Literatures«, *Organization Studies*, 14/3, pp. 375-394.

Dunning John H., 1981. *International Production and the Multinational Enterprise*. Unwin and Hyman, London.

Dunning John H., 1988. »The Eclectic Paradigm of International Production. A Restatement and Some Possible Extensions«, *Journal of International Business Studies*, Spring 1988, 1-13.

Easton, Geoffrey, 1992. »Introduction« in: Geoffrey Easton and Björn Axelsson, (eds.) *Industrial Networks – A New View of Reality*, Routledge and Co., Kent.

Eisenhardt, Kathleen, 1988. »Building Theories from Case Study Research«. *Academy of Management Review*, Vol. 14, No. 4, 532-550

Ford, David (ed.), 1990. *Understanding Business Markets. Interactions, Relationships, Networks.* The Academic Press, London.

Garvin, David A., 1993. »Building a Learning Organization«, *Harvard Business Review,* July-August, 78-91.

Ghauri P.N. – Henriksen A-G., 1994. »Developing a Network Position in the Baltic States: The Case of Statoil in Estonia«. In P. J. Buckley and P .N. Ghauri, (eds.). *The Economics of Change in East and Central Europe. Its Impact on International Business,* Academic Press, London.

Glaser B.G., and A.L. Strauss, 1967. *The Discovery of Grounded Theory. Strategies for Qualitative Research.* Aldine Publishing Company, Chicago.

Halinen, Aino and Jan-Åke Törnroos, 1995. »The Meaning of Time in the Study of Industrial Buyer-Seller Relationships« In K. Möller and D. Wilson, (eds.). *Business Marketing: An Interaction and Network Perspective,* Kluwer Academic Publishers, Boston, 493-530.

Hallén, Lars, Jan Johanson and Nazeem Seyed-Mohamed, 1991. »Interfirm Adaptation in Business Relationships«, *Journal of Marketing,* Vol. 55, 29-37.

Hovi, Niina, 1995. *Outcomers of interfirm co-operation. A case study of four subcontractors.* Turku school of economics and business administration, Series D-3:1995.

Hunt Shelby D. and Robert M. Morgan, 1994. »Organizational Commitment: One of Many Commitments or Key Mediating Construct«. *Academy of Management Journal,* Vol. 37, No. 6, 1568-1587.

Håkansson, Håkan, (ed.), 1987. *Industrial Technological Development. A Network Approach,* Croom Helm, London.

Håkansson, Håkan, 1989. *Corporate Technological Behaviour. Co-operation and Networks.* Routledge and Co., London.

Håkansson, Håkan and Jan Johanson, 1985. »A Model of Industrial Networks«, Uppsala University, Department of Business Administration, Working Paper.

Håkansson, Håkan and Ivan Snehota, (eds.), 1995. *Developing Relationships in Business Networks.* Routledge and Co., London.

Johanson, Jan and Lars Gunnar Mattson, 1988. »Internationalisation in Industrial Systems – A Network Approach«, in: Neil Hood and Jan-Erik Vahlne, (eds.). *Strategies in Global Competition,* Croom Helm, New York, 287-314.

Keegan, Warren J., 1989. *Global Marketing Management.* Prentice Hall Inc., Englewood Cliffs.

Kim, D. H., 1993. »The Link Between Individual and Organizational Learning«, *Sloan Management Review*, Fall, Vol. 35, No. 1, 37-50.

Kraljic, Peter, 1990. »The Economic Gap Separating East and West«, *McKinsey Quarterly*, Spring 1990, pp. 62-74.

Kojo, Auli and Mari-Leena Köngäs, 1995. *Suomen gateway-asema lännestä arvioituna* (Finland's Gateway Position as Seen from the West). Turku School of Economics and Business Administration. Institute for East-West Trade, B 1/1995.

McGee, John and Howard Thomas, 1988. »Making Sense of Complex Industries«, in Neil Hood and Jan-Erik Vahlne, (eds.). *Strategies in Global Competition*, Croom Helm, New York, 40-78.

Miles, Matthew B. and A. Michael Huberman, 1984. *Qualitative Data Analysis. A Sourcebook of New Methods.* Sage Publications, London.

Morgan, Robert M. and Shelby D. Hunt, 1994. »The Commitment-Trust Theory of Relationship Marketing«, *Journal of Marketing*, Vol. 58 (July 1994), 20-38.

Naisbitt, John, 1995. *The Global Paradox.* Nicolas Bealey Publishing, London.

Nieminen, Jarmo, 1994. »From Stagnation To Dynamism in East-West Business Relations«. Paper presented at the »Third Annual Congress of IMDA«, Penang, Malaysia, June 16-18, 1994.

Parke, Arvind, 1991. »Interfirm Diversity, Organizational Learning, and Longevity in Global Strategic Alliances«, *Journal of International Business Studies*, Vol. 22, No. 4, 579-603.

Porter, Michael E., 1990. *Competitive Advantage of Nations.* MacMillan, New York.

Ring, Peter S. and Andrew H. Van de Ven, 1994. »Developmental Processes of Cooperative Interorganizational Relationships«, *Academy of Management Review*, Vol. 19 No. 1, 90-118.

Strauss, Anselm, 1987. *Qualitative Analysis for Social Scientists.* Cambridge University Press, Cambridge.

Tesch, Renata, 1990 *Qualitative Research. Analysis types and software tools*, The Falmer Press, Basingstoke.

Thorelli, Hans B., 1986. »Networks: Between Markets and Hierarchies«, *Strategic Management Journal*, Vol. 7, 37-51.

Törnroos, Jan-Åke, 1991. *Om Företagets Geografi – en teoretisk och empirisk analys* (About corporate geography – a theoretical and empirical analysis), Diss. Åbo Akademi University, Åbo Academy Press, Åbo.

Usunier, Jean-Claude, 1993. *International Marketing. A Cultural Approach* . Prentice Hall Inc., Hemel Hempstead.

Vahlne J-E – Nordström K.A. – Torbacke S., 1994. »Swedish Multinationals in Central and Eastern Europe – Entry and Subsequent Development«. Forthcoming in; *Journal of East-West Business.*

Van de Ven, Andrew H., 1976. »On the Nature, Formation and Maintenance of Relations Among Organizations«, *Academy of Management Review,* Vol 1, 24-36.

Van de Ven, Andrew H., 1992. »Suggestions for Studying Strategy Process: a Research Note«, *Strategic Management Journal,* Vol. 13, 169-188.

Warner, Malcolm, 1994. »How Russian Managers Learn«, *Journal of General Management,* Vol. 19 No. 4. Summer, 69-88.

Webster, Frederick E., 1992. »The Changing Role of Marketing in the Corporation«, *Journal of Marketing,* Vol. 56 (October), 1-17.

Yin, Robert K., 1984. *Case Study Research. Design and Methods.* Sage Publications, Beverly Hills.

Interviews:

Mr. Tapani Ilmanen, Export Manager, Hartwall Oy, March 18, 1994.

Mr. G. Nyman, Export Manager, Paulig Oy, March 23, 1994.

Mr. J. Lehtonen, Senior Vice President, Valio International April 7, 1994.

Mr. A. Jonsson, Export Manager, Raisio Margariini Oy, April 12, 1994.

Internal reports of the case companies.

10. Generic Routes to Subcontractors' Internationalisation[54]

Poul Houman Andersen,
Per Blenker and Poul Rind Christensen

1. Introduction

The aim of this contribution is to analyse generic traits of especially small and medium sized subcontractors' process of internationalisation. In many ways it diverts strongly from that anticipated in mainstream models of firms' internationalisation process. The idea of different generic routes to subcontractors' internationalisation is proposed. It is framed by the general assumption that international competition is becoming systemic in nature, taking place among essentially vertically integrated business systems. Subcontractors' internationalisation has to be seen in this view. We conclude this chapter with some tentative suggestions on how to view the internationalisation process in a strategic perspective of small subcontractors.

2. The International Activity Configuration of Subcontractors

Conditions of subcontracting are in a radical change these years. Basically this trend is caused by radical changes in the global production infrastructure. First and foremost, the division of labour is becoming more fine-grained. A growing number of specialised enterprises are involved in the transformation process from sources of raw materials to final markets. Competition among end producers tend to be systemic, i.e. depen-

54. This contribution was kindly supported by »Karl Pedersen & Hustrus Industrifond«. It has benefited from discussions with prof. G. Albaum, University of Oregon and prof. M. Teubal, Jerusalem Institute for Israel Studies.

dent on the configuration of the whole supply chain and last but not least on the interactive efficiency embedded with the division of labour.

While subcontracting a few years ago mainly took place inside a local or national frame of reference, the market for subcontracted goods is becoming increasingly international. Partly because of the IT promising extended logistical borderlines and new collaborative perspectives in the use of subcontractors, but mainly because of new sourcing strategies followed by global oriented contractors (Engh and Helberg, 1989; Dicken, 1986). International supply management is no more a sole question of low cost supplies from the Third World countries but as much a search for supplies supporting specialisation and efficiency with the contractor. Trade in semi-fabricated goods within the OECD area has thus flourished. It supports the assumption that subcontracting is changing from a predominantly local/regional phenomenon to become dominated by international market conditions. At the same time a large number of small and medium sized manufacturers operate in the business-to-business markets as subcontractors. At least this is the case in the Scandinavian countries (Anderson and Christensen, 1992; Zirius, 1994; Braunerhjem, 1991; Hovi, 1995). Their competitive profile is – most often – combined through a strong mix of custom-tailoring and specialised operations. Subcontracting is an accessible route for entrepreneurs establishing new ventures, as they are often born into a demand situation defined by a collaborative oriented customer. Empirical evidence supports this: about 40 per cent of newly established Danish firms in 1988 were subcontractors (Maskell, 1991).

Although the internationalisation of markets for subcontracting may offer opportunities to subcontractors, it will most probably also leave many small subcontractors in a squeezed situation. The fact that SME subcontractors are especially vulnerable suggests that they – on the average – are less exposed to international markets than other types of SMEs (Andersson and Christensen, 1992).

The international pattern of trade in subcontracted goods has only recently been subject to extensive studies (Wyckoff, 1993; World Bank, 1987). Theories expanding the explanatory power of international trade theory to include the complex pattern of international trade in components and parts have only been touched lightly upon (Dunning, 1995). Studies of subcontractors' international activity expansion have with few exceptions been implicitly dealt with. This is embedded in analyses and mainstream theories about the internationalisation process of firms.

However, there is every reason to place the specific international orientation and activity management of subcontractors explicitly on the research agenda.

Perspectives on global procurement

The growing importance of subcontracting has been emphasised in two theoretical lines normally positioned wide apart: Studies of global supply management and regional studies of localised industrial dynamics.

The former line looks on global corporations as key players configuring production in renewed ways (Amin and Robins, 1990). Vertical integration and control by ownership are substituted with other types of influence. These are based on a fine-grained division of labour backwards and forward in their chain of value added. Through their strategic use of subcontractors global players expand out sourcing to revitalise competitive potential. Key words are supply chain management, global sourcing, hollow corporations, single sourcing, lean supply and knowledge-based production. Several studies have pointed to the growing importance of subcontracting relative to in-house production (Lamming, 1993; Venkatesan, 1992). Other studies have emphasised the growing importance of knowledge intensive subsupplies based on strongly specialised and technological capabilities (Spekman, 1988; Braunerhjelm, 1991; Christensen et al., 1992). Also systems supplies have increased since they allow the contractor to reduce the number of subcontractors. Fewer subcontractors makes the decentralisation of the management task and the reduction of coordination costs possible for the contractor.

In the latter line of thinking, major contributions have proposed a new era within the industrial organisation of society. It has been promoted under headlines like »The Second Industrial Divide« (Piore and Sabel, 1984) and »Post-Fordism« (Scott, 1988). Densely knitted systems of co-specialised enterprises and subcontractors in a regional setting are seen as ways to provide dynamic alternatives to the traditional system of mass production (Storper, 1995).

The growing importance of international subcontracting may have a potential of bridging the two opposed lines of thought, thereby facilitating new explanations for the dynamics of the international division of labour. However, a more detailed study may take on the importance of international subcontracting and offer a preliminary insight into the patterns followed by subcontractors in their approach to international markets.

The importance of international subcontracting

The USA imports of intermediate goods now amount to 580.5 billion dollars (Montague, 1994). In OECD (Wyckoff, 1993) the globalisation of production networks is being discussed and researchers predict a growth in international procurement activities. A study of procurement practices in multinational corporations (MNCs) in six of the major economies of the OECD seem to support the notions that international subcontracting is growing in significance, see figure 1.

Figure 1: The Extension of global procurement of semifabricated goods (Wyckoff, 1993)

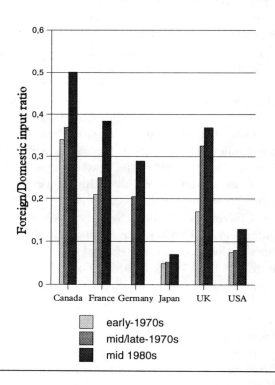

The investigation shows that the use of international supplies for industrial input is taking over from domestic sources. Other sources support this conclusion (Kearney, 1993; Demming, 1993).

Subcontracting: Concepts and typology

Subcontracting is often defined as activities carried out by one firm specified by another firm (the EU Commission, 1989, Andersson, 1990). Moreover, intermediary supplies are often regarded as expansion of the in-house capacity of the contracting firm (MITI, 1989; Harrison and Kellye, 1990). However, the theoretical literature reflects the expanded and changed use of subcontractors. Along with studies of the changing role of subcontractors considered by MNCs, the standard definition of a subcontractor: »a firm producing intermediate inputs based on the specification of the buying firm« – is developed to encompass various degrees of strategic importance of the subcontractors' intermediate input (Andersson 1990, Brege et al, 1993).

Although they traditionally are excluded supplies of standard components are often elements included in a subcontractor arrangement. Partly because of their contribution to the end products and partly because they are an important competitive force to other types of subcontractors.

Adaptations to the needs of specific customers may include other aspects than product modifications. Logistical arrangements; the development of specific technical interfaces and capabilities developed and specific tasks related to the development of new product generations represent other forms of adapting resources to meet the needs of specific customers. The content and strategic importance of the relationship with both the contractor and the subcontractor are greatly affected by these variations. Adaptating to specific industrial customers needs will raise the costs of leaving the relationship. The variety of relationships and practices of subcontractors mushrooming these years therefore suggests that a general definition of subcontracting is insufficient. It does not fully capture the strategic dissimilarities between the different types of vertical collaboration. Neither does it capture the competitive interface between different types of subcontractors. The various interfaces between subcontractors and contractors and their distinctive differences may be captured by a typology of contractors. The typology should display the interplay between the coordination needed and the complexity of the tasks solved. The following typology uses five different types of subcontractors (Blenker and Christensen, 1995).

As seen from the figure, this typology reflects important competitive intersections between the different types of subcontractors. Simulta-

Figure 2. A typology of subcontractors

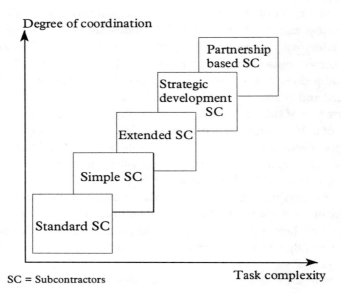

Note: SC = Subcontractors

neously the typology does not suggest a simple relationship between the degree of task complexity and the organisational complexity of interaction. The lack of trust between the parties may cause »excessive« coordination costs, as may distance, divergence of language and cultural dissimilarities. The main characteristics of each type of subcontractor in the typology can briefly be summarised as follows:

Standard Subcontractors are normally high volume suppliers. Users are prepared to adapt to the standards given. This implies a low level of interorganisational coordination and complexity. Economies of scale are important and they often operate in global markets. *Simple Subcontractors* include capacity subcontractors and suppliers of simple components and tasks. Users of contracting are main competitors, since the capacity supplied is also found in-house as well. Contractors charge the subcontractor with a task to be executed according to specifications and sometimes the materials to be processed. The interorganisa-tional coordination needed varies, but it is relatively low. The activities of *Extended Subcontractors* are specialised vis á vis their customers. They tailor-make the deliveries to each contractor. Although contractors normally provide specifications of the tasks, the tasks are often complicated to such a degree that closer mutual coordination is needed. Exit costs often increase for both parties as routines and insight emerge. Deliveries from *Strategic development Subcontractors* have similar characteristics as those of expanded subcontractors, except from the degree of task specialisation. Their prime importance to the contractors is related to their possession of critical competencies or valuable capabilities supporting contractors' internal core skills. Activities are coordinated by dialogue rather than rules. Mutual investments in technical interface and task partitioning are customary. Supplies from *Partnership-based Subcontractors* are fundamental to the contractor. They often play a key role in the development of new product generations. Value is of a long run nature. The need for a detailed task partitioning, exchange of knowledge and mutual investments in the relationship are often prerequisite for extracting value from the relationship. Thus, both parties *have incentives to link up in a stable* and efficient system of coordination.

In view of this typology, subcontractors' perspectives on international market opportunities relates to their position in the typology. This prove correct as far as entry modes and barriers faced are concerned.

Lack of analytical efforts in understanding subcontractors' internationalisation

The increasing internationalisation of the market for intermediate goods implies that industrial marketers and purchasers face a growing array of global opportunities. Subcontractors which have experienced location-specific advantages, will face international competition at close quarters. Simultaneously former domestic customers turn to international procurement in an effort to expand internationally.

Some types of subcontractors are more vulnerable to this pressure than others. Some types are in a better competitive position to respond to market opportunities and threats than are others. Small and medium sized subcontractors may find themselves in a jam due to this pressure. Their ability to operate internationally requires specific competences in how to do business in multiple markets, which however is hard to obtain. One reason would be the comparatively greater difficulties in adapting to the preferences of the customers due to differences in the business practices, technical standards, logistical complexity and foreign languages. A related reason is that international subcontractors must operate in different collaborative regimes posing different and sometimes conflicting routines and practices to them. Research suggests that totally the international subcontracting is concentrated on a few subcontractors.

Two Danish studies revealed, that the turnover generated internationally on the overall level was 5 % of the total of industrial subcontractors' output. However, subcontractors engaged in international activity exported 35 % of their output on average (Andersson and Christensen, 1992; Zirius 1994). Researchers have dealt mainly with these issues under the contemporary orthodoxy of the internationalisation theory. In the following we will assess several important aspects of subcontractors' internationalisation which call for a new theoretical framework. Finally, we will develop a framework containing four ideal[55] routes of internationalisation.

3. Contemporary Orthodoxy Concerning Business Internationalisation

For quite some time students of business internationalisation, have celebrated the behaviourally inspired stages-approach to the internationalisation process. However, the usefulness of this model of how to handle the internationalisation of subcontractors is questionable.

Internationalisation theory: An overview

Researchers often describe the internationalisation process as risk minimisation through learning and the step-wise development of international competence (Johanson and Vahlne 1977 and 1990). Briefly, the stages' approach describes internationalisation as a process starting with simple export and a gradual expansion of the activities to include the internalisation of cross-border transactions. Internationalisation then becomes a process of overcoming managerial mental barriers through the gradual development of international competence. This mechanism of incremental decisions gradually increase foreign resource commitments

---

55. We do not use the term "ideal routes" to describe any normative attributes to subcontractors' internationalization, but in the sense of generic examples, analogeous to Webers' use of ideal types (1949).

which eventually leads to the fully internationalised firm. The fully internationalised firm has substantial resources devoted to foreign market activities and organisational structures to administer the coordination and control of production and marketing activities in a global array of countries (Johanson and Wiedersheim-Paul, 1975).

The stages' approach regards firms as controlled by managerial authority relations, which clearly delimits the boundaries of the firm. Firms are considered as solitary decision units allocating resources independently to meet general market demands. Resource flows are governed internally according to administrative procedures, while resource exchange between firms takes place in the factor and good markets. However, this conceptual model of a firm stands poor against a recent development of the organisation of industrial activities, where firms downsize increasingly, stick to core competence and leave the production of supplementary goods to independent firms. Thus, these firms rest on other levers for activity coordination than those associated with the administrative mode of governance.

International subcontracting reflects this pattern. Industrial subcontractors carry out activities of their internationalisation in ways diverting from the usual view on international firms. In their process of internationalisation industrial subcontractors are usually very close related to their customer. The very concept »subcontractor« suggests that the strategies of such a firm, including its strategy of internationalisation cannot be viewed isolated from the strategies of its counterparts, i.e. the »contractor«. Therefore, industrial subcontractors primarily dedicate their activities to specific contractors, in such a way that it suggests a collaborative process of internationalisation.

Individual elements of activity interact in complex ways to make up the total industrial system. Any attempt to understand these activities from a single actor's point of view would easily fail to grasp the dynamics of the system as a whole. This suggests that subcontractors' internationalisation take place in a systemic manner seldom discussed in the literature. The systemic view focuses on the interdependent vertical system of production. Components are linked through administrative, economic and technical ties which combine production activities within and between legally disjoined entities. Thus, as an analytical unit the enterprise is at the same time too narrow and too wide to use in understanding the factors relevant for the internationalisation of subcontractors. It is too wide, since subcontractors may be committed to the process of internationalisation with respect to particular segments of their customer portfolio, but not necessarily to all. It is too narrow, because the increased degree of vertical specialisation and interdependency between subcontractors and their customers suggest that the internationalisation of the subcontractor is dependent on the international orientation in the system as a whole. The subcontractors' internationalisation is dependent on the collaborative orientation in the system, where the zero-sum optimisation efforts of each firm are replaced by plus-sum considerations which include the interdependence of each firm. The focus is on how firms are involved collaboratively in the game of positional advantages. Its context therefore must be taken into consideration (Ried, 1983)

In total these aspects call for new frameworks in order to analyse the process of internationalisation, which view the firm/environment interface quite differently. Subcontractors' international activity expansion may be viewed as *a process of taking part in the systemic internationalisation of vertical supply chains,* since it depends on the international configuration of the system as a whole – contractors and also supporting layers of subcontractors.

Various routes of internationalisation

Following the systemic view on internationalisation, subcontractors' role in the configuration of international activity chains may differ. In the following section we see four typical routes of subcontractors' partaking in the activity chains.

These are:

- Internationalisation by following domestic customers to the international marketplace
- Internationalisation through integration in the supply chain of an MNC
- Internationalisation in cooperation with domestic or foreign system suppliers
- Independent internationalisation

The motives and the entry modes may differ considerably depending on the different *types of subcontractors.* Simultaneously barriers to internationalisation will often differ along the *routes of internationalisation.* This picture is further complicated as co-evolving motives and barriers may change as the collaborative regime evolves. However, for the sake of convenience, we introduce four generic routes of internationalisation. They are often initiated by an indirect engagement in the contractors' international activity expansion. Several functions may be involved when contractors pass on claims for international standards to subcontractors.

Route one: Following domestic customers

Some subcontractors start their international activities by following domestic customers to their international marketplace. This route is especially used by suppliers of strategic importance to the contractor. Critical inputs from subcontractors are often an essential part of the strategic backbone of an internationalised firm. If crowned with success a growing part of the turnover of the internationalised contractor will stem from foreign activities. As the contractor expands his foreign business, it may strengthen his market position by making a stronger adaptation to local market needs. This will affect the relationship with previous subcontractors in a number of ways. As a consequence of a more rigorous adaptation to local market needs subcontractors who follow customers out will compete increasingly with local suppliers in the target market. Legal or contractual claims on local supplies and also economies of proximity explains this mechanism. For certain categories of subsupplies such factors will create vital barriers to this route of internationalisation. However, subcontractors of a strong strategic value to the contractors' performance may be upheld if they master a functional adaption to needed international standards. As such, they become indirect exporters and their organisation and management adapts to international ways of functioning.

Exhibit 1: Sabroe International

Sabroe A/S is a Danish multinational within the business area of industrial cold store construction, compressors and naval refrigerator equipment. Danish subcontractors usually deliver to the Danish domicile. However, if the required quality standards are not met, the subcontractors are now requested to make deliveries directly to points of sale.

Further along the line of international engagement of the contractor more claims may be back warded to them: Claims to after sales service on delivered components; direct delivery to foreign points of production. Eventually the subcontractor may be urged to locate service facilities or a production unit in key market points of the contractor. However, in those cases which we have knowledge of, such a foreign investment related directly to a specific customer is based on a guaranty of procurement matching the years of pay-back. The contractor may even support initial investments needed. IKEA is a case in point. They have given financially support to the development of production and logistical skills by Scandinavian subcontractors to support the IKEA supply chain on the North American market in an effort to position themselves on this market. In such cases internationalisation forces basic changes on to the collaborative regime. It develops into a partnership-based relationship.

As opposed to strategic development subcontractors or subcontractors already in partnership with their customer, simple subcontractors may often be trapped in the stage of indirect internationalisation. Sometimes they expel them from the supply chain, since their type of supply may be vulnerable to competition and claims for local supplies. Expanded subcontractors are vulnerable to interactive barriers during the internationalisation process, since their supplies are often of limited strategic value to the contractor and since their capacity to undertake international obligations is often limited.

Route two: Internationalisation through integration in the supply chain of a MNC

Deliveries to a multinational corporation or one of its divisions may affect the internationalisation of a small subcontractor. Firstly because deliveries to one division may blue-stamp deliveries to other divisions of the MNC and to third party contractors as well. Secondly because MNCs often have both resources and interest in supporting the development of the subcontractors capabilities. Thirdly because relations to one division or buying centre inside the MNC may introduce the subcontractor to a corporate network with new business opportunities coherent to the lines of business already established. This is the case of Schröder Plast illustrated below in exhibit two.

Exhibit 2: Schröder Plast: An example of dependent internationalization of subcontractors

---

In the 1980s, Schröder Plast A/S made contact with the IBM procurment office in Copenhagen. Schröder Plast had a successful production of plastic caps for printers and sockets. They managed to develop an integrated manufacturing process in which the entire socket could be made in one moulding process. IBMs procurement office introduced Schröder Plast to the internal market of IBM in Europe and later on in the USA.

The role of MNCs as route of internationalisation is triggered as more MNCs outsource production of components. The general idea is to attract subcontractors who support areas of key competence, i.e. suppliers with excellent skills complementary to core competences vested in the business units of the contractor. Subcontractors experienced in for example logistical matters, with a well-established reputation or substantial production capacity may also be targeted. Therefore especially subcontractors with highly specialised technical skills or specialised skills in production processes use the internal network of multinationals to promote their international activity expansion. However, as exhibit three illustrates, a lack of scale of production – or capacity of outbound logistics – may become a major barrier to this route.

Exhibit 3: Kaiser Plast A/S

Kaiser Plast is an advanced but minor producer of spray-plast components for the instrument and appliance industry. The central procurement office of Siemens got into contact with Kaiser Plast for a specific procurement. Kaiser Plast was taken through a vendor audit procedure and failed only due to lack of production capacity.

Subcontractors with simple capacity supplies or a simple co-specialisation may easily end up with delivering to only one division of the contractor. Often, standard component suppliers shall be of a substantial size to use the internal net of the MNC. Competing SME standard subcontractors may in principle set up a collaborative venture to utilise joint capacity (Hovi, 1995).

Procurement practices among divisions within a MNC may be unco-ordinated and differ strongly. This may create interactive barriers to subcontractors international expansion. Furthermore, personal rela-tions between staff of the subcontractor and the MNC buying centre strongly influence continuity, climate and the build up of routines throughout the interaction process. Since MNCs often have a high turn-over of staff within their buying centres, the international expansion of the subcontractor may be disrupted.

Route three: Internationalisation in cooperation with domestic or foreign systems suppliers

Systems supplies are rather in important to large international contrac-tors, thus resulting in the development of a new layer of system suppli-ers.

> *Small Danish subcontractors have only few hopes of direct deliveries to the large German automobile makers. However, chances of in-clusion are good with German system suppliers developing these years. This is reasoned by the fact that cost cutting in procurement is heavy these years. Huge numbers of first tier subcontractors are squeezed out of the market and every body is hunting new routines and competences. In this situation Danish subcontractors within business areas such as plastics, fine mechanics and eventually elec-tronics have favourable positions vis à vis German system suppliers.* (Interview with the Danish Consul General C. Smith, München, June 1994)

Since deliveries of complete subsystems is frequently based on several fields of competence, horizontal collaboration between subcontractors with mutually supporting but »sticky« knowledge gain in importance. Through system supplies, »sticky«, i.e. not easily transferable knowledge (von Hippel, 1990) developed in the fine grained interaction between co-specialised SMEs in specific regional areas, is often lifted into inter-action with the »sticky« knowledge of global contractors. Through hori-zontal collaboration with other co-specialised subcontractors in the re-gional hinterland – or internationally – SME subcontractors may be in-volved in international system supplies through the collaboration with subcontractors taking over the management of whole supplies of subsystems. The creation of or the inclusion of system suppliers in a group is no doubt a route of internationalisation gaining importance for SME subcontractors. In Denmark several recent collaborative ventures give evidence to this. Among them is the case of »Steel Product Group« as outlined below in exhibit four.

Exhibit 4: Steel Product Group Denmark

> Steel Product Group Denmark is established by four co-specialized sub-contractors in the city of Horsens.
> Steel Product Group Denmark is the joint marketing organization of the four enterprises. SPGD organize joint tenders to international system supplies. It has also become the organizer of the technical interface between the four enterprises as well as capacity sharing arrangements.
> Since the establishment of the group turnover has more than doubled and export are three times up.

MNCs even locate divisions and subsidiaries in areas where competent subcontractors can enter into information flows, resources and skills embedded in the regional industrial system (Grøn, 1985). PV Baker, Tetra Laval, Phillips (Medical equipment division) and Maxon (Telecommunications) all exemplify MNCs' locating of units in Denmark close to skilled enterprises of interest.

The route of internationalisation via systems supplies is open to most categories of subcontractors. However, standard subcontractors may find this route too narrow to gain scale advantages in production. A few major barriers to internationalisation may be identified. A major one relating to the managerial capacity of the collaborative venture is to take away the task of coordination from the contractor; the ability to establish a coherent documentation in relation to the auditing undertaken by contractors and finally the collaborative commitment especially when it is a question of market investments.

Route four: The independent internationalisation

Motives to internationalise independently depends on the type of subcontractor in question. For simple and expanded subcontractors a strong dependence on one or on few contractors in the home market may motivate the attempt to develop business with foreign contractors.

Expected risk associated with the transfer of knowledge to other contractors in the same market may also motivate a subcontractor to search for contractors in other – foreign – markets. In relation to standard subcontractors we may experience scale of economics in production as a motive of central importance. The route of independent internationalisation for a standard subcontractor is the one most similar to traditional models of firms' internationalisation. The strong specialisation in skills, knowledge and technology in the categories of partnership-based or strategic development subcontractors may motivate a search for a threshold market and thus motivate the search for international contractors.

A central issue in the business of international subcontracting is indeed to create interactive regimes supporting the systemic efficiency of the production chain. Often this involves a strong element of interactive learning and adoption of production routines, technical interfaces as well as administrative practices. Therefore the replacement of suppliers may be costly, also since the auditing of suitable subcontractors is costly. Thus, some major barrier facing subcontractors on the route of independent internationalisation consist of the network of established relations.

An overview of routes, motives of and barriers to subcontractors internationalisation

In table A below the five prototypes of subcontractors are characterised by their major route of internationalisation (++), possible routes (+) and antagonistic routes (–) of internationalisation. Each prototype has a brief description of their motives to go international, well aware that specific motives may vary widely. At the same token each route of internationalisation is shortly characterised by major barriers of specific importance to that route.

As indicated in the table, more major routes are open to Strategic development and Partnership-based subcontractors compared to Standard, Simple and Expanded subcontractors. Overall the table suggests that as the degree of interorganisational coordination raises more major routes to internationalisation are open to the subcontractor. The given overview also indicates that the route of independent internationalisa-

Table A. Routes of international activity expansion. Motives and barriers.

Subcontractor: Route:	Standard	Simple	Expanded	Strategic development	Partnership based	Major barriers
Follow	(−)	(+)	(+)	(++)	(++)	Customer is trapped in the market
MNC	(+)	(−)	(−)	(++)	(++)	Disintegrated MNC network
Systems supplies	(−)	(++)	(++)	(++)	(+)	Lack of coordination capacity. Dominant partner management
Independent	(++)	(+)	(+)	(−)	(−)	Difficult to position
Motives:	Economics of Scale	Expansion with established contractors. Spread of customers' portfolio	Spread of portfolio. Further spe- cialisation	Expand the base of compe- tence. Avoid spill- over effects in R&D	Join suit- able part- ners & expand interactive regimes	

tion is – more or less -closed to all categories of subcontractors except for the Standard subcontractors.

Motives

Economies of scale are a driving force for standard subcontractors. Therefore, the route of independent internationalisation might be the only one open to them. The route via MNCs may sometimes be viable, namely when the internal market of the MNC is large vis á vis the subcontractor's.

For simple and expanded subcontractors strong dependence on one or on few contractors in the home market may be a strong motive. Since the suggested major route to internationalisation is relatively risky, the process of internationalisation may be leading to strategic considerations concerning the future position of the subcontractor.

Since the »Strategic development« subcontractor is based on the development of tight collaborative links with their contractors, the route of independent internationalisation is blocked. However, cases may exist where technology and knowledge embedded with the enterprise are so strong that this route becomes favourable. In general, two motives may be stipulated, namely a) deepening the position as a critical supplier and b) creating new channels for knowledge generation.

To partnership-based subcontractors they envisage that the choice of suitable interactive regimes is decisive, i.e. interactive regimes in corresponding or supportive to the collaborative regimes in which they are already involved.

Barriers

Many barriers to internationalisation are specific to subcontractors. The ability – or managerial capacity – to work in different collaborative regimes may turn out to be a major internal barrier to the subcontractor. Since auditing is expected to play an important role in future procurement strategies in international subcontracting, also the ability to certify procedures, quality and logistic capacity may also be an important internal barrier. As exit costs rise and single sourcing are gaining in importance in subcontracting, the phase of auditing is inclined to create competitive pressure.

It involves a certain risk for those subcontractors accompanying their contractor to international markets, as the contractor may be trapped in the market(s) selected. For those carried to international markets by multinationals, the organisational structure of the multinational may be a major barrier. Each division may have its own procurement centre and policy. In many MNCs procurement officers often change positions. This may disrupt invested positions and the established trust within the relationship and it may even disrupt established business.

The establishment of system supplies implies a strong managerial task of horizontal coordination between subcontractors involved in the supply of subsystems. Minor subcontractors may lack capacity to stand up to these claims. A dominant partner may manage system supplies by taking on the task of coordinating other subcontractors. This may hamper the development of market knowledge inside the collaborative venture.

The route of independent internationalisation is demanding and may be blocked by the lack of internal resources. It may also be a difficult route since the position created by established subcontractors may be tight. Replacing subcontractors is costly.

4. Strategic Perspectives on Subcontractors' Internationalisation

The relational position of the industrial subcontractors implies the accept of reduced and increased degrees of freedom. Being part of a vertical supply system, strategy means less room for strategic manoeuvring of the individual subcontractor. Taking part in international activity chains however, opens up for several strategic possibilities for the subcontractor.

Being situated in local regions and also in international resource chains the subcontractor has a dual position, which offer different and sometimes opposite logic of how to conduct business. The internationalisation of the subcontractor thus depends on the ability to combine and manage external relations. It also suggests that a vital aspect of the internationalisation process is the ability to cope with varying and sometimes opposing logics of industrial structures and management practices. Overcoming these paradoxes forms a situation of knowledge development for subcontractors traditionally associated with internationalisation (Johanson and Vahlne 1990). As indicated the number of options feasible to different types of subcontractors differs. Subcontractors involved in partnership-based supplies or strategic development supplies have more major routes available than standard subcontractors, simple and expanded subcontractors. International subcontracting is a strong challenge to small and medium sized subcontractors. They must deliver a firm specific advantage superior to suppliers in the contractors' local hinterland and simultaneously cope with geographical, cultural and institutional barriers which can harm the superiority of their basic capability.

The managerial implications of specific routes to internationalisation concern the development of organisational competence in terms of organisational interpretive schemes (Weick 1979) or routines (Nelson, 1991). These are the specific behavioural patterns in which experience is transformed into organisational skills. They can be retrieved to be used in adopting to changing market conditions and consequently they are central for developing the position of subcontractors in the process of internationalisation. Each subcontractors' position is determined by some minimum of product specific characteristics and a minimum of relations specific characteristics. Therefore, the space for strategic positioning is to be found inside the lines indicated in figure 3.

Figur 3. Routes to Internationalization

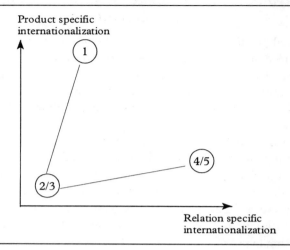

Standard subcontractors (1) route of internationalisation is in general terms characterised by a major focus on the product; the knowledge and flexibility embedded with the product and the potential barriers of internationalisation related to specifications of the product. The strategic position along this route is determined by the value of the product to the international contractors vis à vis competing suppliers. However, as the slope of the line says, some relational problems are inescapable. Logistical problems may have to be solved in collaboration with the contractor. After sales service toward contractors are unavoidable although modulation or high stability of the product may solve problems.

The position of Strategic Development subcontractor's (4) and Partnership Based subcontractor's (5) route of internationalisation includes very much active contribution to the interaction with international contractors. Knowledge, skills and innovative potential of critical importance to the contractor are disembodied. It is embedded with the organisation and released through the interaction with contractors. Interactive learning is important to build up routines and conductive interfaces. In turn this creates important exit barriers. The interactive competence has to be documentated and proved. The strategic position is based on the ability to stand up to the collaborative regime set by the contractor.

As indicated in the figure simple subcontractors (2) and expanded subcontractors (3) are – in general – positioned at a strategic cross road to the international market. On one hand their relationship specific position is not so specialised, that important exit cost can be imposed.

Although exceptions may be seen, they seldom posses competence and skills that are inimitable. Their contribution to knowledge building and to the development of new products with the contractor is limited. On the other hand their product is not a standard product although it may have the potentials. Therefore these – most often small and medium sized – enterprises are in a position, where decisions of international activity expansion are very much one of considering the strategic position in the typology of subcontractors.

Simple and expanded subcontractors are often in a squeezed competitive position. From one side, there is an ongoing pressure towards standardisation. On the other side, there is a pressure from knowledge based strategic subcontractors, being able to deliver more specialised contribution that can support the development of the contractor or support the total chain of value-added.

5. Conclusions

In this contribution we have proposed that the main divergence between standard models of internationalisation and the international activity expansion of subcontractors have to be found in the co-specialisation of activities in the subcontractor relationship. The functional dimensions of the collaborative interface between contractors and subcontractors hold the key for understanding the differences in subcontractors' internationalisation processes. In their internationalisation efforts, subcontractors rely on the combined efforts of a number of interdependencies to attract value from their basic market contribution. Analytically, this calls for an approach where the focus is on the interaction of components in the joint creation of value-added throughout the business chain formed partly by the contractor and partly by the subcontractor. To pursue the analytical path further, our focus should therefore concentrate on the functional co-specialisation of activities in the subcontractor relationship. In this way we may develop an understanding of the systemic character of the internationalisation process, i.e. how functional co-specialisations toward contractors enables the subcontractor to adjust a facilitating structure and in this sense gradually develop international competencies which may feed back on its other activities.

Although considerations concerning entry mode and internal barriers may vary considerably among subcontractors, it is reasonable to believe that a central managerial issue to all subcontractors wanting to expand their international activity, is the question of which collaborative regimes the subcontractor will be introduced to.

The development of collaborative regimes may always be uncertain. However, this uncertainty will be stronger when the new collaborative venture is international. Partly because of differences in collaborative traditions, spoken language and say technical and administrative standards. Partly because new collaborative regimes may disrupt established routines and collaborative patterns and partly because of other disadvantages of international subcontractors, compared with locally positioned subcontractors.

Furthermore our contribution has – apart from its initial discussion on subcontractors internationalisation – pointed to the need of studying the interplay between small and medium sized subcontractors and large global operating contractors. The fact that system supplies gain importance, thus forcing horizontal collaboration on to subcontractors in the local and regional hinterland around the world underlines this.

A final theoretical conclusion may be in place. We need more systemic frames of reference including the technical, collaborative and territorial dimensions as a setting for further studies of the interorganisational dynamics in international supply chains. Studies along these lines may have the potential of linking hitherto antagonistic lines of studies on industrial districts and the role of global players. As such, the study of international subcontracting has a potential to bridge diverse understandings of how international supply systems are configured.

References:

Amin, A. and Robbins, K., 1990. Flexible specialisation and small firms in Italy: Myth and realities. In: Pyke, F., Becattini, G. and Sengenberg, W. (eds.). *Industrial Districts and Inter-Firm Cooperation in Italy*, ILO, Geneva.

Andersen, P. H., 1995. *»Collaborative Internationalization of SMEs«*, DJØF Publishing, Cph.

Andersen, P. H., 1995. »Danske Underleverandørers fremtidige rolle i det globale Produktionssystem« in Finn Valentin, m.fl: *»Strategiske Virksomhedsrelationer«*, Er- hvervsministeriet.

Andersson, G., 1990. *»Underleverandörsroller«*, Working paper, Högskolan i Växjö.

Anderson, J. and P.R. Christensen, 1992. *»Underleverandører i Østjylland«*, Working Paper, the Institute for SME Research, Auning.

Blenker, P. and Christensen P.R., 1995. »Interactive Strategies in Supply Chains – A Double-edged Portfolio Approach to SME Subcontractors Position Analysis«, In: *Entrepreneurship and Regional Development*, Vol. 7, 249-264.

Braunerhjelm, P., 1991. *Svenska underleverantörer och småföretag i det nya Europa. Struktur, kompetens och internationalisering*. Industriens utredningsinstitut, Almqvist and Wiksel International. Stockholm.

Brege, S., O. Brandes, J. Lilliencreutz and H. Brandes, 1993. *»Supplier Strategies in Buyer-Dominated Networks«*, Working Paper, University of Linköping.

Christensen, P. R., J. Andersson and P. Blenker, 1992. *»Industriens Brug af Underleverandører«*, Industri- og Handelsstyrelsen, Kbh.

Cyert, R. and J. G. March, 1963. *»A Behavioural Theory of The Firm«*, Prentice-Hall. International.

Dicken, P., 1986. *»Global Shift: Industrial Change in A Turbulent World«*, Harper and Row, London.

Engh, Ø. and R. Helberg, 1989. »Betydelige fordele med et tettere Leverandørsamarbeid«, *Norsk Harvard no. 3*.

Grøn, J. H., 1985. *»Virksomheder-Arbejde-Regioner«*, Sydjydsk Universitetsforlag, Esbjerg.

Hallén, L., 1982. *»International Industrial Purchasing: Channels, Interaction and Governance Structures«*, Licentiate Thesis, Acta Universitatis Upsaliensis, Studia Oeconomiae Negotiorum, (13), Uppsala University.

Hovi, N., 1995. »*Outcomes of Interfirm Co-operation – A case study of four Subcontractors*«, Publications of the Turku School of Economics and Business Administration, Series D-3.

Johanson J. and J.-E. Vahlne, 1977. »The Internationalization Process of The Firm:A Model of Knowledge development and Increasing Foreign Market Commitment«, *Journal of International Business Studies*, Spring/Summer, pp. 23-32.

Johanson, J. and J.-E. Vahlne, 1990. »The Mechanism of Internationalization«, *International Marketing Review*, Vol. 7 (4), pp. 11-24.

Johanson, J. and F. Wiedersheim-Paul, 1975. »The Internationalization of the Firm – Four Swedish Cases«, *Journal of Management Studies*, October, pp. 305-322.

Hymer, S.H., 1976. »*International Operations of National Firms: A Study of Foreign Direct Investments*«, Boston, MIT Press.

Kearney, A. T., 1993. »*Logistics Exellence in Europe*«, ELA Study Report.

Lamming, R. C., 1993. »*Beyond Partnership: Strategies for for Innovation and Lean Supply*«, Prentice-Hall International, UK.

March, J. G. and H. Simon, 1958. »*Organizations*«, Prentice Hall International.

Maskell, P., 1991. »*Nyetableringer i Industrien – og industristrukturens udvikling*«, Handelshøjskolens Forlag, Cph.

Ministry of International Trade and Industry (MITI), Small and Medium-sized Enterprise Agency, 1989. »*Small Business in Japan*«, Tokyo.

Montague, B., 1994. »Gap isn't Likely to Disappear«, *USA Today*, p. 3B (Feb. 21).

Nelson, R. R., 1991. »Why do Firms differ and how does it matter«, *Strategic Management Journal*,Vol. (12), pp. 61-74.

Piore, M. and C. Sabel, 1984. »*The Second Industrial Divide*«, Basic Books, NY.

Ried, S., 1983. »Firm Internationalization, Transaction Costs and Strategic Choice«, *International Marketing Review*, Winter, pp. 44-56.

Sabel, C., 1994. »Learning by Monitoring: The Institutions of Economic Development« in N. Smelser and R. Swedberg: »*Handbook of Economic Sociology*«, Princeton Publishing, NY.

Scott, A., 1988. »*Metropolis. From the Division of Labour to urban Form*«, University of California Press, LA.

Spekman, R. E., 1988. »Strategic Supplier Selection: Understanding Long-Term Buyer Relationships«, *Business Horizons*, Vol. 31, No. 4, pp. 75-81.

Storper, M., 1995. The Resurgence of Regional Economies, Ten Years Later: The regiona as a nexus of untraded interdependensies. *European Journal of Regional Studies,* Vol. 2, Number 3.

Venkatesan, R., 1992. »To make or not to make – Strategic Sourcing«, *Harvard Business Review,* Nov-Dec, pp. 98-107.

Von Hippel, E., 1990. »Task Partitioning: An innovation Process Variable«, *Research Policy* 19, pp. 407-418.

Weick, K.E., 1979. »*The Social Psychology of Organizing*«, Prentice-Hall International, NY.

Wyckoff, A. W., 1993. »The International Expansion of Productive Networks«, *The OECD Observer,* no. 180, pp. 8-13.

Zirius International, 1994. »*Fremtidens Underleverandører*«, Research Report.

11. Towards a Firm-Based Model of Foreign Direct Investment

Trond Randøy

1. Introduction

During the period of 1983-1989 the world FDI (Foreign Direct Investment) outflows have increased by an astonishing compound annual rate of 29% per year; that is three times the growth rate of world trade (9.4%) and four times the rate of world output (7.8%) (UNCTC, 1992a; UNCTC, 1992b)[56]. Slower economic growth in the developed countries produced a temporary slowdown in the growth of FDI outflows during 1991 and 1992, with annual changes of -17% and -11%, respectively (UNCTAD, 1994). However, in 1993 the FDI outflows bounced back to an annual growth rate of 11%[57]. By the end of 1993 the estimated total stock of FDI amounted to $2125 billion. Since 1985 the gap between the growth of export and that of FDI has widened significantly. This dramatic shift spurred DeAnne Julius to suggest that *»as a means of international economic integration, foreign direct investment is in its take-off phase; perhaps in a position comparable to world trade at the end of the 1940s«* (1990: 36).

When a firm makes an FDI in manufacturing this implies that it emphasises internal growth rather than external growth through market intermediates (e.g. upstream subcontracting or downstream export sale). An FDI implies a high degree of equity control, an extensive foreign market resource commitment, and commonly it involves foreign production. The Economist (1993) points out how growth in FDI indirectly contradicts the dominating management recommendations of the 1980s. FDI has increased despite the focus on subcontracting, decomposing the value chain, and reliance on »core competencies«.

---

56. The UNCTC numbers are in current prices.
57. Includes only France, Germany, the United Kingdom and the United States, which together account for about two-thirds of worldwide outflows.

There are at least three good reasons why one single theory cannot capture all aspects of the phenomena of FDI. First, international production is carried out for a number of reasons and motives. Foreign market involvement can be described in both economic and strategic management terminology, as has been suggested by Dunning (1993a)[58]. One theory might be appropriate for one motive, but useless in relation to other motives. One purpose of this chapter is to identify how different theories address various strategic factors.

Second, the different theories address different aspects of the international firm. Cantwell *et al.* (1986) point out how the economic theory of international production has capitalised on different branches of economic theory. Third, international production can be analysed at three different levels: macroeconomic (addressing broad national and international trends), mesoeconomic (considering the interaction between the firm- and the industry-level), and the microeconomic (individual firms) level. We focus the discussion on the micro-level, i.e. the internationalisation of individual firms, or even units within those firms (divisions).

The chapter is organised as follows. First, we use three Norwegian cases to explore the effect of strategic factors on foreign market involvement decisions. Second, we extend Dunning's (1988, 1993a) eclectic paradigm to develop a conceptual model of market involvement. Third, we suggest some specific hypotheses derived from our conceptual framework for foreign direct investment, or foreign market involvement.

2. Three Norwegian Cases

We believe that the understanding of strategic factors is underdeveloped in the literature. However, the comprehension of firm-specific, location-specific, and transaction-specific factors is much more developed. In order to address the effect of strategic factors we have performed three extensive case studies. These studies specifically concern strategic factors related to firm's choice of foreign market involvement.

Our three case studies of larger Norwegian firms/divisions were: (1) Hafslund Nycomed's contrast media division, (2) the fertiliser division of Norsk Hydro, and (3) the cement/building materials division of

---

58. According to Dunning (1993a: 93) the *"future modelling of MNE activity must also pay more attention to strategic-related variables. .. The full incorporation of strategic-related variables into a general theory or paradigm of MNE has yet to be accomplished."*

Aker[59]. In 1992 each of these divisions had revenues between NOK 3.9 billion and approximately NOK 28 billion (US$ 4 billion), of which at least 69% was generated abroad. As a baseline for our analysis we used Dunning's (1988) *»established theory of the multinational enterprise«* (Buckley 1990:657). We discovered that on the firm/divisional level of analysis we missed out on important explanatory variables. Without considering strategic factors we obtained an incomplete understanding of foreign market involvement. In our three cases these strategic factors were complementary to the existence of ownership-, location-, and transaction-specific advantages, as previously suggested by Dunning.

In the case of the fertiliser division of Norsk Hydro, the main strategic motive was to construct an integrated network of subsidiaries across Europe, i.e. horizontal integration of FDIs. Rather than an owner-specific advantage based on its multinationality (as discussed by Dunning, 1993b), it was a specific strategic intention that determined Norsk Hydro's choice of foreign market involvement. In the early 1980s the company sought to achieve cross-national synergy by acquiring a number of wholly owned companies across Europe. The strategic intention was that these acquisitions should then facilitate a restructuring of the European fertiliser industry and provide Norsk Hydro with international scale and scope advantages. These competitive advantages could only be achieved with considerable intra-subsidiary integration, which made joint ventures or strategic alliances an unattractive option.

The same advantages were also sought in the case of the cement/building materials division of Aker. In addition, another important motive was to preserve a pan-European oligopolistic market. This is an argument which is well known from the »market collusion« theory of Hymer (1960). One approach for Aker to realise its new strategy was to strengthen the strategic alliance with the largest Swedish and Finnish cement producer, i.e. a horizontal integration of FDIs. Aker and Euroc, the Swedish producer, were able to take over a major British producer (Castle Cement) and then substantially increase their European market strength.

Hafslund Nycomed, a pharmaceutical firm, provides the third case. In order to strengthen the firm's core competence in its highly successful imaging drugs, Hafslund Nycomed wanted to buy into emerging technologies as well as improve distribution access in foreign markets, i.e. a

---

59. Extensively documented in Randøy (1992a), Nielsen and Randøy (1992) and Randøy (1992b), respectively.

vertical integration FDI. From 1988 on Hafslund Nycomed acquired a
number of wholly owned subsidiaries in Denmark, Austria, France and
the U.S. Unlike the logic of Dunning's eclectic paradigm, which emphasises the need for capitalising on a firm's *existing* firm-specific assets/skills,
Hafslund Nycomed acquired these companies in order to *create or enhance* such a competitive advantage. Transaction-cost reasons, as well as
the tacitness of the acquired competence, made it necessary to buy these
companies 100%. Neither licensing nor joint ventures provided the necessary organisational capacity to facilitate the desired resource transfer.

3. A Model of Foreign Market Involvement

Buckley and Brooke (1992: 15) point out how »*the motives, the process of
direct investment and the entry strategy [mode] into a particular foreign market vary greatly according to the characteristics of the entrant firm, its past relationship to the market and the nature of the foreign market.* « In our model
of foreign market involvement we capitalise on the above quotation. We
have included factors related to »motives« (strategic factors), »the process of direct investment« (particularly the transaction-specific factors),
»characteristics of the entrant firm« (firm-specific factors), and »the nature of the foreign market« (location-specific factors). Each of these factors are part of our model of foreign market involvement. However, we
have not fully incorporated what Buckley and Brooke describe as the
»past relationship to the market«, although »international experience« is
included in our model.

The economic theory of internationalisation centres on how present
conditions, such as firm-specific advantages and transaction costs, affect the choice of international market involvement. The behavioural
theory of internationalisation is primarily concerned with factors associated with the past, such as firm-specific experience and established
growth patterns. A combination of these two perspectives does not,
however, provide a sufficient explanation for why companies choose a
particular operational mode. By adding strategic factor we are able to
consider factors associated with the future. Dunning (1993a: 93) points
out how »*strategic management is essentially concerned with the ways in
which managers act to achieve their* long-term objectives *[author's empha-
sis] in conditions of market failures*«. A company might not have the firm-
specific skills nor the international experience to justify an FDI, but it
can still be appropriate to choose a particular market involvement mode

because of strategic considerations. Such an investment might be necessary in order to facilitate the creation of a future competitive advantage.
Kim and Hwang (1992: 29) question the *»underlying assumption that
each entry decision is made in isolation and is driven essentially by efficiency
considerations at the level of the individual entrant or subsidiary unit«*. Norsk
Hydro's significant investments in the European fertiliser industry cannot sufficiently be explained with reference to economic and behavioural considerations (Nielsen and Randøy, 1992). The potential competitive advantages associated with restructuring the fertiliser industry,
which created international advantages of scale and scope, were a paramount strategic motive behind the billion (NOK) size investments during the early 1980s.

Dunning's eclectic paradigm (Dunning 1981, 1988, 1993a) is one
important input for the conceptual model of international market involvement. However, using Dunning's framework creates some specific
challenges for model development. First, the paradigm is very comprehensive. Second, it covers multiple levels of analysis, and third, it does
not incorporate strategic considerations[60]. Fourth, the relationships between the constructs is not explicitly modelled. In order to simplify the
market involvement model we focus on the most important constructs.
Unfortunately, Dunning does not make an attempt to summarise the
eclectic paradigm in terms of a shorter list of constructs[61], as most of
the factors are highly interrelated. The principal hypothesis of the eclectic approach (1981: 79) is that a firm will engage in FDI if the following
three conditions are satisfied:

(i)   Possessing *a net ownership-specific advantage* (or firm-specific ad-
      vantage as we refer to it) implies that a firm has a competitive ad-
      vantage vis-a-vis domestic companies. This advantage must be
      greater than the disadvantages of operating in a foreign country.
      Bain's (1956) classical work on industrial economics of barriers to
      entry, and used in an international context by Hymer (1960), ex-
      plains the concept of ownership advantages. Dunning points out
      how these advantages originate from either *size (present or cumula-
      tive), monopolistic power,* and/or *better resource capabilities* (as exclu-
      sive resource possessions, trademarks, patents or unique skills).

---

60. An interesting critique of Dunning's eclectic paradigm is presented by Itaki (1991).
61. A comprehensive overview of the factors associated with the eclectic paradigm is presented by Dunning (1993a: 81).

Porter (1980) uses the same industrial organisational perspective to identify a firm's *sustainable competitive advantage*. In financial terms, a net ownership advantage conveys that a firm, in serving a particular market, can obtain a rate of return *above* the risk adjusted cost of capital derived from the capital market.

(ii) In classical economic terms, utilising an *internalisation incentive advantage* (or transaction-specific factors as we have label these factors) means either to actively or passively to exploit the existence of market failures. This advantage can help minimize »*the costs of running the economic system*« (Arrow, 1969). The question is how different *institutional arrangements*, such as wholly owned subsidiaries or sales subsidiaries, affect the efficiency of the economic activity. The multinational enterprise can circumvent market failure by internalising markets for know-how, trade-names, management, or other specific skills.

(iii) *Location-specific variables* determine where the economic activity should be situated. Localisation-related advantages stem from differences in national factor endowments and relative factor prices, as described by trade theory. Additional factors recently discussed by Porter (1990) are closeness to the market, possible interaction with customers, suppliers, etc., and the quality of national infrastructure. Other important factors affecting the optimal localisation are transportation and other communication costs, initially pointed out by Weber (1929).

The proposed model (Figure 1) is naturally a simplification, as we are not attempting to cover all relevant aspects of international market involvement decisions. In the literature we focus on those theories and empirical findings that relate to the firm/division-level of analysis. Dunning (1990) points out how the eclectic paradigm does not address the importance of strategic or dynamic factors. By introducing global strategic variables, Kim and Hwang (1992) have successfully extended the previous framework of transactional and environmental factors, as pointed out by Gatignon and Anderson (1988). Kim and Hwang identified three global strategic variables: (1) global concentration, (2) global synergy and (3) global strategic motivation. We point out that only one of these strategic variables concerns the firm's own strategic motives (#3), as the others were related to global environmental factors. Kim and Hwang's survey examined 96 foreign entry launches by U.S. MNEs. Considering strategic factors is a natural adaptation of the strategic management theory to the theory of the international firm.

Figure 1: Our conceptual model of foreign market involvement

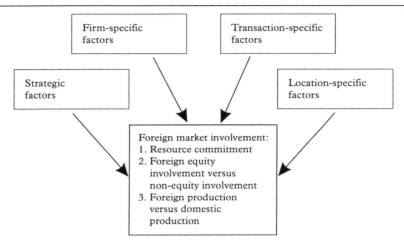

Agarwal and Ramaswami (1992) point out how a number of empirical studies have implicitly or explicitly used Dunning's eclectic framework in explaining the choice between joint venture and FDI (Kogut and Singh, 1988), licensing and FDI (Caves 1982; Davidson and McFetridge 1985), and extent of foreign direct investment (Dunning 1980; Kimura 1989: Sabi 1988; Terpstra and Yu 1988; Yu and Ito 1988). The research of Agarwal and Ramaswami (1992) on 285 leasing firms supports the main predictions of Dunning's eclectic paradigm. One common limitation of these studies is that the dependent variable is either based on one measure (extent of foreign production relative to total production) or is dichotomous, such as licensing versus FDI.

As shown by Figure 1, we use three measures for the dependent variable, namely, (1) foreign market resource commitment, (2) level of equity control, and (3) degree of foreign production. A number of alternative classifications for the dependent variable are provided by previous research. The distinction between export (without ownership), FDI and licensing has been endorsed by Buckley and Casson (1976). The international marketing literature has particularly discussed the issue of exporting, joint ventures and licensing (e.g. Anderson and Gatignon, 1986). The international business literature has centred on the MNE and the proportion of foreign over domestic production. Joint ventures, as another alternative to FDI, have emerged as an important class of market involvement during the 1980s (i.e. Kogut 1988, Contractor and Lorange 1988).

In this chapter we identify three underlying dimensions, or measures, for foreign market involvement, namely the *degree of control,* the *resource commitment,* and the level of *foreign production.* For most of the stated hypotheses (H1-H4) we have specific predictions for *each* of these three dimensions of the dependent variables. Kim and Hwang (1992) and Hill, Kim and Hwang (1990) discuss how each of these different market involvements varies according to the level of control (Clavet 1984; Caves 1982; Davidson 1982; Root 1987) and resource commitment (Vernon 1979). The level of control refers to the level of ownership, i.e., legal control over foreign production. By control we imply that the foreign owner has authority over operational and strategic decision-making. FDI is the market involvement mode that provides the firm with the highest level of control. On the other hand exporting or licensing gives the firm little such ownership control. The level of foreign production is really a measure for the level of local value added activities.

The third measure of the dependent variable, the degree of foreign market resource commitment, reflects the actual resources the firm has allocated to one particular market. Resource commitment refers to the level of dedicated assets that cannot be transferred without loss of economic value. Anderson and Gatignon (1986) point out how FDI represents the typical high commitment and high control mode, whereas licensing is on the opposite end of the spectrum. Exporting is also associated with a low level of commitment and control. Joint venturing is positioned (dependent on the ownership share) between licensing and FDI. Strategic alliances commonly take the form of equity joint ventures, licensing agreements, or long-term co-operation. By a country-specific resource commitment we mean the »extent of economic involvement in that particular country«.

3.1 Hypotheses related to strategic factor

Cantwell (1991), Dunning (1993a) and Oxelheim (1993) point out that a number of surveys and case studies indicate that MNC's strategic motives for FDI[62] can be grouped in five; (1) market-driven and market-seeking, (2) factor-driven and raw materials seeking, (3) production efficiency-driven and global integration seeking, (4) technology-driven and knowledge seeking, and (5) political safety seeking and the pursuit for reduced corporate risk, i.e. diversification-driven. A number of these motives fit well into Dunning's eclectic paradigm of firm-, location-, and transaction-specific factors. A good example of such a strategic variable is the linkage between the motive of the »market seeker« and the company's home-based firm-specific competitive advantage. The »market seeking« motive is well covered by our discussion of firm-specific factors. We do not address the motive of raw material seeking since Brainard's (1993) research reveals that factor endowments across countries has little impact on the use of FDI. Production efficiency seeking (or efficiency seeking as labelled by Dunning, 1993a) concerns the creation of competitive advantages based on activities such as up-stream intermediate product sourcing or down-stream assembly. In order to capture the gains from production efficiency, a number of scholars point out that the firm needs to internalise these transfers or transactions (e.g. Teece, 1981, Hennart, 1982; Dunning, 1993a, 1993b). We discuss this in relation to the transaction-specific factors.

We have identified three strategic variables that are inadequately covered by Dunning's eclectic paradigm. It is our contention that the strategic motive of seeking global integration or synergy goes beyond utilisation of production efficiency in order to reduce transaction costs. Thus, we consider »seeking global integration« as a separate strategic factor (H1a). Another strategic factor that is not captured adequately by existing studies, is knowledge seeking, or what Dunning (1993b) labels as strategic assets and capability seekers (H1b). This variable goes beyond the firm-specific factors that utilise existing resources and capabilities, such as brand-names and know-how. We are also addressing the strategic factor of reduced macro-economic uncertainty (H1c). This diversification motive is also not sufficiently covered by either firm- or location-specific factors.

Our first hypothesis concerns global or international integration (H1a). Such an advantage is based on the benefits of »*transnational integration resulting from specialisation, interchange, and scale*« (Kobrin 1991: 17). From a study of executives of U.S. MNCs, Kim and Hwang (1992)

---

62. We use FDI as a proxy for an extensive foreign market resource commitment.

identified the significance of »global synergy seeking.« An MNC that pursues global integration, and thus global organisational synergy, is motivated by factors beyond the narrow calculus of country-by-country efficiency. This has been identified by a number of researchers (e.g. Hout, Porter and Rudden, 1982: Hamel and Prahalad,1985; Kim and Mauborgne, 1988). These arguments are prevalent within two research streams; the international market power (industrial organisation) perspective, and the resource based perspective on strategic management. The first research stream focus on the efficiency reducing aspects, whereas the second focus on the efficiency enhancing aspects of global integration. A strategic motive of enhanced global integration can be identified by activities such as positioning for future expansion, creating strategic options (Lessard, 1982), maintaining international oligopolistic competition[63], and utilising international scale or scope advantages (Porter, 1986; Chandler, 1990; Bartlett and Ghoshal, 1989). International integration can lead to enhanced innovation through multiple stimulus from different countries (Baumol, Panzer and Willig, 1982). Hedlund (1986) argues that the necessary country-level »sacrifices« for the benefit of the whole organisation makes global integration inaccessible without considerable resource commitment.

H1a: Other things being equal, the higher the motivation for global integration, the more a firm will favour a high foreign market resource commitment and equity involvement.

Prahalad and Doz (1987) suggest that the advantages of global integration (tested by H1a) and the need for national responsiveness (tested by H1b), are two independent constructs. We therefore test the motive of national adaptation (i.e. a response to the need of national responsiveness) on a firm's foreign market involvement. National adaptation of an MNE refers to the degree by which activities, such as marketing, production, R&D etc., are adapted to local contingencies (Jarillo and Martínez, 1990). The desire for national adaptation is motivated by factors such as differences in national factor markets, distributive patterns, political regimes (i.e., government and business interaction), local consumer preferences, etc.

---

63. Interestingly,Yamin (1991) argues that Hymer was more concerned about cross-border market collusion than multi-country exchanges of firm-specific advantages.

We argue that hierarchical control (FDI or sales subsidiary) is a costly and unfavourable means to develop and exploit such a strategic objective. Hout et al.(1982) and Hill, Kim and Hwang (1990) also suggest that a multi-domestic strategy, i.e., one focusing on national adaptation, does not favour the use of a high control/high commitment mode, such as FDI. In line with the above arguments, we propose that a strategy of national adaptation also favours local production in a foreign market. We argue that locally controlled companies are more knowledgeable, and thus better implementors of an adaptation strategy.

H1b: Other thing being equal, the higher the motivation for national adaptation, the more a firm will favour a low degree of foreign market resource commitment, non-equity involvement, and disfavour foreign production.

Our next hypothesis (H1c) links the concept of »advantage seeking« (related to process and product technology) to our three measures for the dependent variable »foreign market involvement«. Our use of »advantage seeking investments« concerns involvement where the purpose of the foreign market involvement is specifically to seek product and/or process technology. Porter (1990) emphasises how domestic rivalry, advanced factor input, demanding customers, and strong supporting industries facilitate the creation of internationally competitive firms. However, Porter's »diamond« framework does not properly recognise how MNEs affect cross-country transfers of capabilities and resources (Dunning, 1990). Forsgren (1989) emphasises how a firm's internationalisation potential is very much embedded in the firm's extended network. McClain (1986) identified how a number of European investments in the United States were carried out in order to expose European firms to the innovative stimuli of the U.S. market (i.e. strong rivalry and demanding customers). These arguments imply that a considerable equity position and foreign production were prerequisites for a successful knowledge transfer. The whole logic of making an FDI in order to seek complementary competitive advantages, rather then merely utilising such an advantage, is totally contrary to the traditional explanations based on the industrial organisation or internalisation perspectives. Our third hypothesis captures this point. One such Norwegian example is the acquisition of the Silicon Valley-based Salutar Inc. by Hafslund Nycomed. This investment provided the company with complementary technology which could lead to economies of scope.

> *H1c: Other things being equal, the higher the motivation for strategic advantage seeking, the more a firm will favour an extensive foreign market resource commitment, equity involvement, and foreign production.*

3.2 Hypotheses related to firm-specific factors

Dunning (1993a) argues that a firm must possess superior assets and/or skills that can earn economic return to counter the disadvantages of involvement in a particular foreign market. This issue is being particularly discussed in relation to the market power perspective. If a company has the skills and assets to develop differentiated products, then sharing these resources through market transactions may carry a significant risk. This risk is often increased in a cross-border setting as the interorganisational infrastructure of international business is often less developed and more prone to frequent changes (Van de Ven and Poole, 1989). These factors make it advantageous to use a foreign market involvement mode with a high degree of ownership control.

Dunning's firm-specific advantages capitalise particularly on industrial organisation theory, or the international market power perspective, dating back to the work of Hymer (1960). With reference to this perspective, FDI is primarily undertaken to exploit product or factor market imperfections. We distinguish between those firm-specific advantages that are based on differentiation (hypothesis H2a), scale and scope economies (hypothesis H2b), and international experience (hypothesis H2c).

A number of studies have identified the association between FDI and a high level of product differentiation (Anderson and Coughlan 1987; Caves 1982; Davidson, 1982). Most of these studies have used research and development, or advertising expenditures, as proxies for the ability to develop differentiated products. The advantages of differentiation can be created in any part of the firm's value-chain, thus suggesting that the owner needs to keep control over production, as well as marketing and research.

> *H2a: Other things being equal, the higher the differentiation capacity, the more a firm will favour a foreign market involvement*

with a high degree of resource commitment and equity involve-ment.

A number of studies built on the market power (industrial organisation) perspective have discussed the role of international oligopolistic competition on the choice of foreign market involvement (Knickerbocker, 1973; Calvet, 1981, Yamin, 1991). MNEs are often most transparent in industries where a small number of competitors challenge each other in a number of markets. Our case research on the international strategic behaviour of Aker's cement activities suggests such behaviour.

In Dunning's eclectic framework, the benefit of having multinational experience is a distinct firm-specific advantage. International or global integration, as opposed to the mere cross-border co-ordination of similar activities, implies rationalisation by standardising products, centralising research and development, or the vertical or horizontal integration of production. A number of empirical studies have used size as a proxy for scale or scope advantages. Empirical evidence indicates that firm size has a positive impact on the use of FDI (Buckley and Casson 1976; Cho 1985; Caves and Mehra 1986; Kimura 1989; Terpstra and Yu 1988; Yu and Ito 1988). The argument is that the foreign firm needs to overcome the disadvantages associated with its foreign origin, such that it needs scale advantages to absorb the higher cost of marketing, as well as costs associated with enforcing patents and contracts.

H2b: Other things being equal, the more a firm possesses international scale and scope advantages, the more it will favour high foreign market resource commitment, equity involvement, and foreign production.

Firm-specific international experience has been shown to influence entry mode choices, particularly as discussed by the internationalisation process perspective (e.g. Johanson and Vahlne, 1977). Dunning includes international experience as a firm-specific advantage. Davidson (1980) and Agarwal and Ramaswami (1992) point out how firms with limited international experience tend to overstate risk, while understating the potential returns of operating abroad. Typically, the less experienced company prefers low control modes such as exporting. When the firm gains more international experience, it tends to move towards more direct investments (Bilkey, 1978). According to Hill et al (1990) and

Anderson and Gatignon's (1986) the internationally inexperienced firm has a lower ability to estimate risk and return related to foreign market involvement. The result of this is that firms with little experience have less of a desire to commit resources (including production) and gain ownership control in foreign markets.

> *H2c: Other things being equal, the greater the international expe-*
> *rience, the more a firm will favour a high foreign market resource*
> *commitment, equity involvement, and foreign production.*

3.3 Hypotheses related to location-specific factors

According to normative theory, the MNE is expected to minimize risk and maximize return on international investments. This implies that attractive markets are best served through a high degree of ownership control (i.e. FDI).

The literature suggests that a number of location-specific or environmentally derived variables affect choice of foreign market involvement. Hofstede (1980) points out how national differences in culture, taste, and literacy require the MNE to make costly adaptations. The larger the differences the more costly the needed adaptation. However, diversity might also be a source of innovation. In modelling choice of foreign market entry Kim and Hwang (1992) used the following location variables: demand uncertainty, competition intensity, location unfamiliarity, and country risk. Agarwal and Ramaswami (1992) focused on two location-related variables, market potential and investment risk, in order to model foreign market entry. We limit our discussion to two location-specific concepts: location familiarity and market attractiveness. The »location familiarity« variable concerns the firm's ability manage a specific cultural diversity (between home and host country). The »market attractiveness« concerns a whole set of national factors that might potentially effect the choice of foreign market involvement.

A number of previous studies have argued that an unfamiliar environment would disfavour FDI (e.g. Anderson and Coughlan, 1987; Kobrin, 1983; Kogut and Singh, 1988; Johanson and Vahlne, 1977). Most of these studies have capitalised on Hofstede's (1980) conceptual research on cultural similarities. Hill, Kim and Hwang (1990) argue that not knowing or being uncomfortable with a host environment makes executives unwilling to make extensive commitments, such as foreign production. According to Root (1987), a long cultural distance creates information needs and thus greater costs. Hill et al (1990) explicitly points out how MNEs are more inclined to use non-equity involvements in culturally distant locations.

> *H3a: Other things being equal, the more a location (country) being served is unfamiliar, the more a firm will favour a low degree of foreign market resource commitment, non-equity involvement, and disfavour foreign production.*

Market attractiveness has been found to be an important determinant of FDI (e.g. Terpstra and Yu 1988). In attractive markets FDI is expected to provide the greatest potential for long-term profit. One reason for this effect is that managers perceive contracts (i.e. export contracts or licensing agreements) to have a shorter time-horizon then an FDI. Kim and Hwang (1992) identified how the intensity of competition apparently did not have a significant effect on choice of entry mode.

Harrigan (1985a, 1985b) argues that the characteristics of the competitive situation has an impact on possible desire for vertical integration, i.e. an FDI involvement. Vertical integration provides the firm with greater strategic flexibility in a situation of contractual risk. We expect that attractive markets enhance the desire for a higher foreign market commitment. Although we can see how this affects the desire for equity control, we do not see how this can enhance foreign production.

> *H3b: Other things being equal, the higher the attractiveness of a foreign market, the more a firm will favour a high foreign market resource commitment, equity involvement, and foreign production.*

3.4 Hypotheses related to transaction-specific factors

In this section we specifically look at how transaction costs affect the choice of foreign market involvement. Previous research suggests that there are two sources of transaction costs related to foreign market involvement (Hill, Hwang and Hill, 1990; and Kim and Hwang, 1992). First, there is the loss of economic value due to the mere tacit nature of the know-how being transferred (H4a). Second, transaction costs occur because of the costs related to drafting, negotiating, monitoring, and enforcing contracts with a possibly opportunistic counterpart (H4b).

The first kind of transaction cost occurs irrespective of the existence of opportunism, whereas the second kind attempts to measure the effect of opportunism.

For hypothesis H4a we are focusing on the effect from tacit knowledge of the firm on choice of foreign market involvement. We are capitalising on the resource-based perspective of strategic management, and the evolutionary theory of the firm (e.g. Nelson and Winter, 1982). This perspective specifically looks for the »core competencies« of the corporation (Prahalad and Hamel, 1990). The effect of tacit know-how on entry mode and market involvement decisions has been tested by Kim and Hwang (1992) and Kogut and Zander (1993), respectively. Both verified the importance of this factor. Kogut and Zander point out that *»it is the difference in knowledge and the embedded capabilities between the creator and the users (possessed with complementary skills) which determine the firm boundary, not market failure itself«* (1993: 631). They question the assumption that the main function of a firm is merely to internalise markets, as assumed by the internalisation and the transaction cost theory. We expect that the existence of know-how would enhance the use of equity-based service modes (FDI), as the transfer costs in an open market become too large. Furthermore, this would also encourage the firm to increase its resource commitment. Our a priori hypothesis related to foreign production and the tacitness of know-how is that such production enhances the advantages of vertical control.

> *H4a: Other things being equal, the greater the tacitness of a firm's resources the more a firm will favour a high foreign market resource commitment, equity involvement, and foreign production.*

Our last hypothesis concerns the effect from contractual risk on choice of foreign market involvement mode, whereas our previous hypothesis (H4a) considered the complexity or difficulty of transferring resources and capabilities. Williamson (1985) points out how low-control market involvements (export or licensing) can reap the benefits of scale economies of the marketplace. The marketplace operates without the bureaucratic cost of hierarchies. This implies that with negligible asset specificity a company can achieve economies of scale without integration. According to the transaction cost theory (Coase, 1937) internalisation only becomes an option where markets fail to provide the appropriate signal to the transactional parties. These market distortions occur when markets are not able to predict future contingencies (problem of bounded rationality/external uncertainty) or cannot provide market participants with alternative transactions (small number bargaining/opportunism).

Transaction costs are often hard to measure and estimate (Buckley and Casson, 1985). Therefore, researchers have recommended the use of contractual risk associated with sharing the firm's assets and skills (Dunning, 1980). Focusing on the risk of transferring skills and assets is consistent with the transaction cost considerations of the resource-based perspective of strategy (Hill and Kim 1988).

Davidson and McFetridge's (1985) study looked at how asset specificity affected intra-firm and market transactions in 32 U.S. MNEs during the period of 1945-1978. They found that newer and more advanced technology was more commonly transferred internally. These findings support the appropriateness of using transaction cost considerations in FDI theory. Gatignon and Anderson (1988) used data from the 180 largest U.S. MNEs to test the effect of transaction costs on the degree of vertical integration. The study found support for a significant and positive relationship between the proprietary products and processes, and the degree of vertical control. This suggest that there is a positive relationship between contractual risk, a natural consequence of proprietary products and processes, and foreign production.

H4b: Other things being equal, the higher the contractual risk of sharing a firm's resources, the more a division will favour a high foreign market resource commitment, equity involvement, and foreign production.

4. Conclusion

This chapter attempt to develop a firm-based conceptual model of FDI. We are explicitly discussing FDI in relation to three underlying dimensions: (1) level of equity control, (2) level of foreign production, and (3) level of foreign market resource commitment. We have specifically outlined hypotheses related to our conceptual model (see Table 1). The major components of this model is strategic factors (H1a-c), firm-specific factors (H2a-c), location-specific factors (H3a-b), and transaction-specific factors (H4a-b). Table 1 summarises how we expect the independent variables to favour/disfavour a high foreign market resource commitment, favour/disfavour equity involvement, and favour/disfavour foreign production.

Table 1: Summary of hypothesized direct effects on foreign market involvement.

	Favours a high degree of resource commitment	Favours equity involvement	Favours foreign production
Strategic factors			
H1a: Seeking global synergy	+	+	no hypothesis
H1b: Seeking localisation	−	−	−
H1c: Seeking potential advantages	+	+	+
Firm-specific factors			
H2a: Differentiation capacity	+	+	+
H2b: Scale and scope advantages	+	+	+
H2c: International experience	+	+	+
Location-specific factors			
H3a: Perceived cultural distance	−	−	−
H3b: High market attractiveness	+	+	no hypothesis
Transaction-specific factors			
H4a: High degree of tacitness of know-how	+	+	+
H4b: Low contractual risk	−	−	−

References

Agarwal, S. and S.N. Ramaswami, 1992. »Choice of foreign market entry mode: Impact of ownership, location and internalization factors«. *Journal of International Business Studies*, Vol. 23 (1), 1-28.

Anderson, E. and A.T. Coughlan. 1987. »International market entry and expansion via independent or integrated channels of distribution«. *Journal of Marketing*, Vol. 51 (January), 71-82.

Anderson, E. and H. Gatignon. 1986. »Modes of foreign entry: A transaction cost analysis and propositions«. *Journal of International Business Studies*, Vol. 17 (Fall), 1-26.

Bain, J.S. 1956. *Barriers to new competition*. Cambridge, Mass: MIT Press.

Bartlett, C. and S. Ghoshal. 1989. *Managing Across Borders – The transnational solution*. Boston: Harvard Business School Press.

Bilkey, W.J. 1978. »An attempted integration of the literature on the export behavior of firms«, *Journal of International Business Studies*, Vol. 9 (1), 33-46.

Buckley, P. J. 1990. »Problems and developments in the core theory of international business«, *Journal of International Business Studies*, Vol. 21, 657-66.

Buckley, P.J. and M. Z. Brooke. 1992. *International business studies: An overview*. Oxford: Blackwell Publishers.

Buckley, P.J. and M. Casson. 1976. *The future of the multinational enterprise*. London: Macmillan.

Buckley, P.J. and M. Casson. 1985. *The economic theory of multinational enterprise*: selected papers, London: Macmillan.

Calvet, A.L. 1981. »A synthesis of foreign direct investment theories and theories of the multinational enterprise«. *Journal of International Business Studies*, Vol. 12 Spring/Summer, 43-59.

Caves, R.E. 1982. *Multinational enterprise and Economic Analysis*. Cambridge: Cambridge University Press.

Caves, R.E and S. Mehra. 1986. »Entry of foreign multinationals into US manufacturing industry«. *In Competition in Global Industries*, Porter, M.E. Boston: Harvard Business School Press.

Cho, K.R. 1985. *Multinational banks: Their identities and determinants*. Ann Arbor: UMI Research Press.

Coase, R.H. 1937. »The nature of the firm«, *Economica*, (New Series), Vol. 4, 386-405.

Contractor, F. and P. Lorange, editors, 1988. *Cooperative strategies in international business.* Lexington, Mass.: D.C. Heath.

Davidson, W.H. 1980. »The location of foreign direct investments activity: Country characteristics and experience effects«. *Journal of International Business Studies,* Vol. 11, 9-11.

Davidson, W.H. 1982. *Global strategic management.* New York: Wiley.

Davidson, W.H and D. McFetridge. 1985. »Key characteristics in the choice of international transfer mode«. *Journal of International Business Studies,* Vol. 16 (Summer), 5-22.

Dunning, J.H. 1980. »Towards an eclectic theory of international production: some empirical tests«. *Journal of International Business Studies,* Vol. 11 (1) Spring/Summer, 9-31.

Dunning, J.H. 1981. *International production and the multinational enterprise.* London: George Allen and Uniwin.

Dunning, J H. 1988. »The eclectic paradigm of international production: A restatement and some possible extensions«, *Journal of International Business Studies,* Vol. 19 (Spring), 1-31.

Dunning, J. H. 1990. *Global strategy and the theory of international production: An exploratory note.* Unpublished manuscript. Reading and Rutgers University.

Dunning, J. H. 1993a. *Multinational enterprises and the global economy.* Workingham: Addision-Wesley Publishing.

Dunning, J. H. 1993b. International Direct Investment Patterns. In *The global race for foreign direct investment: prospects for the future.* L. Oxelheim., editor, Heidelberg: Springer-Verlag.

Dunning, J. H. and G. Norman. 1987. »The location choice of offices of international companies«. *Environment and Planning,* Vol. A, 19, 613-31. *The Economist,* »Everybody's monster: A survey of multinationals«. March 27, 1993.

Franko, L.G.1976. *The European multinationals.* London: Harper and Row.

Forsgren, M. 1989. *Managing the Internationalization Process: The Swedish Case.* New York: Routledge.

Gatignon, H. and E. Anderson. 1988. »The multinational corporation's degree of control over foreign subsidiaries: An empirical test of transaction cost explanations«, *Journal of Law, Economics and Organization,* Vol. (2) 4 Fall, 305-336.

Gencturk, E.F. 1990. *Explaining international marketing involvement: A multidisciplinary perspective.* Unpublished Ph.D dissertation. University of Minnesota.

Harrigan, K.R. 1985a. »Vertical integration and corporate strategy«. *Academy of Management Journal*, Vol. 28 (2), 397-425.

Harrigan, K.R. 1985b. »Exit barriers and vertical integration«. *Academy of Management Journal*, Vol. 28 (3), 686-697.

Hedlund, G. 1986. »The hypermodern MNC – a heterarchy?« *Human Resource Management*, Vol. 25 (1), 9-35.

Hennart, J.-F. 1982. *A Theory of Multinational Enterprise.* Ann Arbor, MI: University of Michigan Press.

Hill, C.W. and W.C. Kim. 1988. »Searching for a dynamic theory of the multinational enterprise: a transaction cost model«. *Strategic Management Journal*, Vol. 9, 93-104.

Hill, C.W., P. Hwang and W.C. Kim. 1990. »An eclectic theory of the choice of international entry mode«. *Strategic Management Journal*, Vol. 11, 117-128.

Hofstede, G. 1980. *Cultures consequence: International differences in work-related values.* Beverley Hills, CA: Sage.

Hout, T, M.E. Porter and E.Rudden. 1982. »How global companies win out«. *Harvard Business Review*, Vol. 60, Sept.-Oct., 98-108.

Hymer, S. 1960 (published 1976). *The international operations of national firms.* Cambridge Mass.: MIT Press.

Jensen, M. and W. Meckling. 1976. »Theory of the firm: managerial behavior, agency costs and ownership structure«. *Journal of Financial Economics*, October: 305-360.

Johanson, J. and J-E. Vahlne 1977. »The Internationalisation process of the firm – a model of knowledge development and increased market commitments«, *Journal of International Business Studies*, Vol. 8, Spring-Summer, 23-32.

Julius, DeAnne. 1990. *Global companies and public policy: The growing challenge of foreign direct investment,* London: Royal Institute of International Affairs/Pinter Publishers.

Kim, W.C and P. Hwang. 1992. »Global strategy and multinationals entry mode choice«. *Journal of International Business Studies*, Vol. 23, 29-54.

Kimura, Y. 1989. »Firm specific strategic advantages and foreign direct investment behavior of firms: the case of Japanese semi-conductor firms«. *Journal of International Business Studies*, Vol. 20 (Summer), 296-314.

Knickerbocker, F.T. 1973. *Oligopolistic reactions and multinational enterprise*. Boston. Mass.: Harvard Business School.

Kobrin, S.J. 1991. »Determinants of global integration«. *Strategic Management Journal*, Vol. 12 (special issue: summer), 17-32.

Kogut, B. 1983. »Foreign direct investments as a sequential process«. In *The Multinational in the 1980s*, Kindleberger, C.P. and D.B. Audretsch, editors, Cambridge, MA.: MIT Press.

Kogut, B. 1988. »Joint ventures: theoretical and empirical perspectives«. *Strategic Management Journal*, Vol. 9, (4), 319-332.

Kogut, B. and A. Singh. 1988. »The effect of national culture on the choice of entry mode«. *Journal of International Business Studies*, Vol. 19 (Fall), 411-32.

Kogut, B. and U. Zander. 1993. »Knowledge of the firm and the evolutionary theory of the multinational corporation«. *Journal of International Business Studies*, Vol. 24 (4), 625-646.

Lessard, D.R. 1982. »Multinational diversification and direct foreign investment«. In *Multinational Business Finance*, Eiteman, D.K. and A. Stonehill, editors. MA: Addison-Wesley.

Li, J. and S. Guisinger. 1992. »The globalization of service Multinationals in the 'Triad'«. *Journal of International Business Studies*, Vol. 23 (4), 675-696.

McClain, D. 1986. »Direct investments in the United States: The European Experience«, in Gray, H.P., editor, *Uncle Sam as Host*, Greenwich, Conn.: JAI Press.

Melin, L. 1992. »Internationalization as a strategy process«, *Strategic Management Journal*, Vol. 13 (Winter special issue), 99-118.

Nielsen, L. and T. Randøy. 1992. *Kunstgjødselindustrien*. Research Report no. 70/92 Centre for Research in Economics and Business Administration: Bergen-Norway.

Oxelheim, L. 1993. Editor. *The global race for foreign direct investment: prospects for the future*. Heidelberg: Springer-Verlag.

Pfeffer, J. 1982. *Organizations and organization theory*. Cambridge, Mass.: Ballinger Publishing Company.

Porter, M. E. 1980. *Competitive strategy*. New York: The Free Press.

Porter, M. E. 1986. *Competition in Global Industries*, Boston: Harvard Business School Press.

Porter, M. E. 1990. *The competitive advantage of nations*. New York: Macmillan Press.

Prahalad, C.K. and Y. Doz. 1987. *The Multinational Mission.* London: The Free Press.

Prahalad, C.K. and G. Hamel. 1990, The core competence of the corporation. *Harvard Business Review,* May/June, 79-91.

Randøy, T. 1992. *The Norwegian Cement Industry: an industry study.* Research Report no. 71/92. Centre for Research in Economics and Business Administration: Bergen-Norway.

Root, F.R. 1987. *Entry Strategies of International Markets.* Lexington, MA.: Lexington Books.

Sabi, M. 1988. »An application of the theory of foreign direct investment to multinational banking in LDCs«. *Journal of International Business Studies,* Vol. 19 (Fall), 433-48.

Teece, D.J. 1981. »The Multinational enterprise: Market failure and market power considerations«, *Sloan Management Review,* Vol. 22 (Spring), 3-18.

Terpstra, V. and C-H. Yu. 1988. »Determinants of foreign investment of U.S. advertising agencies«, *Journal of International Business Studies,* Vol. 19 (Spring), 33-46.

United Nations Centre on Transnational Corporations. 1992a. *World investment report:* New York: United Nations Publications.

United Nations Centre on Transnational Corporations. 1992b. *The determinants of foreign direct investment.* New York: United Nations Publications.

United Nations, Conference on Trade and Development, Programme on Transnational Corporations. *World Investment Report 1994.* New York: United Nations Publications.

Van de Ven, A.H. and M.S. Poole 1989. »Paradoxical requirements for a theory of organizational change«. In A.H. Van de Ven, H. Angle and M.S. Poole, editors, *Research on the management of innovation: The Minnesota studies.* Cambridge: Ballinger.

Vernon, R. 1979. The product cycle hypothesis in a new international environment, *Oxford Bulletin of Economics and Statistics.* Vol. 41, 255-267.

Weber, 1929. *Theory of the location of Industries.* Chicago: University of Chicago Press.

Williamson, O.E. 1985. *The Economic Institutions of Capitalism.* New York: Free Press.

Yamin, M. 1991. In Pitelis, C. N. and R. Sugden, editors, *The nature of the transnational firm*. London, Routledge.

Yu, C-H. and K. Ito. 1988. »Oligopolistic reaction and foreign direct investment: The case of the U.S. tire and textile industries«. *Journal of International Business Studies*, Vol. 19 (Fall), 449-60.

12. Ownership Structures of Finnish Firms' Foreign Subsidiaries in EU Countries[64]

Jorma Larimo

1. Introduction

Since the 1960s the growth in the foreign operation of firms has been especially rapid in the form of foreign direct investments (FDIs). The growth in investment outflows was especially rapid in 1987-1990. The economic recession in several OECD countries slackened FDI flows in 1991 and 1992. However, in 1993-1995 there has again been growth in the FDI flows (see e.g. United Nations 1995). About 30 per cent of the FDI inflows in the late 1960s and almost 40 per cent of the inflows in the late 1980s were directed into Western European countries, mainly to various EU countries (see e.g. Dunning 1993). The increase in foreign investments in EU countries during the 1980s has been regarded as a direct result of the progress towards the Single European Market and the negotiations for European Monetary Union (see e.g. OECD 1989).

The cumulative FDI outflows by Finnish firms grew from USD 605 million in 1971-1980 to USD 12 150 million in 1981-1990. If the cumulative FDI outflows of different OECD countries in the periods 1971-1980 and 1981-1990 are compared, the highest growth rate was found in Finland – more than twenty times greater in the latter than in the former period. Other Nordic countries and EU countries have had a significant role as targets for FDIs by Finnish (and by other Nordic) firms. Of the Finnish FDI outflows in 1980-86. 36 % and in 1990-91 almost 50 % were directed into EU countries (see Appendix 1). Of the Swedish FDI outflows the share of EU countries was even higher than

64. The author wants to express his sincere thanks to Anna Rantala and Marita Anttila for their help in the data collection and coding and for Jari Partanen for his great help in the methodological issues. Furthermore, the author wants to express his sincere thanks for Ingmar Björkman for his comments. Finally, the financial support provided by the Academy of Finland is gratefully acknowledged.

in Finland and in 1990 Sweden was the largest foreign investor in EU countries measured by the value of acquisitions (see Oxelheim & Gärtner 1994 and Statistiska Centralbyrån 1994). Because of this significant orientation of investments into various EU countries, the FDI behaviour in those FDIs is of great interest.

In the literature on FDI and the multinational enterprise the focus has been on the question why manufacturing firms would choose to establish foreign subsidiaries rather than exploiting their firm-specific advantages by exporting or by using licensing. However, once a firm has decided to make an FDI it also faces the choice of e.g. ownership structure of the subsidiary. The main alternatives are a wholly owned subsidiary or a joint venture with one partner or several partners. Several explanations have been have been presented for the choice of the structure: transaction cost analysis, behavioural approach, strategy approach, and bargaining power approach. Of these approaches the first one has most often been used as the framework in previous empirical studies.

The main goal of this chapter is to analyse the ownership structure decisions made by Finnish firms in their FDIs made in the EU countries. The ownership structure (arrangement) decision has been chosen as the focus because of the central importance of this decision in FDIs. The importance of choosing an appropriate ownership structure lies to a great extent in its impact on the level of control held by a firm over the use of its assets. As a joint venture entails sharing control with joint venture partners, the level of control is normally higher in wholly owned subsidiaries than in joint ventures, although control can also be gained by means other than ownership (see e.g. Schaan 1988; and Luostarinen and Welch 1990).

In the next section general theoretical aspects of the ownership arrangement decision are discussed. Section four summarises the theoretical and empirical literature on ownership strategies and identifies the crucial variables. In section five the methodology and the data are discussed. Section six discusses the results and section seven summarises the study and presents some conclusions.

2. Literature Review

The main decision relating to the ownership arrangement is whether to choose a wholly-owned subsidiary (WOS) or a joint venture (JV). In the FDI literature, perhaps the most commonly cited reason or motive for the choice of a WOS is control. Because there is no partner in the unit, there is no shared decision-making and the firm can alone control all the firm's specific assets which constitute the competitive advantage of the firm and keep and plan the use of the profits generated by the foreign unit. The main drawback of the WOS is that it demands that the investing firm has all the needed financial and/or managerial resources to implement the FDI and manage the foreign unit.

The most commonly cited reasons or motives for the choice of a JV arrangement in the FDI literature have been: to gain rapid market entry, to increase economies of scale, to gain local know- how and local image, to obtain vital raw materials, to spread the risks and to meet the host government's demands. The host government's demands have been especially important in FDIs made in LDCs, whereas in FDIs made in OECD countries, know-how and resources of the partner or spreading the risks have been of greater importance (see e.g. Beamish 1985). The greatest problems with the JV arrangement are the decrease in the control possibilities of the unit and possible conflicts between the partners. An additional problem in JVs is that the incentives for the firm to contribute all that the venture needs are not as strong as when it has full ownership, i.e. the firm will »shirk« from its commitments to contribute capabilities (see Gomes-Casseres 1985).

The issue of ownership structure in FDIs has received much attention in recent years. Several explanations have been presented for the choice of the structure: transaction cost analysis (Buckley and Casson 1988; Gatignon and Anderson 1988; Hennart 1988); behavioural approach (Björkman 1990; Johanson and Vahlne 1992), business strategy (Kogut 1988; Hill, Hwang and Kim 1990), and bargaining power (Gomes-Casseres 1990). Although these explanations or approaches differ in many respects, particularly in terms of emphasis put on the various explanatory factors, they do not provide clearly conflicting predictions. Thus, they should be regarded as complementary rather than conflicting.

Transaction cost theory can perhaps be constituted as a mainstream explanation of the MNE. The essence of the theory is that MNEs evolve as a response to market imperfections for various types of cross-border transactions (see e.g. Buckley and Casson 1976, Rugman 1981, Williamson 1981, and Hennart 1981). The central tenet of transaction cost theory is that firms choose governance structures in order to promote asset utilisation while safeguarding against hazards. Because of incomplete information and opportunistic tendencies, there are transaction costs caused by drafting, negotiating, monitoring, and enforcing agreements between economic actors (Williamson 1985). The theory suggests that complete integration of foreign operations is more likely if the basis of the MNE's advantage lies in areas such as valuable product brands, and complex products and production processes, or when the making of the FDI involves investment commitments that greatly increase switching costs. According to the approach a JV alternative is an efficient arrangement when two conditions are simultaneously met (see Hennart 1991): 1) markets for the intermediate goods held by each party are failing, and 2) acquiring or replicating the assets needed for the unit is more expensive than obtaining a right to their use through a JV agreement. If markets for intermediate goods (know-how, raw materials, parts and components, etc.) held by both potential partners were not simultaneously failing, the parties would coordinate their interdependence through market exchange or through contracts. When markets do fail, incentives for opportunistic behaviour can be reduced by making parties co-owners in the venture.

The focus of the behavioural approach is on the decision-makers' knowledge of foreign markets, and on the perceptions, opinions, beliefs and attitudes based on this knowledge (see e.g. Aharoni 1966; Johanson and Vahlne 1977 and 1992). The behavioural approach suggests a positive relationship between the decision-makers' knowledge of foreign markets and the level of the firm's resource commitments to these foreign markets (Luostarinen and Welch 1990). The reason is that lack of information and knowledge about particular markets and/or operation modes creates uncertainty and this heightens the risk perceived by decision-makers. The decision-makers are regarded as highly risk-averse and they are cautious about committing substantial resources to a new mode of operation and to an economically or culturally new or strange foreign market. However, the cautiousness decreases as more knowledge is acquired. According to the behavioural approach, a WOS is the preferred ownership structure in economically and culturally similar countries and in cases where the investing firm has either more operation mode specific and/or target country specific knowledge.

According to the strategy approach, the issue of ownership arrangement is primarily viewed as a question of level of control that is needed in order to coordinate global strategic action (Hill, Hwang and Kim 1990). A key feature of the global strategy is that the value chain of the firm is configurated in such a way that the value added at each stage is maximized. In the presence of location-specific scale economies this leads to breaking up the value chain so that the various activities are conducted in different countries (Porter and Rudden 1982, Yip 1989 and Dunning 1993). If the firm pursues a global strategy this means that the firm has to require a high degree of control, i.e. they prefer WOSs in order to achieve coordination of the global manufacturing system. The interests of a local partner could be very different, especially in cases where the unit is planned to support the global production network of the foreign firm and even a loss in the operation of the unit may be temporarily accepted.

The so-called bargaining power approach takes into consideration also the interests of the host country government. A firm may prefer WOS, but if the host government's policy is to encourage JVs, then the final ownership structure of the subsidiary is likely to be determined in negotiations between the two parties. In this process the final outcome of the negotiations is influenced by the relative bargaining power of the parties (see e.g. Fagre and Wells 1982, Gomes-Casseres 1990).

The focus in this chapter is on FDIs made by Finnish firms in EU markets. Most of the Finnish firms are relatively small in an international sense. The bargaining power approach is better suited to explain FDIs made by large MNEs, because the absolute size of the investments by them is usually much larger than in FDIs made by SMEs. Furthermore, the bargaining power approach corresponds with FDIs made in LDCs where there are often more limitations for foreign investments than in OECD countries. The strategy approach would need a questionnaire survey in order to clarify in more detail different aspects related to the strategy of the firm and nature of the industry. Therefore the focus in this chapter will mainly be on aspects related to the transaction cost and behavioural approach.

In Table 1 there is a summary of the main features of the empirical studies focusing on ownership structures in FDIs made totally or mainly in OECD countries. The results in these studies indicate that 20 to 44 percent of the units have been JVs and 56 to 80 percent WOSs. According to the results in previous studies dealing with Finnish FDIs in OECD countries, the share of JVs has been 30-40 percent (see Larimo 1993a, 1993b; and Hennart & Larimo 1995). Thus both in FDIs made by Finnish firms and by firms of other origin, WOSs seem to have been clearly more common than JVs. As can be seen from the table, several of the previous studies have focused either on FDIs made by large US based firms or on FDIs made in the USA. As stated before, in this study the focus is on FDIs made by Finnish firms in various EU countries. None of the previous studies has totally focused on FDIs made in EU countries. Finally, it can be noted that in most studies the binomial logistic regression has been used as the method of analysis.

3. The Determinants of Ownership Strategies

The size of the investing firm may affect the degree of ownership the firm will take in a foreign subsidiary. The traditional argument is that small firms do not have the necessary resources to put up the whole capital of a greenfield plant or to make a full acquisition of an existing firm. Hence the greater the size of the parent, the lower the probability that it will joint venture.

There is, however, another argument that leads to the opposite prediction that large firms will prefer JVs. As firms grow, they tend to diversify. Assume that the foreign investor wants to combine the services of some of its assets with a local EU firm. The larger the foreign firm, the more likely is the situation that a merger with the EU firm might create two types of problems. First, the merger may raise antitrust problems. Second, the addition of the EU target to an already large and diversified firm may increase the cost of managing the merged unit. By contrast, a JV between the foreign investor and the EU firm may be better received by antitrust authorities. Moreover, a JV makes it possible to obtain services of assets without owning (and having to manage) them. Hence large firms may prefer JVs to full acquisitions (Kay, Robe and Zagnolli 1987).

The empirical findings in different studies have also been mixed. In the studies by Stopford and Wells (1972), Gomes-Casseres (1985) and Kogut and Singh (1988b) a positive relationship was found between size of the investing firm and degree of ownership, but the opposite in the studies by Zejan (1988), Agarwal and Ramaswami (1990), Sanna-Randaccio (1990), and Larimo (1993a and 1993b). Hence, no sign is expected for the relationship between size of the investing firm and degree of ownership.

If the successful commercialisation of a product requires the combination of technology held by two separate firms, and the market for both of these technology inputs is subject to high transaction costs, a JV alternative is apparently the preferred ownership arrangement. Tyebjee

Table 1. Main features of the empirical studies related to the ownership arrangement in FDIs.

Study	Origin of investors	Target country(ies) of FDIs	Number of reviewed FDIs	Research period	Wholly-owned n %	Joint ventures n %	Statistical methods used in the study
Stopford & Wells (1972)	USA	OECD, LDC	n/a1	FDIs made before 1968	n/a	n/a	stepwise & multiple
Stopford & Haberich (1978)	the UK	OECD, LDC	1950	FDIs made before 1971	1304 66.9	646 33.1	not used
Gomes-Casseres (1985)	USA	OECD, LDC	1877	units in operation in 1975	n/a	n/a	binomial logistic regression
Gomes-Casseres (1989)	USA	OECD, LDC	1532	units in operation in 1975	n/a	n/a	binomial logistic regression
Kogut & Singh (1985)	mainly OECD	USA	n/a	FDIs made in 1981-83	n/a	n/a	binomial logistic regression
Kogut & Singh (1988a)	mainly OECD	USA	108	FDIs made in 1981-84	n/a	n/a	binomial logistic regression
Kogut & Singh (1988b)	mainly OECD	USA	228	FDIs made in 1981-85	n/a	n/a	multinomial logistic regression
Gatignon & Andersson (1988)	USA	OECD, LDC	1267	FDIs made in 1960-75	965 76.2	302 23.8	binomial and multinomial logistic regression
Zejan (1988)	Sweden	OECD	403	units in operation in 1974	n/a	n/a	binomial logistic regression
Agarwal & Ramaswami (1990)	USA	OECD, LDC	183	FDIs made in 1985-89	n/a	n/a	multinomial logistic regression
Sanna-Randaccio (1990)	Italy	OECD, LDC	288	FDIs made in 1974-86	n/a	n/a	binomial logistic regression
Hennart (1991)	Japan	USA	158	units in operation in 1985	101 64.0	57 36.0	binomial logistic regression
Larimo (1993a)	Finland	OECD	120	FDIs made in 1977-88	81 67.5	39 32.5	binomial logistic regression
Larimo (1993b)	Finland	OECD	196	FDIs made in 1977-90	128 65.3	68 34.7	binomial logistic regression
Tang (1994)	Japan	USA & Canada	109	FDIs made in 1981-90	73 67.0	36 33.0	binomial logistic regression
Benito (1995)	Norway	OECD, LDC	174	FDIs made in 1910-84	100 57.5	74 42.5	binomial logistic regression
Hennart & Larimo (1995)	Finland & Japan	USA	401	FDIs made in 1977-93	248 61.8	153 38.2	binomial logistic regression
Bell (1996)	the Netherlands	OECD, LDC	168	FDIs made in late 1980s and early 1990s	93 55.4	75 44.6	binomial, multinomial, and ordered logistic regression

1 n/a = not available – the total amount is not mentioned ; FDIs made by 187 US based MNEs before 1968.

(1988) found that six of 21 JVs set up by Japanese firms in the United States had been established to combine Japanese and American technology. If, as Ferguson (1981) argues, the need to obtain tacit technology through JVs varies directly with a firm's R&D intensity, then there will be an inverse relationship between R&D intensity and the propensity to joint venture. Kogut and Singh (1988a) found this to be true in the case of foreign direct investors in the United States.

However, an investor that possesses the full complement of know-how to operate internationally has strong incentives to keep complete control and to enter through WOSs. If knowledge is difficult to transact in markets, then transferring significant amounts of knowledge to a JV is likely to create problems. Unless the innovator is willing to provide knowledge for free, conflict with the partner is likely to arise over the price to be assigned to the knowledge. There are too significant risks that the recipient may use the know-how to later compete with the former partner (Hladik 1985). Gatignon and Anderson (1988), and Gomes-Casseres (1989) found that various proxies for the R&D intensity of the U.S. investor were correlated with the propensity to choose WOSs.

Because of the contradictory predictions, it is difficult to predict whether a parent's R&D intensity increases or decreases its probability of joint venturing. This may explain why in previous studies dealing with Finnish FDIs (Larimo 1992 and 1993b), Japanese FDIs (Hennart 1991), and Dutch FDIs (Bell 1996) a parent's R&D intensity had no significant impact on its choice between WOS and JV. Based on above no sign is expected for the relationship between R&D intensity and degree of ownership.

In cases where foreign firms try to gain access to local natural resources, the preferred alternative is apparently a JV. In resource based industries first movers, which are usually local firms, benefit from differential rents. Hence JVs may be an efficient way to access natural resources. In non-resource based industries a similar need to joint venture as in resource based industries should not exist. These assumptions have received support in several previous studies (see e.g. Gomes-Casseres 1985, Hennart 1991, and Larimo, 1993b). Thus,

H 1. WOSs are less likely in resource intensive industries.

The more diversified a firm is the more likely that the firm does not possess enough product and/ or production specific knowledge in all fields of industries it operates in to manage a foreign unit alone. The previous empirical results also have been relatively unanimous about the direction of the relationship between degree of diversity and degree of ownership, although only results by Gomes-Casseres (1985) and Zejan (1988) have indicated statistically significant support. However,

H 2. The more concentrated the investors' operation, the more likely they will enter with WOSs.

Limited or total lack of international FDI experience increases pressure to gain the operation mode specific and target country specific knowledge of how to manage a foreign unit. One way to limit the financial and management risks related to the FDI is to share the ownership with a local firm. Increased international experience, especially experience from FDIs, gives knowledge of how to plan and manage foreign units and reduces operation mode specific uncertainty. Based on this accumulated knowledge, the parent apparently wants to avoid sharing in decision-making and therefore prefers a WOS. On the other hand, based on accumulated international experience, firms also learn how to evaluate and deal with foreign partners and therefore highly experienced firms may be better able to exploit the benefits of co-operation than firms having no or limited international experience. Because also the previous results are mixed, no hypothesis is stated about the relationship between international experience and degree of ownership.

International operation mode specific knowledge is one way to gain experience, another is target country specific experience. Target country specific experience reduces perceived uncertainty and gives to the investing firm knowledge of how to manage a unit in the target country. The more intensive the firm's previous operation in the target country, the more knowledgeable it is about target country conditions, and the less need it has for a JV partner. Hence,

H 3. The more intensive the investors' previous operation in the target country market, the more likely they will enter with WOSs.

A large sized target country market offers better potential for demand than small market size and, especially if the markets are growing, decreases the perceived risks related to a FDI. Thus a big size of markets apparently leads to the preference for a WOS (see e.g. Stopford and

Habrich 1978). Further, countries having large size are usually strategically more important to the investing firm than countries having small market size. The greater the strategic importance of some target market, the greater apparently is the desire to avoid shared decision-making. But, on the other hand, it may be difficult for a foreign firm to enter a large foreign market on its own, especially if the investment requires a lot of resources for local sales networks, after sales services etc. A large economic size of the target markets also often means better availability of potential JV partners. Thus there are contrary arguments as to whether a large size of target country market would lead to the preference for a WOS or for a JV. The results in previous studies also have been mixed (see Larimo 1993b). However, most studies have indicated support for a positive relationship between economic size and share of ownership. Thus it seems that the greater potential and strategic importance of large markets have weighted more than the possible risks. Hence,

H 4. The larger the target country market size, the more likely it is that the investing firms will enter with WOSs.

If there is rivalry among foreign firms in a growing industry, this may lead to the preference for an acquisition instead of a greenfield investment, since in a rapidly growing market the opportunity costs of a delayed entry is high. However, because full acquisitions involve higher management costs than partial ones, firms may prefer JVs. If foreign firms are competing against local firms, JVs may speed up entry by eliminating start-up and integration costs attached to wholly owned acquisitions (and greenfield investments). Thus JVs should be the preferred alternative in high-growth markets and WOSs in low-growth markets and JVs. Hence,

H 5. Foreign investors will choose WOSs to enter low-growth markets.

The problems in transferring home management techniques and values, management of the labor force etc. increase the greater the cultural distance is between home and target country of the FDI. Because executives perceive higher uncertainty in more distant cultures, it has often been argued that the greater the cultural distance, the lower the degree of control an entrant should demand. Sharing the ownership of the subsidiary with a local firm e.g. reduces learning costs because the management of the JV's labor force can be entrusted to the local partner (Kogut and Singh 1988b).

The results in previous studies have also supported a negative relationship between cultural distance and share of ownership chosen (e.g. Benito 1995 and Bell 1996) although the results have not indicated statistically significant influence in the previous studies dealing with Finnish FDIs (Larimo 1992 and 1993b). However,

> *H 6. The shorter the cultural distance between Finland and the target country, the more likely that they will enter the target country through WOSs.*

Target country specific knowledge is one type of tacit knowledge and another is how to operate in a given industry. If the investing firm has the industry-specific knowledge, there is no pressure to seek a partner. However, if the firm does not have the needed knowledge, it is difficult to acquire it in the market, but it can be obtained from a JV partner. When a firm enters a foreign market by producing a product there which it does not manufacture at home, there is not only a need for industry-specific knowledge, but also a need for access to distribution channels. In that case, a JV with a local incumbent manufacturer may be the most efficient way to obtain the complementary inputs. The results in previous studies seem to be very unanimous that if the foreign unit produces the same product(s) that the parent manufactures at home the parent was more likely to prefer a WOS. Hence,

> *H 7. Investors who manufacture a product in the target country that they also manufacture at home are more likely to enter with WOSs.*

On a priori grounds, the degree of ownership taken in a subsidiary should not hinge on whether entry was through greenfield or through acquisition. The degree of ownership depends on the parent's need for control, and that control can be attained by either a greenfield investment or an acquisition. Gomes-Casseres (1985), however, found that staged acquisitions were more common than staged greenfield investments, and this means that we would expect shared ownership to be associated with acquisitions. However, the results by Benito (1995) indicated the opposite. Previous results dealing with Finnish subsidiaries in OECD countries indicated that WOSs subsidiaries were more likely if the entry had been through greenfield investment and JVs if the entry had been through acquisition, but the influence of the form of entry on ownership was not statistically significant (Larimo 1993a and 1993b). Hennart and Park (1993) found in their study that the percentage of the subsidiary owned by Japanese investors had no influence on their choice between entering the United States through a greenfield investment or through an acquisition. Similar findings were also made in the study by Tang (1994) dealing with Japanese FDIs in United States and Canada and by Benito (1995) dealing with Norwegian FDIs. Hence,

H 8. *Whether entry is through greenfield or acquisition should have no impact on the choice between entry through WOS or JV.*

Finally, the timing of the FDI may also influence the ownership strategy. Various statistics seem to indicate that the use of JVs has clearly increased in the late 1970s and 1980s in both the domestic and international context (see e.g. Harrigan 1988 and Anderson 1990). U.S., Japanese and U.K. data shows, too, that in general the number of JVs has been expanding more rapidly than that of WOSs (see Dunning 1993). Factors behind the increased use of JVs have been the escalating costs of R&D and marketing activities, the shortening of product life cycles, the increase in speed of technical obsolescence, the technological convergence of the leading industrial countries and, outside OECD countries, the opening up of territories previously closed to all forms of FDI (Dunning 1993). In the European context an additional central factor behind increased amount of JVs seems to have been the increased competition which has forced both foreign investing firms and local firms to seek partners. This seems to have been the case especially in the Western European markets after the middle 1980s because of the intensified EU integration process (see e.g. Commission of the European Communities 1989). Apparently the pressure for JVs is especially great in cases where the more intensive internationalisation of the firms has started relatively recently, because of the need to secure market positions quickly. In cases where the more intensive internationalisation of the firm has started already long ago, WOS may also have been the preferred ownership arrangement in FDIs made recently, in spite of the increased competition due to accumulated experience. Furthermore, it seems that the

importance of the rationalisation of the operation at a country or broader level as a motive for the FDI has increased in the 1980's and the rationalisation measures are usually easier to realise if the foreign unit is
wholly-owned. Previous Finnish studies have indicated slight support to
the preference for WOSs in more recent FDIs, but the relationship was
statistically insignificant. Thus no hypothesis is made of the expected relationship between timing of the FDI and degree of ownership chosen.

There is in Appendix 2 a summary of the findings in the 18 empirical
studies dealing with the choice between JV and WOS, which are presented in Table 1. All the same variables as in this study have previously
been included in two previous studies (Larimo 1993a and 1993b). It is
noteworthy is that none of the included variables has had statistically
significant impact in all studies where the variable has been included.

4. Sample, Methodology and Operationalisation of the Measures

Ownership is captured in the study by a dummy variable which receives
a value of one if the Finnish firm owned 95 % or more of the subsidiary's
equity, and zero if it owned at least 10 %, but not more than 94 %. The
95 % cut-off point has been chosen because the firm usually has de facto
total decision power also in situations where the share of ownership is
somewhat under 100 %, and the 95 % cut-off point has been used in several other studies (e.g. in Stopford and Wells 1972, Gatignon and
Anderson 1988, Gomes-Casseres 1989, and Hennart 1991).

Because of the nature of the dependent variable, the binomial logit
model is used in the analysis. In the binomial logistic model the probability of certain type of ownership arrangement is explained by the reviewed variables. The regression coefficients estimate the impact of independent variables on the probability that the foreign unit is wholly-owned. A positive sign for the coefficient means that the variable increases the probability of WOS and a negative sign that the variable increases the probability of a JV. The model can be expressed as

$$P\,(\,y_i = 1) = 1\,/\,(1 + \exp\,(\,-a - X_i B\,)$$

where yi is the dependent variable, Xi is vector of independent variables
for the ith observation, a is intercept parameter, and B is the vector of
regression parameters (Amemiya 1981).

In summary it can be stated that the main criterion for the choice was that similar types of operationalisations were used as have commonly been used in various previous studies dealing with ownership arrangement in FDIs or FDI behaviour in general.

Table 2 lists the independent variables of the study, the operationalisations of the variables, and their expected signs. Data for all variables were obtained from the firm's annual reports and through two surveys sent to them (for details of the surveys see Larimo 1987 and 1993a). In summary it can be stated that the main criterion for the choice was that similar types of operationalisations were used as have commonly been used in various previous studies dealing with ownership arrangement in FDIs or FDI behaviour in general. For earlier operation in the target country (EAROP), economic size of the target country (ECONSIZE), and type of the investment (TYPE) a positive sign is expected and for the industry of the subsidiary (INDUSTRY), degree of diversification of the parent (DIVER), economic growth rate in the target country (ECONGROWTH), and cultural distance (CULTDIS) a negative sign is expected. For the size of the investing firm (SIZE), research and development intensity of the firm (R&D), international operation experience of the investing firm (INTEX), and timing of the investment no sign is expected, and form of entry is expected to be non-significant.

The sample is based on information collected from the annual reports of the Finnish firms and on mail surveys and interviews conducted by the author during several years (see above). The time period for the study was restricted to cover years 1965-1995. Older FDIs were excluded because of problems of finding the needed parent firm related information. Furthermore, there were very few FDIs made by Finnish firms in EU countries before 1965. The EU covers in the study all those countries which were EU member countries before 1995. Thus Austria and Sweden which joined the EU at the beginning of 1995 (as also Finland) are not included in the study. Those countries which joined the EU after 1965 are included for the whole time period. This is done because there were extremely few FDIs in those countries before their joining the EU.

Altogether 415 manufacturing FDIs made by 225 Finnish firms during 1965-1995 in various EU countries covered by the study were identified. Of those FDIs 152 (36.6%) were JVs and 263 (63.4%) were WOSs. The ownership arrangement distribution shows that Finnish firms have in a majority of cases preferred total ownership in EU coun-

Table 2. Summary of the measures used and their operationalisations.

Variable name	Description
SIZE	Global sales of the investing firm (FIM million) in the year preceding the FDI converted into FIM value in 1992. A logarithmic function of the 1992 is used. No sign.
R&D	Percentage of the R & D costs of the turnover of the firm (low=under 1%, medium=1-2.9% and high=3% or more). No sign.
INDUSTRY	Field of industry of the unit (in resource-based industry = 1 ; food and
resource based	beverages, SIC 20, textile mills, SIC 22, wood except furniture, SIC 22, pulp and paper, SIC 26, petroleum, SIC 29, rubber, SIC 30, and primary metals, SIC 33 ; in non-resource based industry = 0). Negative sign.
DIVER	Degree of diversification of the investing firm (number of three level SIC codes where the firm operates. Negative sign.
INTEX	International operation experience of the investing firm (number of manufacturing FDIs made by the firm prior making the reviewed investment). No sign.
EAROP	Mode of earlier operation in the target country (no earlier operation=1, exports, sales subsidiary etc. =2, manufacturing unit=3; 4= two previous manufacturing units; 5=three or more previous manufacturing units). Positive sign.
CULTDIS	Cultural distance to the target country (cultural distance between Finland and the target country counted based on the results by Hofstede, 1980, and using the formula by Kogut and Singh, 1988b). Negative sign.
ECONSIZE	Economic size of the target country (total GDP in the target country in the year preceding the investment). A logarithmic function is used. Positive sign.
ECONGROWTH	Growth of GDP in the target country (growth of total GDP during the three years preceding the investment, percent change). Negative sign.
TYPE: related	Type of the investment (unrelated=1; related=0). Positive sign.
FORM	Form of investment (acquisition =1; greenfield=0). No sign (insignificant).
TIMING	Year of the investment (1965=1, 1966=2 ...1995=31). No sign.

tries. The results related to the distribution between JVs and WOSs indicates that the behaviour of Finnish firms in EU countries has been relatively similar to that in OECD countries in general and to the ownership arrangement behaviour of firms of other origin than Finnish in their FDIs (see Larimo 1993b).

Table 3 presents some descriptive statistics for independent variables in the sample. A clear majority of the FDIs were made in the form of an acquisition, indicating the worldwide trend related to the form of entry, especially in OECD countries. Furthermore, FDIs in non-resource based industries were more common than investments in resource-based industries. Almost 40% of the FDIs were made either in SIC 26 (paper and allied products) or in SIC 35 (non-electrical machinery). Almost all of the FDIs were preceded by earlier operation in the target country (in one-third of cases by one or even several FDIs), and a clear majority were related types of investments. Finally, most of the investments were made in the 1980s and 1990s, clearly over half after 1986.

Table 3. Descriptive statistics for independent variables.

DESCRIPTION	MEAN	SD	MIN	MAX	DISTRIBUTION	
SIZE	8129.00	9132.00	89.00	61352.00		
R & D	1.95	1.37	0.50	18.40		
INDUSTRY	0.43	0.50	0.00	1.00	1: 176	0: 229
DIVER	13.40	6.40	1.00	28.00		
INTEX	19.10	15.70	1.00	66.00		
EAROP	3.14	1.19	1.00	5.00		
ECONSIZE	357.80	23.90	17.50	775.90		
ECONGROWTH	2.61	1.31	-0.41	6.65		
CULTDIST	1.32	0.60	0.36	2.96		
TYPE: common	0.91	0.28	0.00	1.00	1: 370	0: 35
FORM: acquisition	0.78	1.42	0.00	1.00	1: 315	0: 90
TIMING	22.80	5.58	1.00	31.00		

Appendix 3 presents the correlations between the independent variables. The values of correlations exceeding 0.5-0.6 are usually noteworthy. In no case did the correlations exceed 0.5. The highest correlations were found between SIZE and INTEX (0.458) and DIVER and IN-TEX (0.466). In most of the other cases the correlations were clearly lower. Thus the problems of multi-collinearity in the study should be very low.

5. Empirical Results

The results of the binomial logistic regression are presented in Table 4. The estimated coefficients represent the utility of choosing full over shared equity: a positive coefficient means that full ownership will be chosen and a negative coefficient signifies the opposite. The model has a good overall explanatory power with a chi-square of 34.338 with 12 DF (p=0.0006). Another way of measuring how well a maximum likelihood model fits the data is to use the model to classify observations. The ability to classify can be judged againts the classification rate that would have been obtained by change. The rate is equal to $a2 + (1 - a) 2$, where a is the proportion of JVs in the sample. In the present case the baseline rate is 53.6%. The results show that 62.9% of the observations are correctly classified, a rate higher than would be expected by the proportional change criterion. The classification table (see Table 5) shows that the model tends to somewhat over-predict WOSs and to under-predict JVs. Logistic models usually tend to overclassify in the largest category, i.e. here WOS (Amemiya 1981). The sensitivity rate describes the ability of the model to correctly predict event responses, i.e. positives (WOSs). The model's specifity rate describes the ability of the model to correctly predict the no-event responses, i.e. negatives (JVs). The sensitivity rate of the model is clearly better than the specifity rate of the model (the former 85.2% and the latter only 24.3%), i.e. the ability of the model to predict JVs clearly leaves room for improvement.

Table 4. Expected signs of the impact on the ownership arrangement and pa-
rameter estimates for binomial logit model: wholly owned units vs.
joint ventures.

Variable name	Expected sign Estimate	Parameter	Pr > Chi-Squarel
INTERCEPT		5.7882	0.0076***
SIZE	?	-1.34E6	0.9220
R & D	?	0.0211	0.8061
INDUSTRY	−	-0.5125	0.0293**
DIVER	−	-0.0209	0.3136
INTEX	?	-0.0016	0.8780
EAROP	+	0.3268	0.0008***
ECONSIZE	+	0.00022	0.0126**
ECONGROWTH	−	-0.1679	0.0515*
CULTDIS	−	-0.1260	0.5365
TYPE: related	+	0.0218	0.9510
FORM	ns	-0.2048	0.9731
TIMING	?	-0.0641	0.0076***

1 *statistically significant at the 0.1 level, ** significant at the 0.05 level, *** significant at the 0.01 level.

In all cases the reviewed variables had the expected signs. Five of the eleven variables expected to influence the ownership decision had statistically significant impact: INDUSTRY, EAROP, ECONSIZE, ECONGROWTH, and TIMING. The coefficient for INDUSTRY is significant at the 0.05 level and has a negative sign, indicating that Finnish firms which enter in resource intensive industries have a higher propensity to joint venture. The coefficient of EAROP is significant at the 0.05 level and has a positive sign, indicating that the more intensive the earlier operation in the target country is, the more probable that the investing firm prefers a WOS. Thus accumulation of target country specific experience reduces uncertainty and the need for a local partner in the unit. The coefficient for ECONSIZE is significant at the 0.05 level and positive, indicating that Finnish firms have preferred WOSs in EU countries having large size. Apparently the preference for WOSs has partly been dependent on the great potential of large markets (and in this sense the reduced uncertainty) and partly on the fact that large markets are usually strategically very important to the investing firm and therefore there is a greater desire to avoid shared decision-making than in small markets.

Table 5. Classification table for the sample based on ownership arrangement.

	Predicted		
	Wholly owned	Joint venture	Total
Wholly owned	224	39	263
Joint venture	37	115	152
Total	261	154	415
	Sensitivity: 85.2%	Specificity: 24.3%	Correct: 62.9%

The coefficient for ECONGROWTH is significant at the 0.1 level and negative, indicating that high economic growth leads to the preference for a JV. Thus, because the opportunity costs of a delayed entry is high in markets which are growing rapidly, firms try to speed up the entry using a JV arrangement. The coefficient for TIMING is significant at the 0.01 level and negative. No sign was expected for TIMING. The results indicate that JVs have been relatively more common in recent FDIs than in older investments. Thus the escalating costs of R&D and marketing activities, the shortening of product life cycles, the increase in speed of technical obsolescence, and increased competition seem to have forced Finnish firms to seek partners in EU markets especially after the middle 1980s. Apparently the pressure for JVs has been especially great in cases where the more intensive internationalisation of the firms has started in the late 1980s and early 1990s, because of the need to secure market positions quickly.

The coefficients for DIVER, CULTDIS and TYPE are all insignificant. Thus it seems that whether the parent is concentrated in its operation in only one or a few types of products or if it is highly diversified; whether the FDI is made in a culturally close or more distant country, or whether the FDI is a related or unrelated type of investment has not significantly affected the ownership structure behaviour by Finnish firms in EU countries. The sign for form of entry was negative, but totally insignificant as was expected. Thus the results give support to the view that whether entry is through greenfield or acquisition has no impact on the choice between entry through WOS or JV. The results in previous studies have also indicated that the influence of DIVER, CULTDIS and TYPE has not been statistically significant.

In addition to TIMING, no sign was expected for the SIZE, R&D and INTEX. In the case of SIZE the coefficient is negative, but the p-value of the variable is totally insignificant. Thus the size of the Finnish parent firm has not influenced the ownership arrangement behaviour in EU countries. The results in previous studies have indicated that large size of the Finnish parent has increased the preference for JVs, especially in the U.S. markets (see Hennart and Larimo 1995). Hence it seems that there has been a clear difference in the behaviour of Finnish firms in the EU and the U.S. markets. One has to remember, however, that the results in the U.S. markets seem to have been influenced relatively much by the behaviour of the Neste corporation.

The sign for R&D is positive and for the INTEX negative, but the p-values are in both cases insig- nificant. Thus, the impact of the R&D -intensity and previous FDI experience seem to have been very small on the ownership arrangement strategy decisions made by Finnish firms in EU markets. Similar results have also been found in previous studies dealing with Finnish FDIs in OECD markets.

Finally, it was expected that the degree of ownership taken in a subsidiary should not hinge on whether entry was through greenfield or through acquisition. The results show that the coefficient for FORM is negative, but totally insignificant. Thus, the results support the view that the degree of ownership depends on the parent's need for control, and that control can be attained by either a greenfield investment or an acquisition.

For R&D, INTEX and/or ECONGROWTH results in some studies have indicated a U-shaped relationship (see e.g. Bell 1996 and Sanna-Randaccio 1990). Therefore another run was made where those variables were squared. The results of this did not, however, lend support to a U-shaped relationship in any of the three cases.

6. Summary and Conclusions

The main goal of this chapter was to analyse the determinants of ownership arrangement behaviour by Finnish firms in their manufacturing investments made in EU countries. On the basis of theoretical argumentation and the results of previous studies, assumptions of the expected impact were developed to be tested in the empirical part.

The hypotheses investigated in this study were primarily based on the transaction cost and behaviour theories. The transaction cost cost approach places great emphasis on retaining control if proprietary assets are at risk. The approach suggests that complete integration of foreign operations is more likely if the basis of the MNE advantage lies in the areas such as valuable product brands, and complex products and production processes, or when the making of the FDI involves investment commitments that greatly increase switching costs. The core of the behavioural approach is the effects of uncertainty and lack of knowledge in shaping the actions taken by companies when entering foreign markets. According to this approach the ownership structure depends mainly on two factors: on the unfamiliarity of the foreign market, and the firms' prior experience of foreign operations.

The empirical part of the study was based on 415 manufacturing FDIs made in various EU countries between 1965 and 1995. Of the reviewed FDIs 263 (63.4%) were WOSs and 152 (36.6%) JVs. Thus Finnish firms have usually preferred WOSs. The result about the relationship between WOSs and JVs was relatively similar to the findings in previous Finnish and other studies. A binomial logistic model was used in the analysis of the impact of different variables on the ownership arrangement. The overall explanatory power of the model was relatively low. This was somewhat surprising, because for several variables more detailed values could be used in this study than in previous Finnish studies.

The expected signs were in all cases supported by the results. In five cases the reviewed variables had statistically significant impact. First, JVs were the preferred ownership structures in resource based industries. Secondly, the more intensive the investors' earlier operation in the target country, the greater was the preference for WOSs. Thirdly, the larger the economic size of the target country, the greater the preference for WOSs. Fourhtly, the higher the economic growth in the target country, the greater the preference for JVs. Fifthly, the preference for JVs had increased in more recent FDIs. Of these five variables, intensity of earlier operation and timing of the FDI had the strongest impact on the ownership structures. Furthermore, as was expected, the form of entry did not significantly influence the ownership arrangement decision. This gives support to the view that the degree of ownership wanted can be received independent of the form of entry.

The main difference in the results between this and earlier studies analysing ownership behaviour by Finnish firms was that size of the investing firm did not have statistically significant impact on the results. One possible explanation for the difference is that this study did not include the USA as the previous studies have, and that there may be some differences in the behaviour in the EU countries and the USA. Thus, further research is needed with sufficiently large samples, including FDIs made by Finnish firms in both areas. The results in foreign studies have indicated mixed results about the relationship between size of the investing firm and degree of ownership in the foreign unit.

From the theoretical point of view it can be stated that neither the transaction cost theory nor the behavioural approach received very strong support from the results. However, the results were more supportive of the behavioural than the transaction approach. One drawback of this study was that variables related to the strategy approach were actually not included. Thus, in future studies more variables related to the strategy approach should also be included in the analysis.

Appendix 1. Finnish outward Foreign net direct investment flows by countries in 1976, 1983-1995 (million FIM, current prices). (Compiled on the basis of notifications in 1977-1996 by Bank of Finland).

Host country	1976	1983	1984	1985	1986	1987	1988	1989	1990	1991	1992	1993	1994[3]	1995[3]
Austria 1	0	5	5	0	2	16	2	-3	6	7	0	20	595	
Norway	2	26	29	104	129	123	284	371	1014	587	-272	244	48	-63
Sweden 1	7	106	802	191	1590	448	2292	2398	2535	703	966	3765	591	
Switzerland	21	1	515	76	2	131	252	192	17	72	586	-290	-295	-1104
EFTA	**30**	**138**	**1351**	**371**	**1723**	**718**	**2830**	**2958**	**3572**	**1369**	**1280**	**3739**	**938**	**-1167**
Netherland	6	73	70	468	313	226	289	1572	1935	355	-50	-325	5007	-248
Belgium 2	19	28	98	45	336	389	293	118	397	804	960	1889	838	-665
Spain	-1	14	7	44	20	127	70	150	373	311	562	824	981	50
Ireland	0	8	18	7	281	-126	-31	5	146	246	55	97	83	370
Great-Britain	19	208	300	85	168	197	1236	1031	1405	794	894	1518	5322	1593
Italy	0	37	0	18	5	88	54	150	106	391	315	330	85	100
Greece		.	8	0	1	0	4	6	13	0	2	-1	1	.
Luxembourg 2	.	.	.	-41	11	6	19	430	162	-46	126	-57	-135	218
Portugal	0	0	0	0	0	0	12	73	116	272	117	1068	-160	38
France	13	81	31	104	52	327	239	382	1442	678	1046	812	1360	537
Germany	14	96	83	55	49	190	1136	525	401	406	740	3294	1086	533
Denmark	1	67	46	76	90	639	417	373	162	70	-128	47	4930	561
Austria														193
Sweden														952
EU	**71**	**612**	**661**	**861**	**1326**	**2063**	**3800**	**4815**	**6658**	**4281**	**4729**	**13281**	**20584**	**4232**
The USA	5	582	217	469	255	492	1922	3056	1747	1197	453	1382	694	2073
Others	13	119	250	375	337	465	515	2344	1761	760	891	-152	1684	-14

1) Austria and Sweden have been members of EU from the beginning of 1995

2) The figures of Belgium include Luxembourg in 1976, 1983 and 1984.

3) The figures for 1994 and 1995 are preliminary.

Appendix 2. Overview of the findings of the empirical studies which have focused on the choice between JVs and WOSs totally or mainly in OECD countries

	1	2	3	4	5	6	7	8	9	10	11	12	13	14	15	16	17	18
SIZE	ns	.	+	.	+	.	+	.	−	−	−	.	−	−	.	+	−	ns
R & D	ns	.	.	.	ns	−	−	.	ns	−	+	ns	ns	ns	−	ns	−	ns
INDUSTRY:Resource based	.	.	−	.	.	.	.	.	.	.	.	−	−	−	.	.	−	ns
DIVER	ns	ns	−	.	ns	.	.	.	−	.	.	.	ns	ns	.	.	.	.
INTEX	ns	.	+	.	ns	.	ns	.	+	−	−	.	ns	ns	+	ns	.	+
EAROP	.	.	.	.	.	.	ns	.	.	.	.	+	+	+	ns	.	ns	−
ECONSIZE	.	.	−	−	.	.'	.	.	−	ns	+	.	+	+	.	−	.	−
EGONGROWTH	.	.	.	.	−	.	−	.	.	.	.	−	ns	ns	.	.	ns	−
DULTDIS	.	.	.	.	.	.	.	−	.	−	.	.	ns	ns	.	−	−	−
TYPE: Releted	ns	.	+	+	.	.	.	.	ns	.	.	+	ns	ns	ns	.	ns	ns
FORM: Acquisition	.	.	−	.	.	.	.	.	.	.	.	ns	−	−	ns	ns	ns	.
TIMING	.	.	.	.	.	.	.	.	.	.	.	.	ns	ns	.	.	.	.

+ = increases pfobability of a WOS
− = increases probability of a JV
ns = nonsignificant
. = not reviewed in the study

1 Stopford & Wells (1972)
2 Stopford & Haberich (1978)
3 Gomes-Cassers (1985)
4 - " - (1989)
5 Kogut & Singh (1985)
6 - " - (1988a)
7 - " - (1988b)
8 Gatignon & Andersson (1988)
9 Zejan (1988)

10 Agarwal & Ramanswami (1990)
11 Sanna-Randaccio (1990)
12 Hennart (1991)
13 Larimo (1993a)
14 Larimo (1993b)
15 Tang (1994)
16 Benito (1995)
17 Hennart & Larimo (1995) (overall results in the study)
18 Bell (1996)

Appendix 3. Correlation matrix
(Spearman rank correlation coefficients, n= 415)

	SIZE	R & D	INDUS-TRY	DIVER	INTEX	EAROP	ECON-SIZE	ECONG.	CULTDIS	TYPE	FORM	TIMING
SIZE	1.000											
R & D	0.014	1.000										
INDUSTRY	-0.024	-0.263	1.000									
DIVER	0.396	0.132	0.086	1.000								
INTEX	0.458	0.064	-0.008	0.466	1.000							
EAROP	0.298	0.042	0.053	0.369	0.391	1.000						
ECONSIZE	0.022	0.129	-0.058	0.091	0.193	0.236	1.000					
ECONG.	-0.040	0.100	-0.058	-0.030	-0.013	-0.068	-0.011	1.000				
CULTDIS	0.201	-0.015	0.047	-0.000	0.020	0.012	0.033	0.149	1.000			
TYPE	0.027	0.015	0.181	0.012	0.072	-0.022	-0.054	-0.054	0.036	1.000		
FORM	-0.138	-0.062	0.025	-0.017	-0.088	-0.100	0.107	-0.169	-0.133	-0.059	1.000	
TIMING	0.297	0.103	-0.088	0.125	0.414	0.237	0.219	-0.172	0.029	-0.033	-0.052	1.000

References

Agarwal, S. & S. Ramaswami, 1990. *Effects of Market Potential and Socio-cultural Distance on the Choice of Joint Ventures.* Paper presented at the annual meeting of European International Business Association, Madrid, December 1990.

Aharoni, Yair, 1966. *The Foreign Investment Decision Process.* Harvard University Press, Boston.

Amemiya, T, 1981. »Qualitative Response Models: A Survey«, *Journal of Economic Literature,* Vol. 19, 1483-1536.

Anderson, E. & H. Gatignon, 1990. »Two firms, one frontier: On assessing joint venture performance«, *Sloan Management Review,* Vol. 31, No. 2, 19-30.

Beamish, Paul W., 1985. »The characteristics of joint ventures in developed and developing countries«, *Columbia Journal of World Business,* Vol. 20, No. 3, 13-19.

Bell, John, 1996. *Joint or single venturing? An eclectic approach to foreign entry mode choice.* Ph.D. dissertation, Tilburg University.

Benito, Gabriel, 1995. *Studies in the Foreign Direct Investment and Divestment Behavior of Norwegian Manufacturing Companies.* Doctoral dissertation, Norwegian School of Management.

Björkman, Ingmar, 1990. »Foreign Direct Investments: An Organizational Learning Perspective«, *Finnish Journal of Business Economics,* Vol. 39, No. 4, 271-294.

Buckley, P. & M. Casson, 1976. *The Future of the Multinational Enterprise.* MacMillan Press, London.

Buckley, P. & M. Casson, 1988. »A Theory of Cooperation in International Business«, in F. Contractor & P. Lorange,(eds.). *Cooperative Strategies in International Business,* 31-55. Lexington Books, Lexington, Massachusetts.

Comission of the European Communities, 1989. Facing the challenges of the early 1990s. Annual economic report 1989-90. *The Community economy at the turn of the decade.* Analytical Studies No. 42. Comission of the European Communities, Brussels.

Dunning, John, 1993. *Multinational Enterprises and the Global Economy.* Addison Wesley, New York.

Fagre, N. & L. T. Wells, 1982. »Bargaining power of multinationals and host governments«, *Journal of International Business Studies,* Vol. 13, No. 2, 9-23.

Ferguson, R., 1981. *The Nature of Joint Ventures in American Manufacturing Sector.* PhD dissertation, Harvard University.

Franco, Lawrence G., 1971. *Joint Venture Survival in Multinational Corporations.* Praeger, New York.

Gatignon, H. & E. Anderson, 1988. »The multinational corporation degree of control over subsidiaries: An empirical test of a transaction cost explanation«, *Journal of Law, Economics and Organization,* Vol. 4, 305-336.

Gomes-Casseres, Benjamin, 1985. *Multinational Ownership Strategies.* Ph.D. dissertation, Harvard Business School.

Gomes-Casseres, Benjamin, 1989. »Ownership structures of foreign subsidiaries: Theory and evidence«, *Journal of Economic Behavior and Organization,* Vol. 11, 1-25.

Harrigan, Katryn, 1988. »Strategic alliances and partner asymmetries«, in F. Contractor & P. Lorandge, (eds.). *Cooperative Strategies in International Business,* 205-226. Lexington Books, Lexington, Massachusetts.

Hennart, Jean-Francois, 1991. »The Transaction Costs Theory of Joint Ventures: An Empirical Study of Japanese Subsidiaries in the United States«, *Management Science,* Vol. 37: 4, 483-497.

Hennart, J.-F. & J. Larimo (1995). *The Impact of Culture on the Strategy of Multinational Enterprises. Does National Origin Affect Ownership Decisions?* Proceedings of the University of Vaasa. Discussion Papers 185. Vaasa.

Hennart, J.-F. & Y.R. Park (1993). »Greenfield vs. Acquisition: The Strategy of Japanese Investors in the United States«, *Management Science,* Vol. 37: 4, 483-497.

Hill, C. W. L., P. Hwang & W. C. Kim, 1990. »An Eclectic Theory of the Choice of International Entry Mode«, *Strategic Management Journal,* Vol. 11, No. 2, 117-128.

Hladik, K., 1985. International Joint Ventures: An Economic Analysis of U.S. Foreign Business Partnerhips.

Hofstede, Geert, 1980. *Culture's Consequences.* Sage, Beverly Hills, CA.

Johanson, J. & J.-E. Vahlne, 1977. »The Internationalization Process of the Firm: A Model of Knowledge Development and Increasing Commitments«, *Journal of International Business Studies,* Vol. 8, No. 1, 23-32.

Johanson J. & J.-E. Vahlne, 1992. »Management of Foreign Market Entry«, *Scandinavian International Business Review,* Vol. 1, No. 1, 9-27.

Kay, N. & J.-P. Robe & P. Zagnolli, 1987. *An approach to the analysis of joint ventures.* Working Paper, European University Institute.

Kogut, Bruce, 1988. »A study of the life cycle of joint ventures«, in F. Contractor & P. Lorance, (eds.). *Co-operative Strategies in International Business,* 165-185. Lexington Books, Lexington, Massachusetts.

Kogut, B. & H. Singh, 1985. *Entering the United States by acquisition or joint venture: Country patterns and cultural characteristics.* Paper presented at the joint EIBA-AIB meeting, London, november 1985.

Kogut , B. & H. Singh, 1988a. »Entering the United States by Joint Venture: Competitive Rivalry and Industry Structure« in F. Contractor and P. Lorange, (eds.). *Co-operative Strategies in International Business,* 241-251. Lexinghton Books, Lexinghton, Massachusetts.

Kogut, B. & H. Singh, 1988b. »The effect of national culture on the choice of entry mode«, *Journal of International Business Studies,* Vol. 19, No. 3, 411–432.

Larimo, Jorma, 1987. *The foreign direct investment decision process. An empirical study of the foreign direct investment decision behaviour of Finnish firms.* Proceedings of the University of Vaasa, Research Papers No. 124.

Larimo, Jorma, 1993a. *Foreign direct investment behaviour and performance. An analysis of Finnish direct manufacturing investments in OECD countries.* Acta Wasaensia No. 32, University of Vaasa.

Larimo, Jorma, 1993b. »Ownership arrangement in foreign direct investments: Behavior of Finnish firms in OECD countries«, in V. Simeos, (ed.). *International Business and Europe After 1992,* Proceedings of the 19th Annual Conference of European International Business Association, Vol. 2, 289-323.

Luostarinen, R. & L. Welch, 1990. *International Business Operations.* Export Consulting KY, Helsinki.

OECD, 1989. *Investment Incentives and Disincentives Effects on International Direct Investments.* OECD, Paris.

Oxelheim, L. & R. Gärtner, 1994. *Changes in the production pattern of small outside countries as a response to the EC 1992 program.* Institute of Economic Research Working Paper 6. Lund University.

Rugman, Alan, 1981. *Inside the Multinationals:* The Economics of Internal Markets. Croom Helm, London.

Sanna-Randaccio, Francesca, 1990. *The Ownership Structure of Foreign Subsidiaries: Evidence from the Italian Multinationals.* Paper presented at the annual meeting of European International Business Association, Madrid, December 1990.

Schaan, Jean-Louis, 1988. »How to Control a Joint Venture even as a Minority Partner«, *Journal of General Management,* Vol. 14, No. 1, 4-16.

Statistiska Centralbyrån, 1994. *Årsredovisning för Sveriges utrikeshandel* 1993-1994. SCB-Tryck, örebro.

Stopford, J. M. & K.O.Haberich, 1978. »Ownership and control of foreign operations«, in Gertman & Leontiades, (eds.). *European Research in International Business,* 141-167. North-Holland, New York.

Stopford, J. & L. Wells, 1972. *Managing the Multinational Enterprise.* Basic Books, New York.

Tang, Yiming, 1994. *Entry-mode choice between a wholly owned subsidiary or an equity joint venture by Japanese manufacturing entrants in North America.* Ph.D. dissertation, York University.

Tyebjee, T. , 1988. »Japan's Joint Ventures in the United States«, in F. Contractor & P. Lorange, (eds.). *Co-operative Strategies in International Business,* 457-472. Lexinghton Books, Lexinghton, Massachusetts.

United Nations (1995). World Investment Report 1995. *Transnational Corporations and Competitiveness.* United Nations, New York and Geneva.

Williamson, Oliver E. , 1981. »The Modern Corporation: Origins, Evolution, Attributes«, *Journal of Economic Literature,* Vol. 19, December, 1537-1568.

Williamson, Oliver E., 1985. *The Economic Institutions of Capitalism.* The Free Press, New York.

Zejan, Mario C. , 1988. *Studies in the behavior of Swedish multinationals.* Ekonomiska studier utgivna av Nationalekonomiska Institutionen Handelshögskolan vid Göteborgs Universitet 23. Göteborg.

13. Why are Foreign Subsidiaries Divested?

A Conceptual Framework[65]

Gabriel R. G. Benito

1. Introduction

Foreign direct investment (FDI) is usually defined as a cross-border investment made by a company for the purpose of acquiring a lasting equity interest in a foreign enterprise, and thereby exert a considerable degree of influence on the operations of that enterprise. A FDI represents in other words a long-term commitment to a foreign operation. Exits – or divestments – seem nevertheless to be far from uncommon. Boddewyn (1979) – one of the first international business scholars who paid attention to foreign divestment – mentions that while the 180 largest U.S. based multinationals added some 4,700 subsidiaries to their networks between the years 1967 to 1975, more than 2,400 affiliates were divested during the same period. Some more recent studies suggest that the number of divestments is indeed quite significant: for example, Padmanabhan (1993) identified 421 divestments of European subsidiaries by U.K. companies in the 1983-1992 period; Häkkinen (1994) reports that Finnish companies had divested almost 900 foreign subsidiaries in the period 1978-1992; and Barkema, Bell, and Pennings (1996) in a study of the longevity of FDIs made by large Dutch multinationals found that of 225 FDIs made in the period 1966-1988, just over half of them were still in existence in 1988.

While a vast theoretical and empirical literature examining the determinants of entry into foreign operations has emerged in recent years[66],

65. The author thanks Mats Forsgren, Geir Gripsrud, Steen Thomsen and Lawrence S. Welch for valuable comments and suggestions on an earlier version of this paper.
66. See Cantwell (1991) for a review of this literature.

considerably less attention has been given to the decision to exit. Difficulty in getting appropriate data may, in part, explain why relatively few empirical studies have been conducted on divestment. Studies of exits typically require longitudinal data sets, which are notoriously difficult to obtain (Audretsch and Mahmood, 1994). Moreover, because exits often are regarded as an admission of failure, companies tend to treat divestment issues with secrecy (Hamilton and Chow, 1993). One should, however, attempt to overcome such difficulties. From the viewpoint of an investor company, more knowledge about which factors are likely to influence the longevity and success of a foreign venture may contribute to a better assessment of potential FDI projects. Likewise, incoming FDI is generally regarded as vital in order to develop an economy. Host countries want to retain the stock of FDI in the country, and if possible, to attract new foreign investment. Again, knowledge about the determinants of divestment should provide useful clues about adequate policy measures and appropriate government action. Thus, given both the magnitude and the importance of foreign divestment, studies about this issue are certainly warranted.

This chapter discusses why and under what circumstances foreign divestment is likely to take place[67]. While empirical work certainly is commendable, it is particularly important that – given the relative lack of research in this area – attention is given to theoretical development at this stage. Hence, the aim of this chapter is to develop a conceptual framework for understanding foreign divestments. The frame of reference underlying this endeavor will be relatively broad. It will not be confined to a particular field like economics, management, or strategy. Although valuable contributions have come from all of these fields, arguably they only provide partial insights about why firms may choose to divest. Therefore, an attempt is made to integrate the various contributions found in the literature into a simple, yet unifying framework, which in turn could serve as an adequate theoretical platform for future empirical studies about this issue.

This chapter is organised as follows. The next section discusses the concept of divestment and gives a short overview of the literature on this topic. Based on the literature review a conceptual framework is then

---

67. Notice that this chapter does not deal with the question of *how* divestments take place, i.e. the divestment process itself, and the organizational and managerial processes leading to and resulting from the decision to undertake such action. For an interesting article about these issues, see Doz and Prahalad (1987).

presented. A discussion of a number of factors, and their possible impact on foreign divestment behaviour, follows. Some final remarks close the chapter.

2. Divestment of Foreign Operations

2.1. What is foreign divestment?

In general, foreign divestment refers to the dismantling of an ownership relation across national borders. The unwinding of foreign operations can come about in various ways. It is useful to distinguish between forced and deliberate divestitures. The term forced divestment applies to the seizure of foreign-owned property, i.e. actions referred to as nationalisation, socialisation, expropriation, and confiscation, in which change of ownership is forced upon the investor (Kobrin, 1980; Akhter and Choudhry, 1993). Deliberate divestment on the other hand, is based on strategic considerations leading to the voluntary liquidation or sale of all or a major part of an active operation in another country (Boddewyn, 1979). Although forced divestments will be touched upon occasionally, the focus of this chapter is on deliberate divestment.

2.2. Previous literature on divestment

Closing down a foreign plant, or selling it off to another company, is the end result of strategic decisions concerning the reallocation or concentration of productive resources at a national, regional, or global level, a change of foreign market servicing mode, e.g. from local production to export, or a complete withdrawal from a host country. The literature suggests that the reasons, or triggers, underlying such strategic decisions, and more specifically, why divestment in some cases is chosen as the course of action, are numerous. In a recent overview of the literature on divestment, Chow and Hamilton (1993) identify three main streams; industrial organisation, finance, and corporate strategy.

The industrial organisation (IO) literature has been concerned with, on the one hand, incentives to exit and, on the other, impediments to exit (Siegfried and Evans, 1994). Although the empirical evidence is, partly because of measurement problems, not conclusive, the most obvious incentive to exit is low profits, or outright unprofitability, which in turn are due to high costs, permanent decreases in demand, or the entry into an industry by aggressive, more efficient, new competitors (Siegfried and Evans, 1994). The existence of specific assets, i.e. assets which do not have valuable alternative uses (Williamson, 1985), constitute on the other hand an important impediment to exit (Caves and Porter, 1976). Even though sunk costs can, from a purely economic perspective, be seen as an »irrational« barrier to exit, in reality they may function as a perceptual exit barrier (Staw, 1981). Shapiro and Khemani (1987) argue that the role of such investments is often to deter entry by signalling a credible *ex ante* commitment by incumbents to stay in an industry or market. However, what serves as an entry deterrent, also deters exit *ex post* (Eaton and Lipsey, 1980). Specific assets can be either tangible or intangible. In general, the empirical evidence indicates that durable tangible specific assets, such as high sunk cost in machinery, discourage exit (Siegfried and Evans, 1994). In a similar vein, intangible assets such as goodwill, advertising and research and development intensity, firm-specific human capital, and even emotional attachment to the firm and/or industry, can also operate as exit barriers by raising the perceived cost of leaving the arena (Caves and Porter, 1976). An additional exit barrier is interrelatedness between units, such as joint production and distribution facilities, which could prevent what may, in a strict sense, seem as an unprofitable unit from being divested because it may contribute positively to the company's overall activities. Finally, the IO literature suggests that divestment may depend on diversification. Caves and Porter (1976) argue that owners of independent plants have a lower opportunity cost, and are therefore willing to accept a lower rate of return than operations belonging to a multi-plant/multi-industry company would be expected to achieve. Moreover, divestment is facilitated in diversified companies since decisions are likely to be made by top-managers which are geographically and/or emotionally remote from the units under consideration for divestiture (Wright and Thompson, 1987).

Several contributions to the divestment literature have taken a strategic management perspective. Harrigan (1980) looks at divestment through the lens of a product life-cycle approach, and argues that divestment is one of several strategic options for »declining« industries. In particular, she advocates divestment as an appropriate route in »end game« situations characterised by high volatility and uncertainty regarding future returns. Others treat divestment from a corporate portfolio perspective: a company can be regarded as a portfolio of assets, products, and activities, which should be continuously under review from both financial and strategic points of view (Chow and Hamilton, 1993). The contention that poorly performing units are likely candidates for divestiture, is supported in a number of studies (Duhaime and Grant, 1984; Hamilton and Chow, 1993). Moreover, these studies also suggest that corporate level financial performance influences divestment. For example, in their study of 208 divestments made by large New Zealand companies during 1985-1990, Hamilton and Chow (1993) report that the necessity of meeting corporate liquidity requirements was among the most important objectives motivating divestment. However, in addition to the narrow – or short-term – financial considerations, which are undoubtedly important, strategic considerations also play an important role in the decision to divest. In particular, following Rumelt's (1974) study on the relationship between strategy and performance, numerous empirical studies have found that corporate expansion into related industries leads to better performance and superior survival rates than expansion into unrelated industries (Bane and Neubauer, 1981; Lecraw, 1984; Morck, Shleifer and Vishny, 1990; Pennings, Barkema, and Douma, 1994). Similarly, interview based studies report that low interdependency between units (Duhaime and Grant, 1984), and the need to focus on core activities (Hamilton and Chow, 1993), strongly motivate the decision to divest. Thus, although there are examples of companies that have evolved into large conglomerates, in general, studies suggest that firms are inclined to, and are probably better off, by staying close to their specific competencies. Taking a transaction cost approach to strategic management, Reve (1990) even argues that besides the need for protecting the assets constituting the strategic core – which always should be governed within the boundaries of the firm – there are, since all complementary assets can be secured by means of various forms of alliances, no compelling economic reasons for corporate expansion through ownership.

Finally, a third strand of literature – financial studies of divestment – has primarily looked at the effects on share prices of divestment decisions. Although the available evidence is limited, particularly for foreign divestments, it appears that divestment often increases the market value of a company (Padmanabhan, 1993). One obvious reason is that divested units simply are poor performers. Another, and somewhat more subtle, explanation is offered by Fatemi (1984) who argues that monitoring and bonding costs are higher for international operations than for domestic ones. Foreign divestments may, by reducing such costs, affect shareholder wealth positively. An explanation closely linked to the strategy literature is provided by Weston (1989) who points out that operations might be divested for other reasons than poor performance. As already noted, corporate diversification strategies appear to be particularly likely to foster divestiture as time passes by. For example, the synergistic value of units that were originally acquired in order to achieve synergies with a company's core business, may weaken, or even disappear, over time. In a similar vein, highly diversified companies may reach a point where a greater degree of relatedness between units is needed. In such cases, both the original acquisition and the subsequent divestment may have a positive impact on the market value of a company.

To date, the number of studies dealing specifically with foreign divestment is quite limited. In the 1970s, a high number of nationalisations in developing countries led to several studies on forced divestment (see for example Kobrin, 1980). In the 1980s, although concerns were raised about the instability of the then increasingly popular cooperative ventures (Kogut, 1988; Blodgett, 1992), and about the integration problems posed by international acquisitions (Nahavandi and Malekzadeh, 1988; Olie, 1990), few studies of foreign divestments were actually undertaken. Recently, two studies (Li, 1995; Barkema *et al.*, 1996) have investigated the relationship between cultural and experiential aspects of foreign expansion and divestitures. The basic contention in these studies is that while internationalisation exposes companies to an array of difficulties regardless of the actual mode of entry used or the location of the foreign unit, problems are likely to increase when foreign entries are made in culturally distant locations, and/or they are made by acquisition or joint venture. Acquisitions and joint ventures involve »double layered acculturation« in which both another corporate culture and a foreign national culture have to be dealt with. That such processes are difficult, and in turn may lead to inferior performance, is shown in the studies by Li (1995) and Barkema *et al.* (1996) which report that the probability of divestment is higher in such cases. Moreover, in line with several studies of domestic exits, the results from Li's study also indicate that international diversification entails a higher risk of subsequent exit than foreign ventures within the parent company's main line of business.

3. A Framework

3.1. Incentives to exit versus barriers to exit

Since the purpose of operating a foreign unit – as any other commercial activity – is, after all, to make a profit (or at least a contribution to profit), it seems that a natural starting point in a discussion of divestments would be to look at the economic basis for such actions. Even though the frequency of foreign divestments is increasing, it is nevertheless reasonable to assume that divestments probably play a rather minor part in the recurrent strategic considerations of most firms. As pointed out by Cyert and March (1963) the behaviour of firms, while purposeful, is not fully rational due to cognitive and organisational constraints imposed on decision-makers, which inter alia lead to a selective attention to the myriad of problems that confront them at any point in time. Firms will usually not regard a particular unit as a candidate for divestment if its performance is perceived as satisfactory. That sort of attention is likely to be foremost if a unit's operations are not running as smoothly as, or are less profitable than, expected. Therefore, in order for divestment to be taken into consideration as a possible course of action there must be a positive incentive to exit (Siegfried and Evans, 1994). In general, a positive incentive to exit, *Iexit*, will exist whenever current profits Π_t, or expected profits $E(\Pi)_T$ over the relevant period of time T, fail to meet the rate of return Π^* which is deemed as satisfactory (for example according to budget or an industry norm) by a firm, i.e.

$$I_{\text{exit}} > 0 : [\Pi_t ; E(\Pi)_T] < \Pi^*. \tag{1}$$

However, as pointed out in recent industrial organisation literature (see for example Siegfried and Evans, 1994), leaving on-going operations is not a straightforward – or easy – task due to a number of impediments or barriers to exit. As noted previously, barriers to exit, B_{exit}, are primarily due to the existence of assets – tangible and/or intangible – whose value V_t is higher when employed in their current use than in its best alternative use V^A. In addition there may be switching costs SC of a more perceptual kind – for example, decision makers' inability to find viable alternatives other than continuing the current operations – or even of an emotional character such as the company owners' attachment to an industry, a particular unit, or a line of products. Positive barriers to exit, i.e. $B_{\text{exit}} > 0$, can then be defined as,

$$B_{exit} > 0 : [(V_t - V^A) + SC] > 0. \tag{2}$$

As a result, even if the condition expressed in (1) holds – that is, there are positive incentives to exit in a given situation – that does not constitute a sufficient condition for exit since B_{exit} may also be significant. As stated in (3), an additional necessary condition for exit to take place is that the magnitude of the incentives to exit is also larger than that of the barriers to exit;

$$I_{exit} > B_{exit}. \tag{3}$$

Although incentives to exit are not a sufficient condition to make divestment a viable course of action, their role as a necessary condition is evident. In order to illustrate how the opposing forces of incentives versus barriers to exit affect the decision to stay or exit, the situations of high and low values of I_{exit} and B_{exit} respectively, have been put into a simple 2×2 matrix as shown in figure 1. As can be seen, incentives to exit seemingly play the dominant role as »triggers of action«: staying in business is the preferred option if $I_{exit} = 0$, regardless of the value of B_{exit}, as well as if $I_{exit} > 0$ and $B_{exit} = 0$. Only if high values appear for both factors in conjunction do barriers to exit have a possible impact on such decisions (see quadrant IV.).

Figure 1. The decision to stay or exit as a function of incentives and barriers to exit.

| | | Barriers to exit (B_{exit}) | |
		None	High
Incentives to **exit** (I_{exit})	None	I. Stay	II. Stay
	High	III. Exit	IV. If $I_{exit} > B_{exit}$: exit, otherwise : stay

3.2 Factors underlying the decision to divest

The notions of incentives and barriers to exit represent an useful way of approaching the question of why foreign operations are divested, principally because they provide an analytical tool for framing the problem. However, in terms of their explanatory value they constitute rather »empty« concepts. Therefore in order to further pursue the question of why foreign divestments take place, it is necessary to take a closer look at the specific factors that may influence incentives and barriers to exit in foreign contexts, and thereby, the probability of exiting from a foreign operation.

In the literature, a number of factors have been suggested as having an impact on exits and divestments. The economics (IO) literature focuses above all on the performance of a unit, and on the competitive environment in which it operates, suggesting that adverse changes in these factors increase the probability of exit. The strategic management literature gives particular importance to the strategic relation between a given unit and the core business of its parent, suggesting that diversification moves are much more likely to be divested at some later stage. The, admittedly scarce, international business literature brings attention to the problems of conducting activities in a foreign setting, and contends that the difficulties of running such operations, although moderated by the international experience of the firms in charge, are likely to increase if operations are located in very unfamiliar settings and/or the chosen method of operation entails a complex integration process (as often will be the case for joint ventures and acquisitions) before a unit is fully operative. Taken together, it seems that the essential factors suggested in the various contributions from economics, strategy, and international business, can be put together into four main groups:

- The stability and predictability of the environment – competitively and politically – in which a foreign unit operates.
- The attractiveness of current operations, which is dependent on the current and expected performance of a foreign unit.
- The governance problems associated with foreign operations, which are dependent on the mode of operation chosen for a given activity, the unfamiliarity of the foreign context and, finally, of the parent company's ability to deal with such problems.

– The strategic fit between the parent company and a foreign affiliate, i.e. the degree of relatedness between the parent company and a foreign unit, and whether the parent is a company with a well defined core-business or not.

What most of the literature (that is, apart from the IO literature) largely disregards, however, is that the influence of these factors (i.e. environmental stability, attractiveness of current operations, strategic fit, and governance issues) on the probability of exiting from a foreign operation is not direct, but moderated by their respective effects on the incentives and barriers to exit. Bringing these factors together while taking incentives and barriers to exit into consideration, results in the framework shown in figure 2: the probability of exit depends on the relative strength of incentives versus barriers to exit – as expressed in (3) – which again vary across the various factors mentioned above.

It should be noted that at the level of the four main factors, the framework is, in fact, rather general and should be applicable to foreign and well as domestic exit. This should be regarded as a strength of the mod-

Figure 2. Divestment of foreign operations: A framework.

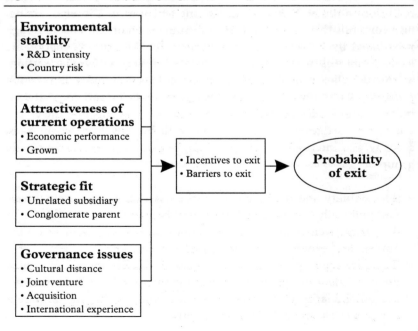

el. While the particularities of foreign operations will shape the actual content and importance of the various determinants of exit, the underlying logic of divestment should be independent of whether the context is foreign or domestic (Shapiro, 1983)[68]. The role of various factors is examined in more detail below.

3.3 Environmental stability

Boddewyn (1983b) contends that the economic underpinnings of divestment can be seen as the reversal of FDI. Analogous to deterioration of the performance of a domestic unit, the adequacy and profitability of FDI as an operation method might be eroded, *inter alia* as a result of changes in the environment of the operation. Taking Dunning's so-called »eclectic theory of international production« (see e.g. Dunning, 1980) as the starting point, Boddewyn argues that foreign divestment is likely to take place whenever any of the necessary conditions for FDI set out in Dunning's theory cease to be present. More specifically, foreign divestment is likely if, *i*) a firm loses its net competitive advantages over firms of other nationalities, i.e. the ownership advantage factor has been eroded, or *ii*) even if the firm retains net competitive advantages, it no longer finds it beneficial to use them itself, but rather selling or renting them to foreign firms, i.e. internalisation benefits are no longer present, and/or *iii*) the firm no longer finds it profitable to utilise its internalised net competitive advantage outside its home country since it is cheaper to serve foreign markets by exports and/or the home market by local production, i.e. foreign location ad-

---

68. Boddewyn (1983a) argues that there are three main differences between domestic and foreign divestments. First, performance appraisal may be less straightforward and more ambiguous in a foreign context making it more difficult to know both when to retain a unit and when to divest. Second, foreign barriers to exit are likely to be lower because *i*) most FDIs are relatively small when compared to their domestic counterparts, *ii*) alternative ways of serving a foreign market usually exist (importing, licensing, management contracts, etc.), *iii*) the emotional involvement in any given foreign subsidiary is normally lower than for domestic plants, and *iv*) divestment decisions are taken at headquarters located at a longer distance from the divestment candidate. Third, it may be easier to gain acceptance and justification for foreign divestments throughout the organization since divestment can be rationalized by motives, such as perceived political risk, that are difficult to verify, and because the »victims« are far away – both spatially and emotionally – hence making divestment more impersonal. Overall then, it appears that foreign divestment can be an easier course of action when compared with domestic divestment (this is supported by Pennings, Barkema and Douma (1994) in their study of Dutch companies).

vantages are no longer present (Boddewyn, 1983b, pp. 347-48). The latter point will be discussed in the next section. Of interest here is the erosion of ownership and internalisation advantages which result from changes in the competitive and political environment in which the company operates. Two factors in particular – R & D intensity, and country risk – are likely to have profound impact on the environmental stability of a foreign operation.

R & D intensity

Ownership advantages are largely due to investments in research and development, and marketing activities such as advertising. Such investments result in a number of rent-yielding assets possessed by the firms, including superior products and production processes, valuable brand names, and special managerial and marketing skills (Buckley and Casson, 1976). Markets for such assets are typically imperfect because of uncertainty problems and the public, information, and intangible good nature of the assets. Hence, instead of relying on market transactions in order to capture the rents inherent in the assets, firms by-pass imperfections in external markets by internalising those operations which employ such assets. FDI is then a special case of integration in general; the internalisation of markets across national boundaries results in FDI (Balasubramanyam, 1985). However, while research and development intensity, as predicted, in some studies has been found to encourage FDI (e.g. Grubaugh, 1987), investments in R & D are in many ways a »double edged sword«. On the one hand, perceived barriers to exit are likely to increase due to large sunk investments made in research, and in the development and marketing of new products. On the other hand, industries that are research and development intensive constitute at the same time rapidly changing competitive environments (Audretsch, 1994). Advantages gained at any point in time may disappear fairly rapidly (Shapiro, 1983). Moreover, further investments in R & D undertaken in order to retain a competitive edge may, due to the high risks involved in R & D projects, in fact increase the risk of subsequent failure. Somewhat paradoxically, strategic action to promote survival exposes the firm to considerable – and inescapable – risks (Hannan and Freeman, 1984); »jumping off« the technology and product development race is not a viable alternative for firms in rapidly changing, technology intensive, industries. That would probably terminate their presence in such industries even faster.

Country risk

One major difference when compared to domestic operations is that in a foreign context the competitive ability of a firm is to a very large extent dependent on actions and events that lie beyond its scope of control, in particular the behaviour of given host countries with regard to economic policy, discriminatory government action, and other adverse changes in the regulatory environment. In general, FDIs face higher risk due to potential abrupt changes in the economic, social, and political conditions of a host country. One may, of course, argue that country risk or political risk is primarily a matter of concern *ex ante*, i.e. when the foreign investor is scanning various potential locations for making a FDI, but before an actual commitment to a particular site has been made. Clearly, FDIs are less likely to be made in countries with high political risk than in countries considered as »safe« (Agarwal, 1980): in order to attract FDI »risky« countries ought, but are often unable, to offer a firm the opportunity to obtain a higher return. However, although *ex ante* considerations certainly are important, FDIs are nevertheless frequently made in countries with moderate, and even high, political risk.

Country risk may operate as a determinant of divestment in several ways. First, and most obviously, political risk can become manifest in the sense that adverse host country action, for example expropriation, actually takes place. Although negotiations between the firm and the host country government may occasionally lead to a continuance of operations, usually the firm faces a *fait accompli* where the firm is basically left with no alternative other than to divest. Second, in addition to leading to forced divestment, political risk may even influence deliberate and voluntary divestment. That may happen if the political risk of a host country changes in a negative direction, which in turn affects the perceived benefit of continuing a given foreign venture. Finally, would the situation arise that a company wants to exit from a country, country risk may heighten the barriers to exit because a sale of the affiliate is likely to attract few buyers – even at a low price.

3.4 Attractiveness of current operations

Economic performance of the foreign unit

A foreign subsidiary's ability to produce a net contribution to the profits of a multinational company provides a strong impetus to the decision of whether it should be retained or divested. Unsatisfactory performance is probably the most obvious reason why particular units are sold off or shut down (or, in some cases, declared bankrupt). However, while good performance provides a rationale for keeping a unit, it might also lower the perceived barriers to exit because owners may see an opportunity to obtain a good price for the unit while it is performing well. Recent research indicates that the units most likely to be sold off are those with high productivity. After all, potential acquirers generally look for businesses doing well rather than those performing poorly.

Economic growth in the host country
Another attractiveness factor pertains to the more general economic conditions of a particular location. According to the »eclectic theory« of international production, a host country needs to have specific location advantages that lead firms to invest in that country rather than in another country or produce at home and export. There are various types of location advantages. First, trade barriers and transport costs, which increase the costs of exporting from a home base, give rise to country or location specific advantages that favor FDI (Culem, 1988). Second, and conversely, barriers to factor movements and factor usage, such as controls on repatriation of profits, local content requirements, and restrictions on ownership, shift the relative profitability of market servicing modes in favor of exports. Finally, as shown in many studies, countries enjoying favorable economic conditions are in general more attractive to inward FDI. In particular, findings from survey research (Majundar, 1980) as well as econometric studies (Kravis and Lipsey, 1982; Meredith, 1984; Culem, 1988; Veugelers, 1990) suggest that market size and market growth have an important impact on international investment location decisions. Along these lines, one may expect that the ability of a host country to remain attractive for FDI is dependent on the growth of its economy[69]. Thus, given that the initial investments were

69. The last decade has witnessed a development toward both fewer trade restrictions and fewer impediments to FDI, which in turn has resulted in a noticeable growth in trade as well as FDI. However, fewer restrictions on FDI, while clearly beneficial to new FDI, does not necessarily affect the existing stock of FDI in a host country. Hence this factor is of little relevance here. On the other hand, trade liberalization should, in theory, lead to a greater propensity to divest. Nevertheless, since the most significant developments toward freer trade have taken place at a global level (GATT/WTO), any increasing tendency to divest operations motivated by liberalization of trade is probably fairly uniformly distributed across countries. Thus, although an upward trend of divestment can be expected, it seems difficult to make any well-grounded predictions on which operations that are most likely to be divested.

undertaken on the basis of a given market size, which at that point in time was considered as sufficiently attractive for FDI, further growth would, ceteris paribus, make a given site even more attractive[70]. Moreover, since host countries compete with each other for FDI, in order to retain FDI a host country must attain growth rates that are considered to be sufficiently high compared to other potential locations. However, the attractiveness of operations located in high growth countries is not judged solely by the current owners but by other investors as well, which, in turn, would make such operations more likely targets for take-overs. Conversely, it may be difficult to dispose of units located in low growth countries, hence increasing the barriers to exit from such countries.

3.5 Governance issues

Another important difference between domestic and foreign ventures is that foreign operations take place in cultures which, to varying degrees, are lesser known. Internationalising companies have to learn about and adjust to foreign cultures, and are more likely to fail whenever the required acculturation is more demanding (Barkema *et al.*, 1996). The literature points out that the extent to which acculturation is needed, and to what extent problems associated with acculturation are likely to arise, depends principally on cultural distance, the mode of operation, and the experience of the company.

Cultural distance
Although any outward movement from the home country probably entails some degree of moving into lesser known territory, such movements vary considerably; from entering a neighboring country to entering a culturally highly dissimilar country located far away. Cultural similarity between the home and the host country should facilitate the implementation of the decision to establish a subsidiary abroad, since important components of the FDI package, such as the transfer of technology and managerial competence, are made easier when the countries in question are not too dissimilar (Kedia and Bhagat, 1988). Moreover, closeness between the countries may, due to easier monitoring and coordination of production and marketing activities in the various locations, alleviate problems at the later operative stages. As a consequence,

70. Note that the opposite may apply for cost motivated FDIs.

the incidence of problems that may in turn motivate the dissolution of a venture is likely to be higher when a FDI is made in culturally distant countries. A related line of reasoning focuses on the relation between distance and barriers to exit. Boddewyn (1983a) argues that barriers to exit are lower in a foreign than in a domestic context because decision makers at company headquarters are both physically and emotionally more detached from the units being considered for divestment. Hence, if perceived barriers to exit are dependent on distance, one might expect that this would hold true for foreign ventures as well. Exit barriers should then be lower for remote foreign units than for units located in neighboring and/ culturally close countries.

Operation method
Foreign entries often involve a joint venture with a foreign partner or the acquisition of an already existing operation in the host country. In such cases at least two different corporate cultures have to be integrated to ensure success (Buckley and Casson, 1988). Processes of integration are often subject to numerous problems even in a purely domestic context. Whenever a joint venture is set up with a foreign partner or a foreign firm is acquired, both national and corporate cultures have an impact on the venture (Barkema *et al.*, 1996). While one important reason for teaming-up with a foreign partner may certainly be to reduce barriers to entry into that country (for example by giving rapid access to knowledge about local markets, see for example Hennart, 1988), at the same time the problems associated with the integration process are compounded. In particular, the potential problems of reconciling institutionalised organisational practices, such as decision-making procedures and corporate policies, will be larger and arise more often as the combined effects of different national and organisational cultures have to be overcome (Nahavandi and Malekzadeh, 1988; Olie, 1990; Barkema *et al.*, 1996). It may therefore not be surprising that international joint ventures often are unstable or rated as unsuccessful by the partners involved (Harrigan, 1988; Kogut, 1988). Chowdhury (1992) finds that international joint ventures are more unstable than wholly-owned subsidiaries in terms of major reorganisations of ownership, but comparable to wholly-owned subsidiaries in terms of exit rates and longevity. Finally, Li (1995) and Barkema *et al.* (1996) report that ventures involving »double layered acculturation« – that is, acquisitions as well as joint ventures – experience lower longevity than wholly-owned greenfield investments.

An additional problem is that managerial attachment takes time to build, which puts joint ventures and acquisitions in a difficult situation in the often critical initial phases of the integration process. A lack of commitment from many in the parent company may even endure – especially among managers who for various reasons were against the acquisition or joint venture project. In contrast, internal start-ups are often vigorously defended – even when less successful – by managers reluctant to divest what they have themselves created (Li, 1995).

Experience
Problems related to lack of knowledge about foreign sites, cultural distance, and the integration process itself, are not necessarily constant. As firms expand abroad they acquire knowledge about foreign markets, about how to run manufacturing operations abroad, and about how to deal with partners that do not share the same cultural background (Welch and Luostarinen, 1988). For example, the study of Barkema *et al.* (1996) suggests that prior experience in the same foreign country is a successful path of learning in the case of joint ventures and acquisitions. Furthermore, they report that the general foreign experience level of a firm, measured as the number of prior FDIs undertaken by the same firm regardless of their location, as well as prior experience from countries that are culturally fairly similar (i.e. belong to the same »cultural block«) provide positive learning effects in the sense that the longevity of ventures is improved. As pointed out by Björkman (1990), this can be interpreted as a process of experiential learning – firms learn from experience which aspects of their environment to focus on, how to operate in that environment, and how to search for solutions to problems that emerge – that becomes institutionalised in the organisation in the form of various norms, operational routines, and decision-making procedures.

Experience can improve the longevity of foreign ventures in several ways. First, experienced firms are probably better market and partner »scanners« than novices in the international arena. More accurate evaluations of potential sites and cooperation partners for a FDI should, in turn, reduce the risk for subsequent divestment. Second, as experience is accumulated it becomes easier to avoid many of the problems involved in running foreign subsidiaries, and to find workable solutions if problems should arise after all. Finally, international operations take place in environments that are often subject to what might be regarded as dramatic changes; for example, sudden changes in exchange rates and prices. The interpretation of such events and how to respond to them can vary greatly depending on how experienced the decision-makers are. An event that from the viewpoint of an inexperienced firm is perceived as being quite extraordinary, may be interpreted by an experienced firm as being normal fluctuation which therefore raises few concerns, or as being a problem that can be solved if appropriate action is taken. Thus, higher experience levels may result in a more tolerant approach to deviations from the expected – which can be regarded as an increase in the barriers to exit – or even lead to adjustments of what is seen as a satisfactory rate of return – which would lower the incentives to exit.

3.6 Strategic fit

As pointed out in much of the literature, diversification frequently seems to lead to divestment. At the level of given expansion projects it appears that, in particular, diversification into unrelated industries is at risk (see for example Pennings *et al.*, 1994). Various explanations have been suggested such as that economies of scale and scope are rarely achieved by unrelated moves (Lecraw, 1984), that they expose the firm to an unfamiliar context thereby increasing the probability of making mistakes (Pennings *et al.*, 1994), that it is difficult to build the inter-firm linkages that are needed in order to successfully compete over time in many industries (Pennings *et al.*, 1994), and that unrelated expansion increases the governance cost of a company without necessarily contributing to lower production costs or higher returns (Reve, 1990).

Another line of reasoning focuses on the company level arguing that diversification by itself increases the propensity to divest. For example, Wright and Thompson (1987) maintain that, due to lack of emotional attachment, perceived barriers to exit are lower in diversified companies than in single-industry companies. Moreover, Caves and Porter (1976) suggest that diversified companies may demand a higher rate of return than that accepted by single-industry companies. The main reason is that the flexibility enjoyed by diversified companies can be used to rapidly reallocate resources. Thus, if a given venture fails to achieve the target rate of return, it may be sold-off quickly and the cash reinvested in other projects. Single-industry companies, on the other hand, often face substantial exit barriers due to sunk costs in specific assets, which in turn may lead to the acceptance of low returns – or even negative results – over prolonged periods of time.

3.7 Effects on the probability of exit

The discussion so far has mostly been confined to the likely effects of a number of factors concerning the incentives and barriers to exit. However, what is of main interest is how these effects in combination, in turn influence the probability of exit from foreign operations. Based on the simple analytical considerations presented in section 3.1., the likely impact of each of the individual factors discussed in the preceding sections on the decision to retain or divest a unit, has been summarised in table 1.

Table 1. Expected impact on the probability of divestment of foreign operations.

Factors	Incentives to exit	Barriers to exit	Impact on probability of foreign divestment[*)]
Stability			
R&D intensity	Higher	Higher	No clear prediction (depends on I_{exit} / B_{exit})
Country risk	Higher	Higher	No clear prediction (depends on I_{exit} / B_{exit})
Attractiveness			
Performance	Lower	Lower	No clear prediction (depends on I_{exit} / B_{exit})
Growth	Lower	Lower	No clear prediction (depends on I_{exit} / B_{exit})
Governance issues			
Cultural distance	Higher	Lower	Positive
Joint venture	Higher	Lower	Positive
Acquisition	Higher	Lower	Positive
Experience	Lower	Higher	Negative
Strategic fit			
Unrelated affiliate	Higher	Lower	Positive
Conglomerate parent	Higher	Lower	Positive

Notes:
[*)] »positive«: increased probability
»negative«: decreased probability

Although the suggested framework captures the essential findings in previous studies, it should be noted that factors other than those discussed above may also have an impact on whether foreign ventures are divested – and they should therefore be included as control variables in future empirical studies.

First, size of the parent company may have an impact. Several studies show that size of the parent company correlates with the propensity to undertake FDIs (Grubaugh, 1987), with whether FDIs made are greenfield investments or acquisitions (Kogut and Singh, 1988), and with the ownership structure of foreign affiliates (Gatignon and Anderson, 1988). However, the effect of size on exit is not clear-cut. For example, one may argue that large firms have more resources in terms of managerial capacity, financial resources, etc., and therefore have a greater capacity to sustain less successful ventures. On the other hand, large firms are usually more diversified than small firms, they often have a larger number of foreign affiliates, and the relative size (i.e. as a fraction of the total size of a company) of given foreign units tends to decrease. In contrast to a small multinational with only a few subsidiaries, a large multinational company may therefore be much less dependent on any single foreign operation. Consequently, barriers to exit may be lower for large firms than for small firms rather than the opposite. Thus, while Pennings *et al.* (1994) find that size of the parent company increases the longevity of ventures, Li (1995), reports mixed results across industries.

Another potentially important control variable is the age of the subsidiary. As pointed out by population ecologists, organisational mortality rates tend to decrease with age (Hannan and Freeman, 1984). The »liability of newness« factor (Stinchcombe, 1965) has both organisational and market aspects. On the market side, the period of time from start-up to profitability is often considerable for new ventures. They are therefore occasionally prematurely terminated by impatient investors. Moreover, since new operations are often perceived as riskier than operations that have »proved themselves« in the market place, they may face difficulties in getting access to – or having to pay a higher price for – the resources that are needed for survival. On the organisational side, external and internal legitimacy increases with age. Over time, organisations tend to develop dense webs of exchange, to develop close relationships with centers of power and, in general, to acquire an aura of inevitability (Hannan and Freeman, 1984, p. 158). Dissolution is hence made more difficult. On the other hand, »old« subsidiaries are more likely than newly established subsidiaries to use less efficient technology, and to produce and market products that are in the mature and declining phases of the product life cycle. This provides a rationale for divesting »old« subsidiaries that may override even significant age-dependent barriers to exit (Harrigan, 1980).

4. Some Final Remarks

Although there are clear indications that the magnitude of foreign divestment that takes place is quite considerable, the question of what might influence whether foreign subsidiaries are divested or not has until recently been left largely unexplored, both theoretically and empirically. This chapter has attempted to shed some light on this subject by presenting a conceptual framework which may serve as the starting point for future empirical studies. Based on industrial organisation reasoning, the framework suggests that the probability of actually exiting from an operation should be seen as the outcome of an interplay between two countervailing forces; incentives to exit and barriers to exit. However, many of the factors suggested as determinants of exit have been taken from the literature on strategy and international business.

There are several avenues for future research. First, empirical research is needed to assess the validity of the various propositions embedded in the framework. Second, there is scope for theoretical refinements. The discussion has basically depended on *ceteris paribus* assumptions, and more attention should be given to possible interrelationships between the various factors. Furthermore, potentially important factors may have been overlooked. Third, in order to gain more knowledge about how and why divestments are made, more attention should be given to the perceptions of the actual decision-makers. After all, such decisions are taken on the basis of the perceptions, motives, and opinions held by owners and higher-rank managers. In-depth case studies would be particularly valuable in order to investigate in more detail how such decisions are made, and the role of divestments in corporate strategy.

References

Agarwal, J. P. 1980. »Determinants of Foreign Direct Investment: A Survey«, *Weltwirtschaftliches Archiv*, Vol. 116, 739-73.

Akhter, S. H. and Y. A. Choudhry, 1993. »Forced Withdrawal from a Country Market: Managing Political Risk«, *Business Horizons*, Vol. 36, 47-54.

Audretsch, D. B. 1994. »Business Survival and the Decision to Exit«, *Journal of The Economics of Business*, Vol. 1, 125-37.

Audretsch, D. B. and T. Mahmood, 1994. »The Rate of Hazard Confronting New Firms and Plants in U.S. Manufacturing«, *Review of Industrial Organization*, Vol. 9, 41-56.

Balasubramanyam, V. N. 1985. »Foreign Direct Investment and the International Transfer of Technology«, in D. Greeneway, ed. *Current Issues in International Trade: Theory and Policy*, Macmillan, London, 159-81.

Bane, W. T. and F.-F. Neubauer, 1981. »Diversification and the Failure of New Activities«, *Strategic Management Journal*, Vol. 2, 219-33.

Barkema, H. G., Bell, J. and J. M. Pennings, 1996. »Foreign Entry, Cultural Barriers, and Learning«, *Strategic Management Journal*, Vol. 17, 151-66.

Björkman, I. 1990. »Foreign Direct Investments: An Organizational Learning Perspective«, *Finnish Journal of Business Economics*, Vol. 39, 271-94.

Blodgett, L. L. 1992. »Factors in the Instability of International Joint Ventures: An Event History Analysis«, *Strategic Management Journal*, Vol. 13, 475-81.

Boddewyn, J. J. 1979. »Foreign Divestment: Magnitude and Factors«, *Journal of International Business Studies*, Vol. 10, 21-27.

Boddewyn, J. J. 1983a. »Foreign and Domestic Divestment and Investment Decisions: Like or Unlike?«, *Journal of International Business Studies*, Vol. 14, 23-35.

Boddewyn, J. J. 1983b. »Foreign Direct Divestment Theory: Is It the Reverse of FDI Theory?«, *Weltwirtschaftliches Archiv*, Vol. 119, 345-55.

Buckley, P. J. and M. Casson, 1976. *The Future of The Multinational Enterprise*. Macmillan, London.

Buckley, P. J. and M. Casson, 1988. »A Theory of Cooperation in International Business«, in F. Contractor and P. Lorange, eds. *Cooperative Strategies in International Business.* Lexington Books, Lexington, 31-55.

Cantwell, J. 1991. »A Survey of Theories of International Production«, in C. N. Pitelis and R. Sugden, eds. *The Nature of The Transnational Firm.* Routledge, London, 16-63.

Caves, R. E. and M. E. Porter, 1976. »Barriers to Exit«, in R. Masson and P. D. Qualls, eds. *Essays in Industrial Organization in Honor of Joe S. Bain.* Ballinger, Cambridge, 36-69.

Chow, Y. K. and R. T. Hamilton, 1993. »Corporate Divestment: An Overview«, *Journal of Managerial Psychology*, Vol. 8, 9-13.

Chowdhury, J. 1992. »Performance of International Joint Ventures and Wholly Owned Foreign Subsidiaries: A Comparative Perspective«, *Management International Review*, Vol. 32, 115-33.

Culem, C. G. 1988. »The Locational Determinants of Direct Investments among Industrialized Countries«, *European Economic Review*, Vol. 32, 885-904.

Cyert, R. M. and J. G. March, 1963. *A Behavioral Theory of the Firm.* Prentice-Hall, Englewood Cliffs.

Doz, Y. L. and C. K. Prahalad, 1987. »A Process Model of Strategic Redirection in Large Complex Firms: The Case of Multinational Corporations«, in A. Pettigrew, ed. *The Management of Strategic Change.* Basil Blackwell, London, 64-83.

Duhaime, I. M. and J. H. Grant, 1984. »Factors Influencing Divestment Decision-Making: Evidence from a Field Study«, *Strategic Management Journal*, Vol. 5, 301-18.

Dunning, J. H. 1980. »Toward an Eclectic Theory of International Production«, *Journal of International Business Studies*, Vol. 11, 9-31.

Eaton, B. C. and R. G. Lipsey, 1980. »Exit Barriers Are Entry Barriers: The Durability of Capital as a Barrier to Entry«, *Bell Journal of Economics*, Vol. 12, 721-29.

Fatemi, A. 1984. »Shareholder Benefits from Corporate International Diversification«, *Journal of Finance*, Vol. 39, 1325-44.

Gatignon, H. and E. Anderson, 1988. »The Multinational Corporation's Degree of Control over Foreign Subsidiaries: An Empirical Test of a Transaction Cost Explanation«, *Journal of Law, Economics, and Organization*, Vol. 4, 305-36.

Grubaugh, S. G. 1987. »Determinants of Foreign Direct Investment«, *Review of Economics and Statistics*, Vol. 69, 149-52.

Häkkinen, T. 1994. *Divestments of Foreign Subsidiaries of Finnish Manufacturing Companies*. CIBR Research Report Series X-3, Helsinki School of Economics and Business Administration, Helsinki.

Hamilton, R. T. and Y. K. Chow, 1993. »Why Managers Divest: Evidence from New Zealand's Largest Companies«, *Strategic Management Journal*, Vol. 14, 479-84.

Hannan, M. T. and J. Freeman, 1984. »Structural Inertia and Organizational Change«, *American Sociological Review*, Vol. 49, 149-64.

Harrigan, K. R. 1980. *Strategies For Declining Businesses*, Lexington Books, Lexington.

Harrigan, K. R. 1988. »Strategic Alliances and Partner Asymmetries«, in F. Contractor and P. Lorange, eds. *Cooperative Strategies in International Business*. Lexington Books, Lexington, 205-26.

Hennart, J.-F. 1988. »A Transaction Cost Theory of Equity Joint Ventures«, *Strategic Management Journal*, Vol. 9, 361-74.

Kedia, B. L. and R. S. Bhagat, 1988. »Cultural Constraints on Transfers of Technology across Nations: Implications for Research in International Comparative Management«, *Academy of Management Review*, Vol. 13, 559-71.

Kobrin, S. J. 1980. »Foreign Enterprise and Forced Divestment in LDCs«, *International Organization*, Vol. 34, 65-88.

Kogut, B. 1988. »Joint Ventures: Theoretical and Empirical Perspectives«, *Strategic Management Journal*, Vol. 9, 319-32.

Kogut, B. and H. Singh, 1988. »The Effect of National Culture on the Choice of Entry Mode«, *Journal of International Business Studies*, Vol. 19, 411-32.

Kravis, I. B. and R. E. Lipsey, 1982. »The Location of Overseas Production and Production for Export by U.S. Multinational Firms«, *Journal of International Economics*, Vol. 12, 201-23.

Lecraw, D. J. 1984. »Diversification Strategy and Performance«, *Journal of Industrial Economics*, Vol. 33, 179-98.

Li, J. 1995. »Foreign Entry and Survival: Effects of Strategic Choices on Performance in International Markets«, *Strategic Management Journal*, Vol. 16, 333-51.

Majundar, B. A. 1980. »A Case Study of The Industrial Organization Theory of Direct Foreign Investment« *Weltwirtschaftliches Archiv*, Vol. 116, 353-64.

Mcguckin, R. H. and S. V. Nguyen, 1995. »On Productivity and Plant Ownership Change: New Evidence from the Longitudinal Research Database«, *Rand Journal of Economics*, Vol. 26, 257-76.

Meredith, L. 1984. »U.S. Multinational Investment in Canadian Manufacturing Industries«, *Review of Economics and Statistics*, Vol. 66, 111-19.

Morck, R., Shleifer, A. and R. N. Vishny, 1990. »Do Managerial Objectives Drive Bad Acquisitions?«, *Journal of Finance*, Vol. 45, 31-48.

Nahavandi, A. and A. R. Malekzadeh, 1988. »Acculturation in Mergers and Acquisitions«, *Academy of Management Review*, Vol. 13, 79-90.

Olie, R. 1990. »Culture and Integration Problems in International Mergers and Acquisitions«, *European Management Journal*, Vol. 8, 206-15.

Padmanabhan, P. 1993. »The Impact of European Divestment Announcements on Shareholder Wealth: Evidence From the U.K.«, *Journal of Multinational Financial Management*, Vol. 2, 185-208.

Pennings, J., Barkema, H. and S. Douma, 1994. »Organizational Learning and Diversification«, *Academy of Management Journal*, Vol. 37, 608-40.

Reve, T. 1990. »The Firm as a Nexus of Internal and External Contracts«, in M. Aoki, B. Gustafsson and O. E. Williamson, eds. *The Firm as a Nexus of Treaties*. Sage Publications, London, 133-61.

Rumelt, R. 1974. *Strategy, Structure and Economic Performance*. Harvard University Press, Cambridge.

Siegfried, J. J. and L. B. Evans, 1994. »Empirical Studies of Entry and Exit: A Survey of the Evidence«, *Review of Industrial Organization*, Vol. 9, 121-55.

Shapiro, D. 1983. »Entry, Exit, and the Theory of the Multinational Corporation«, in C. P. Kindleberger and D. B. Audretsch, eds. *The Multinational Corporation in the 1980s*. MIT Press, Cambridge, 103-22.

Shapiro, D. and R. S. Khemani, 1987. »The Determinants of Entry and Exit Reconsidered«, *International Journal of Industrial Organization*, Vol. 5, 15-26.

Staw, B. M. 1981. »The Escalation of Commitment to a Course of Action«, *Academy of Management Review*, Vol. 6, 577-87.

Stinchcombe, A. S. (1965) Social Structure and Organizations, in J. G. March, ed. *Handbook of Organizations.* Rand Mcnally, Chicago (Reprinted in Stinchcombe, A. L. (1986) *Stratification and Organization: Selected Papers.* Cambridge University Press/Norwegian University Press, Cambridge/Oslo, 196-220).

Veugelers, R. 1990. »Locational Determinants and Rankings of Host Countries: An Empirical Assessment«, *KYKLOS,* Vol. 44, 363-82.

Welch, L. S. and R. Luostarinen, 1988. »Internationalization: Evolution of a Concept«, *Journal of General Management,* Vol. 14, 34-55.

Weston, J. F. 1989. »Divestitures: Mistakes or Learning?«, *Journal of Applied Corporate Finance,* Vol. 2, 68-76.

Williamson, O. E. 1985. *The Economic Institutions of Capitalism,* The Free Press, New York.

Wright, W. and S. Thompson, 1987. »Divestment and The Control of Divisionalised Firms«, *Accounting and Business Research,* Vol. 17, 259-67.

Part III

Managing the
International Firm

14. Towards Explaining Human Resource Management Practices in International Joint Ventures – The Case of Chinese-Western Joint Ventures[71]

Ingmar Björkman

1. Introduction

Joint ventures (JVs) have become an important element in many companies' international operations. In spite of an impressive amount of research on JVs with at least one foreign parent organisation, few efforts have been made at explaining the Human Resource Management (HRM) practices that are found in such ventures. In the present chapter both the HRM practices -such as appointments, performance appraisal, reward systems, training and development, and dismissal and retention- found at a specific point of time and how they change over time are of interest.[72] We are also interested in both commonly found features of joint venture practices and the variance within the total population. The aim of the chapter is to evaluate what different perspectives within organisation theory may contribute to explanatory research on the HRM practices that are found in international joint ventures, and to suggest a framework for future research. By doing so the chapter aims at responding to recent calls for an integration of organisation theory and the operations of multinational corporations (Ghoshal and Westney, 1993).

71. The first version of this chapter was written during a visit at ESSEC, Paris, and I would like to thank ESSEC and in particular everybody in the Department of Strategy and Management for their support. I would also like to thank Mats Forsgren, Cynthia Hardy, and Bo-Magnus Salenius for their comments on earlier drafts.
72. Rather than analyzing *how* certain practices are implemented and perceived, the chapter analyzes *what* kind of practices are found in international JVs. Thus, the chapter deals predominantly with the choice of HRM practices.

The chapter will analyse the following perspectives within organisation theory: institutionalisation theory (DiMaggio and Powell, 1983; Scott, 1987), resource dependence (Pfeffer and Salancik, 1978), an efficiency-based perspective drawing on theories such as the transaction cost perspective (Williamson, 1985), political process models (e.g. Boddewyn and Brewer, 1994), and organisational learning (Levitt and March, 1988).[73] Each of the theoretical perspectives differ considerably in their approach towards analysing the focal empirical questions. They are based on different assumptions, tend to use different levels of analysis, focus on somewhat different issues, and differ in the methodologies that are likely to be utilised in empirical research. The perspectives will be discussed in terms of the following dimensions: Which assumptions are the perspectives based on? At which level of analysis are the perspectives utilised? How are processual issues dealt with? Which hypotheses can be developed concerning HRM practices in international joint ventures?

The case of Chinese-Western JVs is used for the purpose of illustration. Recent years have seen a dramatic increase in the number of equity JVs in China. Although a number of studies have recently analysed the HRM practices in Chinese domestic organisations (e.g. Warner, 1993; Child, 1994; 1995; Easterby-Smith, Malina, and Lu, 1995; Brown and Branine, 1995) and the overall management practices in Chinese-Western JVs (e.g. Child, 1991; Child and Markóczy, 1993; Björkman, 1994), somewhat less attention has been paid to HRM practices in Chinese-Western JVs (for a few exceptions, see Child et al, 1990; Child and Markóczy, 1993; Björkman and Schaap, 1994a). The focus here is on HRM practices related to the domestic employees in the JVs.

The chapter attempts to analyse the potential contribution of each of the theoretical perspectives to research on HRM practices in Chinese-Western joint ventures. Data from a study on 33 Chinese-Western joint ventures as well as previously published research is used in a very preliminary evaluation of the perspectives. An analytical evaluation of the potential usefulness of the perspectives is also undertaken. The chapter

---

73. The need for MNC adaptation to local conditions has often been seen to stem from cross-cultural differences in norms and values (see e.g. Schneider, 1986; Lachmann, Nedd, and Hinings, 1994). The work of Hofstede (1980; 1991) has often been used in this respect. In the present chapter, cultural factors are discussed in conjunction with, among others, the institutionalization, the efficiency, and the organizational learning perspectives.

is structured as follows: first, the HRM practices that have been found in the present and earlier studies on Chinese-Western JVs are briefly described. The subsequent section outlines theoretical perspectives within organisation theory, whereafter each of the perspectives are evaluated. The chapter ends with a suggested framework for future research.

2. HRM Activities in Chinese-Western Joint Ventures

The findings presented in this chapter are from the author's research on Chinese-western joint ventures (see Björkman, 1994; 1995; Björkman and Schaap, 1994a; 1994b) as well as from other studies on this phenomenon, in particular research carried out by John Child and his associates (Child et al, 1990; Child, 1991; Child and Marcóczy, 1993; Child, 1994; see also Warner, 1993; Sharma and Wallström-Pan, Ch. 14). The focal study consisted of semi-structured interviews carried out with 40 expatriate and six Chinese managers in 33 Chinese-western joint ventures. In most cases, the top foreign manager was interviewed. Interviews lasted between one and four hours, often preceded or followed by an informal meal, during which the discussion typically centred round the management of the joint venture. Most interviews were tape recorded. With the exception of four service producing companies, the joint ventures were undertaking manufacturing operations. They were located in Beijing, Tianjin, and Shanghai, and Liaoning, Jiangsu, Shaanxi, Fujian, and Guangdong provinces. Data gathering was conducted in 1992. During the interviews, respondents were asked, among other things, to describe how different HRM issues related to the Chinese employees were handled in their company. Recruitment, training and development, assessment and reward systems, and dismissal and retention were among the topics that were discussed. The respondents were asked to describe practice and how it had changed over time in their JV. It should be noted that data was not elicited with the intention to evaluate the explanatory power of different organisation theories.

HRM practices typically differed considerably from those in the foreign parent organisations. Many of the joint ventures were under pressure from the Chinese authorities and the Chinese partner to take on an overly large number of employees, and many Western respondents viewed it as a problem that the Chinese managers tended to suggest predominately relatives or other people with which they had personal relationships (*guanxi*) for positions within the company (regardless of whether the candidates had the necessary qualifications). The JVs were restricted in their hiring and firing decisions, and were in some instances under pressure to employ relatives or associates of government officials (see also Casati, 1991; Greene, 1991). Also concerning the choice of persons for training and development, *guanxi* seemed an important element. Many experienced difficulties in obtaining an approval to introduce »western« incentive and assessment systems, and several of those who had introduced such systems were complaining about the implementation problems and about the fact that they did not seem to be efficient. Similar results have been reported in other studies (see Child and Markóczy, 1993; Sharma and Wallström-Pan, Ch. 14).

The HRM practices described above were found in many joint ventures, but there were nevertheless considerable differences within the sample, for instance in terms of training and development practices. There were also changes taking place over time. We will later present additional data on the HRM practices that have been observed in Chinese-Western JVs.

The next section describes different perspectives within organisation theory. Our intention is to discuss how each perspective may be used to analyse HRM practices in a sample of international JVs. The subsequent part of the chapter will then consist of a preliminary evaluation of the ability of different perspectives to account for the findings on Chinese-Western JVs.

3. A Brief Description of the Theoretical Perspectives

3.1 The institutionalisation perspective

The institutionalisation perspective takes as its point of departure that organisations are under pressure to adapt and be consistent with their institutional environment. They are assumed to search for legitimacy and recognition, and they do so by adopting structures and practices defined as appropriate in their environment. In other words, organisations are expected to gradually resemble other organisations in the same environment. By doing so they increase their likelihood of external recognition, and therefore survival.

DiMaggio and Powell (1983) suggest that there are three major ways in which isomorphism is produced: coercive isomorphism, where a powerful constituency (typically the government) imposes certain patterns on the organisation; mimetic isomorphism, where organisations in situations of uncertainty adopt the pattern exhibited by »successful« organisations in their environment; and normative isomorphism, where professional organisations act as the dissiminators of appropriate organisational patterns which then are adopted by organisations which are under the influence of the professional organisations. More recently, additional isomorpic processes have been identified (Scott, 1987); these can be categorised into those which focus on the role of external institutional agencies in the environment, and those which emphasise the processes whereby those within organisations come to take certain externally validated patterns for granted and value them as ends in themselves (Westney, 1993: 55-56). This review will focus on the external institutions and the institutional pressure they exert on the focal organisation.

Institutional theorists have usually assumed a rather passive adaptation on the part of organisations to their institutional environments (DiMaggio, 1988), though some writers do suggest that organisational decision makers may consciously try to increase the legitimacy of their organisation by adhering -at least on the surface- to institutionalised patterns (Meyer and Rowan, 1977; Oliver, 1991). The level of analysis within the institutional perspective is the organisational field, i.e. »those organisations« that, in the aggregate, constitute a recognised area of institutional life« (DiMaggio and Powell, 1983: 148). Much research within the institutionalisation perspective has focused on the outcomes of institutionalisation processes, typically the way in which a certain organisational pattern has been spread within an organisational field.

Turning to the question of HRM practices in an international joint ventures, it should probably be seen as being under institutional influence from both parent organisations and from the local environment (Rosenzweig and Singh, 1991; Arias and Guillen, 1992; Westney, 1993; Rosenzweig and Nohria, 1994). The institutionalisation perspective draws our intention to the coersive, mimetic, and normative forces that influence organisational practices. Both the local environment and the foreign owner[74] may exert coersive pressure on the joint venture, that is,

---

74. For reasons of simplification it is assumed throughout the chapter that joint ventures have one foreign and one domestic owner. In reality they relatively often have more than two owners. However, in most cases there is one principal foreign and one principal local parent organization.

the venture will be under formal or informal pressure to adopt certain practices.

Several mimetic processes may influence the practices of joint ventures. First, expatriate managers bring with them taken-for-granted views of the kind of HRM practices that are efficient. Being uncertain about the kind of practices that are efficient in the joint venture, they may attempt to introduce these practices also in the new environment (Brooke and Remmers, 1970; Bartlett and Ghoshal, 1989). The taken-for-granted views may, in turn, have its roots in e.g. corporate and/or home country cultures (Westney, 1993). Secondly, MNC units may mimic the organisational patterns exhibited by foreign companies in their local environment. Many Western managers interact socially with other expatriates, and such interaction can provide the vehicle for a diffusion of »rationalised myths« (Meyer and Rowan, 1977) concerning appropriate practices. Thirdly, companies may mimic domestic Chinese companies. Rooted in their own past, the Chinese employees have taken-for-granted views about management practices which may influence the patterns that they would suggest for, and actually enact in joint ventures.

In addition to coersive and mimetic isomorphic processes, it is also possible that normative processes may be of some importance. For instance, consultance firms and professional associations such as the US-China Business Council may spread certain notions about appropriate management policies in China.

Based on the discussion above, the following hypotheses are forwarded:

i)   *joint ventures with the same foreign parent organisation are likely to exhibit similar HRM practices (as the result of coersive and/or mimetic pressure from the foreign parent organisation)*

ii) *joint ventures with foreign parent organisations from different home countries will tend to differ in their HRM practices in China (as the result of coersive and/or mimetic pressure from the foreign parent organisation)*

iii) *the closer the joint ventures are in terms in geographical location and business operations, the more likely joint ventures are to exhibit similar HRM practices to those of other companies (as the result of coersive pressure from the Chinese government and/or parent organisation, or mimetic pressure from the Chinese parent organisation)*

iv) *the greater perceived uncertainty concerning what constitutes appropri-*

ate HRM practices, the more likely joint ventures will be to adopt the practices of joint ventures seen as successful (as the result of mimetic processes)

v)   compared with joint ventures established as greenfield operations, joint ventures which have been established based on existing operations will have HRM practices that more closely resemble those of local companies than those of the Western partner (as the result of coersive and/or mimetic pressure from the local parent organisation)

vi)   joint ventures whose top executives are members of the same professional organisation and/or are employing the same consultants will be more likely to exhibit similar HRM practices than other joint ventures (as the result of normative processes)

3.2 The resource dependence perspective

At the core of the resource dependence perspective (Pfeffer and Salancik, 1978) is the assumption that actors have conflicting interests. In the context of joint ventures it can, for instance, be presumed that the Chinese and foreign owners have at least partly conflicting objectives and that certain HRM practices can help a partner fulfill its objectives. As argued by Geringer and Frayne (1990), by controlling HRM issues such as staffing, training, and compensation systems a partner organisation may attain more of its objectives than the other partner. The joint venture (and its owners) may also have objectives which differ from those of Chinese government organisations.

Another assumption of the resource dependence perspective is that the outcome of conflicts are determined by the relative power that each party possesses. This power, in turn, is determined by the extent to which the actor controls resources which are of high value to the other actor. The actual process whereby power is utilised in political processes is not of interest, neither is the question of how the actors perceive power relations. It is rather assumed that the possession of power (typically as measured by some structural measure such as the number of board members or possession of a valuable resource) is sufficient to produce a certain outcome, thus:

i)   the stronger the relative power of one of the actors, the greater the likelihood that the joint venture will adopt HRM practices preferred by this actor

3.3 An economic efficiency perspective

Probably the most common assumption in management studies is that organisations tend to adopt the practices which are efficient from an economic point of view. In Whitley's terms:

> »While economic rationalists may accept that firms are complex social organisations whose constitution and activities reflect the conceptions and values of owners and/or their agents as well as employees, they consider competitive pressures to be so strong that efficient forms of business organisation and »rational« strategic choices quickly dominate all market economies whatever cultural and institutional variations may exist between them. Thus differences between owners' and managers' beliefs and preferences are essentially irrelevant to economic outcomes in this view because all competing firms are constrained to follow the logic of efficient market processes.« (Whitley, 1992: 121)

Calculated rationality is seen as the basis for management. The subsidiary and/or the MNC as a whole is commonly the level of analysis. The assumptions made within this perspective render the process irrelevant, and therefore the actual practices constituted the sole interest of the researcher. Transaction cost theory (Williamson, 1985) is a typical example of theories which are based on this assumption. Using this line of reasoning to the question of management practices, it is assumed that joint ventures will use the most efficient practices. For example, if a joint venture has extensive transactions with other parts of the foreign parent organisation in terms of e.g. shipments of components and entire products, service, marketing and sales assistance, there may be transaction cost advantages in standardising some HRM practices across units. Consequently, it is expected that high transaction levels will be correlated with standardisation of policies also within local subsidiaries.[75] Similarly, if scale or scope advantages can be obtained in e.g. production or marketing, MNCs will tend to standardise (and/or integrate) these activities on an international basis (see e.g. Porter, 1986). Other contin-

---

75. To the extent that joint ventures are of great importance to the parent organization, standardization of practices may also be viewed as one way for parent organizations to control their foreign units.

gencies may also influence the degree of adaptation. For example, characteristics of the subsidiary's operations may render certain management practices more efficient. For example, research on Japanese subsidiaries in the US found a fit between technology type and HRM practices (Kujawa, 1983).

In addition to MNC and joint venture characteristics, differences between the parent country and the host country environment can also be included in efficiency-based analyses. The greater the difference, because the costs of transfer will be higher and the efficiency of the practices will be lower, the lower probability that MNCs will transfer parent company practices to the local unit. It may for instance be hypothesised that the lower the cultural distance is between the parent organisation and the overseas setting, the more likely MNCs are to implement parent company practices in their subsidiaries (see e.g. Beechler and Yang, 1994; Lachmann, Nedd, and Hinings, 1994). Below are some examples of hypotheses that may be investigated in empirical research:

i)   *the higher levels of transactions with the parent organisations, the more likely joint ventures are to adopt the HRM practices of their parents*[76]

ii) *the more different the operational characteristics of the joint ventures, the more likely they are to differ in terms of HRM practices*

iii) *the lower the cultural distance is between the parent organisation and the overseas setting, the more likely the MNCs are to transfer HRM practices to their overseas units*

3.4 The political process perspective

One of the basic assumptions of the political process perspective is similar to that made within the resource dependency perspective, namely that actors have conflicting interests. The main difference between the perspectives is that the process perspective assumes that the outcome of conflicting interest is not pre-determined by some measure of the power held by the actors involved (although power is not without importance), but rather that the political actions undertaken by the actors may influence the outcome. The sequence of events is thus of utmost importance. Actors may also invest in developing their political competence in terms

---

76. It should be noted that a similar hypothesis can be developed within institutionalization theory.

of, among others, intelligence, access to decision makers, and bargaining skills (Boddewyn and Brewer, 1994).

A number of actors can be imagined within the context of joint ventures: one vs. the other parent organisation; the joint venture and/or one or both parent organisations vs. different Chinese constituencies (at individual, group, local, regional, and central levels, all of which may have different and partly contradictory objectives); the joint venture vs. the parent organisations; and two (groups of) top executives within the joint venture. Based on the political perspective we will expect actors to engage in active political behaviour when faced by action alternatives that are not congruent with their objectives. For instance, the foreign parent organisation may decide not to give in to Chinese pressure concerning HRM practices in the joint venture but rather to engage in political strategies such as compromise, avoidance, defiance, and manipulation of the parties from which they are under pressure (see Oliver, 1991). Such behaviour may take place through joint venture employees, but may also include collaboration with other joint ventures, MNCs, and possibly even with the home government of the MNC. Although it is difficult to develop general propositions within this perspective, the following propositions are probably consistent with most of the literature:

i) *actors will be more likely to engage in political action in situations where the outcome of the political process is uncertain, in situations which are not seen as zero-sum but rather as positive sum situations, and when the actors have developed political competence (cf. Boddewyn and Brewer, 1994)*

ii) *the higher the perceived gains to be attained from political action, the higher the likelihood that actors will engage in political actions (cf. Boddewyn and Brewer, 1994)*

iii) *the higher the political competency of the actors, the more likely they are to achieve their objectives through political action*

3.5 The organisational learning perspective

The basic tenet of organisational learning as interpreted in this chapter is that organisational actions are history-dependent. The organisational learning perspective is thus different from some other theoretical perspectives for analysing organisational patterns:

»Theories of organisational learning can be distinguished from theories of analysis and choice which emphasise anticipatory calculation and intention... from theories of conflict and bargaining which emphasise strategic action, power, and exchange... and from theories of variation and selection which emphasise differential birth and survival rates of invariant forms.«
(Levitt and March, 1988: 319)

Learning can be analysed both in terms of cognition and behaviour. There is presumably a relatively close linkage between the beliefs that people have, and the actions they take (although people may be more or less conscious about the beliefs that they hold). Changes in cognition tend to precede behavioural changes, though members may be taught a certain behaviour without necessarily learning the rationale behind the behaviour. It has also been suggested that particularly in situations seen as novel people may not have any strong beliefs about what action to take. After they have acted, however, beliefs consistent with their actions tend to develop (Weick, 1979), thus they »learn« that certain practices are appropriate. Subsequently they are likely to act accordingly.

People learn from their own experience, but experience is often a poor teacher. People are presumably resistant to change their beliefs concerning e.g. the appropriateness of a certain management practice. A search for new solutions tends to be triggered mainly when existing organisational routines have ceased to work, i.e. learning is often problem-driven (Cyert and March, 1963). However, aspiration levels tend to adjust to performance; a rapid drop in aspiration level may therefore substitute for a search for new superior solutions (March, 1988). Learning tends to take place in the neighborhood of the perceived problems. The simultaneous occurrence of possible solutions and perceived problems may also lead to the implementation of new practices (Cohen, March, and Olsen, 1972; Mintzberg, Raisinghani, and Theoret, 1976). In addition to experiential internal learning, the entrance of new members is an important way in which organisations learn. Organisations can also learn from the experience of other organisations, including joint venture partners, customers and users, and competitors. The distinction between mimetic and normative processes within the institutionalisation perspective, and organisational learning becomes increasingly blurred when it is also acknowledged that firms learn from other learning organisations.

Learning can be analysed at different levels, e.g. at the individual, group, and organisational levels of analysis. The distinction between these levels is often somewhat unclear. The learning of key individuals is frequently used as a proxy for organisational learning, in spite of the problems that obviously exist in transferring what has been learnt within organisations. It is often assumed that individuals and organisations differ in their learning capabilities. The research interest within the learning perspective covers both the process of learning and its outcome. Within organisational studies, scholars working within the learning perspective have typically used case studies. Most commonly it is economic efficiency that has been analysed in terms of learning, but it may also be used to analyse learning concerning organisational legitimacy and power.

Organisation theory scholars working within the learning perspective have relatively seldom formulated general propositions and have rather analysed learning as it occurs in different organisational settings. We will therefore refrain from presenting any propositions or hypotheses.

4. A Preliminary Evaluation of the Perspectives

4.1 The institutionalisation perspective

The institutionalisation perspective draws our attention to some isomorphic forces that seem to influence how joint ventures are managed. There were obviously coersive pressures from the Chinese authorities and owners on joint venture decision makers. The ventures had to conform with many formal and informal rules and regulations, some of which were public, some not (so called *neibu* regulations). The Chinese managers in particular felt this pressure, and it seemed quite clear that they felt a fear of punishment if not adhering to signals from the Chinese authorities and owners (see Child and Markóczy, 1993; Björkman, 1994.) The overall coersive pressure on joint ventures had been reduced in the final period preceding the point of data gathering in mid-1992. There were considerable regional differences. Government organisations in the southern and coastal regions seemed to exert less pressure. The general autonomy granted to the JV by the Chinese parent organisation appears to be an important determinant of the coersive pressure.

There were also indications that some foreign managers were under pressure from their parent organisations to introduce Western HRM practices and systems in the joint venture. In particular joint ventures

with North American parent organisations seemed likely to try to introduce »US« management practices in their ventures (Child et al [1990]
report similar findings). This seems to be at least party an outcome of
parent organisation expectations in this direction, although some uncer-
tainty-induced mimetic processes may also have been at play. Future research on, among others, joint ventures with the same foreign parent organisation would shed additional light on this issue. It seems that at least
some local mimicing behaviour took place. Most Western managers in-
teracted socially with other expatriates, and some respondents referred
to networks of foreigner managers where business issues were discussed.
Nevertheless, few interviewees actually admitted that they had copied
practices from other organisations. It is plausible that much of this influence was unconscious, that is, foreign managers may actually have
believed that they themselves had developed new ideas concerning management practices when in fact the ideas stemmed from discussions with
managers in other (successful) foreign investment companies.

It was quite evident that the joint venture practices were strongly influenced by the functioning of domestic Chinese companies. Rooted in
their own past, the Chinese employees had taken-for-granted views
about management practices. It would, in fact, be surprising if this
would not have influenced the patterns that they suggested for, and actually enacted in JVs. As with the Western managers, there may have
been mimetic processes among the Chinese employees working in JVs.
A well-functioning intra-industry grape-vine existed in China, and Chinese employees were well informed about the practices in other companies. It should also be noted that many domestic employees apparently
felt great uncertainty concerning what constituted appropriate HRM
practices. Several Chinese managers were reluctant to change practices
which during earlier periods had been endorsed by Chinese constituencies. Unfortunately, no data was available neither to verify nor to dismiss
this possibility that there were mimetic processes taking place within this
social field. Neither does the fact that there was no clear indication of
normative institutionalisation necessarily mean that it has not occurred.

In summary, significant support for the existence of institutionalisation processes was found in the present and in earlier studies (see Child
and Markóczy, 1993), but more research on the institutionalisation perspective is clearly warranted.

Although the institutionalisation did obtain empirical support, some
limitations of the institutionalisation perspective need to be mentioned.

First, the perspective de-emphasises agency. There is ample evidence that large organisations are able to influence the institutions in their environment (Oliver, 1991), both through purposeful political activies and through the fact that other organisations mimic their actions and structures. For instance, a large JV located in an inland province used considerable political actions to get a government approval for using »job fairs« to attract new people to the company. Subsequent to the successful recruitment fair, the government endorsed the idea. The action of the part of the JV thus led to the institutionalisation of a new practice within the province. The institutionalisation perspective also de-emphasises agency and change processes within the organisation. The JV managers were under several institutional pressures, several of which were contradictory. The typical situation was that the Chinese and foreign managers experienced different and contradictory expectations. In order to analyse how such conflicting pressures are handled within the JV itself we need to draw on other theoretical perspectives, such as resource dependence or the political process perspective.

Secondly, the perspective does not necessarily explain why *certain* HRM practices begin to be seen as appropriate, and why certain practices become de-institutionalised. Thirdly, defining the appropriate boundaries of an organisational field is a major methodological problem. An organisational field is characterised by a recognition that the actors share a similar set of activities. Interviews with decision makers have sometimes been carried out to ascertain which elements of the institutional environment they are most sensitive to (e.g. Gupta, Dirsmith, and Fogarty, 1994), but this obviously requires extensive field work. The definition of organisational fields is particularly difficult in Chinese-Western JVs due to the multitude of potential sources of institutionalisation.

4.2 Resource dependence

By focusing on the sources of power, the resource dependence perspective seems to provide some insight into how conflicts between the parents concerning appropriate HRM practices were solved. It did make a difference if the foreign partner had a majority position in the JV, in particular if the Western partner had explicitly been given management responsibility. However, the resource dependence perspective fails to show how power is mobilised, i.e. process aspects are not dealt with.

Neither are political activies paid attention to. In reality, there was considerable political activity ongoing in the joint ventures and it did in a significant way influence the outcome of conflicts. For instance, in most ventures Western managers needed to obtain the support of either JV managers or Chinese parent company executives to carry out changes within the organisation. To the extent that they managed to rally such support they were able to implement these changes, otherwise not.

One possible limitation of the applicability of this perspective is that it assumes that the parties really have certain objectives. This may of course not be the case for all aspects of JV operations. For example, a few Chinese investors seemed to be pre-dominately interested in the profitability of the JV, not how it was achieved through certain management practices. Furthermore, the dependency relationships may be far from self-evident. For example, many Chinese employees in the coastal areas seemed to be uncertain whether they, in terms of their future career, were more dependent on their Western superiors or the Chinese parent organisation. To the extent that employees changed their perceptions, this reportedly had significant effects on their behaviour. In-depth analyses, preferably real-time longitudinal work would shed additional light on such processes.

4.3 Efficency-based explanations

In the present sample there were some, although relatively few clear indications that efficiency-based variables would explain variances in management practices. For instance, there was no indication that the amout of transactions with the parent organisations had influenced HRM practices. However, as no quantitative data on transactions was, based on an ex post judgement it is difficult to evaluate whether this factor may have influenced JV practices.

On the other hand, there was some data congruent with that expected within an efficiency perspective. There was some indication that the kind of operations undertaken by the joint venture has led to differences in management practices. Companies whose operations were characterised by clear work methods and output standards for the production process were more likely to have bonus systems based on quantitative measures of individual productivity. Additionally, joint ventures operating in locations where the values and norms had become more »Westernized« (i.e. in the coastal regions) seemed more likely to have more »Western« management practices.

It must be noted, however, that especially the latter finding can be interpreted within several theoretical perspectives. In fact, the interviews indicate that it was perhaps more institutional and political rather than efficiency reasons why joint ventures along the coast of China were more likely to exhibit »Western« management practices (cf. the discussion in the section on the institutionalisation perspective). A limitation of the efficiency perspective is that it does not pay attention to the processes leading up to changes in practices. Thereby, the data is open for a number of alternative interpretations. The perspective also ignores the question of whether practices are approved by the parent organisations or government constituencies because of political/institutional reasons. Finally, the calculated rationality assumption made within the efficiency perspective has been criticised in the organisation literature, and this criticism will not be repeated here.

4.4 The political process perspective

In many of the joint ventures there were political processes congruent with those expected within the political process perspective. Thus, over all, actors seemed more likely to engage in political action in situations where the outcome of the political process was uncertain, when the actors had developed political competence, and when the stakes were high. In the present sample, there were several examples of politically adroit Western managers who managed despite some resistance to implement changes. Different strategies were used. In some companies Western executives had developed a good working relationship either with the top Chinese manager in the joint venture or with the Chinese chairman of the board. These relationships were drawn upon to investigate up-front the possibilities for certain changes, and to work behind the scene on obtaining support for changes favored by the expatriate. How to sell the ideas was seen as crucial, especially in joint ventures where the foreign company did not have management control. Some Western managers suggested that it was better not to present a fully fledged proposal, but rather to point out how some other companies handled similar issues, perhaps even suggesting overseas visits to look into the issue. Eventually the Chinese might present change suggestions which (hopefully) were in line with those favored by the Western managers. This procedure would also give the Chinese manager 'face'. Conversely, there were several examples of Western managers who apparently had not learnt how to handle the political processes well (see also Björkman, 1994)

Some of the limitations of the political process perspective are similar to those discussed in the section on the resource dependence perspective. First, the aims of the parties are not (necessarily) problematised. In other words, why do for instance the foreign partner want to introduce certain HRM practices in the joint ventures or the Chinese owner oppose these practices? Furthermore, it assumes that both parties really have an agenda that they want to pursue. Secondly, the perspective is better suited to real time and ex post analyses of political processes and their outcome than to predicting a priori the actors who take part in political processes, the strategies they use, not to speak of the outcome of political processes. Thus, some researchers may hold it against this perspective that it is difficult to predict the management practices that the JV will eventually end up with.

4.5 The organisational learning perspective

It was evident in most interviews with joint venture managers that some kind of learning constantly took place within the ventures. When attempting to introduce Western management practices, Western managers learnt appropriate political strategies to pursue in order to get the practices implemented (cf. the previous section). They also went through a learning process concerning how to actually make policies work subsequent to approvals from the Chinese top managers or parent organisation. For instance, several Western managers had noted great difficulties in introducing individual performance appraisals. A common problem had been that the Chinese superiors tended to give virtually everybody the same bonus, seemingly because of considerations related to personal relationships (*guanxi*) and 'face'. The Western managers had tried several ways to induce the Chinese employees to increase the differences, e.g. by forcing the appraisor to divide people into high, medium, and low performers, and by refusing to accepts the appraisals unless the differences were sufficiently great. In some companies, the Western managers had started to take the formal responsibility for the appraisal, thus relieving the Chinese employees of some of the negative aspects of appraising their fellow employees.

The learning perspective has been criticised for being content-free, i.e. the object of learning remains unspecified. As pointed out by Doz and Prahaled (1993) learning may differ depending on what is being learnt (which is also one of the inherent problems in developing general propositions within this perspective). The multitude of historical factors that influence learning makes it very difficult to obtain generalisable results. Thus the perspective may be used to explain why some outcome has occurred, even though it would have been difficult to foresee, prior to the fact, the particular chain of events that lead to organisational learning. It may be highly unlikely that an identical sequence of events may occur in the future.

5. A Suggested Framework for Processual Analysis

One of the starting point of this chapter was that an appropriate theoretical framework should enable us to explain the HRM practices found at a specific point of time as well as their change over time. The latter of these issues has so far not received the attention that it arguably deserves. In particular, little effort has been made to understand how sequences of incidents and actions at different levels of analysis influence the practices that can be observed in individual organisations. Consequently, the framework for future research which is suggested here builds mainly on the theoretical perspectives within organisation theory which have an interest in process issues.

The suggested framework draws on the institutionalisation, political process, and the learning perspective. It is suggested that research should pay attention to three levels of analysis: organisational fields, the joint venture as a whole, and the individual and groups of managers in the joint venture. The focus is on the two latter levels of analysis. Attention should be paid to the way in which the higher level of analysis sets constraints on the activities taking place at lower levels, and how activities at lower levels may influence structures at higher levels (cf. Aldrich, 1992: 30). In a similar vein, different processes may take place at different levels and a crucial source of change may be the changes taking place at other levels (Pettigrew, 1992).

It is assumed that the joint ventures are under, in particular, coercive institutional pressure from the parent organisations and from Chinese government organisations. The local institutional pressures are likely to change over time as a result of general societal changes but also because of the actions taken by, among others, foreign investment enterprises refusing to conform to the isomorphic processes in the organisational field. JVs may also collaborate to change through political actions the institutional demands placed upon them. The institutional environment is likely to differ in different locations within the country in question, a fact which should be born in mind in empirical analyses. Mimetic and normative processes may also be identified within the organisational field.

At the organisational level of analysis it is presumed that legitimacy (including efficiency) are important aims of the JV as a whole, and that political actions may be used to deal with the external demands placed on the joint venture. External political actions are particularly likely when there is consensus among the JV top managers that there is a conflict between institutional demands and other aims of the organisation.

JVs are expected to learn over time which practices are the most efficient ones and how to spread such practices within the organisation. The practices are over time likely to become institutionalised within the organisation in the form or informal and formal routines. JVs are also expected to learn over time how to engage successfully in externally oriented political activities.

Empirically, data is needed on the perceived coersive institutionalisation pressures from the parent organisations and from local government organisations, its content and how it differs from practices seen to contribute to other goals (such as efficiency) within the JV. Data is also needed on the perceived consequences of non-compliance. In order to investigate mimetic processes, in depth interviews with top managers are necessary. Such interviews may reveal the extent to which the top management group perceives uncertainty concerning the »right« HRM practices, and therefore mimic other organisations. These organisations can be both other units within the Chinese or foreign parent organisation, and other foreign investment companies.

At the third level of analysis, individuals and groups of individuals are seen to be driven primarily by the aim of increasing their personal legitimacy. Thus, employees are likely to suggest and enact HRM practices thought to be legitimate in the eyes fo those whom they see as their most important superiors. Their view of the person(s) who constitutes the most important superior may change over time as may the extent to which managers feel that they are under the scrutiny of their superiors.

To the extent that employees have different notions of appropriate HRM practices, political processes tend to follow. Politically adroit employees are more likely than to produce changes in HRM practices than are employees who are not politically competent. Individuals are likely to learn, albeit imperfectly, political skills over time.

Organisation members are also expected to learn over time, although imperfectly, which HRM practices are the most efficient ones. Management changes within JVs may influence learning as it provides a vehicle for de-learning old practices, and for introducing new views about appropriate practices. To the extent that new knowledge is internalised by other managers within the organisation, this learning may produce changes at the JV level of analysis. Empirically data is needed on the perceptions that managers have of the success/failure of the management practices within the organisation and on the circumstances that may have compelled organisational members to critically evaluate the effectiveness of their HRM practices.

The framework outlined above appears to be consistent with existing limited data on HRM practices in Chinese-Western joint ventures. There are however a of number specific issues within this framework that have not been addressed in previous research. Among others, the following questions could be posed in future research:

– joint venture and individual managers' learning concerning the political strategies used to handle demands from parent organisations (cf. Lyles and Reger, 1993) and government organisations (cf. Boddewyn and Brewer, 1994)
– learning concerning what constitutes efficient HRM practices in joint ventures which differ considerably in their operational characteristics and in their geographical locations
– individual employee strategies to handle conflicting views concerning appropriate practices: can certain patterns be found in terms of e.g. structural characteristics of the joint venture or the personal characteristics of the employees?
– the extent to which mimetic vs. coercive processes are at play in the institutional pressure on Chinese and foreign managers

A final comments should be made concerning the research strategy used in future studies. Thus far studies have either consisted of broad surveys or cross-sectional interviews with managers. There is an urgent need for in depth longitudinal research and comparative analysis of some strategically selected cases. It is in fact a pre-requisite for the kind of processual research that has been suggested in this section (see also Pettigrew, 1992; Van de Ven, 1992). Nonetheless, surveys may obviously be used as an important complement.

6. Conclusions

The principal aim of this chapter has been to discuss to what extent different perspectives within organisation theory may contribute to research on HRM practices in international joint ventures. The chapter has discussed institutionalisation theory, resource dependence, an efficiency-based perspective to organisational analysis, a political process perspective, and an organisational learning perspective. The perspectives were evaluated analytically, and in light of the findings in research on HRM practices in Chinese-Western JVs. In this preliminary evaluation of the perspectives all were found to have at least some potential explanatory power. An important conclusion is therefore that future work on both Chinese-Western joint ventures and international joint ventures in general may benefit from using an eclectic theoretical framwork. We are finally calling for longitudinal research on the emergence of HRM practices in international joint ventures. A framework for such research has been presented earlier in this chapter.

References

Aldrich, H.E., 1992. »Incommensurable paradigms? Vital signs from three perspectives«, in M. Reed and M. Hughes, (eds.). *Rethinking organization: New directions in organization theory and analysis.* Sage, London.

Arias, M.E. and M.F. Guillen, 1992. *The transfer of organizational management techniques across borders: Combining neo-institutional and comparative perspectives.* INSEAD, Fontainebleau. Working chapter No. 92/41/OB.

Bartlett, C.A. and S. Ghoshal, 1989. *Managing across borders: The transnational solution.* Harvard University Press, Cambridge, MA.

Beechler, S. and J.Z. Yang, 1994. »The transfer of Japanese-style management to American subsidiaries: Contingencies, constraints, and competencies«, *Journal of International Business Studies,* Vol. 25, 467-492.

Björkman, I., 1994. »Role perception and behavior among Chinese managers in Sino-Western joint ventures«, in S. Stewart, (ed.). *Advances in Chinese Industrial Studies.* JAI Press, Greenwich, Conn.

Björkman, I., 1995. »The board of directors in Sino-Western joint ventures«, *Corporate Governance,* Vol. 3, 156-166.

Björkman, I. and A. Schaap, 1994a. »Human resource management practices in Sino-Western joint ventures«, *The Finnish Journal of Business Economics,* Vol. 43, 111-125.

Björkman, I. and A. Schaap, 1994b. »Outsiders in the Middle Kingdom: Expatriate managers in Sino-Western joint ventures«, *European Management Journal,* Vol. 12, No. 2, 147-153.

Boddewyn, J.J. and T.L. Brewer, 1994: »International-business political behavior: New theoretical directions«, *Academy of Management Review,* Vol. 19, 119-143.

Brewster, C., 1993. »The paradox of adjustment: UK and Swedish expatriates in Sweden and the UK«, *Human Resource Management Journal,* Vol. 4, 49-62.

Brooke, M.Z. and H.L. Remmers, 1970. *The strategy of multinational enterprise.* Elsevier, New York.

Brown, D.H. & M. Branine, 1995. »Managing people in China's foreign trade corporations: some evidence of change«, *International Journal of Human Resource Management,* Vol. 6, 159-175.

Casati, C., 1991. »Satisfying labor laws – and needs«, *China Business Review*, July-August, 16-22.

Child, J., 1991. »A foreign perspective on the management of people in China«, *International Journal of Human Resource Management*, Vol. 2, 93-107.

Child, J., M. Boisot, J. Ireland, Z. Li and J. Watts, 1990. *The management of equity joint ventures in China.* China-Europe Management Institute, Beijing.

Child, J. and L. Markóczy, 1993. »Host-country managerial behaviour and learning in Chinese and Hungarian joint ventures«, *Journal of Management Studies*, Vol. 30, 611-631.

Child, J., 1994. *Management in China during the age of reform.* Cambridge University Press, Cambridge.

Child, J., 1995. »Changes in the structure and prediction of earnings in Chinese state enterprises during the economic reform.« *International Journal of Human Resource Management*, Vol. 6, 1-30.

Cohen, M., J.G. March, and J.P. Olsen, 1972. »A garbage-can model of organizational choice«, *Administrative Science Quarterly*, Vol. 17, 1-15.

Cyert, R. and J.G. March, 1963. *A behavioral theory of the firm.* Prentice-Hall. Englewood Cliffs, NJ.

DiMaggio, P.J., 1988. »Interest and agency in institutional theory«, in L.G. Zucker, (ed.). *Institutional patterns and organizations: Culture and environment.* Ballinger, Cambridge, MA.

DiMaggio, P.J. and W.W. Powell, 1983. »The iron cage revisited: institutional isomorphism and collective rationality in organizational fields«, *American Sociological Review*, Vol. 48, 147-160.

Doz, Y. and C.K. Prahaled, 1993. »Managing DMNCs: A search for a new paradigm«, in S. Ghoshal and D.E. Westney. (eds.). *Organization Theory and the Multinational Corporation.* St. Martin's Press, New York.

Easterby-Smith, M., D. Malina, and Y. Lu, 1995. »How culture-sensitive is HRM? A comparative analysis of practice in Chinese and UK companies«, *International Journal of Human Resource Management*, Vol. 6, 31-59.

Geringer, J.M. and C.A. Frayne, 1990. »Human resource management and international joint venture control: a parent company perspective«, *Management International Review.* Special Issue, 103-120.

Ghoshal, S. and D.E. Westney, 1993. »Introduction and overview«, in S. Ghoshal and D.E. Westney, (eds.). *Organization Theory and the Multinational Corporation*. St. Martin's Press, New York.

Greene, J.L., 1991. »FIEs face new labor obstacles«, *The China Business Review*, January-February, 8-12.

Gupta, P.P., M.W. Dirsmith, and T.J. Fogarthy, 1994. »Coordination and control in a government agency: Contingency and institutional perspectives on GAO audits«, *Administrative Science Quarterly*, Vol. 39, 264-285.

Hofstede, G., 1980. *Culture's consequences: International differences in work related values.* Sage, Beverly Hills.

Hofstede, G., 1991. *Cultures and organizations.* McGraw-Hill, London.

Kujawa, D., 1983. »Technology strategy and industrial relations: Case studies of Japanese multinationals in the United States«, *Journal of International Busienss Studies*, Vol. 14. No. 3, 9-22.

Lachman, R., A. Nedd, and B. Hinings, 1994. »Analyzing cross-national management and organizations: A theoretical framework«, *Management Science*, Vol. 40, 40-55.

Levitt, B. and J.G. March, 1988. »Organizational learning«, in, *Annual Review of Sociology.* Vol. 14.

Lyles, M.A. and R.K. Reger, 1993. »Managing for autonomy in joint ventures: A longitudinal study of upward influence«, *Journal of Management Studies*, Vol. 30, 383-404.

March, J.G., 1988. *Decisions and organizations.* Basil Blackwell, Oxford.

March, J.G. and J.P. Olsen, 1976. *Ambiguity and Choice in Organizations.* Universitetsforlaget, Oslo.

Meyer, J.W. and B. Rowan, 1977. »Institutionalized organizations: formal structure as myth and ceremony«, *American Journal of Sociology*, Vol. 83, 340-360.

Mintzberg, H., D. Raisinghani, and A. Theoret, 1976. »The structure of »unstructured« decision processes«, *Administrative Science Quarterly*, Vol. 21, 246-275.

Newman, W.H., 1992. »»Focused joint ventures« in transforming economies«, *Academy of Management Executive*, Vol. 6, No. 1, 67-75.

Oliver, C., 1991. »Strategic responses to institutional processes«, *Academy of Management Review*, Vol. 16, 145-179.

Pettigrew, A.M., 1992. »The character and significance of strategy process research«, *Strategic Management Journal*, Vol. 13, Winter Special Issue, 5-16.

Pfeffer, J. and G.R. Salancik, 1978. *The external control of organizations: A resource dependence perspective.* Harper & Row, New York.

Porter, M., 1986. *Competition in global industries.* Harvard Business School Press, Boston, MA.

Rosenzweig, P.M. and N. Nohria, 1994. »Influences on human resource management practices in Multinational Corporations«, *Journal of International Business Studies.* Vol. 25, 229-251.

Rosenzweig, P.M. and J.V. Singh, 1991. »Organizational environments and the multinational enterprise«, *Academy of Management Review,* Vol. 16, 340-361.

Schneider, S., 1986. »National vs. corporate culture: Implications for human resource management«, *Human Resource Management,* Vol. 27, 133-148.

Scott, W.R., 1987. »The adolescence of institutional theory«, *Administrative Science Quarterly,* Vol. 32, 493-511.

Sharma, D.D. and C. Wallström-Pan: »Internal Management in Sino-Swedish Joint Ventures«, in I. Björkman and M. Forsgren, (eds.). *The Nature of the International Firm – A Nordic Perspective on International Business Research.* Copenhagen Business School Press.

Shenkar, O. and M.A. von Glinow, 1994. »Paradoxes of organizational theory and research: Using the case of China to illustrate national contingency«, *Management Science,* Vol. 40, 56-71.

Van de Ven, A.H., 1992. »Suggestions for stuyding strategy process: A resarch note«, *Strategic Management Journal,* Vol. 13, 169-188.

Warner, M., 1993. »Human resource management 'with Chinese characteristics'«, *International Journal of Human Resource Management,* Vol. 4, 45-65.

Weick, K.E., 1979. *The social psychology of organizing.* Addison-Wesley, Reading, MA.

Westney, D.E., 1993. »Institutionalization theory and the multinational corporation«, in S. Ghoshal and D.E. Westney, (eds.). *Organization Theory and the Multinational Corporation.* St. Martin's Press, New York.

Whitley, R., 1992. »The social construction of organizations and markets: The comparative analysis of business recipes«, in M. Reed and M. Hughes, (eds.). *Rethinking organization: New directions in organization theory and analysis.* Sage, London.

Williamson, O.E., 1985. *The economic institution of capitalism.* Free Press, New York.

15. Internal Management of Sino-Swedish Joint Ventures

D. Deo Sharma and Carolina Wallström-Pan

1. Background

Joint Ventures (JVs) are an increasingly common feature in international business (Contractor, 1990). In the previous years a number of transnational corporations (TNCs) have established JVs in China. Some JVs work well, others face difficulties. A number of questions are relevant; how are internal affairs in these JVs managed? What problems face these operations and for what reasons? The purpose of this study is to investigate and analyse the internal management process in Sino-Swedish JVs. We investigate what works and what does not work, and the causes of this. A secondary purpose is to examine the extent to which Swedish management practices are applicable in a very different society such as China. This chapter also elucidates the problems that expatriate managers face in their efforts to institute Western management practices in China. Our approach is that the problems facing Sino-Swedish JVs emanate from two main sources, (a) cultural factors – the traditional Chinese culture embedded in Confucianism and Taoism, and (b) structural factors – the legacies of the Maoist era's industrial governance systems, e. g., its evaluation and reporting systems. This view is very similar to the view expressed by Child and Markoczy (1993) and Hoon-Halbauer (1994). In a similar vein Milford (1995) writes, 'Emforcement of technology transfer laws should be matched to the Chinese experience......... For these reasons, it is important to examine both the history of Chinese culture and Chinese Communist perspectives regarding rights and laws as relating to individuals' (p. 80).

The importance of national culture in international management is well established (Hofstede, 1984; Jaeger and Kanungo, 1990). China is no exception (Garatt, 1981; Redding, 1990). During our interviews employees repeatedly stated that differences in the Swedish and the Chinese work cultures are causing tensions, misinterpretations and misunderstandings. Our interviews show that the logic's of the Maoist era industrial governance system is important in explaining the management processes in Sino-Swedish JVs. Therefore, understanding culture based differences as well as the Maoist era's industrial governance systems is important. Our analysis combines these aspects.

In the past researchers have paid some attention to JVs in China. Zamet and Bovarick (1986), Campbell (1988), Child (1991) and Davidson (1987) investigated the difficulties associated with managing JVs and human resources in China. They report that problems are related to the communist system of the country. Garatt (1981) elucidate the influence of the Mao era and Confucian culture in China. At a more general level previous studies on JVs have investigated such aspects as the theory of JVs (Beamish and Bank, 1987; Hennart, 1988), motives for forming JVs (Killing, 1983; Harrigan, 1985; Contractor, 1986; 1989), management and control of JVs (Beamish, 1984; Harrigan, 1986), and JV performance (Kogut, 1987). These studies are structural. An exception is the work by Hoon-Halbauer (1994) who emphasised the process aspects and studied the internal working of two JVs in China. We need more similar studies. Our study aims to fill part of this gap and will provide additional knowledge on the internal management of JVs in China in particular, but also JVs in general. By doing so we limit ourselves from issues such as the relationships between the owners in the JVs, and the influence of the parent companies on the JVs.

2. Model and Method

As stated earlier, internal management of Sino-Swedish JVs in China is problematic partly due to cultural factors and partly due to structural factors. The reason being that the Chinese culture or mental and psychological disposition of a Chinese differ from that of a Swede. Culture is defined and studied in many ways (Roberts, 1970; Adler, 1983; Dymsza and Negandhi, 1983). In this chapter, following Hofstede (1984 a), culture is defined as the collective mental programming of people. Culture refers to subjective and objective organisational culture (Buono and Bowditch, 1989). The former are the beliefs, expectations, and shared assumptions by which the participants in an organisation perceive norms, values and roles in the organisation. The mental framework of the members of an organisation and the leadership style constitute the subjective culture of an organisation. Objective culture is the artefacts developed by organisations, e. g., the location of a firm. We investigate the orientation and the assumptions held by the expatriate and local staff in the JVs, the leadership style, and concern for product and service quality. Since the subjective cultures of the Chinese and the expatriate staff in JVs are different, a clash of culture occurs. In international JVs clash of cultures occurs when (1) the degree of shared beliefs, values, and norms are low, (2) the shared beliefs, values, and norms are highly localised within the JVs, and (3) the shared beliefs, values, and norms lack a clear ordering (ibid., 1989).

The nature of the cultural in JVs can be identified along the dimensions of Power distance, Collectivism vs. individualism, Uncertainty avoidance (Hofstede, 1984), and Long-range vs. Short-range thinking (Bond, 1986).

2.1 Power distance

Societies differ in the distribution of power between individuals (Richman, 1965). Societies with a 'large power distance' accept centralisation and authoritarian leadership, hierarchy is strong and obedience is a virtue. Companies in such countries centralise the power to a few hands, subordinates are dependent, there are many levels of superiors, differences in financial rewards are large, and superiors enjoy privileges. The ideal manager is a benevolent autocrat. Visible symbols of status boost managerial power, and give subordinates a higher status compared to subordinates in other companies. In countries with a small power difference, power is distributed equally, the subordinates' dependence on their superiors is limited and consultation between manager and subordinate is preferred (Hofstede, 1983).

In Sweden the power distance is small. In China the power distance is large. This means different relations and reactions by subordinates toward their superiors in the two countries. The Chinese accept inequalities but feel that power should be moderated by obligations. This has an impact on how orders are carried out, the need for titles and other symbols of status and authority and the use of different managerial techniques. A large power distance, however, does not automatically imply that the upper levels in a company hierarchy have the effective power to issue orders to the workers and get them implemented (Hoon-Halbau-

er, 1994). The subordinates' power may be supported by external actors located in the environment that supply a higher level of legitimacy
(Parson, 1956). In the Chinese case such an external source of support
is the State through its communist ideology, and the Communist Party
(Party) through its power to participate in the functioning of commercial firms. The power of the State is supported by its control over the
credit system, banks, and the other scarce resources (Child, 1991).
These are scarce resources in China. Control over scarce resources is a
source of power (Pfeffer and Salancik, 1978). In China the influence of
power based on hierarchy is also reduced by, as will be discussed later,
guanxi or relationships. What meaning is given to rules is dependent on
the (lack of) connections enjoyed by a person. There exist a conviction
in China that people, not rules, ought to determine the actions of people
in society.

2.2 Collectivism vs. individualism

In an individualist country the relations between individuals are loose.
In a collectivist country the individual is integrated in strong, well knit-
together groups, which protect that person throughout his life in exchange for unconditional loyalty (Pye, 1985). China is a collective country with a fundamental Confucian assumption that man exists in relationship to others. As Milford (1995) notes, 'The concept of individual
rights is absent, both in ancient Chinese culture, and in modern day So-
cialism in PRC (p. 13). Similarly, (Pendleton,1993) states that in China,
'(A)dvocacy of Individual rights is anathema to community harmony –
'the nail that stands up must be hammered down' (p. 120).

Chinese believe that it is the state that grants rights to individuals.
These rights should be granted to those who are loyal and friendly to the
State. The disloyal should be deprived of these rights (Huang, 1990).
The Western starting point of the unique individual is alien to the Chinese (Bonds, 1986). In a collectivistic culture it is important to stay in
harmony with the social surroundings, a direct confrontation with another person is strange and unwanted. According to Hofstede (1984 a)
a 'no' is seldom used as that would create a confrontation. 'Yes', on the
other hand, is not always a consent either. In this kind of culture the individual adjusts to others, and few personal opinions are expressed.
Consultation is needed if there is no group opinion on a question. In individualist cultures it is a virtue to be frank and honest. Confrontation

is healthy. The individual is expected to, and encouraged to, develop his own ideas and opinions. Collectivism leads to 'social loafing' (Latane, Williams, and Harkins, 1979; Harkins and Petty, 1982; Woldon and Gargano, 1988).

Conflict avoidance is important in China. Chinese people first present the common problems and contextual constraints which are binding on all the participants, before stating their own position. To Westerners this is vague, but it helps the Chinese to avoid a polarisation of different positions, and helps to uphold harmony within the group. Shame is felt by the whole group when someone in a collectivistic culture does something wrong. Hiding faults is important to save 'face'. To lose face means to be humiliated. But it is also possible in the Chinese culture to 'give face' which means to honour and give prestige to someone. 'Face' describes the proper relation to people around an individual. The corresponding quality in an individualistic culture is 'self-respect' (Hofstede, 1984 a). In the individualist culture only the person who has done the misdeed feels guilt. The honour of the group is more important than the issue at hand in a collectivist culture. The individual's actual position on an issue is subordinated to his desire to protect the group's integrity by side-stepping open disagreement. Collectivists also achieve satisfaction and a feeling of achievement from group (Earley, 1989). The solution for the individual is to imitate the responses of other. The conformity of ideas and beliefs of the Chinese are therefore in many parts a false pretence. The Chinese themselves know when another Chinese is acting in this way and will themselves act accordingly. A foreigner will only with difficulty observe the false conformity and become angry because no one is prepared to speak their mind, or because 'promises' are not kept, and deals are not honoured.

Management in an individualist culture is management of individuals. It is possible to move individuals around, and financial rewards are distributed according to the individual's performance. Management in a collectivist society is management of groups. The Chinese prefer a leadership style in which the leader maintains a harmonious, considerate relationship with the followers, defines clear-cut tasks for each member of the group, and takes skilled and decisive action. The communication between superiors and subordinates is subtle in a collectivist culture. Criticism, for instance, are aired indirectly through middle hands. To be open and frank is considered insensitive. It is important first to arrange proper personal relations; the work to be done comes second. It is easy to become an 'outsider' person if one fails to act in accordance with the traits of the collectivist society. In individualist societies the task is more important than the individual (Hofstede, 1984b).

2.3 Uncertainty Avoidance

Uncertainty avoidance is the extent to which the members of a culture feel threatened by uncertain or unknown situations (Hofstede, 1984 a). This feeling can be expressed as stress or anxiety and a need for predictions. Chinese avoid uncertainty, they are more expressive, communicate with their hands and it is acceptable to show emotions. These societies are less achievement oriented (Weber, 1951). In the less anxious cultures aggression and emotions are not openly expressed, instead they are internalised. In this kind of society there is a lack of mental stimuli. In countries with little uncertainty avoidance people seem to be calm, easy-going, idly, restrained, and lazy (Hofstede, 1984 a).

The traits of a culture with high uncertainty avoidance fit China. They consume enormous amounts of tea, are easy-going and restrained and avoid embarrassment and loss of face. Chinese surround themselves with many formal rules. In China relations between employer and employee are regulated by written and unwritten rules. People in such societies feel comfortable in a structured environment, where as little as possible is left to chance. There is a fear of formal rules in countries with small uncertainty avoidance (Hofstede, 1984b). To solve problems without the need of formal rules gives people pride. The paradox is that in these countries with fewer rules, the rules are more adhered to than in countries with many rules. That rules and laws are primarily 'ritualistic' and the rule of who ever is in power is also evident from the fact that since 1948 China have adopted four radically different constitutions. These constitutions reflect the agenda of the rulers. For example, the 1954 constitution contained 19 articles on the rights of the individuals. The 1975 constitution 'reflected Mao's desire on a straight Socialist path' (Milford, 1995, p. 82) and had only four articles on individuals rights. In China law is the 'weapon of the dictatorship' (Ladany, 1991). Milford (1995) claims that 'Chinese culture has disdain for law' (p. 92). In the Chinese culture a higher value is placed on 'ritual and status above purposeful activity' (Pye, 1985, p. 61). Also, in societies with less uncertainty avoidance people don't feel a need always to be busy, as in countries with strong uncertainty avoidance. In the former type, people are more tolerant towards dissenting ideas.

2.4 Long-range vs. short-range thinking

China is a 'long-range thinking' society. The basic values of long-range thinking are endurance, the arranging of relations according to status, frugality, to feel a sense of shame, to protect one's face, respect for traditions, reciprocity with regards to greetings, privileges and gifts (Bond, 1986). In addition, Western thinking is analytic while the Chinese thinking is synthetic, that is, putting things together to form a whole. In China the analysis is more intuitive than in the West. Since this dimension is connected to future, in the discussion section we integrate this with the remaining dimensions.

2.5 Some traits of chinese and scandinavian management

In China Confucianism and Taoism have inculcated values of law and relationship building. The Chinese feel that law is the last resort socially and ethically inferior to other ways of solving disputes (Chew, 1994). These other means are heavenly reason, the way, morality, ritual property, and customs. Thus in China 'Public positive law was meant to buttress, rather than supersede, the more desirable means to guide society' (Alford, 1995, p. 10). Furthermore, law is 'one of the countless methods of governing, which could be used and constituted at will by the ruler' (Lubman, 1991, p 334). The Maoist ideology failed to break this. The emphasis on relations in China has created some special concepts regarding the interaction of individuals, e. .g, *Guanxi* – relationship and connections, *Renqing* – favour, *Mianzi* – face, and *Bao* – reciprocity (Bond, 1986). In Sino-Swedish JVs *Guanxi*, and *Mianzi* are important.

Guanxi & Mianzi

Guanxi is informal, unofficial relationship utilised to get things done, from simple tasks to major life choices (Kolenda, 1990). It is a power relationship as well as one's control over a valuable good or access to it (Pye, 1985). China functions on relationships based on a common birth place, descent, working together, or belonging to the same organisation (Bond, 1986). *Guanxi* is supported by increasing social interaction between two people, e. g., by visiting and giving gifts. With connections everything is possible. Without *gaunxi* hardly anything gets done. Creating and strengthening *guanxi* is common in the business world (Davis, Leung, Luk and Wong, 1995). An individual's power and status can guarantee an allocator's help, *renqing*. Face or *mianzi* works in order to enhance people's position. *Mianzi* also concerns aspects such as recognition, reputation, and prestige. A person losing face loses integrity. Saving face is important and is a mechanism to control the Chinese people in their workplace. One can enhance one's own or other people's face and save one's own or other people's face. Face and the interaction of individuals involve both collectivism and power distance. Saving face may inhibit Chinese managers from making decisions, especially when they are unsure of the outcome. Chinese managers are frequently assigned tasks more due to connections than due to professionalism. Research on interpersonal relations shows that factors such as friendship (Love, 1981), personal acquaintance (Kinstrom and Mainstone, 1985; Freeberg, 1969) and the other interpersonal relationships (Tsui and Barry, 1995) between the evaluators and those to be evaluated adversely affect a proper evaluation. As discussed later, in China other values such as loyalty to the Party, are important in the evaluation process and to secure high management positions. This is problematic. If the unprofessional managers are later demoted problems arise. Where should he be placed in the organisational hierarchy? Should he be counted among the juniors? What is to be done with his salary and privileges?

Relationships are used to secure jobs and other benefits for friends and relatives. Reciprocity is important. Respect for age and position are vital in social and economic dealings. In return superiors supply security to subordinates (Anzizu and Chen, 1988). Commercial ventures, for example, are expected to supply housing and other basic facilities to the workers. Anzizu and Chen (ibid., 1988) argue that traditional Chinese culture is mixed with the ideology of Mao leading to characteristics such as assisting the weak rather than penalising them, and supplying (lifetime job) security to workers. Because of the importance of connections the distribution of rewards is personalised and based on Party interest (Chan, undated). This results in the undesirable consequences such as poor quality, lack of motivation, and poor discipline in organisations. Also in China there is the feeling that, 'The threat is omnipresent and lurks in the future, and therefore any significant erosion of authority is always dangerous – a view that inclines Asians towards accepting what for the Western mind would appear to be authoritarianism' (Pye, 1985, p. 38). Chinese managers are scared of delegating decision making power to subordinates.

Institutional Set-up

The authority of the Chinese managers is restricted. The managerial role played by the Party in managing firms is widespread (Lockett, 1990). Party members are an independent and parallel centre of power and form a sub-culture. For the same reason Chinese managers and workers lack skills and professionalism to execute their tasks (Child, 1990). To gain high positions are connections and Party membership important. Responsibilities and interpretation of rules are personalised and unclear and informal structures are more important than formal structures. The distribution of power, rewards, and responsibilities are frequently based on informal processes (Walder, 1991; Björkman, 1994). The Party stands beyond the law. Chew (1994) states that in practice, express legal principles have frequently been over-shadowed by Party policies. The law becomes the tool of the Party and the socialist state. One consequence is that decision making within Chinese firms is closed and based on clique-building. Another consequence is that it is difficult to pin-point responsibility for the decisions made in the firm. The reporting and evaluation systems are diffused.

Conflicts and Confusion

For the above mentioned reasons it is difficult to introduce new and superior managerial practices. Introducing new organisational culture means that the respected behaviour patters of to-day are discarded overnight. Ambiguities at different levels in the firm develops. The roots of these ambiguities lie in impending changes. These may concern any or all three levels: (a) technical changes, e. g., changes in the division of work and related technical issues, (b) structural changes, i. e., redesigning the organisation, its reward and punishment system, and (c) behavioural changes, i. e., changes in the attitudes and beliefs held by the members of the firm (Gordon, 1987). Impending changes are undesirable also because in China, '(L)earning from and copying the past masters....were to be encouraged and did not have the negative connotations that such copying would carry in the West. In fact , Chinese though sought, to varying degrees, to limit originality' (Milford, 1995, p. 81).

The above also illustrates that for Chinese, China is the centre of the world. Chinese may find it difficult to appreciate the value of imported knowledge. This sentiment was expressed by the Chinese king Qianlong, on 3 October, 1793 in a reply to King George of England, 'We possess all things. I set no value on objects strange or ingenious, and have no use for your country's manufacturer'.

Any of the technical, structural and behavioural changes results in ambiguity being felt by the members in the JVs. These concern the place of the organisation as well as inter-group formal and informal relationships and exchange within the JV, the effect(s) on individuals and groups with regard to the distribution of rewards, power, and authority. These ambiguities may generate conflicts and hostility between the agents of change (in JVs the expatriates) and those effected by these changes. A feeling of 'us' and 'them' develops. Conflicts result in hostility and disruption in operations. Otherwise this may come to the surface in the form of 'passive resistance'. The prevailing organisational culture resists the threatening features of the new culture (Buono and Bowditch, 1989). A polarisation based on the supporters of the old and the new culture occurs. Groups with divergent organisational cultures develop. These groups may be based on young vs. old, local vs. expatriates, department X vs. department Y, and in the Chinese case members of the Party vs. non-members. This affects the dealings with foreigners in general but expatriates in particular. Chinese managers show a feeling of 'Chineseness (= we are Chinese)'. This results in a lack of communication with and trust in expatriates. Conflicts, tension, and power struggles erupt. Members of the organisation get confused and frustrated which leads to a breakdown in the functioning of the organisation.

Scandinavian Management

Scandinavian management style contains a large element of 'human touch'. It is human oriented, democratic, decentralised, individual based and contains a high degree of flexibility. Employees are assigned a high degree of freedom and responsibility when it comes to executing their tasks and making decisions. Controlling the workers is based on feedback, training and education, and the delegation of authority. Reliance on punishment is limited. In addition, rules and their implementation are more objective. Evaluation is less dependent on individuals. The group is assigned a central place in work planning, decision making, and control. Workers are motivated more by providing opportuni-

ties to learn and achieve self-satisfaction than supplying higher monetary rewards.

2.6 Data collection

The information for this chapter was collected in 1994. Thirty interviews lasting over 100 hours in five JVs were conducted. These interviews give a comprehensive view of the process in which internal management in these JVs functions. We conducted a series of interviews
with the staff on all levels, including workers, secretaries, middle- and
top level managers. The questions concerned negotiations, contracting,
partners, implementation, management, and culture. In this way we develop a picture of the companies' situations at the outset and their
progress up until the time of the interviews. One of the authors is fluent
in Chinese language, she conducted interviews with the Chinese staff.

We asked people at different levels within the same functions and the
same company similar questions. This gave the data extra reliability. If
a problem is frequent then several people will perceive it. From this it is
possible to generalise. We tried to study the actual actions of people during our short visits with the companies: who speaks to whom, who goes
to look for whom when a problem arises, etc., to find out the informal
lines of communication and the state of that communication. We also
spent around a week at each JV to get a picture of the situation. We
didn't have the opportunity to speak to someone from every sub-depart-
ment within the main departments. These shortcomings in collecting
data are due to limited resources and time. As a whole our data is large
and broad.

3. Market and Company Presentation

Ericsson Radio Systems Ltd (ERA) in the summer of 1994 had two
manufacturing JVs in China, namely, Guangzhou Ericsson Communication Company Ltd. (GEC) and Ericsson Nanjing Communication
Company Ltd. (ENC). The main products are Radio Base Stations for
mobile systems, AXE-switch boards for mobile networks and for offices.
GEC is owned by ERA (56%) and three Chinese partners. GEC has
about 40 employees, ten of whom are expatriates. The company is functionally organised. The Personnel Department deals with the personal
acts which are only to be handled by Party members with special per-

mission. The Marketing Department has four expatriates and three local assistants. In the Operations Department there are about 10 people, most of whom are expatriates. The Financial Department consists of one Hong-Kong expatriate and one local accountant. There are special problems in China that make work difficult. The Manufacturing Department employ's 15 people. The Production Manager is an expatriate, all the others are local Chinese. They assemble and test RBS transceivers, which are imported from Sweden. Some of the quality and test engineers received training in Sweden. It is difficult to convince the Chinese of the superiority of Ericsson people and why expatriates are needed. Certain quality requirements are new to the Chinese.

ENC is owned by ERA (52%), Nanjing Radio Factory (NRF) (45%), and a third Chinese party. There is a Swedish President and a Chinese vice General Manager. ENC has 110 local employees and 20 expatriates. ENC is functionally organised. The manager of Personnel is a Party member. The Department of Administration has a Chinese manager. The Supply and Manufacturing Department is responsible for the assembly and testing of transceivers for mobile communication systems. Assembly workers are trained by their Chinese supervisor who, together with some engineers, has been trained for a month in Sweden. The Marketing Department has eight employees of whom five are expatriates. The Finance Department has five staff members, two Swedes and three Chinese.

We studied five JVs by ABB. These have over 1000 employees in China, Hong-Kong included. ABB produces and sells electrical equipment for power and transportation sectors. ABB has established a business school in China. The school provides management training. ABB has appointed the General Manager, Production Manager, and Financial Manager.

Sino-Swedish Pharmaceutical Co. (SSPC) is a JV between Astra, Pharmacia, Swedefund and China National Pharmaceutical Industry Corporation. The contract for this JV was signed in 1982, and production started in 1987. The stock is shared equally, between Sweden and China. SSPC produces anti asthma and cardiovascular medicines and intravenous nutrition products, for the Chinese market. SSPC has about 600 employees. The company has had some difficult years and some of the products have been difficult to sell. Only the Production Manager is Swedish, the other managers are Chinese.

Tetra Pac – Beijing Pulp & Paper Experimental Mill (BPPEM) was earlier owned by Beijing Municipality. In 1984 the contract was signed for the technology transfer of Tetra Pac machines to BPPEM. Soon after we collected data Tetra Pac will have a majority share and the right to appoint General Manager, Production Manager and Finance Manger in BPPEM.

4. Analysis: Managing Sino-Swedish JVs

4.1 Power distance

As described earlier, the Chinese accept centralisation and authoritarian leadership more easily than Swedes. Differences in wages and privileges between managers and their subordinates are great. In practice, as one expatriate points out, Chinese Managers work their subordinates by threat and coercion. Also, in China symbols of status, titles, business cards, cellular telephones, expense accounts, and cars are important boosters of managerial power. If a manager is perceived as having high status and power, his subordinate's status is automatically raised as well. It gives 'face' to the subordinate, something that in China is an important means of competition in, for instance, marketing and operations (see Collectivism vs. Individualism).

Professionalism and Leadership
In the studied cases the level of professionalism among many of the Chinese Managers is low. Most importantly in China it is still almost impossible to reach higher positions without being a honoured member of the Party. During several periods, Party membership and heritage (preferably landless peasant or industrial worker), were the only ways to get any kind of skilled work or reach a managerial position. During Mao's leadership the slogan was 'better red than expert'. Although efforts are being made to introduce more experts in the JVs, old ways of doing things still prevail. In all the JVs the Personnel Managers are Party members. Each employee has a detailed personal file containing his life history. These files are opened by specially authorised Party Members. In the choice of Personnel Manager it is therefore more important that he or she is a 'card-carrying member' than has a suitable background in professional terms. Also, the older generation has never been allowed a free hand in running a company. Their old ways are still shining through and make them look foolish and unprofessional in We-

stern eyes. Old generation Chinese still dominate managerial levels. A leadership built on threat and coercion is detrimental to more independent ways of working, in which individuals take the responsibility for their work. To achieve success it is important not only to train the workers, but also to train the managers and help them rid themselves of the old habits.

In all the cases the affects of the subjective culture of expatriates and the Chinese is visible. The Chinese managers feel that they are doing all that they should be doing, that is, working for the best of the JVs, earning profits, and producing goods and services. Expatriate managers feel different and complain. One expatriate says, 'The goal of the West is survival, the goal of the East is profit'. A polarisation between the expatriates and the Chinese managers occurs. An expatriate asserts that Chinese hardly care about the company, are not motivated to do a good job or to learn from expatriates. The Chinese managers are less competent and ritualistic. The Chinese managers consider the expatriate staff lazy. Confusion prevails. The expatriates complain that the Chinese hardly care about the plant, their own work, and that they neglect development, repair, and maintenance. If the Chinese make a certain profit, they are happy. As proof, an expatriate described what happened in 1993. At the end of November the sales budget of the year was reached. Customers were waiting for products, but the Chinese management stopped production, as the target for that year was already achieved. Other JVs experience problems with supervisors not giving proper orders or being afraid of giving orders. Due to a large power distance and the dual hierarchy system- one based on Party membership and the other based on company hierarchy – there is a fear of workers with Party membership and supervisors feel uncomfortable about giving orders to workers who are Party members.

Face

A common problem in the studied JVs are the middle aged Chinese managers. A middle aged Chinese manager in one JV, for example, is criticised for failing to see the needs of the core functions. He was trying to steer everyone else' work. He was accused of not knowing how a JV works. The Chinese manager has no previous experience of a JV. And as he is a department manager, he needs to show off his abilities and power by taking over other departments' responsibilities. Otherwise the employees will not respect him. It is impossible for a person in his position to say 'I am wrong'. In addition, a middle-aged Chinese manager does not accept to be told what to do. A similar problem is illustrated by the way the Chinese managers treat the 'overseas' Chinese women in two of the JVs. Despite their high education and experience from working abroad, these women are looked down upon and treated without respect by the Chinese managers. To them the two overseas Chinese are 'just Chinese'. Both ladies are 'very' young in the eyes of the Chinese, despite the fact that they have very high positions within the company and earn salaries comparable to the other expatriates. For a senior Chinese manager this is unacceptable. He has worked his whole life for what he has got, he is a man, maybe even a Party member, yet these young Chinese women earn more than he does, and have an equally high position within the company. They are supposed to have a subordinate relation to all men. Lastly, the two ladies have studied abroad. The Chinese managers feel that foreigners don't respect Chinese education. Accepting that foreign education is superior to the Chinese education is a loss of face for the older generation. This loss of face is also connected with collectivism.

Titles and Commissions
In China fancy titles, commissions and bribes are the result of a high power distance. Fancy titles and money create respect for the bearer. In JVs a lack of respect for a person makes it difficult to get orders carried out. One expatriate states, 'Experts who sit on the side to help production but are not actually supervisor do not get any respect from the Chinese...... No one goes to them for advise, unless they have some kind of position or title'. Titles are important all the expatriates we interviewed agreed. Within JVs status and fancy titles give authority to instructions on how to run the equipment and when checking how the equipment is treated. A subordinate is not listened to by people of higher status. Chinese employees hesitate to follow the orders of an expatriate expert, if that person does not have a higher status than the Chinese himself. If there is a Chinese manager within the department, the Chinese employees often check with him first, regardless of his status, before following the advice or order of the expatriate. Some of the expatriates expressed the view that Chinese employees ask the Chinese boss if it is OK to carry out a certain order of an expatriate. (see also »Subculture«).

In JVs Chinese managers think, for example, that Swedes are lazy. That the expatriates take a week or two off at almost any time is abhorrent to them. Who is then going to work? How can someone just leave a managing position empty for two weeks? The differences in importance put upon their work between Swedes and the Chinese are obvious. For Chinese being at the work place is more important than actually working. Their behaviour is ritualistic. To Chinese managers Swedish managers 'lack work morale' and give an impression of laziness and lack of interest in their work and responsibilities.

Delegating Authority

The large power distance in combination with uncertainty avoidance make Chinese companies have many formal and unwritten rules. The expatriates want the Chinese employees to take their responsibility and rely less on rules and detailed job specifications. The expatriates feel that Chinese managers control their subordinates as much as possible. One managers says, 'The Chinese are not used to delegation. Traditionally they want to have a totally clear cut area of responsibility, and they do not act outside their own area of responsibility. They want clear job description'. In the JVs the Chinese employees speak of the need of more detailed job descriptions and a more formal organisation. One Chinese employee describes, 'We must have authority of regulations........A formal system. Here we only have an informal management system'.

Expatriates try to delegate responsibility and check their subordinates occasionally or when something goes wrong. It is difficult to change the Chinese management's behaviour, as it is a result of perceived uncertainty and anxiety. On the other hand, the Chinese are not guided by short term returns. They are willing to learn, improve product quality and do a better job. The Chinese owners are more interested in learning technology and skills. The Swedish firms are interested in establishing a foothold in the expanding Chinese market.

Swedish managers deal with these issues of a lack in professionalism and leadership in different ways. ABB established a management school in China. This school is providing training to the Chinese managers. A more frequently used method is to supply the Chinese staff with opportunities to learn better skills and send the Chinese abroad for training. Almost all the JVs send Chinese abroad to improve their professionalism and expertise. A less Scandinavian method is paying a higher salary to Chinese employees. Frequently, the Chinese employees are paid around a 30 % higher salary than the going market rate. Other firms also pay incentive bonuses to the better performing employees. Higher salaries and bonuses improve the status of the Chinese employees in the society. Another ingredient of the Scandinavian management style is meetings between the employees and management. These meetings are easy to hold as they are in line with the Chinese system of management and the Chinese state ideology.

4.2 Collectivism vs. individualism

Differences between collectivism and individualism causes a great deal of trouble in JVs. In the JVs Chinese employees do not, for instance, openly criticise a manager or how things are done. But they do it indirectly by some sort of behaviour that will tell others where he stands or by voicing criticism through a middleman. Swedes use conflicts as a way of solving problems. This is not working in China. In China the relation between employer and employee is perceived in moral terms, as a family relation. A lot of rules exist, but need not be followed. The implications are many. In the JVs there are many intricacies with the wage system, for instance. In Sweden benefits are distributed according to performance, in China social ranking in the group, such as Party membership or a seat on the union board is a more common system of distributing benefits. A Swedish manager might give a benefit to the 'wrong' person and severely damage his relation to those considered of high ranking in the hierarchy. If someone loses face because of this, it may lead to reprisals from the hurt party.

Chinese managers rely on 'group consent', when making a decision. Although this consent is of the more superficial kind, the ritual is performed and it serves its purpose of relating to everyone what the management is planning to do, so that no one will be taken by surprise and not support the management's decision. Furthermore, the Chinese are suspicious toward their Western partner in the beginning, but they do want to build a friendly relation, based on mutual respect and trust. A lack of trust and communication leads to unwillingness to understand each others' intentions, needs, and actions. A good communication is realised when everyone can share information together and in their own language. This is just as important on the workers' level as on management level. In the JVs there was a great deal of 'backbiting' going on between different groups. There is a Western camp and a Chinese camp. The Chinese get news written in Chinese on a board, the Westerners get nothing. There were no contact between Westerners and Chinese on a private basis. The Chinese management even tried to discourage private relations. Communications are made difficult due to language problems. Lastly, in some JVs problems arise due to conflicts between 'mainland' Chinese and 'Hong-Kong' Chinese. The latter feel that the mainland Chinese are inferior, whereas the former see the Hong-Kong Chinese as traitors and blood suckers who once left the country but are now returning to suck the blood of the country.

These problems arise partly because for the Chinese, China is the centre of the world. The farther away one goes from the big metropolises and the foreign influence, the stronger this attitude gets. Foreigners failing to follow the Chinese rules and culture are not accepted in China. The feeling of 'them' and 'us' is strong. An expatriate likened the Chinese to an orchestra director. He says, 'They will always manage everything, you have no chance of showing them the way, they will show you the way. In all contacts, in all work, if they approve, or if they want what you are selling, or what you say, then it will be successful. You have no chance to get through if they do not agree completely'. This is a result of the collectivist trait in China. This collectivism is encouraged by the Party. The feeling of 'us' and 'them' creates a fear of everything new. This fear shows in different ways. There are, for instance, clear guidelines issued by the local Party office on how to deal with foreigners in different situations. The expatriate mentioned above has experienced some of these in business relations.

Subcultures

The expatriate managers feel that there is a sort of subculture among the Chinese within their companies. Chinese employees rather look up a Chinese manager when there is a problem, even if that manager works within another department. The expatriate managers and some Chinese feel that the control of the company is more in the hands of the Chinese than the expatriates. The reason is partly language, since it is easier for a Chinese to express himself in Chinese than in English. But the situation is also related to collectivism. In China, problems are solved among Chinese. Looking for help from the expatriates is a loss of face for the whole Chinese group, an acceptance that the Chinese are unable to solve the problem.

The Chinese employees try to cover their backs in order to avoid trouble and the old authorities are still working in the background. In one JV, for example, the Secretary of the Party branch literally forbade the Chinese employees to associate in private with the Westerners. The Party members are expected to encourage the workers to do a good job. But the nominations for 'best worker' regularly go to Party members, who are supposed to act as models for the rest of the work force. But the Party workers do not encourage others to produce more. Party group meetings during work hours do anything but encourage the other workers to perform their best. These meetings have been discontinued. One Party member describes the situation, 'The Party is creating subculture. The Party has become a spiritual organisation or group.....If you are a member of the Party then you have many more chances'. Party members have both official and unofficial tasks in JVs. This creates a 'dual' power structure in JVs, one based on management position and the other based on Party membership. The latter is frequently more important. Changing the system causes conflicts. As young Chinese are appointed as middle level managers an ambiguity develops. Old timers feel threatened by the expatriates as well by the young Chinese. Conflicts arise. Chinese working closely with the foreigners, such as interpreters, secretaries and supervisors, are exposed to great pressure from the Party organisation. Those are the ones that are blamed if something goes wrong and other workers are nasty to them if they have a good and friendly relation with foreigners. Very often these positions are filled by Party members, as they are considered to have a high morale. But this create ambiguities. Who should they report to – the Party or higher level managers in the company? This also makes it difficult to exercise managerial authority. How much decision making power do the Chinese managers really have? How, when, and on whom should this authority be used and for what purpose? The authority structure of the JVs is blurred. ABB tried to solve this problem by placing their JVs in coastal cities with a historical record of contacts with foreigners.

One JV is experiencing a 'pre-organisational power structure'. Before the current expatriates arrived, some Chinese were given jobs. After the formal organisation structure was laid out some of these positions are no longer needed. But it is difficult to move these people to lower positions. They are related with the Chinese management. Sending them to junior positions will reduce their salary and benefits. This is unacceptable to the Chinese managers.

The above problems get serious because of communications difficulties, particularly between departments. Because collectivist cultures build decision-making on a consensus, new ideas have to be 'sold' to the Chinese for a long time before they have a chance to get accepted. This demands great amounts of information being dispersed within the company. In the JVs this is made difficult by the fact that everything has to be translated. The Chinese employees are informed in Chinese via a blackboard. The expatriates are seldom able to study that information. In one of the JVs, for instance, the Production Manager, who reads Chinese, got the news of a salary increase this way. There was no official message about the raise to him, or any of the other expatriate managers, prior to him reading it on the blackboard.

Quality and Professionalism

In China quality seldom receives attention. The story is that when the Swedish expert at one of the JVs goes on holiday, all foreigners in Beijing stop buying their products on that same day! When he comes back they wait three days before buying the products again. During those three days he has been at his office, he has checked the cleaning of the machines, and killed all the bacteria. Only then do buyers return. There is a slack in the quality of the cleaning in the plant. The same holds true in other JVs. The Chinese management may also distribute products without recording them, loosen on the product quality and send the staff members to other companies to train those companies' staff, while the production at JV is standing still. The money from these kind of transactions may remain unaccounted for. The fact that relations are more important than the task in China, is a contributing factor to the difficulty to get the Chinese to accept quality thinking. Frequent criticism is voiced against the Departments of Administration at ENC and SSPC, which are unable to abide by demands put to them. The work in the Storerooms is criticised. Patience is required. Expatriate managers get nowhere with anger, which only creates disharmony and may even hurt their social position. To reveal feelings of anger towards the employees is uncommon in China, as it shows vulnerability and shakes the social order. One solution is to hire young Chinese. A manager at SSPC says, 'We don't hire people with work experience. Most of our employees come directly from the university, and we train them here at the company so that we get what we want. The right attitude is the most difficult thing to achieve'.

Problems related to preventive maintenance of buildings and machinery exist. As one expatriate manager says, 'There are numerous problems with the buildings and doors. In over 80% of the toilets the flush does not work. No one takes the responsibility for the failures'. A similar problem exists in the store rooms. The Chinese way is to run things until they break down. The above exposes an unwillingness and inability on the part of the older Chinese managers to learn and improve their career opportunities. They are more trapped in traditional Chinese culture and Maoist values. Fresh, young, and non-Party members are more accommodating and willing to learn. The cultural features of China interfere even at this level. The traditional values of China hinder young managers from being bold and stand against older managers. The 'unwillingness' of the young Chinese managers is also contingent upon their unwillingness to come in conflict with the norms and values of Chinese society. The recruitment and promotion of young and career seeking managers results in a cultural pluralism and, in the short – and middle time perspective, cultural clash within JVs. A polarisation occurs which makes introducing new managerial practices difficult.

The low Chinese professionalism is rooted in the collectivist system. Changing this culture is not easy. If an expatriate want to make the Chinese employees independent decision makers, then it is important not to forget to always be there, to protect that person if things go wrong.

Guanxi

An ugly aspect of business in China is that of corruption which takes many shapes. There are occasions when to save face Chinese managers accept bribery. Another type of corruption is the theft, selling or copying of company products, raw materials or company secrets by employees. Counterfeit foreign products being produced and sold in China are common. Employees steal expensive, often imported, raw material and sell it to laboratories that try to copy the products for Chinese use. Some Swedish firms have also seen products similar to theirs, in almost identical packages and capsules, being sold in China. Often this is done in active co-operation with the Chinese employees. Lastly, in one JV they have problems with the Marketing Department, run by a Chinese manager. The Marketing Department spends money on sales promotion, but with no improvement in actual sales. It was discovered that much commission had been handed arbitrarily.

Elements of the Scandinavian style of management are apparent here. The emphasis is to decentralise decision making allowing the Chinese workers freedom in making decisions. All the JVs make efforts to develop a two way flow of information and communication. These efforts are made easy as the Chinese are accustomed to group meetings. As described earlier, regular meetings between managers and employees are held in all the JVs. However, these efforts have achieved only limited success. One major problem is language. Also Chinese meetings are different from Scandinavian meetings. The Scandinavian managers in the JVs do not speak Chinese. The Chinese workers do not speak any foreign language. A two way communication is difficult. The Chinese workers are unable to forward complaints directly to the Scandinavian managers. On the other hand, the workers are afraid to complain to the Chinese managers.

Efforts are also made to introduce a degree of individualism in managing the JVs. First, more productive workers are paid bonuses. All the JVs have installed formal and objective evaluation, reporting and control systems. The feedback from these evaluations is distributed to the workers. Evaluations are used to determine the individual based bonuses. Paying individual based bonuses is neither very Chinese nor very Scandinavian.

4.3 Introducing changes

After the formation of the five JVs the expatriate managers have tried to introduce changes in the cultural values and norms of the Chinese employees. Increasingly Chinese managers and other employees are recruited on the basis of their competence and experience and not on the basis of their connections, relationships and Party membership. These changes conflict with traditional and Maoist values and norms in China. These changes introduce ambiguities in JVs. Technical and managerial changes exert a different demand on the Chinese workers and managers concerning product quality, cleaning, inventory control, and the procurement of components and systems. The expatriate management has also initiated a process to change internal accounting, reporting systems, and evaluation systems in the JVs. Intuition based evaluations have been substituted by a more formal evaluation. New production technology is making old knowledge obsolete and the old workers feel 'worthless'. Their prestige and privileges in the Chinese society are being threatened. Similarly, a competence based staffing policy is threatening older managers. These policies are reducing the power distance within the JVs allowing workers greater independence in decision making. Also, by not supplying the Chinese workers with housing facilities the five JVs are departing from the established cultural traditions of the Maoist era. This is traumatic for a majority of the Chinese, but especially for those Chinese that consider China the centre of the world. The Chinese workers are confused over their own role in the JVs, their decision making authority and responsibility. Old workers and Party members still feel that they have 'unlimited' power. The younger generation, on the other hand, underestimates its decision making power. Ambiguity and confusion prevail.

Our case studies show that the transition in the JVs concern all three aspects, namely, structural, technical and behavioural. The experience of the five JVs shows that introducing changes on the technological side is less problematic. The Chinese staff is willing to and capable of learning Western technologies. Changing behavioural aspects is more difficult as these are linked to social values and impinge upon individual prestige, social status, and psychological well being. These changes generate, what Buono and Bowditch (1989) call role ambiguity. This is a stressful situation for people affected by changes.

Many of these issues arise because the legal status of the five local firms is that of a JV. The Chinese partner, but the Swedish firms also see the local firm as their own, an extension of the parent firm. Both the Chinese and the Swedish parent firms expect to inculcate their own cultural values and norms in the JVs. Neither the legal contract between the parent companies nor any other document impinges upon these issues. It is merely presumed that the Chinese expect to learn from their Western partners. On technical issues there is an agreement that the Swedish firms are to supply and install modern production processes in the JVs. But on managerial issues no such agreement exists.

The problems related to introducing new and modern management methods are more serious during the transition period. During this period the older Chinese management still work for the JVs. Introducing new management methods creates a feeling among them that they are not needed in the firm. A sense of disloyalty results and a vicious circle is created. The more rapidly the Western management methods are introduced, the more the feeling of disloyalty. On the other hand, a failure to introduce new production and management methods will lead to low productivity, inferior quality production, and bad services to the clients. Managing the transition is a real challenge in Sino-Swedish JVs.

5. Conclusions and Future Research Issues

The JVs studied in this paper illustrate the difficulties involved in managing and operating international JVs. Our study generally supports the findings by other researchers concerning managing operations in China in particular but JVs in general. We find that installing changes at technical levels in JVs are less problematic. Introducing changes in the values, norms, and the work ethics in an alien environment is more difficult. We require more research on how to effectively introduce and manage changes in the values, norms, and work ethics in international JVs. What methods are effective for this purpose? This chapter also shows that managing the transition period is problematic, but crucial. During the transition period JVs in an alien environment are mixtures of foreign and local work cultures and ethics. The existing literature on international business and JVs have paid little attention to these issues. It is important to investigate the qualities that individual managers in JVs possess to be successful in their task. Should international managers be autocratic or democratic to achieve success in managing JVs abroad? Should expatriate managers show cultural sensitivity to local values, norms, and work ethics? If yes, then what are the costs of (not) being sensitive to the host country culture? Additional research issues concern whether JVs should employ mainly locals or expatriates to effectively manage the transition period. It is also important to investigate the impact of previous international experience of expatriates on their ability to effectively manage culturally sensitive issues in international JVs. Are managers with previous international experience more/less successful in managing JVs abroad? Our research shows that the use of monetary incentives to motivate employees in Sino-Swedish JVs is common. Previous researchers found the use of punishment more common. This change may be due to the recent industrial reforms in China. We need more research on these issues.

References

Alford, W. P., 1995, *To Steal A Book Is An Elegant Offence: Intellectual Property Law in Chinese Civilization*. Stanford University Press, Stanford, CA.

Adler, N., 1983. 'A Typology of Management Studies Involving Culture'. *Journal of International Business Studies*, Fall, 29-47.

Anzizu, J. De and D. Chen. 1988. *General Management in China: An Emerging and Complex Task*, paper presented at the International Conference on Management in China Today, Leuven, Belgium, June 20-21.

Beamish, P., 1984. *Joint Venture Performance in Developing Countries*. Unpublished Doctoral Diss., The University of Western Ontario.

Beamish, P. and J. C. Banks, 1987. 'Equity Joint Ventures and the Theory of the Multinational Enterprises', *Journal of International Business Studies*, Vol. XVIII, No. 2, 1-16.

Björkman, I., 1994, 'Role Perceptions and Behaviour Among Chinese Managers in Sino-Western Joint Ventures'. *Advances in Chinese Industrial Studies*, JAI Press, Vol. 4, 285-300.

Buono, A. F. and J. L. Bowditch, 1989. *The Human Side of Mergers and Acquisitions*. Jossey-Bas, San Francisco.

Bond, M. H. (ed.), 1986. *The Psychology of the Chinese People*. Oxford University Press, NY.

Campbell, N., 1988. *A Strategic Guide to Equity Joint Ventures in China*. Pergamon Press, Oxford.

Chang, A., (undated), *Managerial Reforms in Chinese Enterprises, the Roadblocks that Remain*, School of Management, National University of Singapore, Singapore.

Chew, P. K., 1994, 'Political Risk and U.S. Investments in China: Chimera or Protection and Predictability', *Virginia Journal of International Law*, Vol. 30, 615-635.

Child, J., 1990,.'The Character of Chinese Enterprises Management', in: Child, J., and M. Lockett, (eds.). *Reform Policy and the Chinese Enterprises*. JAI Press, London.

Child, J., 1991. 'A Foreign Perspective on the Management of People in China'. *International Journal of Human Resources Management*, Vol. 2, No. 1, 93-107.

Child, J. and M. Markoczy, 1993. 'Host Country Managerial Behaviour and Learning in Chinese and Hungarian Joint Ventures', *Journal of Management Studies*, Vol. 30, No. 4, 611-631.

Contractor, F., 1986. 'Strategic Considerations Behind International Joint Venture', *International Marketing Review*, Vol. 3, 78-85.

Contractor, F., 1990. 'Ownership Patterns of U.S. Joint Ventures Abroad and the Liberalization of Foreign Government Regulations in the 1980s: Evidences From the Benchmark Surveys', *Journal of International Business Studies*, Vol. 21, No. 1, 55-73.

Davidson, W. H., 1987, 'Creating and Managing Joint Ventures in China', *California Management Review*, Summer, 77-94.

Davis, H., T. K. P. Leung, S. T. K. Luk, and Y. Wong, 1995, 'The Benefits of Guanxi: The Value of Relationships in Developing the Chinese Market', *Industrial Marketing Management*, Vol. 24, 207-214.

Dymsza, W. and A. Negandhi, 1983. 'Introduction to Cross-Cultural Management Issue', *Journal of International Business Studies*, Fall, 15-28.

Earley, P. C., 1989. 'Social Loafing and Collectivism: A Comparison of the United States and the People's Republic of China', *Administrative Science Quarterly*, Vol. 34, 565-581.

Franko, L. G., 1989. 'Use of Minority and 50-50 Joint Ventures by United States Multinationals During the 1970s: Interaction of Host Country Policies and Corporate Strategies'. *Journal of International Business Studies*, Vol. XX, No. 1, 19-40.

Freeberg, N. E., 1969, 'Relevance of rater-ratee Acquaintance in the Validity and Reliability of Ratings', *Journal of Applied Psychology*, Vol. 62, 301-310.

Garatt, Bob, 1981, *Contracts in Chinese and Western Management Thinking*. LODJ 2.

Gordon, J. R., 1987. *Organisational Behaviour*. Allon and Bacon.

Harkins, S. and R. E. Petty, 1982. 'The Effects of Task Difficulty and Task Uniqueness on Social Loafing', *Journal of Personality and Social Psychology*, Vol. 43, 1214-1229.

Harrigan, K. R., 1985. *Strategies for Joint Ventures*. D. C. Heath. & Co., Lexington.

Harrigan, K. R., 1986. *Managing for Joint Venture Success*. D. C. Heath & Co., Lexington.

Hennart, J-F, 1988, 'Transition Costs Theory of Equity Joint Ventures'. *Strategic Management Journal*, Vol. 9, 361-374.

Hendryx, S. R., 1986. 'Implementation of a Technology Transfer JV in the People's Republic of China: A Management Perspective', *Columbia Journal of World Business*, Spring, 57-66.

Huang, Yasheng, 1990, 'The Origins of Chinas Pro-Democracy Movement and The Governments Response: A Tale of Two Reforms', *The Fletcher Forum*, Vol. 14.

Hofstede, G., 1983. 'The Cultural Relativity of Organisational Practices and Theories', *Journal of International Business Studies*, Fall, 75 – 90.

Hofstede, G., 1984 a. *Culture's Consequences.* Sage, London.

Hofstede, G., 1984 b. 'Cultural Dimensions In Management & Planning', *Asia Pacific Journal of Management*, January, 81-99.

Hoon-Habauer, S., 1994. *Management of Sino-Foreign Joint Ventures*, Lund University Press, Lund, Sweden.

Jaeger, A. M. and R. N. Kanungo, 1990, *Management in Developing Countries*, Routledge, London.

Kingstrom, P. O. and L. E. Mainstone, 1985, 'An Investigation of the rater-Ratee Acquaintance and Rate Bias', *Academy of Management Journal*, Vol. 28, 641-653.

Killing, P., 1983. *Strategies for Joint Venture Success.* Croom Helm, London.

Kogut, B., 1987. 'Joint Ventures: Theoretical and Empirical Perspectives'. *Strategic Management Journal*, Vol. 9, 319-332.

Kolenda, Helena, 1990, 'One Part, Two Systems: Corruption in the People Republic of China and Attempts to Control it', *Journal of Chinese Law*, Vol. 14, 187-272.

Ladany, L., 1991, Law and Legality in China – The Testament of A China Watcher. Hurst, London.

Latane, B., K. D. Williams and S. Harkins, 1979. 'Many Hands Make Light the Work: The Causes and Consequences of Social Loafing', *Journal of Personal and Social Psychology*, Vol. 37, 822-832,

Lockett, M., 1986. '*Working in the Special Economic Zones: The Cultural and Managerial Challenges*', paper presented at the Chinese Culture and Management Conference, Paris, Jan. 23-24.

Love, K. G., 1981, 'Comparison of Peer Assessment Methods: Reliability, Validity, Friendship Bias, and User Reaction', *Journal of Applied Psychology*, Vol. 66, 451-547.

Lubman, S., 1991, 'Studying Contemporary Chinese Law: Limits, Possibilities and Strategies', *The American Journal of Comparative Law*, Vol. 39, 293-302.

Milford, D. L., 1995, 'Legal aspects of Technology Transfer to the People's Republic of China: Steps Towards Understanding the Chinese Perspective', in: Wilson, T. (ed.), *APUBEF Proceedings*, Fall, 79-99.

Newman, W. H., 1992. 'Launching a Viable JV', *California Management Review*, Fall, 68- 80.

Parson, T., 1956. 'Suggestions for a Sociological Approach to the Theory of Organisations – 1', *Administrative Science Quarterly*, June, 63-85.

Pendleton, M. D., 1993, *Chinese Intellectual Property – Some Global Implications for Legal Culture and National Sovereignty*, EIPR, Vol. 19.

Pye, L., 1985. *Asian Power and Politics*. Harvard University Press, Mass.

Pfeffer, J. & R. Salancik, 1978, *The External Control of Organisation*, Harper & Raw, N.Y.

Redding, S. G., 1990, The Psycho-Social Legacy of China, in: S. G. Redding, (ed.), *The Split of Chinese Captilism*, De Gruyter, N. Y.

Richman, B. M., 1965. 'Significance of Cultural Variables'. *Academy of Management Journal*, Vol. 8, No. 4, 292-308.

Roberts, K. H., 1970. 'On Looking at an Elephant: An Evaluation of Cross-Cultural Research Related to Organizations'. *Psychological Bulletin*, Vol. 74, No. 5, 327-350. Tsui, Anne S. and B. Barry, 1986, 'Interpersonal Affects and Rating Errors', *Academy of Management Journal*, Vol. 29, No. 3, 586-599.

Walder, A. G., 1991. 'Workers, Managers, and the State: The Reform Era and the Political Crisis of 1989'. *China Quarterly*, Vol. 128, 467-492.

Weber, M., 1951, (trans. Gerth, Hans). *The Religion of China*. Free Press, N. Y.

Woldon, E. and E. Gargano,1988. 'Cognitive Loafing: The Effects of Accountability and Shared Responsibility on Cognitive Efforts', *Personality and Psychology Bulletin*, Vol. 14, 159-171.

16. Cross-Border Buyer-Supplier Development Collaborations

Lee Davis

1. Introduction

Multinational corporate »global sourcing strategies« – strategic arrangements by which firms coordinate innovative activities and the sourcing of components supplied for production and marketing – are the focus of increasing attention. The value-added activities of a multinational corporation include materials procurement, R & D, manufacturing, marketing, finance, personnel management, and so forth. Firms can obtain competitive advantage on a global basis by the optimal organization and coordination of these different activities.

The sourcing of innovation is clearly a central aspect of this emerging global strategy. This chapter investigates the special problems and opportunities that arise in cross-border buyer-supplier development collaborations. More specifically, we ask: under what conditions do such collaborations (1) lead to the development of commercially important innovations and (2) enhance competence-building on both sides? Cross-border collaborations are of particular interest in that they would both seem to offer special advantages in developing new products and processes, and at the same time pose the most daunting management challenges. In the following, we present a tentative framework for analysis within which it is intended, in future empirical research, to answer this question.

The term »buyer-supplier development collaborations« is conceived fairly broadly, embracing those partnerships characterized by a medium to high degree of coordination and complexity (Christensen, Andersson and Blenker, 1992). By »commercially important innovation« is meant the generation of a prototype the buyer feels it can use commercially. Competence-building may be defined as the ability to put the knowledge and skills gained during the period of collaboration to other uses, generating new competencies over time.

To give the analysis focus, we will utilize two concepts: core competence, and relational contracting. Buyer-supplier development collaborations, it is contended, are more likely to succeed – in terms of the two above-named goals – if they both occur within the areas of the core competence of both partners, and are informed by a high degree of relational contracting.

We start, in Section 2, with a brief overview of key aspects of interfirm cooperation on R & D. Section 3 considers the relationship between buyers and suppliers in its broader theoretical context, and argues that the concepts of core competence and relational contracting can provide the basis for a fruitful framework for analysis. The next section discusses these concepts in greater detail. Section 5 summarizes the main issues of importance when the buyer-supplier development partnership takes place across national borders. In section 6, four hypotheses are proposed by which to structure the ongoing research agenda.

2. Inter-Firm Cooperation

Interfirm cooperation can take a variety of forms. These can include informal know-how exchange (Von Hippel, 1987), business networks (Håkansson and Johanson, 1988), licensing and joint ventures (Contractor and Lorange, 1988), user-producer relationships (Lundvall, 1985), and complex, multi-faceted partnerships (Häusler *et al.*, 1994).

Depending on the nature of the cooperation, there are a number of advantages to be gained. Collaboration enables firms specializing in fundamentally different technologies to combine this expertise to create totally new products and processes. The partners' considerable costs and risks of developing new technologies can also be shared. Collaboration is a non-binding way to test the possibilities of diversifying into a new field, and may enable the realisation of other strategic aims, including entry into foreign markets, and surmounting regulatory and licensing barriers. Alliances may also be a precursor to the establishment of industry-wide standards.

Yet there are disadvantages as well. Firms risk losing control over their own operations; they sacrifice their independence (Simon, 1992). It can be difficult to devise the framework for a joint project that exists largely in the minds of the development engineers. Since there is a fairly high chance that the cooperation may not succeed, the firm might better have used its resources in another way. It can be difficult to find the right partner – and even then, there is no guarantee that the partner may not later be forced to withdraw. Disputes may emerge over the division of intellectual property rights and other contractual issues (Pisano, 1991). Alliances are not easy to manage, and serious problems of coordination may arise for both management and project staff.

Many studies of inter-firm cooperation have emphasized the role of organizational factors. In his analysis of the Danish EUREKA projects, for example, Kreiner (1993) found that the projects suffered from »turbulence« (a large number of partners withdrew from the projects for internal reasons), a general lack of experience with cooperation, confusion of project goals, and failures by management to deal with and solve problems as they arose. Nevertheless, participants often deemed projects as a success – even if they failed to achieve their stated goal – in that skills and new knowledge were gained that could usefully be applied in other contexts.

For cooperation to work, studies have emphasized the importance of clearly defined project goals, the presence of a strong motivator (a person who enjoys the respect of both sides, believes passionately in the project, and is able to galvanize others to work together), a strong commitment on the part of both partners to the project's success, and the willingness of management in both firms to promote organizational compatibility, including the ability to work in teams and provide continuous feedback.

Buyer-supplier development partnerships, the focus of this chapter, have been relatively unexplored in the literature. Most studies of subcontracting have neglected the specific issues that are important to an understanding of R & D, and most analyses of inter-firm cooperation on R & D have focused on horizontal forms such as joint ventures and strategic alliances. Exceptions include investigations of buyer-supplier development partnerships in pharmaceuticals (Pisano, 1991, and Whittaker and Bower, 1994), food processing and packaging (Bonaccorsi and Lipparini, 1994), electronics (Nishiguchi, 1994), computer systems development (Webb and Cleary, 1993), and automobiles (Turnbull, Oliver and Wilkinson, 1992). Important recent Danish studies include Valentin *et al.* (1995).

Most investigations are either in the form of cases, or focus on aggregate industry-level phenomena. Some analysts have explored the relationship between core competence and the cross-border governance of international alliances; Haugland and Reve (1995), for example, drawing on evidence from Norwegian manufacturing companies, compare the use of hierarchical mechanisms and social or relational mechanisms in terms of linkages between the firms' strategic cores, asset specificity and partner nationality. But no study, to my knowledge, utilizes the approach proposed here.

3. Theoretical Background

To elucidate the main issues, a number of questions must be addressed. How can the value of the knowledge produced in a firm's R & D laboratories be measured? How can firms cooperate in developing an innovation whose value, at the signing of the contract, is essentially unknown? To what extent can the terms of the contract anticipate and deal with unforeseen contingencies? What happens if, midway through the development process, one or both partners change the direction of their innovative focus?

To answer such questions, we need, firstly, to identify *what activities* are to form the basis of the cooperation, and thereby the point of departure for competence-building, and, secondly, how the *contractual relationship* between the two partners is to be structured over time.

The buyer-supplier relationship has been extensively explored in the international business literature. Yet the approach to suppliers differs, based on the particular theory's view of the firm. International industry analysts, for example (e.g. Porter, 1980), have essentially regarded the firm as a collection of entities competing in different product markets. Profitability is derived mainly from participating in an attractive industry, particularly one with high entry barriers. In this literature, managers were encouraged to decentralize decision-making processes and segment their corporations into strategic business units. To cut costs and increase efficiency, many activities could profitably be outsourced. The buyer specified what it wanted, and took competitive bids from several firms. Such arrangements were governed by short-term contracts, with very little knowledge sharing. Competitive bidding ensured market discipline and kept prices down. Suppliers were seen largely as adversaries, with their own interests to defend; Supplier Bargaining Power was one of Porter's Five Forces.

An alternative approach, the resource-based perspective, gained ground particularly during the 1980s and 1990s (e.g. Peteraf, 1993). Proponents criticized industry analysts for their failure to explain why some firms consistently do better than others in certain product markets, and for underestimating the importance of the interrelatedness of the various business activities within the firm. Profitability, they asserted, derived from the ways in which firms apply and combine resources to achieve sustained competitive advantage and earn rents. With regard to suppliers, they contended that industry analysts had been too quick to encourage the outsourcing of activities best preserved within the firm. Yet these analysts, too, viewed suppliers in largely adversarial terms. Outsourcing could dangerously »hollow out« the firm, leaving it dependent on suppliers for key skills and technologies. Sharing information with suppliers might mean that they passed vital secrets to one's competitors. In essence, the resource-based approach can be said to support either an »arms length« approach to suppliers, or vertical integration.

Concern over potential supplier opportunism is also a central pillar of transaction costs economics (Williamson, 1973, 1985, Rubin, 1990). This approach, which investigates how firms can increase efficiency by minimizing transaction costs, holds that the first presumption should always be to buy an input on the open market, as this is the best way to control costs. If this is not possible, the buyer must choose between contracting for the good, or making it itself. With contractual solutions, however, there is a risk that suppliers can exploit buyer dependency by »holding up« the buyer, raising prices or delaying deliveries to extract further concessions. The greater the asset specificity, uncertainty, and frequency of the transactions concerned, the greater the tendency towards internalization. Other writers (Casson, 1982) have emphasized the advantages of internalization to reduce asymmetric information between the two partners and ensure quality. This theory, too, can generally be said to support either an »arms length« approach to suppliers, or vertical integration. Firms can find it difficult to contract for all contingencies – either for fear of the threat of hold-up, or poor quality. The buyer can also never be sure whether its partner will make the necessary investments efficiently.

It is important to emphasize, however, that all of these perspectives recognize the importance of certain benefits of outsourcing. Industry analysts noted that relationships with specialized suppliers could contribute to the development of new business opportunities. The resource-based approach underlined the importance of supplier-provided access to complementary human resources and skills, in particular the opportunity to learn from one's partner. A long-term relationship with a supplier could also in itself lead to competitive advantage, as it is not easily replicable. Transaction costs theorists noted the advantages of access to new technology on attractive terms, and cost- and risk-sharing. The concept of »self-enforcing contracts« (Klein and Leffler, 1981) was developed to characterize informal agreements that were, nevertheless, considered binding by both sides. And where internalization was not feasible, a number of different hybrid organizational forms could be utilized, including strategic alliances, where some functions could be externalized, and some internalized; all such long-term relationships could be governed by a combination of market incentives and hierarchical controls.

It is on the basis of such »openings« in the latter two theoretical frameworks that the arguments presented below are advanced. Firstly, given the emphasis in the resource-based perspective on the combination and utilization of resources (Wernerfelt, 1984; Barney, 1986; Dierickx and Cool, 1989; Grant, 1991), the concept of core competence would appear to be highly useful for our purposes. This concept can help us to ascertain which activities should form the basis of the collaboration, and thereby to detetermine whether the partners intend to cooperate in areas of core – or only marginal – importance. The resource-based perspective is also centrally concerned with the development of skills and competencies: competition is seen as much as a »race to learn« as achieving a strong competitive position.

Our second analytical concept, relational contracting, has been largely elaborated by legal scholars such as Macneil (1974, 1978, 1985) and Macaulay (1963, 1985). It has been further developed in the economics and business literature by Williamson (1973, 1979, 1985), Goldberg (1976a, 1976b), Bolton, Malmrose and Ouchi (1994), and Noorderhaven (1992), among others. In the proposed research agenda, it is intended to focus primarily on the economic analysis of relational contracting, as outlined in section 4.2. (below). In the remainder of this section, we will define what is meant by relational contracting, and place it in the context of the other approaches to contracting.

According to Macneil, a distinction can be made between classical, neoclassical, and relational contracting. The classical approach to contract law, assuming low transaction costs, explores the influence of different legal terms and provisions in environments where the parties can describe and discount the likelihood of all relevant contingencies at the time of the signing of the contract. The characteristics of the parties to the transaction are seen as irrelevant, the nature of the agreement is carefully defined, and remedies for non-compliance are clearly stated.

The neoclassical approach to contract law recognizes, by contrast, that uncertainty and complexity often prevent the parties from accurately allocating all the relevant risks at the time the contract is signed. Instead, analysts investigate methods of reducing transaction costs in complex contractual relationships. Neoclassical contracts formally stipulate what the parties are obligated to do in case of various contingencies (both foreseen and unforeseen). Eventual disputes are resolved through the legal system.

The third approach, relational contracting, makes the same assumptions about uncertainty and complexity but goes even further, arguing that the parties concerned also need the possibility of reconsidering the terms of the contract when they encounter a situation that could not have been taken into account when the agreement was signed. The reference point, as Macneil puts it (1978, p. 890), is »the entire relation as it has developed (through) time. This may or may not include an 'original agreement,' and if it does, may or may not result in great deference being given it«. Disputes are mainly settled by ongoing bargaining among the involved parties.

Notably, in the buyer-supplier development contract, not all contingencies can be foreseen and accounted for; thus the classical approach is unsuitable for our purposes. Neoclassical contracting is also unsuitable, in that disputes can only be resolved through the courts. Given the high degree of uncertainty and complexity, and the central role of innovation, learning, and competence-building in the buyer-supplier development partnership, it is crucial that the parties have ways of accomodating change and solving conflicts within the framework of the ongoing agreement.

Contracts are important, as Macaulay (1985) has written, in that they (1) spell out the legal requirements and possibilities in the case of non-performance, (2) contain a body of clear rules that can facilitate planning, and (3) present a way by which to determine breach of contracts and resolve disputes. Nevertheless: »contract planning and contract law, at best, stand at the margin of long-term business relationships.« Comparatively few contract cases are litigated, and few of those litigated produce adequate compensation. Other sanctions, such as reputation, are often far more effective. This is arguably particularly true as regards the kinds of contracts discussed here.

4. Towards a Framework for Analysis

In this section, we will briefly explore how the two concepts introduced above – core competence and relational contracting – can offer important insights into buyer-supplier development collaborations.

4.1. Core competence

The resource-based perspective sees the firm as a »bundle« of unique resources and capabilities. A central assumption is that firms with superior resources are more efficient. Resources which lead to sustained competitive advantage and generate rents can broadly be characterized as valuable, rare, non-substitutable, and non-imitable. Key elements in this perspective include resource heterogeneity, *ex ante* and *ex post* limits to competition, and imperfect resource mobility (Peteraf, 1993).

The concept of core competencies, as originally conceived by Prahalad and Hamel (1990), can be defined as »the collective learning in the organization, especially how to coordinate diverse production skills and integrate multiple streams of technology«, the »glue that holds the organization together,« and the fundamental driver behind the firm's creation of value. They are what makes the firm essentially different from other firms, and are typically difficult to imitate. Firms can use a variety of »isolating mechanisms« (Rumelt, 1984), such as intellectual property rights and team-embodied skills, to prevent imitation of their core competencies. The concept has been explored empirically, for example, in a series of studies in Hamel and Heine (1994).

As contended by Bettis, Bradley and Hamel in an investigation of outsourcing in the U.S. manufacturing industry (1992), a defensive, incremental approach to outsourcing can initiate a spiral of decline that ultimately leaves firms without the skills and competencies to compete. Economies of scale and scope are reduced in the outsourcing firm while they rise in the supplier firm. Outsourcing separates market knowledge from manufacturing capabilities. Once key skills and competencies are lost, they are difficult to regain, not least because skills and competencies are often tacit.

According to the resource-based perspective, competitive advantage which is not based on replicable and growing distinctive skills will not be sustainable. Learning, particularly firm-specific learning, is critical to the long-term maintenance of competitive advantage. To the extent that R & D is part of a firm's core competencies, thus, outsourcing of R & D would lead to a loss of competitive advantage.

Even so, as indicated earlier, the theory recognizes that outsourcing also offers opportunities. First of all, it is a way to reduce costs, which can lead to an improved competitive position. The financial savings from outsourcing can also be redeployed to enhance remaining core competencies. Outsourcing enables the firm to take advantage of locational advantages in the partner's home country: cheaper labor, needed skills, mineral resources, government subsidies, tax advantages and so forth.

Finally, outsourcing enables the firm to create valuable alliances, bringing fruitful opportunities to learn from one's suppliers. Yet this side of the theory is not well-developed. It is one of the intentions of the research elaborated here to develop this concept to be better applicable to the subject at hand.

4.2. Relational contracting

The relational contract specifies the general terms and goals of the contractual relationship, the criteria by which to decide what to do when unforeseen contingencies arise, who has what power to act, the limits of the range of actions that can be taken, and the mechanisms for resolving disputes. The contract is intended to govern relations which take place over a long period of time, and where the parties will have to deal with each other regularly over a wide range of issues, many of which cannot be foreseen in advance.

Investigations of relational contracting recognize that the length of the agreement, the nature of the contractual restrictions, and the complexity of the issues involved between the time of the signing of the contract and its termination, are of central importance. While the two parties might, at the signing of the contract, desire to specify in considerable detail the rights and obligations of each party given various contingencies, this will often prove too costly. Instead, it will be preferable to use rough formulae or mutual agreement to adjust the contract to the current situation. For instance, with regard to pricing, firms can choose either to fix a price schedule at the beginning of the contract, or agree to leave the question of pricing open to various degrees. In the relational contract, rather than specifying future prices in advance, they can specify a process by which such prices would be determined.

Relational contracting has been deemed particularly appropriate for the analysis of the long-term relationships in the development and procurement of complex defense hardware, the construction of chemical plants embodying substantial state of the art advances, and joint ventures (Goldberg, 1976a). It would thus seem eminently suitable for the analysis of the complex issues involved in buyer-supplier development collaborations. With relational contracting, firms agree to devote their best efforts to the collaboration, to share the costs and benefits, to consult with each other in the event of new developments, and to bargain in good faith should disputes arise. Such contracts, suggest Milgrom and Roberts (1992, p. 131), »can in fact work quite effectively, at least when the potential conflicts are not too great and the parties are not inclined to be too opportunistic in their dealings with one another.«

Important issues to be addressed in the economic analysis of relational contracting include: the types of incentives that are built into these contracts to promote efficiency; the degree to which such incentives lead, in practice, to the desired result; the ways in which relational contracting can enable the parties concerned to deal with development risk and uncertainty; and the effectiveness of relational contracting as compared with other forms of governance.

5. Cross-Border Partnerships

In the theoretical literature on the multinational enterprise (MNE), as we have indicated, the buyer-supplier relationship has mainly been analyzed in terms of the choice between *make or buy*. The buyer can either purchase the needed component on the market, contract with another firm to develop it, or produce the good internally. In much of this literature, buyers are cautioned against forming too close a relationship with their suppliers.

Traditionally, multinational corporations have found it more efficient to create and transfer knowledge within the boundaries of the group, rather than exchange it within the framework of a cooperation with an external partner. Internalization not only deflects supplier opportunism and eases problems of communication and coordination, it also enables economies of scale and quality control (Casson, 1991), and facilitates appropriability (McGee, 1977). Collaborative arrangements have been seen as unwieldy, difficult to manage, and unlikely to produce anything of value.

Yet numerous business analysts, as suggested above, have emphasized the benefits of cooperation (e.g. Contractor and Lorange, 1988, Håkansson, 1987). Its advantages have been documented in empirical studies as well. Japanese firms have, for example, successfully used a more integrated approach (»integrated supply management«), where buyer-supplier new product development occurs within the framework of long-term relationships based on mutual trust (Kotabe, 1992). Clearly, the Japanese model, building as it does on the country's industrial traditions and structure which facilitates cooperation among large groups of enterprises, cannot readily be transferred to the West. But among the sources listed in section 2, both Whittaker and Bower (1994), and Bonaccorsi and Lipparini (1994) found that integrated supply management brought notable benefits to the firms they studied, in terms of the development of valuable innovations and in creating learning spin-offs.

Through buyer-supplier development collaborations, the MNE can be said to expand its boundaries, without actually acquiring the supplier itself. This raises a number of interesting questions for research, not least in light of the complexity of the relationships studied, involving both the MNE as a whole, the subsidiary that is directly involved in the joint effort, and the supplier. Those questions of relevance for the study of international business include the following:

1. To what degree can the experiences of firms from particular countries (for example, the Japanese model) be said to have a broader relevance?
2. In what ways do cultural differences in the cross-border project team affect peoples' ability to work together effectively?
3. How do differences in the laws and legal practices of the countries concerned (with regard to intellectual property rights, conditions of labor, and so forth) affect the relationship between the two firms? How are they resolved in the contract?
4. In what ways do buyer-supplier development collaborations contribute to competence-building in the MNE subsidiary responsible for fielding the buyer's portion of the joint project team? In the MNE as a whole? What conflicts can arise? What happens when there is a shift in priorities affecting general MNE core competencies due to corporate strategy (say, downsizing) or to changes in marketing prospects or technology? To what extent does the cooperation take on a life of its own, with little regard for central management's objectives?

5. What difficulties arise with regard to the diffusion of knowledge created within the subsidiary, as part of its collaborative partnership, to other units within the MNE?
6. To the degree that the collaboration can be said to enable the MNE to expand its boundaries, what problems and opportunities arise as regards the MNE's ability to absorb and utilize supplier resources and competencies?
7. How do collaborations enhance supplier competencies and competence-building? Under what circumstances does the relationship between buyers and suppliers become so intense that supplier core competence advantages become tied to one particular buyer, rendering it difficult if not impossible to deal with alternative buyers? What happens to supplier competence-building if the buyer is drastically restructured, or acquired by another firm?
8. To what extent do MNEs that set up operations outside their domestic market establish links with home country suppliers that have also established foreign facilities? To what degree do buyers and suppliers that have previously worked together successfully on a development project go abroad together? How frequently do MNE subsidiaries establish their own supplier networks abroad that are not part of the corporate group to which they belong?

6. *Some Proposed Hypotheses*

By using the two key concepts introduced earlier – core competence and relational contracting – and further developing and reinterpreting them in terms of the special characteristics of cross-border buyer-supplier development collaborations – it should be possible to generate hypotheses by which to answer the question posed at the beginning of this chapter: Under what conditions will the buyer-supplier cooperation both lead to the development of commercially important innovations, and enhance competence-building?

According to logic of the resource-based perspective, as described above, firms should generally not outsource their core competencies. Nevertheless, it is our contention that this logic does not always – necessarily – apply, particularly with regard to buyer-supplier collaborations involving R & D. What is more important: the loss of potential competitive advantage due to the chance of imitation, or the loss of potential competitive advantage due to the failure to create important new products and products based knowledge sharing?

One could argue, in fact, that *the greater the degree of sharing of core competencies (and knowledge), the greater degree of mutual commitment that the cooperation will succeed – with substantial competitive benefits to follow, for both parties, over the longer term.*

New institutional economic theories often underline the importance of preserving specific assets – investments involving sunk costs undertaken in support of particular transactions and that have a much lower value in other uses – within the firm. Much of the literature on transaction costs and outsourcing, as we have seen, emphasizes that firms should avoid outsourcing activities where there is a high level of asset specificity, due to the risk of supplier opportunism.

Nishiguchi (1994), however, in his comparative analysis of British and Japanese strategic industrial sourcing in electronics, argues that Japanese subcontracting is in fact successful *because* asset specificity is involved. In his sample, asset specificity was notably higher in the Japanese subcontracts than in the British. He argues that »asset specificity seems to be not the cause but the consequence of a strategy,« and that the Japanese contracts were specifically designed to encourage – and take advantage of the gains from – asset specificity.

Could not the same logic be applied to core competence: namely, the greater the amount of core competencies each partner is willing to contribute to the cooperation, the greater each partner has a stake in the project's success, and the greater the willingness on the part of both parties to make the agreement function? Firms working within their core competencies have already assigned these areas high priority, giving them a special incentive for the project to succeed. Dependency, at least in this type of relationship, would seem to constitute a positive force, not a sign of vulnerability.

It would also be interesting to explore the degree to which a high mutual commitment of core competencies to the project might contribute to salvaging something from the partnership, should it fail. The collaboration might fall victim to problems connected with the larger framework of the relationship, in particular changes in the strategic goals of the MNE, leading to a shift in corporate priorities and, consequently, project termination. But would the partners still emerge with at least some competence-building advantages?

Against this background, we propose the following hypothesis:

Hypothesis 1: The more the buyer-supplier development collaboration
involves the core competencies of both parties, the greater
will be the commitment to the collaboration by both
sides, and the greater the amount of competence-building
that will occur.

We can now pursue the logic of this argument further. When firms cooperate, they in essence merge their resources in a given area, leading to
a new combination of heretofore heterogeneous resources. The result of
this combination, particularly when it concerns new product and process development, cannot at its inception be fully known. Much can also
be altered within a very short period. Demand conditions can shift, resulting in the need to adjust the description of the desired project. The
prices of key raw materials can rise, stimulating interest in alternative
sources. Technology can change.

   For this reason, the ongoing relations between the involved parties
become critical. It is here where our second analytical construct, relational contracting, comes into play. While a sense of shared vision and
commitment are necessary for project success, they are not sufficient. It
is equally important that the relationship *per se* is strengthened by the
language, and incentive structure, of the contract. The special value of
relational contracting is that it not only preserves flexibility in the partnership, but also serves as a constant reminder that the project is intended to achieve a specified, commercially viable result. This leads to a second hypothesis:

Hypothesis 2: The more the contract enables continuous mutual adjustments in the relationship between the partners, the greater the likelihood that the collaboration will produce an innovation of commercial value.

In that the cross-border buyer-supplier development partnership involves constituting a project team composed of people from different
nationalities, it would be interesting to investigate the role of cross-cultural differences.

   Project development teams from different countries might have much
that pulls them apart: their nationalities, their traditions, their corporate

cultures, their languages. But if both firms give high priority to the object of the joint effort – if, in the language of this chapter, it involves the core competencies of both partners – this might help the members of the two project teams to bridge the other gaps. Project staffers would know, for one thing, that top management had a strategic interest in the project's success, and was willing to continue to commit the necessary resources. This gives rise to a third hypothesis:

Hypothesis 3: The more the collaboration involves the core competencies of both parties, the less cross-cultural differences in the joint project team matter to the project's success.

Finally, and related to this: in section 5 of this chapter, we enumerated various ways in which existing or potential relationships with suppliers might affect MNE strategies when locating their operations abroad. It would be interesting to investigate the degree to which collaborations among buyers and suppliers who knew each other beforehand – or perhaps even moved abroad together – were more successful (in terms of the two above-defined goals) than collaborations where the partners had no previous experience in working together.

Normally, it is argued that previous positive collaborative experiences benefit future joint efforts. On the other hand, it could be asserted that for the particular types of collaborations investigated here – to the degree that the contract allows for the necessary mutual adjustment along the way – the nature of the previous cooperation would not be that important. Such flexibility could well be enhanced by the use of relational contracting. This leads to the formulation of our fourth hypothesis:

Hypothesis 4: The more the contract enables continuous mutual adjustments in the relationship between the partners, the less it matters to the project's success that the two firms have worked together in the past.

7. Research Method

It should be emphasized that the hypotheses outlined above are of a preliminary nature, and should mainly be seen as a means of structuring on ongoing research agenda. The method for testing these hypotheses also remains to be elaborated. It is intended to study empirical material from industries in areas such as electronics, transportation equipment, scientific and photographic equipment, motor vehicles and parts, aerospace, computers and office equipment, and industrial and farm equipment. The reason is that these industries have in common that the manufactured final product is made up of easily identifiable and separable components. This is different from, for example, chemical processing, where it is difficult to see what characteristics components have.

The case studies will include cooperations between Danish MNE subsidiaries abroad and their local suppliers, and foreign MNE subsidiaries in Denmark that cooperate with local suppliers, along with a control sample of buyer-supplier partnerships within the same country. In-depth interviews with managers and project development staff will be used to gather the relevant information.

8. Conclusion

The continued globalization of business activities, combined with accelerating technological change, should arguably increase the advantages to firms of entering into development collaborations. Advances in telecommunications, computers and transport have led to a more interconnected, open world. Financial deregulation has made capital highly mobile. Shortened product life cycles have generated fiercer competition in technologically intense industries, underlining the benefits of sharing R & D costs and risks. The degree to which these opportunities can be realized in a common development project, however, clearly depends on the ability of the participating firms to resolve the myriad problems involved.

It is expected that the investigation will generate a systematic analytical framework by which to determine why some types of collaborations are more successful than others, and under what circumstances buyers, suppliers, or both partners, respectively, will gain (or lose). The analysis is also expected to provide important insights into differences between collaborations involving Danish Multinational enterprises abroad, and foreign multinational enterprises in Denmark.

References

Barney, Jay B., 1986. »Strategic factor markets: expectations, luck and business strategy,« *Management Science*, 32, 1231-1241.

Bettis, Richard A., Stephen P. Bradley and Gary Hamel, 1992. »Outsourcing and industrial decline,« *Academy of Management Executive*, 6 (1), 7-22.

Bolton, Michele Kremen, Roger Malmrose and William G. Ouchi, 1994. »The organization of innovation in the United States and Japan: neoclassical and relational contracting,« *Journal of Management Studies*, 31, (5) (September), 653-80.

Bonaccorsi, Andrea and Andrea Lipparini, 1994. »Strategic partnerships in new product development: an Italian case study« *Journal of Product Innovation Management*, 11, 134-45.

Casson, Mark, ed., 1991. *Global Research Strategy and International Competitiveness.* (Basil Blackwell, Cambridge).

Casson, Mark, 1982. »Transaction costs and the theory of the multinational enterprise,« in A.M. Rugman, ed., *New Theories of the Multinational Enterprise.* (Croom Helm, London), 24-43.

Christensen, Poul Rind, Jens Andersson og Per Blenker, 1992. *Industriens brug af under leverandører.* (Industri- og Handelsstyrelsen, København).

Contractor, Farok J. and P. Lorange, eds., 1988. *Cooperative Strategies in International Business* (Lexington Books, Lexington Mass.)

Dierickx, Ingeman and Karel Cool, 1989. »Asset stock accumulation and sustainability of competitive advantage,« *Management Science*, 35, 1504-1511.

Goldberg, Victor P., 1976a. »Regulation and administered contracts,« *The Bell Journal of Economics*, 426-448.

Goldberg, Victor P., 1976b. »Toward an expanded economic theory of contract,« *Journal of Economic Issues*, 10 (1), (March), 45-61.

Grant, Robert M., 1991. »The resource-based theory of competitive advantage: implications for strategy formulation,« *California Management Review* (Spring), 33, (3), 114-135.

Gugler, Philippe and John H. Dunning, 1993. »Technology-based cross-border alliances,« in Refik Culpan, ed. *Multinational Strategic Alliances.* New York.

Hamel, Gary and A. Heine, eds., 1994. *Competence-Based Competition* (John Wiley, Chichester).

Haugland, Sven A. and Torger Reve, 1995. »Governance of cross-border partnerships: a contract perspective,« Norwegian School of Economics and Business Administration, unpublished paper, 32 pages.

Håkansson, Håkan, 1990. »Technological collaboration in industrial networks,« *European Management Journal*, 8 (3), (September), 371-379.

Håkansson, Håkan, 1987. *Industrial Technological Development: A Network Approach* (Croom Helm, London).

Håkansson, Håkan and Jan Johanson, 1988. »Formal and informal cooperative strategies in international industrial networks,« in F. Contractor and P. Lorange, eds., *Cooperative Strategies in International Business* (Lexington Books, Lexington, Mass.), 369-90.

Häusler, Jürgen, Hans-Willy Hohn and Susanne Lütz, 1994. »Contingencies of innovative networks: a case study of successful interfirm R & D collaboration,« *Research Policy* 23, 47-66.

Klein, Benjamin and K.B. Leffler, 1981. »The role of market forces in assuring contractual performance,« *Journal of Political Economy*, 89 (August), 615-41.

Kleinknecht, Alfred and Jerome O.N. Reijnen, 1992. »Why do firms cooperate on R & D? An empirical study,« *Research Policy* 21, 347-60.

Kodama, Fumio, 1992. »Technology fusion and the new R & D,« *Harvard Business Review* (July-August), 70-78.

Kotabe, Masaki, 1992. *Global Sourcing Strategy* (Quorum Books, New York).

Kreiner, Kristian, 1993. *EUREKA – på dansk* (Samfundslitteratur, København).

Lundvall, Bengt-Åke, 1985. *Product Innovation and User-Producer Innovation* (Aalborg University Press, Aalborg).

Macaulay, Stewart, 1985. »An empirical view of contract,« *Wisconsin Law Review*, 465-482.

Macaulay, Stewart, 1963. »Non-contractual relations in business,« *American Sociological Review*, 28, 55-67.

Macneil, Ian R., 1985. »Relational contract. What we do and do not know,« *Wisconsin Law Review*.

Macneil, Ian R., 1978. »Contracts: adjustments of long-term economic relations under classical, neoclassical, and relational contract law,« *Northwestern University Law Review*, 72, 854-906.

Macneil, Ian R., 1974. »The many futures of contracts,« *Southern California Law Review*, 47 (May), 691-816.

McGee, Stephen P., 1977. »Multinational corporations, the industry technology cycle and development,« *Journal of World Trade Law,* 2 (4), 297-321.

Milgrom, Paul and John Roberts, 1992. *Economics, Organization and Management* (Prentice-Hall International Editions, Englewood Cliffs, N.J.).

Nishiguchi, Toshihiro, 1994. *Strategic Industrial Sourcing* (Oxford University Press, New York and Oxford).

Noorderhaven, Niels G., 1992. »The problem of contract enforcement in economic organization theory,« *Organization Studies,* 13, 2, 229-243.

Papanastassiou, Marina and Robert Pearce, 1993. »Global-innovation strategies of MNEs and European integration: the role of regional R & D facilities,« in *European International Business Association,* 19th Annual Conference, Lisboa, December.

Peteraf, Margaret, 1993. »The cornerstones of competitive advantage: a resource-based view,« *Strategic Management Journal,* 14, 179-91.

Pisano, Gary P., 1991. »The governance of innovation: vertical integration and collaborative arrangements in the biotechnology industry,« *Research Policy* 20, 237-249.

Porter, Michael E., 1980. *Competitive Strategy.* (Macmillan, New York).

Prahalad, C.K. & Gary Hamel, 1990. »The Core Competence of the Corporation,« *Harvard Business Review,* 66 (May/June), 79-91.

Reve, Torger, 1990. »The firm as a nexus of internal and external contracts,« in Aoki, Masahiko, Gustafsson, and Oliver Williamson, eds, *The Firm as a Nexus of Treaties* (London), 133-161.

Rubin, Paul H., 1990. *Managing Business Transactions.* (The Free Press, New York).

Rumelt, R.P., 1984. »Towards a strategic theory of the firm,« in B. Lamb, ed., *Competitive Strategic Management.* (Prentice-Hall, Englewood Cliffs, N.J), 556-570.

Simon, Hermann, 1992. »Lessons from Germany's midsize giants,« *Harvard Business Review,* (March-April), 115-123.

Strong, Norman and Michael Waterson, 1987. »Principals, agents and information,« in Roger Clarke and Tony McGuinness, eds., *The Economics of the Firm,* (Blackwell, Oxford), 18-41.

Turnbull, Peter, Nick Oliver and Barry Wilkinson, 1992. »Buyer-supplier relations in the UK automotive industry: strategic implications of the Japanese manufacturing model,« *Strategic Management Journal,* 13, 159-68.

Valentin, F., P. Andersen, B. Dalum, T. Pedersen & G. Villumsen, 1995. *Strategiske virksomhedsrelationer.* (Velfærdskommissionen, København). Report 5.

Von Hippel, Eric, 1988. *The Sources of Innovation.* (Oxford University Press, Oxford and New York).

Von Hippel, Eric, 1987. »Cooperation between rivals: informal know-how trading,« *Research Policy* 16, 291-302.

Webb, Janette and David Cleary, 1993. »Supplier-user relationships and the management of expertise in computer systems development,« in Swann, Peter, ed. *New Technologies and the Firm* (Routledge, New York), 102-127.

Wernerfelt, Birger, 1984. »A resource-based view of the firm,« *Strategic Management Journal,* 5: 171-180.

Whittaker, E. and J. Bower, 1994. »A shift to external alliances for product development in the pharmaceutical industry,« *R & D Management* 24 (3), 249-60.

Williamson, Oliver E., 1985. *The Economic Institutions of Capitalism.* (Free Press, New York).

Williamson, Oliver E., 1979. »Transaction-cost economics: the governance of contractual relations,« *Journal of Law and Economics,* 22, 233-61.

Williamson, Oliver E., 1973. »Markets and hierarchies: some elementary considerations,« *American Economic Review,* 63 (May), 316-25.

17. Business Network Connections and the Atmosphere of International Business Relationships

Désirée Blankenburg Holm and Jan Johanson

1. Are Business Relationships Affected by the Surrounding Business Network?

Can we get a better understanding of international business relationships if they are considered in the context of the surrounding business network? Are business relationships affected by any specific type of business network connections? Is the atmosphere of international business relationships influenced by the business network connections of the relationship? Based on exchange network theory and business network concepts this chapter explores how five kinds of network connections affect three different dimensions of the atmosphere of dyadic business relationships. In other relationship studies these atmosphere dimensions have been regarded as important links between relationship antecedent and outcome variables (Håkansson 1982; Hallén and Sandström 1988). The results of the empirical study using data about international business relationships from the IMP data base[77] demonstrate that network connections have effects on the business relationship atmosphere. They show also that different connections have different effects on four different atmosphere dimensions. The results indicate that relationship strategies have to be designed differently depending on the business network contexts.

During the last decade a number of studies have contributed to our understanding of interfirm relationships in business markets (Anderson and Narus, 1990; Anderson and Weitz, 1989; Dwyer, Schurr and Oh, 1987; Frazier, 1983; Håkansson, 1982; Hallén, Johanson and Seyed-Mohamed, 1991; Heide and John, 1988; Morgan and Hunt, 1994).

---

77. The second European International Marketing and Purchasing (IMP) project started in 1988. The research project is undertaken by a number of academic institutions with the aim to gather data on interfirm relationships in eight countries. It builds on previous IMP project reported in Håkansson 1982.

Typically those studies have limited their analysis to the relations among characteristics of the dyadic relation. It has, however, been suggested that dyadic relations in business markets do not exist in isolation but are connected to each other and can fruitfully be considered within a network context (Achrol, Reve and Stern, 1983; Anderson, Håkansson, and Johanson, 1994; Baker 1990; Gadde and Mattsson, 1987; Iacobucci and Hopkins, 1992; Thorelli, 1986; Webster, 1993). The underlying assumption is that the interaction between firms in a dyadic relationship to some extent is contingent on the firm's involvement in relationships with other parties.

Case studies have provided a number of examples of the impact of the surrounding network on single dyadic business relationships (Forsgren and Olsson, 1992; Hertz, 1993; Lee, 1991). But so far no empirical studies have been reported about more general impacts of networks on dyadic relations. This paper is an attempt to explore empirically some important aspects of business relationships and their network connections in such a way that it is possible to analyse the impact of the network. The first section outlines the theoretical conceptualisations of relationships and networks employed. The second section describes how the concepts have been operationalised and how data have been collected and analysed. The following section shows the empirical results of the study. In the final section the results are discussed.

2. *Dyadic Business Relationships in Business Networks*

In the marketing literature the importance of the environment is frequently stressed (Achrol 1991). Usually a generalised conception of the environment as a faceless entity is used, such as political environment, competitive environment or social environment. Thrall (1986) has, however, argued that »the most salient part of the environment of any firm is other firms« (ibid. p.38) and that the environment should be conceptualised as a network of firms involved in exchange relationships. In a similar spirit Ashram, Reve and Stern (1983) distinguish the direct exchange network as the immediate environment of the channel dyad. Morgan and Hunt (1994) also argue that relationship marketing should be seen as part of the developing network paradigm. Moreover, Kogut, Shan and Walker (1992) suggest that make or buy decisions can be analysed in an industry network context. Thus, there is reason to expect that our knowledge about dyadic business relationships, that is exchange relationships between two firms doing business with each can be enhanced by viewing them as embedded in the context of a network structure (Granovetter 1985).

Although attractive, network ideas are in many ways vague and elusive and have to be specified in order to become operational. Several of the studies mentioned at the outset have been based on social exchange theory (Blau 1964; Emerson 1962; Homans 1958; Thibaut and Kelley 1959). This theory has also been generalised from dyadic exchange relations to exchange networks (Cook and Emerson 1978; Willer and Anderson 1981). A number of experimental studies of exchange networks have been conducted and business market research may profit by using some of the findings of the exchange network research (Willer 1992). A basic question is, then, if exchange network theory can be generalised to business networks. In that case, a second question is if exchange network theory can contribute to a better understanding of dyadic business relationships.

2.1 Network connections

In social exchange theory exchange networks are defined as sets of two or more connected exchange relations, where connected means that exchange in one dyadic relation is contingent on exchange or non-exchange in the other (Emerson 1981). If we want to use exchange network theory in studies of business markets we have to be able to identify sets of connected exchange relations in business markets in the sense that business in one business relationship supports business transactions in the other, or alternatively, that business in one is done at the expense of business in the other (Anderson, Håkansson and Johanson 1994). Only if the business relationships are connected in that sense can we really speak about business networks more than metaphorically.

Considering now a focal business relationship between a supplier firm and a customer firm we expect that the firms, in order to get to access to resources controlled by other firms, also are engaged in other relationships than the focal relationship. Evidently, each of the two firms in the dyad is involved in exchange with a number of other suppliers and customers. It is possible that some of those other exchange relationships are connected to the focal business relationship and have an impact – positive or negative – on business in it. Following exchange network theory we call these interdependencies between relationships network connections. First, the customer firm may be engaged in relationships with competitive suppliers having an impact on business with the focal supplier. The customer firm may also be engaged in relationships with suppliers of complementary products, which may be more or less adjusted to the specific characteristics of the focal supplier's products. Moreover, the customer firm probably has customers whose business with the focal customer has an impact on business in the focal relationship.

Correspondingly, the supplier firm may be engaged in relationships with their suppliers and with other customers, all of which may affect business in the focal relationship. In addition, both the supplier firm and the customer firm may have connected relationships with other organisations, such as consultants, banks, public regulating agencies and those relationships may have an impact on the focal relationship. Figure 1 shows a set of relationships potentially connected to a focal business relationship in the sense that they may have an impact on business there. It can be assumed that both the supplier firm and the customer firm recognise and take into consideration the potential impact of the relations to the above mentioned firms or organisations on the focal relationship. The firms can be expected to bring the connected relationships into the focal relationship when they interact.

For the following discussion and analysis we distinguish five kinds of network connections which can be expected to have different impacts on a focal relationship. The first kind is competitive connections (C-

Figure 1. Five kinds of network connection of a focal dyadic relationship

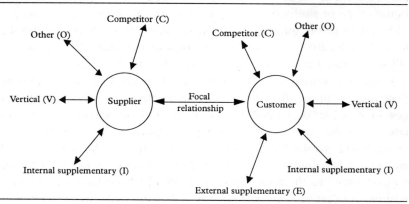

connections) which may occur both on the supplier and the customer side. According to received industrial organisation theory they can be expected to have a negative impact on business in the focal relationship (Scherer 1980). Case studies of business markets, however, have demonstrated that they have positive consequences in some situations (Laage-Hellman 1989). A customer may, for instance, not be willing to buy a new product from a supplier unless there exist competitive suppliers that can be utilised if problems would occur. C-connections on the supplier side refer to the connections between the supplier's relationships with other customers and the focal relationship. Evidently, such connections may have both a positive and a negative effect on business in the focal relationship. Thus, on one hand one customer may require an exclusive relation with the supplier. In that case the supplier's relationships with the two customers are negatively connected. On the other hand, a customer may consider another customer's relationship with the supplier as an indication that the supplier firm is a reliable supplier. In that case, the two customer relationships are positively connected.

The second kind of business network connection is value chain connections (V-connections), that is relationships that are connected along the value chain preceding and following the focal dyad. For instance, a supplier's attractiveness to a customer may be based on its having a specific supplier (Webster 1991). Correspondingly, a customer firm's customer may require that the customer firm has a relationships with a specific supplier firm. In the literature we can find instances of increasing interfirm organising along the value chain in order to enhance efficiency (Kogut 1984). It can be expected that such vertically connected relationships have a distinct impact on the focal relationship.

Figure 1 shows also connected relationships with supplementary suppliers. Being supplementary implies that they have a supporting effect on business in the focal relationship. Two different kinds of supplementary relationships can, however, be distinguished. One concerns the suppliers of supplementary products, such as components that are specifically adapted to the product supplied in the focal relationship. Another, and special, case of supplementarity exists when the supplementarity is a consequence of belonging to the same firm. There may exist another relationship between the two firms that in some way can support the focal relationship. We call this internal supplementarity I-connection as distinct from the external supplementarity or E-connection.

Finally, as suggested by Figure 1 there is reason to consider the importance of connected relationships with various non-commercial organisations or agencies. Thus, for a firm supplying big projects internationally relations to consultants, banks, international organisations, and regulating agencies may have a strong impact on the relationship with a specific customer. We call these ancillary connections A-connections.

Against this background we expect that dyadic business relationships are contingent on C-, V-, E-, I-, and A-connections and that the contingencies of the connections are different.

2.2 The atmosphere of business relationships

Evidently, the wide spectrum of connections listed above can also be expected to affect various aspects of a focal business relationship. In the European International Marketing and Purchasing (IMP) project the atmosphere concept is used to handle the dynamics of business relationships. The atmosphere concept was, in fact, introduced by Williamson (1975) in his early conceptualisation of the transaction-cost approach. He abandoned the concept, but it was used by the IMP group as an intervening variable linking buyer-seller interaction variables – interacting parties, interaction processes, and interaction environment – to each other (Ford 1990; Håkansson 1982). In this chapter we explore how the atmosphere is affected by one aspect of the interaction environment, the network context of the relationship.

Hallén and Sandström (1988) see the atmosphere as the emotional setting in which business between two partners is conducted and suggest that important atmosphere elements are understanding, trust, and power-dependence. Those elements are also stressed in many conceptualisations of relationships and, particularly, those using a social exchange framework (Dwyer, Schurr and Oh 1987). According to Anderson and Narus (1990, p.42) mutual understanding is the distinctive characteristic of working partnerships. Trust is one of the basic concepts in the social exchange framework (Blau 1964; Dwyer, Schurr and Oh 1987). Trust can also be seen as the correlate of opportunism, which is one of the basic concepts in the transaction-cost approach (Williamson 1985). Morgan and Hunt (1994) have demonstrated that trust – together with commitment – is a powerful construct linking relationship antecedent and outcome variables. Power is a fundamental concept in the political economy framework (Stern and Reve 1980) as well as in social exchange and exchange network theory (Cook and Emerson 1978; Markovsky, Willer and Patton 1988). The roles of the understanding, trust and power-dependence differ between models of exchange relationships and it seems to be no clear agreement on the causal relations among them. But, altogether, these characteristics are present in dyadic business relationships, although in varying combinations. This chapter accepts the unclarity and subsumes the different aspects of the business relationships under the heading atmosphere.

2.3 Network connections and relationship atmosphere

The atmosphere elements differ with regard to the impact that can be expected from structural network properties. Mutual understanding concerns the exchange partners' willingness to recognise each other's goals and conditions. Partly this is related to an awareness of the partner's relations to other actors and to what extent those connected relations support or hinder the focal relationship. Mutual understanding can therefore be, at least partially, affected by connections in the exchange network.

Trust has been defined as »willingness to rely on an exchange partner in whom one has confidence« (Moorman, Deshpandé, and Zaltman 1993, p. 82). There seem to be two characteristics of the exchange partner that are relevant, trustworthiness and capability. While trustworthiness primarily is a characteristic of the exchange partner and not related to the network of the exchange partner, capability may as well be a matter of being able to handle network connections. To that extent trust in a focal relationship can be expected to be affected by network connections (Larson 1992).

Power-dependence is a central concept in exchange network theory and there is reason to expect that power in a dyadic relationship is affected by the connected network relations of the parties. Thus, in experimental research Patton and Willer (1990) have demonstrated that an actor, who is exclusively connecting other actors gains in power in relation to the connected actors. Exclusively connected means that the focal actor is exchanging with one of the other actors at the expense of exchange with the other. They have also shown that actors who are inclusively connecting other actors loose in power relative to the connected actors. Inclusively connected means that the focal actor has to exchange with all the connected actors in order to complete the exchange. Since a customer firm according to received industrial organisation theory buys from one supplier at the expense of buying from a competing supplier we should expect that the stronger the customer C-connections, that is the C-connections of the customer, the stronger the power of the customer in relation to the supplier is.

As for the C-connections on the supplier side, the expected relation is more diffuse. C-connection means her an other customer relationship of the supplier than the focal one. Evidently, in some cases such customer relationships are exclusively connected in the sense that the supplier supplies either the focal customer or the connected customer. In that case supplier C-connection can be expected to reduce the power of the customer in relation to the supplier. But it can as well be expected that a supplier's trade with one customer supports his trade with other customers (Larson 1992). By being accepted as a supplier to a customer firm other customer firms may consider the supplier as having the required capability as a supplier. To that extent the customer relationships are inclusively connected and the power relation can be expected to be advantageous to the customer. Thus, supplier C-connections can be regarded as simultaneously exclusively and inclusively connected. Patton and Willer (1990) found, in experiments that the joint effect of inclusion and exclusion is effectively identical to exclusion. Since we cannot isolate inclusion and exclusion from each other in business markets we have no reason to expect that supplier C-connections reduce customer power in the relation.

Supplementary connections are almost by definition inclusively connecting two suppliers to a customer. The customer needs products from both supplementary suppliers. This means that we can expect that supplementary connections reduce customer power.

In general, the stronger the connections of all kinds the more tightly the network is structured and the less discretion is left to the focal actors. Thus, in tightly connected networks we expect strong power-dependence relations.

The overall expected relations between the independent variables network connections and the dependent variables business relationship atmosphere is summarised as follows. Firstly, the discussion above indicates that we have reason to expect that the atmosphere in a focal business relationship is affected by its network connections. Secondly, there is reason to expect that different dimensions of the atmosphere of a focal business relationships are differently affected by its network connections. Thirdly, the power-dependence relation in a focal business relationship is affected more strongly by the network connections than are the other atmosphere dimensions. Fourthly, the atmosphere of a focal business relationship is differently affected by the different network connections of the relationship. In the following sections these relations are explored in a sample of international business relationships.

3. The Empirical Study

The empirical analysis is based on the data base established in the second European International Marketing and Purchasing (IMP) project. Data about the atmosphere of dyadic business relationships of suppliers in Finland, France, Germany, and Sweden with customers in Finland, France, Germany, Italy, Japan, Sweden, UK and U.S.A. was gathered. Thus, overall it is an international set of business relationships that is investigated. The companies in the set belong to different industries ranging from raw materials over components to equipment.

Interviews were made with marketing managers, who were asked to select an important customer relationship which they had personal experience of. Thus the respondents were selected so that their judgement of the relationship would be important for the company's enactment of the relationship. Questions about the focal customer relationship were answered according to a standardised questionnaire together with the interviewer. The present analysis is based on questions about the atmosphere in the focal relationship and about relationships connected to the focal relationship.

The analysis proceeds in the following three steps:

1) On the basis of attitude data about the atmosphere of a sample of 147 dyadic business relationships a factor analysis is conducted to find the best indicators of the atmosphere variables.
2) The strength of network connections are estimated on the basis of interview data about connected relationships.
3) Regression analyses are performed with the atmosphere variables as dependent variables and the different network connections as independent variables. The scores of the relationships in terms of the atmosphere variables are estimated for relationships for which network connection data are available. The sample of customer network connections analysed is 64, of supplier network connections 54, and of total network connections 50.

3.1 Factor analysis on the atmosphere indicators

The factor analysis is conducted on 27 atmosphere indicators which are expected to reflect the three atmosphere variables understanding, trust and power-dependence (app. 1). The factor analysis results in four dimensions, two of which correspond closely to the theoretical variables understanding and trust. The other two dimensions correspond to two different aspects of the theoretical power-dependence variable. One of them reflects the power balance between the relationship partners. We label this variable customer power. The other reflects the feeling that the exchange partners are stuck together and will not change partners. We label it tie strength.

The four dimensions are dependent variables in the following regression analyses. Thus, for each relationship the scores on the atmosphere dimensions are computed.

3.2 Impact of network connections

The estimated impacts of the network connections are based on a set of questions with the following wording »To what extent is your business with this specific customer affected by *your own* relationship with any specific of the following parties:....?« and a corresponding set of questions with the wording »To what extent is your business with this specific customer affected by *his own* relationships with any specific of the following parties:.......?«. The possible alternative network connections that the respondents were asked to identify and the categorisation of them is shown in Table 1. The strength of each connection was measured on a five-grade scale from »not at all« to »very much«.
On that basis we compute the average impact on the focal relationships of the five categories of network connections.

3.3 Regression analyses

The impacts of the network connections are independent variables and the relationship atmosphere dependent variables in the regressions as illustrated in Figure 2.
Three sets of multiple regressions are performed on each of the four dependent variables. In the first set, connected relationships on both the customer and supplier sides are used to compute the network connec-

Table 1. Possible Network Connections

	The supplier's relationship with:	The customer's relationship with:
C-connection	any of the supplier's own other customers.	any supplier of products competing with the focal supplier's.
V-connection	any of the supplier's own suppliers.	any customer of the customer's.
E-connection	(exists only as customer related connection)	any supplier of products supplementary to the focal supplier's.
I-connection	any other unit of the customer's firm. any other unit of the supplier's firm.	any other unit of the customer's firm. any other unit of the supplier's firm.
A-connection	any bank or other financial organisation. any law firm or other legal organisation. any consultant or research organisation. any trade union or other social body. any government agency. any international organsation. any other relevant organisation (specify).	any bank or other financial organisation. any law firm or other legal organisation. any consultant or research organisation. any trade union or other social body. any government agency. any international organsation. any other relevant organisation (specify).

Figure 2. Structure of the relations between network connections and relationship atmosphere

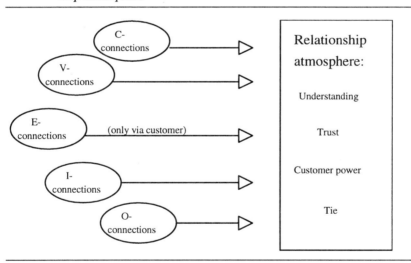

tions. For instance, V-connections are here computed on the basis both of the supplier's connected relationship with own suppliers and of the customer's relationships with own customers. The parameter estimates, t-values and R-squares of the first regression set are shown in Table 2.

Table 2. Impacts of Network Connections on Focal Relationship Atmosphere

Dependent variables **Atmosphere** Factor 1-4 n=50	Parameter estimates and t-values of independent variables					
	Connections via customer and supplier					R2
	C-con- nection	V-con- nection	E-con- nection	I-con- nection	O-con- nection	
»Understanding«	-0.078 (-0.451)	0.083 (0.564)	0.045 (0.363)	0.241 (1.365)	-0.087 (-0.225)	5.1%
»Trust«	-0.260 (-1.476)	0.191 (1.279)	-0.195 (-1.528)	0.136 (0.755)	0.438 (1.103)	12.3%
»Customer power«	0.350 (2.150)*	0.290 (2.157)*	0.048 (0.411)	0.137 (0.825)	-0.250 (-0.676)	21.9%
»Tie«	0.118 (0.861)	0.028 (0.241)	0.271 (2.714)**	0.392 (2.792)**	-0.816 (-2.639)*	35.5%

Notes: [1] T-values in parenthesis [2] *p<0.05; **p<0.01;

First, the table demonstrates that there is no relation between the connections and the atmosphere dimension understanding. There are no significant t-values and R-square is very low. Regarding the atmosphere dimension trust the picture is almost the same although the t-values are closer to 5% significance and R-square is higher.

Table 2 also shows that customer power is significantly (5%-level) related to the independent variable V-connections. This means that the stronger the focal relationship is connected to value-chain relationships the stronger is customer power as perceived by the supplier in the focal dyad. There is no effect from competitive connections to customer power. It is possible that there is a difference depending on whether there is a supplier or a customer C-connection. We shall return to that in the following regression sets. One fifth of the variations in customer power is explained by the five kinds of network connection of the dyad.

The atmosphere dimension tie strength is significantly related to the independent variables E- and I-connections (1%-level) and A-connections (1%-level) with R-square 35.5%. The effect from E-connection means that the more a business relationship is connected to the customers supplementary supplier relationships the stronger is the tie between the partners as perceived by the supplier. The effect from I-connection indicate that the more the parties are engaged in connected relationships with other business units within the own or the counterpart firms the stronger is the tie between them. Finally, the negative effect from A-connection to tie strength means that the more one of the parties is involved in connected relationships with service firms or non-commercial agencies the weaker is the tie in the focal relationship according to the supplier.

The results shown by Table 2 concern the connections both via the customer and via the supplier. The earlier theoretical discussion stressed, however, that there is reason to expect differences between customer connections and supplier connections at least with regard to the impact on customer power.

Tables 3 and 4 demonstrate the corresponding impacts of customer connections (Table 3) and supplier connections (Table 4) separately, so that a comparison can be made.

Table 3. Impacts of Customer Network Connections on Focal Relationship Atmosphere

Dependent variables **Atmosphere** Factor 1-4 n=64	Parameter estimates and t-values of independent variables					
	Customer network connections					
	C-con-nection	V-con-nection	E-con-nection	I-con-nection	O-con-nection	R2
»Understanding«	-0.124 (-1.403)	0.002 (0.031)	0.025 (0.243)	0.153 (1.269)	-0.061 (-0.234)	4.9%
»Trust«	-0.061 (-0.584)	0.189 (1.848)	-0.273 (**-2.190**)*	0.250 (0.729)	-0.203 (-0.645)	12.8%
»Customer Power«	0.199 (**2.361**)*	0.173 (**2.108**)*	0.062 (0.624)	0.093 (0.805)	-0.232 (-0.917)	22.1%
»Tie«	-0.103 (-1.330)	0.030 (0.402)	0.270 (**2.939**)**	0.331 (**3.119**)**	-0.406 (-1.753)	30.9%

Notes: [1] T-values in parenthesis [2] $p<0.05$; $p<0.01$;

On the whole, Table 3 provides a similar picture as Table 2. Once again there is no relation between network connections and the atmosphere dimension understanding. But the tables differ as Table 3 shows a 5% significant effect from E-connection to trust (the negative sign means positive impact on trust). This means that stronger the customer firm is engaged in a relationship which is supplementary to the focal relationship the stronger is the trust in the focal relationship as perceived by the supplier. Although this should be interpreted with caution it is easy to believe that a customer who is involved in relationships with two strongly supplementary suppliers is anxious to establish trust in the relationships.

A second difference is that there is a significant positive effect (5 %
level) from C-connection to customer power. This means that the more
the customer is engaged in a connected relationship with a competitive
supplier the stronger is the customer power in the focal relationship according to the supplier. This is expected on the basis of received industrial organisation theory, but is almost surprising that the effect of competitive relationships is not stronger.

A third difference compared with Table 2 is that there is no significant
effect from A-connection to tie strength. But the difference between the
two tables is quite small. Note also that the R-squares are almost the
same as in Table 2.

*Table 4. Impacts of Supplier Network Connections on Focal Relationship At-
mosphere*

Dependent variables **Atmosphere** Factor 1-4 n=54	*Parameter estimates and t-values of independent variables*				
	Supplier network connections				
	E-con-nection	V-con-nection	I-con-nection	O-con-nection	R2
»Understanding«	0.085 (0.709)	0.075 (0.668)	-0.108 (0.742)	-0.187 (-0.476)	4%
»Trust«	-0.097 (-0.782)	-0.050 (-0.432)	0.063 (0.417)	0.459 (1.128)	3.6%
»Customer Power«	0.048 (0.397)	0.248 (2.160)*	0.130 (0.880)	0.384 (0.961)	14%
»Tie«	0.262 (2.669)*	0.029 (0.313)	0.382 (3.215)**	-1.080 (-3.364)**	35.6%

Notes: [1] T-values in parenthesis [2] *p<0.05; **p<0.01;

Table 4, finally, shows the results of the regressions when supplier network connections are independent variables. Once again the picture is
almost the same. There is no relation between connections and understanding and no between connections and trust. Thus, the supplier
firm does not perceive that trust in the focal relationship is affected by
its own network connections. There is no relation between customer
power and C-connections, but the effect from V-connection to customer power is unchanged. The absence of relation from C-connection to
customer power is not unexpected, since it is reasonable that supplier
C-connections, that is the connections to other customer relationships
of the supplier, have both positive and negative effects on customer

power, and we have no possibility to separate them. The effect from V-connection means that the supplier's connected relationships with its own suppliers have a positive effect on customer power according to the supplier.

Tie strength is positively affected by the strength of the supplier's connected relationships with other customers (5%-level) and by the supplier's connected relationships with other business units in the firms (1%-level), as well as negatively (1%-level) by the supplier's connected relationships with service firms and non-commercial agencies. R-square of this regression is 35%.

Concerning the expectations summarised at the end of the theoretical section, the regression analyses support the expectation that network connections have an impact on a focal business relationship. This means that there is an empirical basis for saying that dyadic business relationships are embedded in business networks.

We can also see that understanding in the relationships is not at all related to the connected relationships. Thus, an interpretation of this finding is that understanding seems to be created by the exchange partners during the course of exchange, independent of the exchange network structure in which the partners are embedded.

Although the results with regard to trust point in the same direction they are, by no means, as unequivocal. We cannot say that trust is independent of network structure. There is a weak significance in the relation between trust and the customer's supplementary connections indicating that if the customer is engaged in a strongly connected supplementary relationship, the trust is stronger in the focal relationship. And there is a relation, albeit not significant, from the customer's value chain connections to the supplier's perceived trust in the focal relationship. There are some weak signs that an actor's trust in a relationship partner is dependent on the partner's network connections.

The power-dependence dimensions of atmosphere are, as was expected, clearly related to the network connections. Thus, competitive and value-chain connections influence the power balance, with a single exception in the case of the supplier's C-connections. Consistently, the power balance is influenced in favour of the customer firm. R-square indicates that 15 and 22 per cent of the variations in power balance can be explained by the business network connections.

Tie strength is clearly conditioned by the network structure. Consistently, there are significant positive influences from both internally and externally connected supplementary relationships and a negative influence from ancillary connected relationships. In addition, there is a positive effect from the supplier's C-connections to bond. As much as one third of the variations in bond can be explained by network connections.

Evidently, we can conclude, in accordance with the second expectation summarising the theoretical section, that the atmosphere dimensions are affected in different ways by the network connections. We can also conclude that the two power-dependence variables are much more closely related to network structure than are understanding and trust.

From the point of view of the independent variables we can clearly see that there are differences between the connections with regard to the impact on the atmosphere. First, customer C-connections have a positive effect on customer power only. V-connections have a consistent positive impact on customer power, as perceived by the supplier, in the focal business relationships, but no impact on any other atmosphere dimensions. I-connections have a consistent positive impact on bond in the focal relationships. E-connections have consistently, when they exist, a positive impact on bond. A-connections, finally, have a consistent negative effect on bond albeit not significant when they are on the customer side.

On the whole the three tables indicate that the similarities of the effects from connections on the supplier and the customer sides are striking. Network organising is almost the same irrespective of supplier or customer side but network organising is different depending on the category of connected relationships and depending on the atmosphere dimension.

4. Discussion

The overall argument of this paper is that viewing dyadic business relationships in a business network context can fruitfully contribute to our understanding of them. The empirical study supports this view. Moreover, since the network concept used in the paper is closely related to the network concept in exchange network theory there is a basis for generalising from that theory to business network settings. Such generalisation, evidently, must be done with caution. Exchange network theory has been validated in experimental laboratories but business network theory must deal with a more ambiguous, complex and fluid business reality. It seems, however, to be a potential for experimental research in which assumptions from business relationship research are governing experimental design. Possibly, business games may be useful for bridging the gap between exchange network laboratories and business network realities.

It is interesting that as much as one third of the variations in bonds between the partners in the focal relationships is explained by the impact of connected network structure. It is also interesting that this is a result of the strengthening impact from externally – other customers in the case of supplier – and internally supplementary connections together with a weakening impact from ancillary relationships. Value chain connections do not contribute at all to the explanation. The more of connections to service firms and non-commercial agencies the less the exchange partners in the focal relationships are committed to each other. In particular, this holds for the supplier's connections. There seem to be reasons for further research about the roles and impacts of relationships with institutional actors in business networks.

There are reasons to be cautious in drawing conclusions from this study. One reason is that the data about both atmosphere and network connections are provided by just one informant, albeit one who is familiar with and responsible for the relationship. Since business relationships may involve a number of persons it could be argued that the atmosphere in some cases is too complex to be evaluated by one single person. The same probably holds for information about network connections. But we mean that the respondent provides the perceptions of both connections and atmosphere that govern the enactment of the relationship.

A particular feature of the study is that it is only based on the judgements of one of the business partners, the supplier firm. This may be the reason why all connection effects on customer power are positive. It is possible that a respondent in charge of marketing is biased so that strong value chain connections, implying tighter network organising, are perceived as strengthening the counterpart's power and reducing the own power. Future research comparing the judgement's of the two exchange partners seems to be fruitful.

Our findings have some interesting managerial implications. First, the study demonstrates that relationship strategies ought to consider the network structure in which the focal relationships are embedded. It in-

dicates also that understanding is created between the exchange partners independent of the surrounding network. Thus, as far as this study
concerns network connections are not obstacles to development of mutual understanding and thereby a working partnership between the partners (Anderson and Narus 1990).

In a similar way the study shows that trust can also be developed
within the relationship in a social exchange process that can overcome
obstacles that are external to the relationship. Both understanding and
trust are more a result of productive interaction processes than of partner selection.

But, this does not mean that the network context is irrelevant. It has
a strong conditioning effect on power balance and ties in the relationship. In that way it sets clear limits on the possibilities to establish and
develop relationships by managing understanding and trust. The relationship atmosphere is a whole, with elements of understanding, trust,
power and bonds, and a relationship strategy cannot focus one and neglect other elements. Thus, if the effects of network structure, via the intervening variables power and tie strength, is not taken into consideration relationship strategies focusing understanding and trust only may
be impossible to realise.

Appendix 1.
Factor analysis on the attitude data on atmosphere

Method: Varimax
Rotated Factor Pattern
Mineigen=1.4 N=148 Missing Values=82 The variance explained by
each factor: Factor 1=4.967, Factor 2=2.797, Factor 3=2.283, Factor
4=1.730

Atmosphere indicators	Factor 1: Under-standing	Factor 2: Trust	Factor 3: Customer power	Factor 4: Mutual commit-ment
The customer has a good understanding of our problems as a supplier.	**0.75053**	-0.08988	0.06633	0.12161
Misunderstandings between our two companies are quite rare.	**0.68491**	-0.23986	-0.08936	-0.03161
We like dealing with this customer.	**0.67683**	-0.24060	0.26173	-0.04263
The customer's motives are generally clear to us.	**0.64465**	-0.19829	-0.00545	0.06796
We are satisfied with the level of attention we receive from this customer.	**0.63927**	0.10237	0.06776	-0.04273
We feel that we can trust this customer completely.	**0.62398**	-0.48502	0.06841	0.04761
It is easy to agree about how to handle the various issues that arise in this relationship.	**0.60234**	-0.20125	-0.04685	-0.01280
We have full confidence in the information provided to us from this customer.	**0.56871**	-0.33673	0.18968	0.16056
We can criticize the customer face-to-face when we con-sider it justified without jeopardizing the relationship.	**0.53781**	-0.03172	-0.03828	-0.10338
Agreements on contract terms are usually reached easily.	**0.51225**	-0.32577	-0.06945	-0.19116
Business with this customer is usually based on mutual trust rather than legal agreements.	**0.48311**	-0.34300	0.20973	-0.09596
We are well aware of this customer's relations with other firms in this market.	**0.38399**	0.20677	0.07728	0.06774
This customer tries to exploit the advantage of our cooperation for his own sake.	-016081	**0.68789**	0.17521	0.14520
Our relations with other companies have caused problems in our relationship with this customer.	-0.10016	**0.57002**	0.23661	-0.12999
This customer withholds important information from us.	**-0.35113**	**0.55867**	0.33186	-009553
We have the upper hand in this relationship.	0.06570	**0.48826**	-0.30619	0.17587
The customer's organisation is rather closed to us when we want to obtain non-routine information.	**-0.34819**	**0.40057**	-0.12005	-0.09955
We are convinced that this customer can handle confidential information from us.	0.38951	**-0.59742**	0.08158	0.02904
If necessary we would go quite far in making concessions to this customer.	0.03849	0.09825	**0.65007**	-0.17525
We feel dependent on this customer.	0.14951	0.12920	**0.58433**	0.23020
Adaptations are more frequently made by us than by this customer.	-0.20767	-0.13217	**0.54071**	-0.01308
We usually make an effort to establish personal contacts with people from the customer's company.	0.08075	0.01723	**0.53546**	-0.00823
We have a feeling of mutual dependence in our relationship with this customer.	0.13201	-0.12490	**0.45423**	0.31722
Our relationship with this customer is instrumental for obtaining information necessary for our other activities in this market.	0.16490	0.14925	**0.33471**	0.11337
Considering everything, we actually have no alternative to this relationship.	-0.18354	-0.01194	0.01273	**0.79267**
It would be very difficult for us to find a replacement for this customer.	-0.15578	-0.01726	0.33858	**0.64422**
It is very unlikely that this customer would stop purchasing from us in the near future.	0.17749	0.13918	-0.10239	**0.53580**

References

Achrol, Ravi S, 1991. »Evolution of the Marketing Organisation: New Forms for Turbulent Environments,« *Journal of Marketing*, Vol. 55 (October), 77-93.

Achrol, Ravi S., Torger Reve and Louis W. Stern, 1983. »The Environment of Marketing Channel Dyads: A Framework for Comparative Analysis,« *Journal of Marketing*, Vol. 47 (Fall), 55-67.

Anderson, James C., Håkan Håkansson and Jan Johanson, 1994. »Dyadic Business Relationships Within a Business Network Context,« *Journal of Marketing*, Vol. 58 (Fall).

Anderson, James C. and James A. Narus, 1990. »A Model of Distributor Firm and Manufacturer Firm Working Partnerships,« *Journal of Marketing*, Vol. 54 (January), 42-58.

Anderson, Erin and Barton Weitz, 1989. »Determinants of Continuity in Conventional Industrial Channel Dyads,« *Marketing Science*, Vol. 8 (Fall), 310-323.

Baker , Wayne E., 1990. »Market Networks and Corporate Behavior,« *American Journal of Sociology*, Vol. 96 (November) 589-625.

Blau, P. M., 1964. *Exchange and Power in Social Life*, New York: Wiley.

Cook, Karen S. and Richard M. Emerson, 1978. »Power, Equity, Commitment in Exchange Networks: Theory and Experimental Results,« *American Sociological Review*, Vol. 43 (October), 721-738.

Dwyer, F. Robert, Paul H. Schurr and Sejo Oh, 1987. »Developing Buyer-Seller Relationships,« *Journal of Marketing*, Vol. 51 (April), 11-27.

Emerson, Richard M., 1972. »Social Exchange Theory,« *Annual Review of Sociology*, Vol. 2, 335-62.

Emerson, Richard M., 1981. »Social Exchange Theory,« in M. Rosenberg and R. Turner, (eds.). *Social Psychology: Sociological Perspectives*, New York: Basic Books, 30-65.

Ford, D. I., (ed.), 1990. *Understanding Business Markets: Interaction, Relationships and Networks*. San Diego: Academic Press.

Forsgren, Mats and Ulf Olsson, 1992. »Power Balancing in an International Business Network,« in M. Forsgren and J. Johanson, (eds.), *Managing Networks in International Business*, Philadelphia: Gordon and Breach.

Frazier, Gary L., 1983. »Interorganizational Exchange Behavior in Marketing Channels: A Broadened Perspective,« *Journal of Marketing*, Vol. 47 (Fall), 68-78.

Gadde, Lars-Erik and Lars-Gunnar Mattsson, 1987. »Stability and Change in Network Relationships,« *International Journal of Research in Marketing*, Vol. 4, 29-41.

Granovetter, Mark, 1985. »Economic Action and Social Structure: The Problem of Embeddedness,« *American Journal of Sociology*, Vol. 91 (November) 481-510.

Håkansson, Håkan, (ed.), 1982. *International Marketing and Purchasing of Industrial Goods: An Interaction Approach*. Chichester: Wiley.

Hallén, Lars, Jan Johanson and Nazeem Seyed-Mohamed, 1991. »Inter-firm Adaptation in Business Relationships,« *Journal of Marketing*, Vol. 55 (April), 29-37.

Hallén, L. and M. Sandström, 1988. »Relationship Atmosphere in International Business,« in P.W. Turnbull and S. Paliwoda, (eds.). *Research Developments in International Marketing*, Manchester: Manchester School of Management.

Heide, Jan B. and George John, 1988. »The Role of Dependence Balancing in Safeguarding Transaction-Specific Assets in Conventional Channels,« *Journal of Marketing*, Vol. 52 (May), 186-92.

Hertz, S., 1993. *The Internationalization Processes of Freight Transport Companies*, Stockholm: The Economic Research Institute.

Homans, George C., 1958. »Social Behavior as Exchange,« *American Journal of Sociology*, Vol. 63 (May), 597-606.

Iacobucci, Dawn and Nigel Hopkins, 1992. »Modeling Dyadic Interactions and Networks in Marketing,« *Journal of Marketing Research*, Vol. 29 (February), 5-17.

Kogut, Bruce, 1984. »Normative Observations on the International Value-Added Chain and Strategic Groups,« *Journal of International Business Studies*, Vol. 16,

Laage-Hellman, Jens, 1989. *Technological Development in Industrial Networks*, Uppsala: Acta Universitatis Upsaliensis.

Larson, Andrea, 1992. »Network Dyads in Entrepreneurial Settings: A Study of the Governance of Exchange Relationships,« *Administrative Science Quarterly*, Vol. 37: 76-104.

Lee, J-W., 1991. *Swedish Firms Entering the Korean Market – Position Development in Distant Industrial Networks*, Uppsala: Department of Business Studies.

Markovsky, Barry, David Willer and Travis Patton, 1988. »Power in Networks,« *American Sociological Review*, Vol. 53 (April), 220-36.

Moorman, Christine, Rohit Deshpandé, and Gerald Zaltman, 1993. »Factors Affecting Trust in Market Research Relationships,« *Journal of Marketing*, Vol. 57 (January), 81-101.

Morgan, Robert M. and Shelby D. Hunt, 1994. »The Commitment-Trust Theory of Relationship Marketing,« *Journal of Marketing*, Vol. 58 (July), 20-38.

Patton, Travis and David Willer, 1990. »Connection and Power in Centralized Exchange Networks,« *Journal of Mathematical Sociology*, Vol. 16 (1), 31-49.

Scherer, F. M., 1980. *Industrial Market Structure and Economic Performance*, Boston, Mass.: Houghton Mifflin Comp.

Thibaut, J.W. and H. Kelley, 1959. *The Social Psychology of Groups*. New York: Wiley.

Thorelli, Hans B., 1986. »Networks: Between Markets and Hierarchies,« *Strategic Management Journal*, Vol. 7 (January-February), 37-51.

Webster, F. E., 1979. *Industrial Marketing Strategy*, New York: Wiley.

Webster, Frederick E., 1993. »The Changing Role of Marketing in the Corporation,« *Journal of Marketing*, Vol. 50 (October), 1-17.

Willer, David, 1992. »Predicting Power in Exchange Networks: A Brief History and Introduction to the Issues,« *Social Networks*, Vol. 14, 187-211.

Willer, D. and B. Anderson, (eds.), 1981. *Networks, Exchange and Coercion*, New York: Elsevier.

Williamson, O. E., 1975. *Markets and Hierarchies: Analysis and Antitrust Implications*, New York: The Free Press.

Williamson, O. E., 1985. *The Economic Institutions of Capitalism. Firms, Markets, Relational Contracting*, New York: The Free Press.

18. Dimensions of Less-Hierarchical Structures in Multinationals

Rebecca Marschan

1. Introduction

A growing body of research has observed new structural forms in multinational corporations (Bartlett and Ghoshal, 1989; Forsgren, 1990; Hedlund, 1986; White and Poynter, 1990). Following the broad school of thought including the transnational corporation (Bartlett and Ghoshal, 1989), the heterarchy (Hedlund, 1986; Hedlund and Rolander, 1990) and the multi-centre firm (Forsgren, 1990; Forsgren et al., 1992), writers in the area have described MNC organisations as flatter and more horizontal than the traditional ones. The intended gains of these organisational forms, referred to as less-hierarchical structures in the present chapter, are shown to stem from enhanced entrepreneurship; increased cost efficiency and resource utilisation; improved decision making and working conditions within the company (Bartlett and Ghoshal, 1990; White and Poynter, 1990).

However, most research in the field seems to overlook the precise examination of what the movement toward a less-hierarchical structure actually entails and how the process is implemented. First, there are few studies with an explicit empirical basis that would concentrate on the structural change process itself. Second, prior research on organisational evolution in multinational corporations (MNCs) has largely focused on headquarters' viewpoint neglecting the subsidiary perspective (Davidson and Haspeslagh, 1982; Franko, 1976; Stopford and Wells, 1972). Third, most studies have a top management approach (e.g. Bartlett and Ghoshal, 1993; 1995a) without incorporating accounts of middle managers and staff, whose perception of the structural change may differ from that at the apex of the organisation. Such isolated studies at one organisational level are likely to result in a more biased understanding of the structural change process than multi-level investigations (Södergren, 1992). Given this, it would seem that there is a need to extend our understanding of the process toward less-hierarchical structures in MNCs.

The principal aim of this chapter is to address the phenomenon of less-hierarchical structures in MNCs by critically examining the models of such organisational forms and the underlying assumptions associated with them. In the current literature, it remains an open question as to whether the process toward a less-hierarchical structure in MNCs involves, for instance, removal of management layers, decrease in the level of bureaucratisation, and delegation of decision making authority to subsidiary staff or only some of these aspects. Empirical data are used to support the argumentation.

2. Models of New Structural Forms in Multinationals

In the current literature, one can identify several models which describe recent structural forms in MNCs: the heterarchy (Hedlund, 1986; Hedlund and Rolander, 1990), the transnational corporation (Bartlett and Ghoshal, 1989), the multi-centre firm (Forsgren, 1990), the horizontal organisation (White and Poynter, 1990) and the multifocal corporation (Doz, 1986). These writers adopt a broad perspective on the organising of foreign operations, since they do not suggest a uniform organisational chart as a structural remedy[78]. Rather, the underlying organisational form of these models varies, but it seems to share elements of formal and informal matrix management (Bartlett and Ghoshal, 1990; Hedlund, 1986). Table 1 summarises the five models reviewed, which describe recent organisational development in MNCs.

As Table 1 shows, scholars investigating recent organisational development in MNCs all describe parallel findings in their own terms and thus there was a need to develop an umbrella concept for the purpose of this chapter. Based on the literature review, it can be concluded that regardless of the subtle differences in emphasis of the different approaches, the above researchers share a general view about the organisational evolution in multinationals: their structures are becoming less hierarchical. The fact that top management of several MNCs have had to reconsider the long-standing principle that 'the parent always knows best' has

---

78. According to the classical approach (Whittingon, 1993), the strategy-structure paradigm explains the evolution of organizational structures (Chandler, 1962). The central assumption of the paradigm is to have one superior structure to match the corporate strategy.

Table 1. Comparison of Five Models of Recent Organizational Development in MNCs

Criteria	Heterarchy	Multi-Centre	Transnational	Multilocal	Horizontal
Literature	Hedlund 1986, Hedlund & Rolander 1990, Hedlund 1993	Forsgren 1990, Forsgren & al. 1992	Bartlett 1986, Bartlett & Ghoshal 1987a, 1987b, 1989, 1995a, 1995b	Doz 1986, Doz & Prahalad 1987a	White & Poynter 1990
Theoretical Frame of Reference	cybernetics, organization theory	resource dependence	strategy-structure paradigm, contingency theory	theories on political influence, diversified MNC	decision-making processes
Focus	innovativeness, change, flexibility	external and internal networks	strategy-structure paradigm, contingency theory	balancing global and local challenges	horizontal exchange of information
Organizational Structure	coinciding knowledge, action and people	multi-centred network of headquarters and subsidiary units	aiming at global efficiency, local responsiveness, transfer of learning	between conventional oraganizational forms and matrix structures	horizontal network of functions
Implications for Strategy	changes in information technology, acquisitions	considering network relationships	industry characteristics	balancing global integration and national responsiveness	achieving globally and locally based advantages
Driving Force	changes in information technology, acquisitions	power structures, politics	industry characteristics	industry characteristics	competitive advantage
Relationships between Units	interdependent, circular, shifting	interdependent	interdependent	interdependent	horizontal, interdependent
Advantages in Relations to Conventional Structures	more efficient, more innovative, entrepreneurship aon a large scale	more efficient, more innovative	better performance, more motivated personnel	stronger competitive advantage	stronger competitive advantage

Source: Adapted from Marschan (1994:10).

required a radical change in the way the entire company is managed, turning it from a hierarchical pyramid into an integrated network (Bartlett and Ghoshal, 1989; Forsgren, 1990).

Consequently, the term 'less-hierarchical structure' is developed to refer to the broad array of models identified in the literature (see Table 1). The less-hierarchical MNC operates like a network, beyond the constraints of formal, bureaucratic structures. Under such a structure, subsidiary units are highly differentiated and functionally interdependent, which results in complex flows of products, people and information (Bartlett and Ghoshal, 1989). These subsidiary units are granted the necessary responsibility and decision making authority for performing strategically important functions, thus revealing the importance of global and regional functional management (Hedlund, 1994). While units across the subsidiary network are geographically very dispersed, they are coordinated and controlled particularly through informal mechanisms, such as organisational culture, interlocking board of directors and personal relationships (Hedlund and Rolander, 1990; Hedlund, 1993; Marschan et al., 1996). Unlike Nohria and Eccles (1992) who define network organisations in terms of personal relationships, the umbrella concept of 'less-hierarchical structures' is clearly broader encompassing also social networks. The advantages of less-hierarchical structures have been widely shown in prior research in terms of increased flexibility in management, innovativeness, efficient use of resources and work satisfaction (Doz and Prahalad, 1987a; Bartlett and Ghoshal, 1989; White and Poynter, 1990).

The term 'less-hierarchical structure' stems from two interrelated factors emphasised in the literature (Bartlett and Ghoshal, 1989; Forsgren, 1990; Hedlund, 1986): (1) the traditional hierarchy between headquarters and its foreign subsidiaries is altered, and (2) the role of formal structure is becoming marginalised. In the less-hierarchical MNC, headquarters transfers some of the key activities with the necessary decision making authority and control to subsidiary level. Thus, there is less of the traditional hierarchy between headquarters and foreign subsidiaries. Still, the division of power needs to be reconsidered, as the new organisation consists of headquarters, the subsidiaries which have become strategic centres, and the subsidiaries that remain as non-centres. Given the multiple centres of control, one would assume that in a less-hierarchical structure power will increasingly affect inter-subsidiary linkages, rather than traditional headquarters-subsidiary relationships (Forsgren, 1990; Forsgren et al., 1992). Obviously, the term 'less-hierarchical' does not refer to complete removal of hierarchy.

In addition to the shift in power between headquarters and foreign subsidiaries, a contributing factor to the use of the term 'less hierarchical' is the diminished role of formal structure[79]. As mentioned earlier, the simultaneous strategic demands in the external business environment would require the designing of highly complex formal structures, which would need to be continuously adapted and changed. Also internally the formal structure is considered incapable of capturing the complex characteristics of the subsidiary network within the MNC. Thus, it is suggested in the relevant literature, that in order to gain more flexibility, the modern MNC gives up the logic of formal structure as well as the hierarchy and symmetry associated with it (Bartlett and Ghoshal, 1990; Egelhoff, 1993; Hedlund and Rolander, 1990). To counterbalance the reduced importance of formal structure, these writers propose that the MNC top management will rely on informal coordination and control devices such as culture and inter-unit communication.

When reviewing the relevant literature, one can claim that the notion of hierarchy on the one hand, and its absence on the other hand, has been highly influential for research and intellectual debate in organisational theory (Hedlund, 1993). Early organisational theorists[80] who investigated principles of management and scientific management, bureaucratic organisations and decision making as well as formal and informal organisations argued in favour of authority, specialisation, written rules and regulations, while others saw benefits in organising work in a less bureaucratic way. For instance, Burns and Stalker (1966, in McPhee 1985) presented such a structural form as the organic organisation, indicating a minimal degree of formality. Likewise, Kanter (1983) identified an integrative type of organisation showing the participative behaviour of key staff.

Clearly then, viewing organisational structures as more or less hierarchical is by no means new. However, the approach has not been widely applied to MNCs. Prior research has largely focused on head-

79. Formal structure indicates the lines of predetermined information exchanges between superiors and subordinates. It defines the relationships of the command structure within the organization (McPhee, 1985; Jablin, 1987).
80. For instance, Chester Barnard, Henri Fayol, Herbert Simon, Frederic Taylor and Max Weber can be called early organizational theorists.

quarters' perspective, as Andersson et al. (1990:1) remark: 'Most literature on international business presents a hierarchic perspective, where the corporate executive committee controls the subsidiaries and makes the main strategic decisions'. Without any doubt, this quotation reflects reality until recent years. Thus, the contribution of the less-hierarchical approach stems from the important position that foreign subsidiaries have become to occupy within the MNC as opposed to the centrality of headquarters. Given the resources and capabilities embedded in foreign subsidiaries, the less-hierarchical approach should allow the organisation as a whole to fully utilise and combine its competences in a way far beyond the possibilities suggested by a hierarchical organisational chart.

3. Dimensions of the Less-Hierarchical Structure

Rather than examining at an aggregate level whether an MNC has adopted a less-hierarchical structure or not, there seems to be a need to explore in greater depth different dimensions of these new organisational forms. Such an approach would allow a more detailed analysis of the structural change process which tend to require readjustment and long periods of recovery (Bartlett, 1983).

In prior research, however, different dimensions of the less-hierarchical structure are seldom precisely and explicitly determined. What emerges in the current literature is the role of decentralisation in the structural change process (Bartlett and Ghoshal, 1989; Forsgren, 1990; Hedlund, 1986). The less-hierarchical MNC transfers certain activities which used to reside at the centre (headquarters) – such as the locus of control of particular strategic functions and the necessary decision making authority – to subsidiary level. Thus, the term centralisation indicates that authority to make important decisions lies towards the 'head' or centre of an organisation, while decentralisation, on the other hand, implies more autonomy, with authority vested in those further removed from the centre (Cummings, 1995: 103). As Morton (1995) observes, with increased turbulence new organisational forms tend to stress forces of decentralisation endeavouring to increase the level of creativity, innovation and individual motivation. Yet few studies in the field move beyond the overall notion of decentralisation, thus leaving the key dimensions of a less-hierarchical structure undefined.

One can argue that, in the narrowest view, decentralisation equals delegation of decision making authority[81] (e.g. Brooke and Remmers, 1978). However, the fine distinction between decentralisation and other closely related concepts such as geographical dispersal, de-bureaucratisation and delayering, for instance, may exist only in the minds of academics. Recent empirical studies show that company representatives tend to define decentralisation in a broader way, encompassing also additional elements rather than solely delegation of decision making. For instance, results of a survey of 48 American manufacturers suggest that removing layers is a structural change which facilitates decentralised decision making (Chilton, 1995). According to the findings of this survey decentralisation and flatter structures are seen to go hand-in-hand.

In a similar vein, based on a qualitative interview study of 40 Swedish companies from different industries, Södergren (1992) regards restructuring, de-bureaucratisation and delegation as the core components of decentralisation. Here restructuring involves, for instance, establishing smaller units that operate as autonomous profit centres; reducing the number of hierarchical levels (i.e. delayering); and delegating work, responsibility and authority (i.e. empowerment) to local business units. The second core component, de-bureaucratisation, refers to a reduction in formal procedures and guidelines. The third component, delegation, means the transfer of decision making authority as well as the assignment of tasks and responsibility (i.e. empowerment) to lower levels. Clearly, Södergren's findings show the multiple dimensions of decentralisation as a concept. However, while Södergren acknowledges the broad scope of decentralisation efforts, issues directly related to MNCs are excluded from her analysis.

Consequently, from the viewpoint of the less-hierarchical MNC, geographical dispersal seems particularly pertinent in addition to delegation of decision making and delayering. In fact, dispersal in MNCs may occur at two levels: within units, for instance from the subsidiary headquarters to its local front line units, and between units, which tends to involve crossing national frontiers. It seems, however, that in the literature on less-hierarchical MNCs dispersal is most commonly understood as the latter, meaning, for instance, transferring core activities across countries, from corporate to divisional headquarters and/or further to subsidiary units (Forsgren, 1990; Hedlund, 1986; Hedlund and Rolan-

81. This narrow view of decentralization was supported by Forsgren at the workshop on Nordic Research in International Business in 8 -9 June 1995 at Copenhagen Business School.

der, 1990). These writers suggest that such dispersal of key functions is likely to involve also shifting the locus of control from the home country abroad. Thus, dispersal is a central dimension of the less-hierarchical structure.

Moreover, de-bureaucratisation appears to be closely associated with decentralisation and the process of moving toward a less-hierarchical structure (Bartlett and Ghoshal, 1990; Hedlund and Rolander, 1990; Södergren, 1992). Many of the daily routines are assumed to be handled in an environment containing self-disciplined employees, who are not constrained by internal regulations and extensive formalisation[82], but rather steered by a culture of trust (Bartlett and Ghoshal, 1995b). For instance, despite the large size of the corporation, Percy Barnevik, the CEO of Asea Brown Boveri (ABB) the Swedish-Swiss engineering multinational, is reported to 'rip down bureaucracy so executives in Atlanta can launch new products without meddling from the headquarters, so power technicians in Sweden can make design changes, and so factory workers in India can alter production methods on their own' (Schares, 1993: 204). His comment reflects the unique management style in ABB, which Bartlett and Ghoshal have widely used as an example of a successful, less-hierarchical corporation (Bartlett and Ghoshal, 1993; 1995a).

Finally, in less-hierarchical structures, differentiation can be considered an essential dimension of organisational change process. As mentioned earlier, subsidiary units are granted highly specialised roles in terms of functional and geographical responsibilities. For instance, in Electrolux, one of its European units coordinates globally component manufacturing and supplies (Hedlund and Rolander, 1990). Several companies have created finance centres and regional research and development units to support the activities of other subsidiaries. Such a development trend shows the importance of global functional management (Hedlund, 1993).

Figure 1 suggests that the less-hierarchical structure comprises the following five dimensions: (1) delegation of decision making authority to appropriate levels; (2) delayering of organisational levels; (3) geographical dispersal of key functions across units in different countries; (4) de-bureaucratisation of formal procedures; and (5) differentiation of

---

82. Formalization, typically credited to Max Weber, who defined it as a method of enhancing organizational efficiency by making job behaviour explicit through, for instance, task specification (Weber, 1947 in Jablin, 1987).

Figure 1. The Five Dimensions of the Less-Hierarchical Structure.

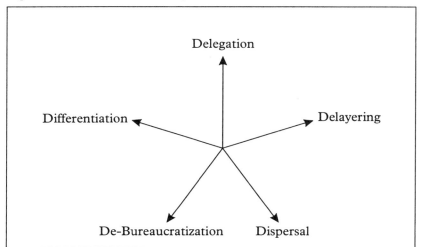

work, responsibility and authority among subsidiary units. Given the influential role of decentralisation in the process of moving toward a less-hierarchical structure, these dimensions are viewed as key factors affecting and enhancing organisational changes.

3.1 Underlying Assumptions

A central assumption in the current literature is that the less-hierarchical structure involves all five dimensions (e.g. Bartlett and Ghoshal, 1990; Hedlund and Rolander, 1990). Writers in the area observe that in truly less-hierarchical MNCs, subsidiary staff are highly involved in decision making and empowered to perform wholly or partly differentiated tasks. Moreover, key responsibilities tend to be geographically dispersed, thus indicating not only physical spread but also transfer of the locus of control from headquarters to subsidiary units. In such MNCs, top management are likely to remove organisational layers and reduce the level of formalisation and bureaucratisation to facilitate the transfer of knowledge and expertise across subsidiary units.

However, as the Finnish multinational KONE Elevators moved toward a less-hierarchical structure, the new organisation did not involve all five dimensions (Marschan, 1994; 1996). To support the structural

Managing the International Firm

change process, the intention of top management was to streamline and improve information flows between subsidiaries by formally channelling communication flows through newly formed, regional engineering centres. The unintended effect, though, was that the new centres created a barrier to horizontal communication flows as they made it more difficult for people within sales subsidiaries in different countries to use their personal relationships (Marschan et al., 1996). Also, for control and co-ordination purposes an additional management layer was introduced. Thus, while the level of delegation, differentiation and dispersal was considerably high in KONE Elevators, the interview data show that the degree of de-bureaucratisation and delayering was perceived to be fairly low, particularly at organisational levels below top management (Marschan, 1996). One can argue that KONE Elevators tried to reorganise according to the normative models of less-hierarchical structures and thus the empirical evidence shows the difficulty of the management and implementation process.

Indeed, Bartlett and Ghoshal (1990) claim that effective implementation of the less-hierarchical structure involves not only structural changes, but also extensive adaptation of other management steering systems. For such radical organisational surgery to succeed, support of the entire staff is necessary. In fact, it is often assumed that lower organisational levels will accept the increase in responsibility and accountability which the organisational change requires (Marschan et al., 1996). Prior research on less-hierarchical structures seems to describe an MNC where a reduction in hierarchy and an increase in common culture leads to a 'happy family solution' (e.g. Bartlett and Ghoshal, 1990; 1993). This positive view of people's attitudes toward decentralisation and empowerment which accompanies the organisational change is seldom questioned or challenged (cf. Marschan et al., 1996; Södergren, 1992). In general, the less-hierarchical structure coupled with decentralisation is perceived as 'good' and morally better than centralisation, which is seen as an inherently evil action[83] (Cummings, 1995; Söder-

83. It should be noted that the various dimensions of the less-hierarchical structure are 'culturally bound'. As Cummings (1995) correctly points out, decentralization is an inherent part of the Western management style coming mainly out of the US. From this perspective, the attributes of the less-hierarchical structure should not be regarded as universally desirable, but rather specific to certain cultural contexts (e.g. Whittington, 1993).

gren, 1990). Clearly then, it seems that the movement toward a less-hierarchical structure tends to be associated with the innate dislike of bureaucracy and perceived degree of efficiency.

Nevertheless, the findings of a study conducted in 200 UK-based organisations suggest that staff support for decentralisation efforts should be reconsidered (Holbeche, 1994). In fact, Holbeche describes the general attitude of the respondents toward decentralisation accompanied by a reduction in hierarchical levels as rather negative. Staff associated decentralisation with the resultant job loss which has tended to follow restructuring. Overall, delayering was found to lead to a decrease in morale, job satisfaction and organisational commitment, fewer promotion prospects and an increase in the amount of work. In short, the respondents in Holbeche's study regarded decentralisation accompanied by delayering as primarily a cost-cutting exercise.

Following this, the attitude toward the less-hierarchical structure as a 'happy family solution' may also be explained by the position the observer occupies within the MNC. Most probably, a comparison of headquarters and subsidiary perspectives may reveal a discrepancy in the perception of the structural change. Hedlund (1994) maintains that transferring key functions from headquarters to subsidiary level may result in an 'ethnocentric backlash' in the implementation stage. From the subsidiary perspective, any lengthening of the lines of communication to the top of the organisation may appear as bureaucratisation when these lines are substituted with an intermediary organisational layer headed by an increasingly lower ranked manager from the home country (Hedlund, 1994). Thus, subsidiary staff may be of the opinion that an ideology of delegation is masking the reality of bureaucratisation and formalisation (e.g. Brooke and Remmers, 1978). As Södergen (1992) correctly notes, decentralisation is a relative concept and thus, the 'average' degree of decentralisation would have little information value when examining structural change processes.

Clearly then, there are several assumptions underlying prior research on less-hierarchical structures. One can argue that writers in the area have predominantly adopted a normative approach, thus underestimating the challenges involved in the management and implementation of these new structural forms (e.g. Bartlett and Ghoshal, 1989; 1990; White and Poynter, 1990).

4. Implications for Further Research

The aim of the previous discussion was to address the phenomenon of new organisational forms in MNCs, referred to as less-hierarchical structures in the present chapter. Most research centres around describing the characteristics and the intended gains of the less-hierarchical structures at a rather general level (e.g. Bartlett and Ghoshal, 1989; White and Poynter, 1990). There seems to be limited the conceptualisation of the term, the structural change process itself and what it actually entails. In this respect the present analysis has focused on examining the dimensions of less-hierarchical structures and the basic assumptions underlying the structural change process. Empirical examples have been advanced to illustrate the complexity of these new organisational forms.

In most research in the field the issue of less-hierarchical structures has been somewhat clouded by the open question as to whether the structural change process in MNCs involves, for instance, removal of management layers, decrease in the level of bureaucratisation, and delegation of decision making authority to subsidiary staff or only some of these aspects. The concentration of prior research on the views of top management perspective rather than broadening the examination to include perceptions of middle management and operative staff has resulted in a more narrow comprehension of less-hierarchical structures than what multi-level investigations would have produced. Indeed, the previous discussion shows that the outcome of the structural change process is a multifaceted interplay between several factors. Moreover, physical distance separating the different units of the MNC further adds complexity to the analysis. In fact, the genuine intention of top management, for instance to delegate decision making authority to foreign units by geographically dispersing key activities may be perceived at subsidiary levels as an attempt to increase bureaucratisation and formalisation. Given this, defining precisely the dimensions of the structural form and stating explicitly the perspective adopted in the analysis, seems to be a suitable approach for examining the process toward a less-hierarchical MNC.

Thus, an effort has been made to conceptualise the less-hierarchical structure. The present chapter adopts the position that such an organisational form comprises five dimensions: (1) delegation of decision making authority to appropriate levels, (2) delayering of organisational levels, (3) dispersal of key functions across units in different countries, (4) de-bureaucratisation of formal rules and procedures, and (5) differentiation of work, responsibility and authority among subsidiary units. These five dimensions are viewed as key factors affecting and enhancing the process of moving toward a less-hierarchical structure.

With few exceptions (e.g. Doz and Prahalad, 1987b), the field of new structural forms in MNCs is characterised by a limited number of longitudinal studies of the process toward a less-hierarchical structure (Melin, 1992). In future research, the structural dimensions presented in this chapter could be used to analyse MNCs in different stages of the process toward a less-hierarchical form. As more effort is devoted to operationalisation of key terms, empirical studies could also include some scaling to measure the relative strength of the structural dimensions in less-hierarchical MNCs as Figure 2 shows.

Figure 2. Two Profiles of the Less-Hierarchical Structure.

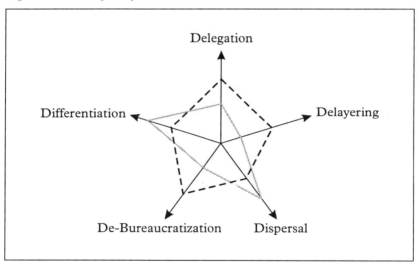

To conclude, the process of moving toward a less-hierarchical structure in MNCs is dynamic and in continuous flux. From this perspective, analysing the structural change process using what have been described as the five structural dimensions may capture shifts in implementation stage and changes in the degree of one dimension. As a response to internal and external changes, some MNCs may recentralise their activities within a certain dimension such as delegation of decision making, leaving otherwise the structure unchanged. Such detailed empirical data would contribute to the understanding of the challenges and difficulties involved in the management and implementation of less-hierarchical MNCs.

References

Andersson, Ulf, Mats Forsgren, Cecilia Pahlberg and Peter Thilenius, 1990. »Global Firms in Internationalized Networks«. In *Proceedings of the 16th Annual Conference of the European International Business Association*, Madrid, December 12th-15th, 1990.

Bartlett, Christopher and Sumantra Ghoshal, 1995a. »Changing the Role of Top Management: Beyond Structure to Processes«, *Harvard Business Review*, January-February, 86-96.

Bartlett, Christopher and Sumantra Ghoshal, 1995b. »Rebuilding Behavioral Context: Turning Process Re-engineering into People Rejuvenation«, *Sloan Management Review*, Fall, 11-23.

Bartlett, Christopher and Sumantra Ghoshal, 1993. »Beyond the M-Form: Toward a Managerial Theory of the Firm«, *Strategic Management Journal*, Vol. 14, 23-46.

Bartlett, Christopher and Sumantra Ghoshal, 1990. »Matrix Management: Not a Structure, a Frame of Mind«, *Harvard Business Review*, July-August, 138-147.

Bartlett, Christopher and Sumantra Ghoshal, 1989. *Managing Across Borders: The Transnational Solution*. Harvard Business School Press, Boston.

Bartlett, Christopher and Sumantra Ghoshal, 1987a. »Managing Across Borders: New Strategic Requirements«, *Sloan Management Review*, Summer, 7-17.

Bartlett, Christopher and Sumantra Ghoshal, 1987b. »Managing Across Borders: New Organizational Responses«, *Sloan Management Review*, Fall, 43-53.

Bartlett, Christopher, 1986. »Building and Managing the Transnational: The New Organizational Challenge«, in M. Porter, (ed.) *Competition in Global Industries*. Harvard Business School Press, Boston.

Bartlett, Christopher, 1983. »MNCs: Get off the Reorganization Merry-Go-Around«, *Harvard Business Review*, March-April, 138-146.

Brooke, Michael and Lee Remmers, 1978. *The Strategy of Multinational Enterprise*. Pitman Publishing, London.

Chilton, Kenneth, 1995. »How American Manufacturers are Facing the Global Marketplace?«, *Business Horizons*, July-August, 10-19.

Cummings, Stephen, 1995. »Centralization and Decentralization: The Never-ending Story of Separation and Betrayal«, *Scandinavian Journal of Management*, Vol. 11, No. 2, 103-117.

Davidson, William and Philippe Haspeslagh, 1982. »Shaping a Global Product Organization«, *Harward Business Review*, July-August, 125-132.

Doz, Yves and C. Prahalad, 1987a. *The Multinational Mission*. Free Press, New York.

Doz, Yves and C. Prahalad, 1987b. »A Process Model of Strategic Redirection in Large Complex Firms: The Case of Multinational Corporations«, in A. Pettigrew, (ed.). *The Management of Strategic Change*. Basil Blackwell, New York.

Doz, Yves, 1986. *Strategic Management in Multinational Companies*. Pergamon Press, Oxford. Ferner, Anthony, Paul Edwards, and Keith Sisson, 1995. »Coming Unstuck? In Search of the 'Corporate Glue' in an International Professional Service Firm«, *Human Resource Management*, Fall, Vol. 34, No. 3, 343-361.

Forsgren, Mats, Ulf Holm and Jan Johansson, 1992. »Internationalization of the Second Degree: The Emergence of European-Based Centres in Swedish Firms«, in S. Young and J. Hamill, (eds.). *Europe and the Multinationals*. Worcester: Edward Elgar Publishing Ltd.

Forsgren, Mats, 1990. »Managing the International Multi-Centre Firm: Case Studies from Sweden«, *European Management Journal*, Vol. 8, 261-267.

Franco, Lawrence, 1976. *The European Multinational*, Greylock Press, Greenwich CT.

Ghoshal, Sumantra, Harry Korine and Gabriel Szulanski, 1994. »Interunit Communication in Multinational Corporations«, *Management Science*. Vol. 40, No. 1, 96-110.

Gupta, Anil and V. Govindarajan, 1991. »Knowledge Flows and the Structure of Control within Multinational Corporations«, *Academy of Management Review*, Vol. 16, No. 4, 768-792.

Hedlund, Gunnar, 1994. *Managing the international firm: Alternative approaches and future trends*. Presentation given in a seminar offered by Institute for International Research in Helsinki, March 22, 1994.

Hedlund, Gunnar, 1993. »Assumptions of Hierarchy and Heterarchy: An Application to Multinational Corporation«, in S. Ghoshal and E. Westney, (eds.). *Organization Theory and the Multinational Corporation*. The Macmillan Press, London.

Hedlund, Gunnar and Dag Rolander, 1990. »Action in Heterarchies: New Approaches to Managing the MNC«, in C. Bartlett, Y. Doz, G. Hedlund, (eds.). *Managing the Global Firm*, Routledge, London.

Hedlund, Gunnar, 1986. »The Hypermodern MNC – a Heterarchy?«, *Human Resource Management,*. Spring, Vol. 25, 9-35.

Holbeche, Linda, 1994. *Career Development in Flatter Structures*, Research Report, Roffey Park Management Institute, Horsham, West Sussex, August.

Jablin, Fredric, 1987. »Formal Organization Structure«, in F. Jablin, L. Putnam, L., (eds.). *Handbook of Organizational Communication: An Interdisciplinary Perspective*, Sage Publications, Newbury Park.

Kanter, Rosabeth, 1983. *The Change Masters: Corporate Entrepreneurs at Work.* Counterpoint, London.

Kearney, A., 1994. *Scandinavian Management Year 2000.* Research Report, A. T. Kearney Management Consultants Oy, Helsinki.

Marschan, Rebecca, Denice Welch, and Lawrence Welch, 1996. »Control in Less-Hierarchical Multinationals: The Role of Personal Networks and Informal Communication«, *International Business Review,* Vol. 5, No. 2, forthcoming.

Marschan, Rebeccca, 1996. *New Structural Forms and Inter-Unit Communication: The Case of Kone Elevators.* Helsinki School of Economics Press, Helsinki.

Marschan, Rebecca, 1994. *New Structural Forms and Inter-Unit Communication in Multinationals: A Process Perspective on Kone Elevators Northern Europe.* Helsinki School of Economics Press, Helsinki.

Martinez, Jon and Carolos Jarillo, 1989. »The Evolution of Research on Coordination Mechanisms in Multinational Corporations«, *Journal of International Business Studies,* Vol. 20, No. 3, 489-514.

McPhee, Robert, 1985. »Formal Structure and Organizational Communication«, in R. McPhee, and P. Tompkins, (eds.). *Organizational Communication: Traditional Themes and New Directions.* Sage Publications, Beverly Hills.

Melin, Leif, 1992. »Internationalization as a Strategy Process«, *Strategic Management Journal,* Vol. 13, 99-118.

Morton, Michael, 1995. »Emerging Organizational Forms: Work and Organization in the 21st Century«, *European Management Journal,* Vol. 13, No. 4, December, 339-344.

Nohria, Nitin and Robert Eccles, 1992. »Face-to-Face: Making Network Organizations Work«, in N. Nohria and R. Eccles, (eds.). *Networks and Organizations: Structure, Form and Action.* Harvard Business School Press, Boston.

Schares, Gail, 1993. »Percy Barnevik's Global Crusade«, *Business Week/ Entreprise*, 204-211.

Stopford, J. and Wells, L., 1972. *Managing the Multinational Entreprise.* Basic Books, New York.

Södergren, Birgitta, 1992. *Decentralisering: Förändring i Företag och Arbetsliv.* Handelshögskolan i Stockholm, Tryck Graphic Systems, Stockholm.

White, Roderic and Thomas Poynter, 1990. »Organizing for Worldwide Advantage«, in C. Bartlett, C., Y. Doz and G. Hedlund, (eds.). *Managing the Global Firm.* Routledge, London.

Whittington, Richard, 1993. *What is Strategy and Does It Matter?* Routledge, London.

19. Cultural Differences and Problems in HQ-Subsidiary Relationships in MNCs

Cecilia Pahlberg

1. Introduction

During the last decades, it has often been argued that barriers between different cultures have diminished (Nordström, 1991, p. 28ff). Cultural integration has been in focus and several researchers have argued that the world, especially within the business community, has become more and more homogeneous (see e.g. Vernon, 1979; Porter, 1980, 1986; Levitt, 1983, Ohmae, 1985). A recent trend, however, is to stress heterogeneity rather than homogeneity and we are experiencing a revitalisation of the interest in national identities and cultures (Salzer, 1994). Not least the animated discussion during the last few years about the future of the European Union shows that cultural differences still exist. Such differences are of special interest in MNCs, whose most characteristic feature is that they consist of units located in many countries.

A number of researchers (see e.g. Bartlett; 1986, Ghoshal and Bartlett, 1990, Hedlund, 1986; Ghoshal and Nohria, 1989; Gupta and Govindarajan, 1991; Nohria and Ghoshal, 1994; Prahalad and Doz, 1987; Rosenzweig and Nohria, 1994) have pointed to the fact that units within multinational firms are not identical. According to Ghoshal and Nohria (1989, p. 323) the MNC is the quintessential case of the dispersed firm with different national subsidiaries often embedded in very heterogeneous environmental conditions (Robock, Simmons and Zwick, 1977). Thus, MNC units are located in different cultural milieus (Hofstede, 1980) and people with different nationalities, belonging to the same firm, have to get along with each other. When people from different cultures work together, misunderstandings are likely to occur (Adler, 1986). Problems due to cultural differences are thus of special interest in firms in which complexity, differentiation and variation in relations between the subsidiaries and HQ are characteristic features (Van Maanen and Laurent, 1993). As Hofstede (1983, p. 75) points out, cultural differences do matter, and cultural differences may become one of the most crucial problems especially for managements in multinational, multicultural firms.

Differences in culture is thus a main factor causing friction between parties in MNCs as cultural differences may lead to a communication gap. In order to get necessary information, individuals in different parts of the firm have to communicate and communication is largely influenced by cultural factors. Hence, people have culturally determined styles and ways of doing business, acquired primarily through their national culture but also through their business, corporate and individually based environments, and a reasonable hypothesis is that it is easier to communicate with people who share the same view of the world. Conflicts are also affected by cultural differences as individuals may have very different approaches to conflict resolution. (Törnroos *et al*, 1993)

Although there are cultural differences between units belonging to the same firm, these differences are not necessarily a handicap. On the contrary, cultural diversity represents one of the most valuable assets in an MNC as each culture has some contribution to offer (see e.g. Ekstedt *et al*, 1994, Laurent, 1991, Van Maanen and Laurent, 1993). To strive for a shared, common culture should not necessarily be a main objective. However, cultural differences must be handled in such a way that they do not create too many problems in the relationship between HQ and subsidiaries. In order to function smoothly, there is a need for understanding between the units in the different cultures. The parties must learn how to cope with the cultural differences that exist.

In this chapter cross-cultural differences within MNCs are in focus and the relationship between headquarters and subsidiaries is studied. There is always a geographical distance but there is also one in a mental sense, between two firms and also between actors in the same organisation (Hallén and Wiedersheim-Paul 1979, 1984). The purpose here is to discuss when cultural differences cause problems in the relationship between HQ and subsidiaries. A common hypothesis is that the greater the differences between countries, the greater the difficulties in understanding each other. As a consequence, the propensity for cultural-related problems should increase with cultural distances. In the following discussion it will be suggested that the picture is more complicated and nuanced. Although cultural differences do exist and affect the relationship between HQ and subsidiaries abroad, a main argument in the following will be that problems in the relationship between HQ and subsidiaries are more related to operational interdependences than to the cultural differences between them. It will also be suggested that actors involved in a relationship by time learn to handle the cultural differences, i.e. an understanding between them develops which reduces the cultural friction.

2. Theoretical Background

According to a number of international business studies there are differences in organisations and management practices between companies in different countries (Hofstede, 1980, Laurent, 1983, Sandström, 1990) and difficulties in international business caused by what has been designated as »culture« have frequently been discussed. What do we mean by »culture« then? The last decade has seen a rapidly growing interest in this subject and a number of different definitions has appeared. Culture has been defined both as something an organisation *is* as well as something it *has* (Smircich, 1983, Sackmann, 1992). Consequently there is no consensus on the concept of culture (Czarniawska-Joerges, 1992, p. 160) and »the organisational culture literature is full of competing and often incompatible views« (Smircich and Calás, 1987, p. 244f). Although the concept of culture does not have *one* definition and meaning, a fundamental distinction can be made whether it is seen as a result of differences between countries or if by »culture« we mean something that can be created in order to hold a firm together. As pointed out by Ghoshal and Westney (1993), from either of these perspectives, the multinational firm is suitable for concept building and empirical research. »The multinational represents a theatre of action at the intersection between two cultures: the culture or subcultures of the MNC organisation and the culture or subcultures of the different countries in which the MNC operates« (Ghoshal and Westney, 1993, p. 19).

A number of researchers have studied the effects of national cultures on different organisations (Erramilli, 1991, Kogut and Singh, 1988, Nordström 1991.) The best known study on cultural differences is probably Hofstede's study (1980) of 40 subsidiaries in one multinational firm[84]. He argues that people within a nation are »collectively mentally programmed«, i.e. they interpret experiences in a certain way that differs from the interpretation in other cultures. These mental programs are developed in childhood and as they are reinforced and institutionalised in legal systems, government, schools, organisations etc., there are no rapid changes in culture (Hofstede, 1983, p. 76). According to Hofstede, cultural differences can be expressed as differences in symbols, heroes, rituals and values, of which the three first can be collected under the term »practices«. Such practices are more superficial than values and can be manipulated through organisational culture. Hence, while national culture mainly refers to differences in values developed early in a person's life, organisational culture is primarily related to practices which have been learnt at work. Besides national and organisational culture, Hofstede identifies a third category, professional culture, which is formed somewhere in between and consists of values and practices to an equal degree. (Hofstede, 1991)

Deeply rooted values which are hard to change is, according to Hofstede, the essence of culture. Such a »culture-specific« argument implies that different societies reflect relatively stable and distinct cultures (Child and Kieser, 1979). However, it is important to remember that within every nation there are cultural differences. Although it might be possible to distinguish some national characteristics it is misleading to use culture and cultural characteristics as a factor connecting *all* inhabitants of a country. With this limitation in mind, the starting-point in this chapter is that different countries reflect different cultures. The more two countries differ, the more difficult it will be for members of these cultures to understand each other, i.e. the larger the cultural distance. As stressed already by Carlson (1966, p. 20), »The firm's knowledge of a foreign market is a function of the cultural distance. The risks involved in doing business with neighbouring countries whose institutions it knows seem much less than those inherent in transactions with strange countries far away«.

According to Hofstede (1980), differences in national cultures vary along four dimensions (individualism vs. collectivism, large vs. small power distance, strong vs. weak uncertainty avoidance and masculinity

84. In the late 1960s and early 1970s, Hofstede collected data from employees in one multinational corporation in 40 countries (116 000 questionnaires) which forms the basis of his book *Culture's Consequences* (1980). Later, supplementary data for another ten countries has increased the number to 50 countries.

vs. femininity), and in his study the position of each country on each of the four dimensions is indicated by a score. In order to capture cultural differences in general between countries, Kogut and Singh (1988) formed a composite index based on the deviation along each of the four cultural dimensions. The more two cultures differ, the higher the cultural distance between them will be. This methodology has been used by Nordström and Vahlne (1992) to illustrate cultural differences between Sweden and 22 other countries (see Appendix). These adjusted Hofstede data show that cultural differences to the neighbouring Nordic countries and to the Netherlands are the smallest, followed by the English speaking countries Canada, Australia, USA and Great Britain. Western European and South American countries then follow, whereas Mexico and Japan, according to this ranking, are most culturally distant from Sweden.

It is often claimed that it is easier to understand people in countries that are culturally close to one's own. Consequently, cultural problems should be less frequent in the relationship between actors in such countries and increase with distance. This will be further discussed and illustrated in the next section where empirical material from a study of Swedish MNCs is used. Problems due to cultural differences in the relationship between HQ and subsidiaries will be related to the cultural distance measurement, based on Hofstede's data which was discussed above. A divergence from the hypothesis above leads to a discussion where interdependence is suggested to be of vital importance. Other aspects of the HQ-subsidiary relationship, such as how long it has existed, the nationality and profession of the actors involved and the power relationship between them, will also be included. The discussion ends in a number of propositions.

3. Methodology and Empirical Results

In an ongoing project at the Department of Business Studies in Uppsala the relationship between HQ and subsidiaries in some of the best known Swedish MNCs, representing forest products, power generation & distribution, gas and petrochemical products, telecommunications, welding consumables and hard materials/tools, is studied. The largest unit has more than 27,000 employees and the smallest about 1,000 (the mean is 8,600 employees). The turnover ranges from 1.7 to 23 billion SEK (the mean is about 8 billion SEK). These companies have a long history of international experience and they are highly internationalised. Almost all subsidiaries have their own production. To broaden the material, two service companies are included, one in the computer industry and one air transport company. These two companies are much smaller, with less than one thousand employees and a turnover of just over 500 million SEK in each company.

The data base contains 57 foreign subsidiaries, located in the following countries: Finland (5), Norway (5), Denmark (4), Germany (7), Great Britain (10), Holland (2), Belgium (3), Switzerland (4), Austria (1), France (5), Spain (2), Italy (6), Turkey (1) and Mexico (2). In other words, Europe dominates. However, studies such as Hofstede's point to the fact that cultural differences between European countries are significant and therefore interesting to study. Further, Laurent (1986, 1991) claims that important differences that exist within Europe have been largely ignored or overlooked. Therefore an emphasis on Europe cannot be seen as a serious constraint.

During the period 1991-1994 we visited the subsidiaries as well as HQ. Headquarters are located in Sweden, whereas the subsidiaries are all abroad. It should be observed that HQ in the study is not the corporate HQ but a divisional management. The reason for this is that in Swedish MNCs, the tendency has been to strengthen the position of the divisions (Hedlund and Åman 1984). Rather than reporting to the CEO, to an increasing extent subsidiaries report to the divisional management. The operative responsibility for the subsidiaries thus lies in the hands of divisional management.

Individuals are the »carriers of culture« which implies that the picture that emerges depends on the characteristics of the respondents (Törnroos *et al*, 1993). Consequently, the selection of representative individuals is crucial. In order to capture how cultural differences are perceived in the subsidiaries, three different functions in each subsidiary have been covered -general management, sales and purchasing. The reason for interviewing the general manager is quite obvious: he can be expected to be the person having most frequent contacts with divisional HQ. The sales and purchasing managers have been chosen as they are also likely to be in contact with and affected by the divisional management. However, these three management categories at subsidiary level are not only involved in relationships with divisional HQ. Their daily operations are probably even more affected by counterparts in their business networks such as suppliers, customers and other important actors, for instance banks, governmental units, research institutes etc. Most of the subsidiaries in this study have their own production units and the relationship with suppliers inside as well as outside the firm is essential for the survival of the unit as are the relationship with the customers. The three functions included can thus be seen as the »core functions« and vital for the existence of each unit. The individuals in charge of each of these functions are considered to be the ones with the most experience of handling relationships with both divisional HQ and counterparts in their local networks. 57 subsidiary managers, 52 purchasing representatives and 57 sales managers participated. At divisional HQ, the chief executive manager (sometimes together with an assistant) answered questions concerning the relationship with each subsidiary in the division included in the study. Four different respondents, representing different functions and levels in the firm, have thus evaluated if cultural differences have caused problems.

3.1 Presentation of results

Above it was suggested that cultural differences do exist and may be of such importance that the relationship between HQ and subsidiaries will be disturbed. In order to study this, the subsidiary respondents were asked to respond to the following statement: »Cultural differences have caused problems in the relationship with the Global Divisional Management« (= divisional HQ). The divisional HQ responded to the same statement concerning their relationship towards each subsidiary. The distribution of answers on a five grade scale ranging from »Fully agree« to »Totally disagree« is shown in Table 1 below. The four respondent categories are shown separately while the percentage figures refer to the total.

The most apparent result is that in more than a third of the relationships, cultural differences have *not* caused problems. If the relationships where the respondents partially disagree with the statement are included, it can be seen that in nearly 2/3 of the relationships, problems due to cultural differences are not essential. This does not mean that cultural differences do not exist, but rather that the parties involved have learned how to handle the differences, or alternatively, do not need to handle them.

However, all relationships between HQ and subsidiaries do not function without problems. Although the majority partially or totally

Table 1: Cultural differences and problems in the relationship between HQ and subsidiaries.

	Div HQ	Sub. manager	Purchasing	Sales	Total	%
Fully agree	2	2	-	2	6	2,7%
Partially agree	16	13	11	10	50	22,4%
Neither nor	9	6	6	4	25	11,2%
Partially disagree	18	11	15	14	58	26,0%
Totally disagree	12	25	20	27	84	37,7%
TOTAL:	57	57	52	57	223	100%

disagree with the statement, one of four agrees totally or partially that cultural differences have such an impact that they have caused problems. Where are these problems most frequent then? Although the variation between the four groups of respondents is small, it can be noted that among divisional HQ there are more respondents who fully or partially agree with the statement and considerably fewer who totally disagree than in the three respondent groups representing the subsidiaries. While divisional managers seem to experience most problems, the fewest problems seem to be experienced by the sales managers. Among the latter, almost 72 per cent totally or partially disagree with the statement.

To what extent is there a positive relation between cultural distance and problems in the HQ-subsidiary relationship? In Figure 1 below is shown how cultural distance in Hofstede's terms (See p. 5 and Appendix) is related to problems in each subsidiary. Hence, the dependent variable shows the four respondents' perception of problems which they relate to cultural differences. The answers to the statement in Table 1 (p. 8) concerning whether cultural differences have caused problems in the relationship (where »Fully agree« correspond to 5 and »Totally disagree« to 1) from three different respondents in each subsidiary as well as divisional HQ have been added. In five subsidiaries, only two of three respondents have answered the question. These subsidiaries are not included in Figure 1. Each point in the figure below represents one subsidiary. In seven cases, two subsidiaries within a country have experienced the same amount of problems, and this is illustrated in the figure.

The points to the left represent subsidiaries in Norway, Denmark, Finland and Holland. In the middle, subsidiaries in Great Britain, Spain, France, Germany and Switzerland are found, and to the right, i.e. on a larger cultural distance from Sweden, are the subsidiaries in Belgium, Italy, Austria and Mexico.

Figure 1. Cultural distance and problems in the relationship

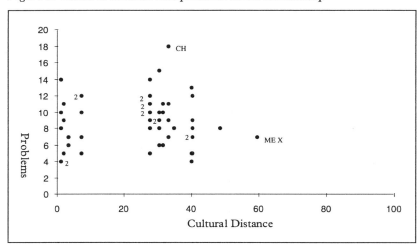

The pattern above indicates that there is no relation between cultural distance and problems. The correlation coefficient is even negative, - 0,06 (Spearman's rank). Thus, in our material there is no support for the hypothesis that problems related to culture increase with cultural distance. But when and where do cultural differences cause problems? In order to discuss this, two of the subsidiaries which differ from the expected pattern will be analysed further.

The picture above indicates that most problems are experienced in the relationship between HQ and a subsidiary in Switzerland, where all four respondents fully or partially agreed with the statement. This subsidiary is followed by subsidiaries in France, Great Britain, Spain and Norway. However, the most distant subsidiary, located in Mexico, does not experience problems due to cultural differences. Hence, cultural differences may affect a relationship negatively although there is a short distance between the actors, while, on the other hand, subsidiaries located in culturally distant countries may experience fewer or no cultural-related problems.

Figure 1 also indicates that subsidiaries located in the same country do not experience cultural differences in the same way. Although some subsidiaries in Switzerland, France, Great Britain, Spain and Norway seem to have problems in their relationships with HQ due to cultural differences, the majority of respondents in other subsidiaries in these countries do not experience problems. Consequently, there are differences between subsidiaries located in the same country. Furthermore, according to our data, there are differences within the same subsidiary as respondents in the same subsidiary experience the existence of problems due to cultural differences between subsidiary and HQ differently.

To sum up, the picture outlined above indicates that problems due to cultural differences call for other explanations than the cultural distance between HQ and subsidiary. In the following it will be suggested that such problems are more related to the character of the specific relationship that exist between HQ and each subsidiary, which in turn mainly is contingent upon how interdependent the actors are.

4. Interdependences

No business unit can function in isolation. On the contrary, each subsidiary is involved in relationships with other actors. Every unit contributes to and receives something from the others, i.e. interdependence is a fundamental trait in all relationships.

In Thompson's seminal work *Organisations in Action* (1967) there is a distinction of interdependence between three categories. Pooled interdependence is the simplest form and implies that each unit contributes and is supported by the whole. While all organisations have pooled interdependence, more complicated organisations also have sequential interdependence, i.e. the order of interdependence between two units is specified. The third and most advanced form stresses the reciprocity between the units and is consequently named reciprocal interdependence. The most complex organisations have pooled, sequential and reciprocal interdependence. According to Thompson, the three types place increasingly more demanding burdens on co-ordination and communication.

Interdependence is not necessarily balanced. In the resource-dependence perspective (see e.g. Pfeffer and Salancik, 1978) it is stressed that in a dyadic, asymmetrical relationship, the less dependent actor is the more powerful. When interdependences in MNCs are discussed, the dyadic relationship between two units, such as HQ and a subsidiary, is too limited. The concept of functional centrality (Astley and Zajac, 1990), i.e. to what extent a specific unit (subsidiary) is important to the function of the whole system (division), seems to be more relevant. According to this view, it is not only other divisional units' dependence on the subsidiary which is in focus, but also the subsidiary's dependence on these other units.

Interdependence is not solely an intraorganisational characteristic involving units within the MNC. Subsidiaries as well as HQ are also interlinked in relationships with actors such as customers and suppliers located outside the legal borders of the company. Each MNC unit can thus be seen as part of a business network consisting of counterparts inside as well as outside the MNC. The relationships with external partners have led to a situation where the boundaries of the MNC are not always clear cut and well delineated (Doz and Prahalad, 1993). However, in the following, a broad distinction between corporate and external interdependence is made.

As was shown in Table 1 (p. 8), most HQ-subsidiary relationships do not seem to be disturbed by the cultural differences that exist between countries. One reason might be that there is a low degree of interaction between the parties involved. Following Thompson (1967), several empirical studies have shown that higher levels of interdependence require more communication (see e.g. Boyacigiller, 1990). According to cross-cultural communication and psychology literature, people behave differently with members of their own culture than with members of foreign cultures, and as is pointed out by Mishler (1965), the greater the cultural differences, the more likely that there will be misunderstandings and barriers to communication (Adler and Graham, 1989). Thus, a high level of interaction increases the risk of conflicts while little contact diminishes that risk (Olie, 1994).

Hence, problems experienced in the relationship between HQ and a subsidiary can be associated with the degree of interaction which in turn is contingent on how interdependent HQ and subsidiary are. When HQ and subsidiary are very dependent on each other they probably interact more regularly and meet each other more often. The propensity for problems to arise due to cultural differences is higher in such a case than in cases when subsidiaries are more independent and involved in their local networks. Thus, when a subsidiary has most of its important relationships with actors outside the firm, i.e. is more involved in its external network, HQ-subsidiary relationship may function without problems, although there is a considerable cultural distance. In such a case, there is probably only limited interaction between them, emotions play a smaller role and the need for cultural understanding is limited. This can be illustrated by the situation in the largest of the Mexican subsidiaries in the above-mentioned project.

The Mexican firm has existed for more than 40 years and has been part of the division for 20 years. It has about 1,600 employees and accounts for 5 per cent of the division's turnover. The most important actors in the subsidiary's network have been identified and it is obvious that the local external network is of high importance. The three most critical suppliers are all external as are two of the three most critical customers. The purchasing and sales managers have evaluated the importance of these most critical suppliers and customers for the subsidiary, as well as the subsidiaries' importance for the suppliers and customers. The results indicate that the degree of interdependence is high. The most important customer, which is external, is considered to play a vital role for the subsidiary when it comes to such critical aspects as technological development, sales volume, information about market activities and also for the creation and maintenance of relations with other counterparts. Although the subsidiary's importance to this customer is somewhat lower, it is still considerable. It can be noted that the customer which belongs to the same firm as the subsidiary is notably less important. The relationship with the suppliers shows a similar pattern with a high degree of interdependence between the subsidiary and all three external suppliers. However, when the importance of this subsidiary for other units within the division is estimated by the divisional HQ, it is stated that the subsidiary has some importance only in connection with creating and maintaining relationships with external counterparts. The subsidiary is dependent on other divisional units only when it comes to technological information. When the subsidiary manager was asked the hypothetical question about the consequences for his unit if the division »ceased to exist«, his answer reveals that there would not be any major negative effects. (The divisional manager is, however, of another opinion.) The low degree of interdependence between the Mexican subsidiary and the rest of the firm to which it belongs should, according to the discussion above, imply that there is a low degree of interaction between HQ and the subsidiary. This is also the case. When visits from HQ to the subsidiaries and the subsidiaries' visits to HQ in Sweden are taken into consideration, our data shows that the Mexican subsidiary is the unit with the fewest personal HQ contacts among the subsidiaries in this division.

In the Swiss subsidiary, the one which experiences most problems of all subsidiaries in the study, the situation is quite the opposite. This subsidiary has 380 employees and accounts for about 25 per cent of the division's turnover. The subsidiary is quite recently acquired – when the interviews were made it had been part of the Swedish division for three years. Even though the Swiss subsidiary does not have a long history within the firm, the degree of interdependence with other units within the division must be considered high. The three most critical suppliers are all within the group, as are two of the three most critical customers. When the importance of the subsidiary for other units in the division is estimated by HQ, this subsidiary is considered to be of higher importance than other subsidiaries within the division. The division's importance for the subsidiary is also substantial. Both divisional HQ and the subsidiary manager state that the business activities would be at danger and the overall consequences would be high for the subsidiary if the division »ceased to exist«. The high degree of interdependence can also be seen in the interaction pattern between this subsidiary and its HQ. The subsidiary has the most frequent personal contacts with HQ among the six subsidiaries in the division included in the study, and, according to HQ, much more time is spent on this unit than on the others in the division.

These short illustrations of the subsidiaries indicate that whether the subsidiaries are mainly involved in the corporate or external network has something to do with how cultural differences affect the relationship. If the degree of corporate interdependence is high, the relationship is more vulnerable to cultural differences than when the subsidiary has most of its critical relationships with actors outside the firm. In the latter case, resources necessary for the firm are mainly obtained through interactions with external units, which enables the subsidiary to function without the rest of the firm. There is no need for HQ to interfere or try to understand the foreign culture. The relationship may function smoothly just because of the fact that they do not need to interact frequently and control can be obtained through written manuals and reports.

According to the respondents in the Mexican subsidiary and its divisional HQ, they seem to find it much easier to get along in comparison with the Swiss subsidiary and its divisional HQ. In the latter firm, the actors have much more difficulties in understanding the other party's way of thinking and divisional HQ especially seems to experience that his and the subsidiary's interests differ regarding such important aspects as marketing, purchasing, product design as well as size and direction of investments in the subsidiary. According to him, there is not agreement about the roles in the relationship and nor are the long-term plans consistent.

From the illustrations above follows that the likelihood for problems in a relationship is higher when there is a high degree of interdependence between HQ and subsidiary. The interaction between the parties is then more frequent than if there is a low degree of interdependence and the cultural differences that exist between the countries have a higher impact. This leads to the following proposition:

Proposition 1: Cultural differences are more likely to cause problems in an HQ-subsidiary relationship when there is a high degree of interdependence between them.

Thus, using Thompson's terminology, the likelihood for problems would increase in cases of reciprocal interdependence where both parties in a relationship are deeply involved in and dependent on each other, while interdependences characterised as being sequential are less likely to cause problems.

4.1 Interdependences in different functions

Just as an MNC does not consist of homogeneous subsidiaries, a subsidiary is not a homogeneous entity. Within each subsidiary, there are different functions, such as production, marketing and sales, which to varying degrees are involved in exchange relationships with other corporate or external counterparts. For example, purchasing in one subsidiary may be conducted mainly from other units belonging to the same MNC, while the products are sold to external customers. In another subsidiary belonging to the same MNC, the situation might be the opposite. Obviously there is a great variety of structures, but the point here is that different functions within a subsidiary can be more interdependent and corporate embedded than others. Thus, respondents within a subsidiary may have different opinions of whether cultural differences cause problems in the relationship with divisional HQ. When we studied the sales and purchasing functions in our material, we found that eleven respondents responsible for purchasing and twelve responsible for sales partially or totally agree with the statement that cultural differences have caused problems in the relationship with divisional HQ. These 23 respondents represent 19 subsidiaries. Thus, only in four subsidiaries, both purchasing and sales directors agree that cultural differences have caused problems. In line with the discussion above, we propose that experiencing problems in the relationship is related to each function's degree of corporate embeddedness.

Proposition 2: The more a subsidiary buys from other units within the division, the higher the propensity for problems due to cultural differences in the HQ-purchasing department relationship will be.

Proposition 3: The more a subsidiary sells to other units within the division, the higher the propensity for problems due to cultural differences in the HQ-sales department relationship will be.

When the concept of culture was discussed in the first part of this chapter, professional culture was mentioned as an aspect between national and organisational culture. Our data indicate that sales and purchasing representatives experience somewhat fewer problems due to cultural differences. One explanation might be that the professional culture is more pronounced for these categories than for the general managers at HQ and subsidiary level and that this facilitates communication. Sales and purchasing representatives probably interact with other sales and purchasing managers in the division and their professional culture helps to reduce cultural differences. Further, it can be expected that their communication mainly concerns operational issues where standard operating procedures are more commonly in use.

5. How Power Affects the Relationship

The power relationship between the parties involved may also affect how cultural differences are perceived. It has been stressed that exchanges between parties lead to interdependences which are not necessarily symmetrical (Emerson, 1962, Blau, 1964). Although all units within a multinational division might be of importance for the functioning of the whole division, some units may be more vital than others. From this follows that the more important a subsidiary is for the division, the higher its power and also its possibilities to have domination over more dependent units will be. Thus, having the upper hand in a relationship makes a unit less vulnerable to influences from others. Cultural differences are less likely to cause problems for such a unit, which is more probably able to impose its cultural values on others. Consequently, the more dependent a party is in an interdependent system, the more likely that this party experiences problems due to cultural differences.

Proposition 4: The more a subsidiary is dependent on the division, the higher the propensity for problems due to cultural differences.

Proposition 5: The more a division is dependent on a subsidiary, the higher the propensity for problems due to cultural differences.

6. How to Handle Cultural Friction

The transfer of managers from the home country, in this case from Sweden to subsidiaries abroad, can be expected to reduce problems due to cultural differences. According to Gates (1994), expatriates tend to be chosen when communication between HQ and the subsidiary is of high importance, while local nationals are selected when the relationship between the subsidiary and its local counterparts is more significant. Among the companies in our study, the majority of the subsidiary managers are locals: 41 of the 57 managers are from the host countries while 15 are Swedes and only one is from a third country. Among the purchasing and sales managers, the share of locals is even higher: 54 of the 57 sales managers and 49 of the 52 people responsible for purchasing are from the country in which the subsidiary is located. Hence, only three respondents in each category are Swedes. It could be expected that the 22 respondents of Swedish origin in the subsidiaries would totally disagree with the statement that cultural differences had caused problems in the relationship with divisional HQ. Although this is the case for most of them, five of the respondents state that cultural differences partially have caused problems in their relationship with HQ. An explanation might be that these five respondents are more influenced by their local surroundings and identify more with the situation in their new countries than with headquarters in Sweden.

In the two subsidiaries described above, one of the respondents in each of the companies is a Swede. While the Swedish subsidiary manager in Mexico does not experience culturally related problems in his relationship with HQ (nor do his two Mexican colleagues), the Swedish sales manager in the Swiss subsidiary agrees with her Swiss colleagues and says that such problems exist.

Using expatriates in the subsidiaries does not necessarily guarantee that cultural differences diminish. Language differences can, however, be eliminated when the actors in a relationship are of the same nationality.

7. Concluding Remarks

In this chapter it has been stressed that cultural differences are a reality in MNCs. The aim has been to discuss *when* cultural differences cause problems between HQ and subsidiaries. A common argument is that problems are more frequent the more different the cultures are. Our data, however, indicate a more complicated picture. Although there might be a considerable cultural distance, this does not necessarily mean problems. As can be seen in the empirical material, the respondents in most HQ-subsidiary relationships do not experience that cultural differences cause major problems. A main point is that these differences do not lead to problems if there is a low degree of interdependence. The network structure in which a subsidiary is embedded seems, in this empirical material, to be more related to cultural problems than the cultural distance between HQ and subsidiary. Subsidiaries which are of lower importance for other units in the firm and with most of their critical counterparts outside the MNC might experience only minor problems due to cultural differences. If there is a low degree of interdependence, the need for HQ to understand the subsidiary's culture is less vital. The subsidiary can be left to handle its business in the external network in which it is involved and personal interaction between HQ and subsidiary is not necessary. The relationship between HQ and a subsidiary which is deeply involved in its local network may function best when it is accepted that the subsidiary lives in a world apart and HQ does not intrude. In such a case the »pull« from the subsidiary's network and its culture is more vital for the subsidiary.

On the other hand, subsidiaries which are important to other units within the firm and have critical relationships with counterparts inside the legal boundaries may experience major problems due to cultural differences. In such a case, HQ and subsidiary are likely to have more interpersonal contacts. The more people have to interact, the more important the cultures, and the higher the propensity for conflicts. Cultural differences between the actors involved may then become more apparent and put a strain on the relationship.

Although it has been suggested that frequent interaction is a cause for problems, it is worth noting that it is probably also a prerequisite for the development of a positive atmosphere. The more interdependent two units are, the more important it is for the actors to understand and trust each other. This does not mean that a »shared culture« must be created, something which was suggested as a main solution for holding firms together especially during the 1980s. Such a »company culture« is – if possible to create – costly, and may as well turn out to be an impediment to change. More important is an atmosphere of mutual understanding, which is certainly not created overnight. Not least the fact that international firms today often grow through mergers and acquisitions makes it difficult for units which often have very different backgrounds to cooperate when they are »forced together«. But as time goes by, the parties in a relationship can hopefully learn how to handle the cultural friction that exists.

Appendix

Adjusted Hofstede data

Norway	1,2		Germany	31,5
Denmark	1,9		Switzerland	33,2
Holland	3,4		Brazil	34,0
Finland	7,1		Turkey	34,6
Canada	17,7		Argentina	35,4
Australia	25,3		Belgium	39,9
USA	25,9		Portugal	40.0
Great Britain	27,6		Italy	40,2
Spain	27,7		Austria	48,4
France	30,3		Mexico	59,4
Chile	30,7		Japan	78,1

Source: Nordström and Vahlne, 1992

A comparison with Nordström's psychic distance study indicates that the similarity between the rankings is quite high. The Spearman rank correlation coefficient is 0.61, significant at the 0.01 level. As the overall pattern between the countries in the studies is about the same, the conclusion is that psychic/cultural distance is rather stable. (Nordström and Vahlne, 1992.)

References

Adler, N., 1986. *International Dimensions of Organizational Behaviour.* Kent Publications, Boston, MA.

Adler, N. and J. Graham, 1989. »Cross-Cultural Interaction. The International Comparison Fallacy?«, *Journal of International Business Studies,* Fall, 515-537.

Astley, G. and E. Zajac, 1990. »Beyond Dyadic Exchange: Functional Interdependence and Sub-unit Power«, *Organization Studies,* Vol. 11, No. 4, 481-501.

Bartlett, C., 1986. »Building and Managing the Transnational: The New Organizational Challenge«, in M. Porter, (ed.). *Competition in Global Industries.* Harvard Business School Press, Boston.

Blau, P., 1964. *Exchange and Power in Social Life.* Wiley, New York.

Boyacigiller, N., 1990. »The Role of Expatriates in the Management of Interdependence, Complexity and Risk in Multinational Corporations«, *Journal of International Business Studies,* Third Quarter, 357-381.

Carlson, S., 1966. »International Business Research«, in L. Engwall, (ed.). *Uppsala Contributions to Business Research,* Acta Universitatis Upsaliensis, 18, 1984, Uppsala.

Child, J. and A. Kieser, 1979. »Organization and Managerial Roles in British and West German Companies: An Examination of the Culture-Free Thesis«, in C. Lammers and D. Hickson, (eds.). *Organizations Alike and Unlike.* Routledge & Kegan Paul Ltd, 251-271.

Czarniawska-Joerges, B., 1992. *Exploring Complex Organizations. A Cultural Perspective,* SAGE Publications, Newbury Park, California.

Doz, Y. and C.K. Prahalad, 1993. »Managing DMNCs: A Search for a New Paradigm«, in S. Ghoshal and E. Westney, (eds.). *Organization Theory and the Multinational Corporation.* St. Martin's Press, London.

Ekstedt, E., R. Henning, R. Andersson, N. Elvander, M. Forsgren, A. Malmberg, and L. Norgren, 1994. »*Kulturell Friktion. Konfliktkälla och förnyelsekraft i en integrerad ekonomi*«. SNS Förlag, Stockholm.

Emerson, R., 1962. »Power-dependence relations«, *American Sociological Review,* No. 27, 31-41.

Erramilli, K., 1991. »The Experience Factor in Foreign Market Entry Behavior of Service Firms«, *Journal of International Business Studies,* Third Quarter, 479-501.

Gates, S., 1994. »The Changing Global Role of The Foreign Subsidiary Manager«, *The Conference Board*, New York.

Ghoshal, S. and C. Bartlett, 1990. »The Multinational Corporation as an Interorganizational Network«, *Academy of Management Review*, Vol. 15, No. 4, 603-625.

Ghoshal, S and N. Nohria, 1989. »Internal Differentiation within Multinational Corporations«, *Strategic Management Journal*, Vol. 10, No.4, 323-337.

Ghoshal, S. and E. Westney, 1993. *Organization Theory and Multinational Corporation*. St. Martin's Press, New York.

Gupta, A. and V. Govindarajan, 1991. »Knowledge Flows and the Structure of Control within Multinational Corporations«, *Academy of Management Review*, Vol. 16, No. 4, 768-792.

Hallén L. and F. Wiedersheim-Paul, 1979. »Psychic Distance and Buyer-Seller Interaction«, *Organisation, Marknad och Samhälle*, Vol. 16, No. 5, 308-324.

Hallén L. and F. Wiedersheim-Paul, 1984. »The Evolution of Psychic Distance in International Business Relationships«, in I. Hägg. and F. Wiedersheim-Paul, (eds.). *Between Market and Hierarchy«*. University of Uppsala.

Hedlund, G., 1986. »The Hypermodern MNC – A Heterarchy?«, *Human Resource Management*, Spring 1986, Vol. 25, No. 1, 9-35.

Hedlund, G. and P. Åman, 1984. *Managing Relationships with Foreign Subsidiaries*. Sveriges Mekanförbund, Stockholm.

Hofstede, G., 1980. *Culture's Consequences. International Differences in Work-Related Values*. SAGE Publications, London.

Hofstede, G., 1983. »The Cultural Relativity of Organizational Practices and Theories«, *Journal of International Business Studies*, Fall 1983, 75- 89.

Hofstede, G., 1991. *Cultures and Organizations. Software of the Mind*. McGraw-Hill International, UK.

Kogut, B. and H. Singh, 1988. »The Effect of National Culture on the Choice of Entry Mode«, *Journal of International Business Studies*, Fall, 1988, 411-432.

Laurent, A., 1983. »The Cultural Diversity of Western Conceptions of Management«, *International Studies of Management and Organization*, Vol. 13, No. 1-2, 75-96.

Laurent, A., 1986. »The Cross-Cultural Puzzle of International Human Resource Management«, *Human Resource Management*, Vol. 25, No. 1, 91-102.

Laurent, A., 1991. »Managing Across Cultures and National Borders«, in S. Makridakis, (ed.). *Single Market Europe Opportunities & Challenges for Business.* Jossey Bass Inc. Publishers.

Levitt, T., 1983. *The Marketing Imagination.* The Free Press, New York.

Mishler, A.L., 1965. »Personal Contact in International Exchanges«, in H.C. Kelman, (ed.). *International Behavior: A Social-Psychological Analysis.* Holt, Rinehart & Winston, New York.

Nohria, N. and S. Ghoshal, 1994. »Differentiated Fit and Shared Values: Alternatives for Managing Headquarters-Subsidiary Relations«, *Strategic Management Journal*, Vol. 15, 491-502.

Nordström, K., 1991. *The Internationalization Process of the Firm – Searching for New Patterns and Explanations.* Dissertation in Business Administration, Institute of International Business, Stockholm School of Economics.

Nordström, K and J-E. Vahlne, 1992. »Is the Globe Shrinking? Psychic Distance and the Establishment of Swedish Sales Subsidiaries During the last 100 Years«. Paper presented at the International Trade and Finance Association's Annual Conference, April 22-25, 1992, Laredo Texas.

Ohmae, K., 1985. *Triad Power: The Coming Shape of Global Competition.* The Free Press.

Olie, R., 1994. »Shades of Culture and Institutions in International Mergers«, *Organization Studies*, Vol. 15, No.3, 381-405.

Pfeffer, J. and G. Salancik, 1978. *The External Control of Organizations: A Resource Dependence Perspective.* Harper and Row, New York.

Porter, M., 1980. *Competitive Strategy – Techniques for Analyzing Industries and Competitors.* The Free Press, New York.

Porter, M., 1986. »Changing Patterns of International Competition«, *California Management Review*, Vol. XXVIII, No. 2, Winter.

Prahalad, C.K. and Y. Doz, 1987. *The Multinational Mission: Balancing Local Demands and Global Vision.* The Free Press, New York.

Robock, S.H., K. Simmons, and J. Zwick, 1977. *International Business and Multinational Enterprises.* Irwin, Homewood, Il.

Rosenzweig, P. and N. Nohria, 1994. »Influences on Human Resource Management Practices in Multinational Corporations«, *Journal of International Business Studies*, Second Quarter, 229-251.

Salzer, M., 1994. *Identity Across Borders: A Study in the IKEA-world.* Dissertation No. 27, Department of Management and Economics, Linköping University.

Sandström, M., 1990. *Atmosphere in International Business Relationships,* Licentiate Thesis, Department of Business Studies, Uppsala University.

Sackmann, S., 1992. »Culture and Subcultures: An Analysis of Organizational Knowledge«, *Administrative Science Quarterly,* Vol. 37, 140-161.

Smircich, L., 1983. »Concepts of Culture and Organizational Analysis«, *Administrative Science Quarterly,* Vol. 28, 339-358.

Smircich, L. and M. Calás, 1987. »Organizational Culture. A Critical Assessment«, in F. Jablin, L. Putnam, K. Roberts and L. Porter, (eds.). *Handbook of Organizational Communication. An Interdisciplinary Perspective.* SAGE Publications, Newbury Park, California.

Thompson, J., 1967. *Organizations in Action.* McGraw-Hill Inc., New York.

Törnroos, J-Å., A. Bonaccorsi and D. Dalli, 1993. »Theoretical Approaches in Understanding Cross-Cultural Business Interaction in Industrial Markets«, in J. Chías and J. Sureda, (eds.). *Proceedings of the 22nd European Marketing Academy Conference – Vol II,* Barcelona, 1417-1448.

Van Maanen, J. and A. Laurent, 1993. »The Flow of Culture: Some Notes on Globalization and the Multinational Corporation«, in S. Ghoshal and E. Westney, (eds.). *Organization Theory and the Multinational Corporation.* St Martin's Press, New York.

Vernon, R., 1979. »The Product Life Cycle. Hypothesis in a New International Environment«, *Oxford Bulletin of Economics and Statistics,* Vol. 41, November, 255-267.

20. Network Infusion in the Multinational Corporation

Mats Forsgren, Ulf Holm and Peter Thilenius

1. Does the Character of the Subsidiary Network Matter to the MNC?

To what extent are an MNC's activities and its development related to the local environments of its subunits? This question is associated with a dominant part of the literature on international business, that focuses on the relation between the corporation and its environment. Although authors seem to regard environment in various ways and relate environment to various problems for an MNC, many seem to concur that one can view the corporation as a more or less open system in which the environment plays an important role (Scott, 1987). A resource/dependence perspective, for example, stresses the external control of the corporation based on the dependence on critical resources controlled by actors in the environment (Pfeffer and Salancik, 1978; Yuchtman and Seashore, 1967). Another area of the literature discusses the role of the environment in creating uncertainty, a problem which affects strategy formulation and how to design the corporate structure in an efficient way (Egelhoff, 1988; Galbraith, 1973; Lawrence and Lorch, 1967).

A general organisational problem related to this view is which role to give to a specific subsidiary of an MNC? On the one hand, the subsidiary »..should be suited to its specific environment« (Lawrence and Lorch, 1967) and, on the other, its role must be consistent in relation to that of the other corporate units (Bartlett and Ghoshal, 1989; Gupta and Govindarajan, 1991). Therefore, one central managerial issue is to specify different roles for the subsidiaries in the MNC. In their »transnational solution«, Bartlett and Ghoshal use the strategic importance of the subsidiary's local environment, in combination with the level of resources and the capabilities, to formulate four generic roles. Gupta and Govindarajan (1991) focus on knowledge flows and use the degree of inflow and outflow to define four types of roles. These notions also relate to the management of a headquarters-subsidiary relationship which must be specifically dealt with to fit the specific context of each subsidiary (Nohria, Gulati and Ghoshal, 1994; Nohria and Ghoshal, 1994).

The common trait of these theories is that they take a managerial perspective. The prime concern is to design the organisation so that the subsidiary holds the right role with regard to the rest of the organisation.

There is also growing interest in regarding the MNC as a set of subunits, each operating in a distinct environment, rather than as a single entity facing a global environment (Ghoshal and Westney, 1993). Related to this view is the assumption that different attributes of an MNC can be explained by the characteristics of the networks within which the different subsidiaries are embedded (Ghoshal and Bartlett, 1990). One such attribute is the relationship between characteristics of, for example, business and technology in the subsidiary network and the subsidiary's business and technological role within the MNC. In this chapter, we assume that there is such a general link. We refer to this as network infusion in the MNC.

However, this can not be understood without an explicit analysis of the subsidiary's relationships with customers, suppliers, competitors and other counterparts in the subsidiary network (Doz & Prahalad, 1993; Ghoshal & Bartlett, 1990). From this, it follows that an MNC consists of many specific subsidiary business networks, all important for several and different reasons. Thus, we consider the environment of an MNC to be complex because it consist of many sub environments which we call local business networks.

The purpose of this chapter is to identify *if* and *what* operative functions matter in the local subsidiary business network, not only for the subsidiary but for the corporation as a whole. This will be done by analysing the link between network functions and the subsidiary role within the MNC division with regard to the corresponding functions. The first issue is to identify what we call strait-functional infusion, which means that a specific operative function in the subsidiary network corresponds to the role of the subsidiary in the division. The second issue is to identify what we call cross-functional infusion, since it can be argued that an operative function of the subsidiary network is connected to the characteristics of other operative functions held by the subsidiary within the MNC. After a theoretical discussion of subsidiary network contexts and infusion in the MNC, operationalisation and analysis of network infusion is conducted based on a sample of 61 subsidiaries in 13 MNC divisions. The chapter ends with a discussion including propositions about the existence and patterns of network infusion and the management of the MNC.

2. The Subsidiary Network Context[85]

The concept network infusion in the MNC implies at least two important components. First, there is the concept of network, in this case meaning the subsidiary's network context, which is the object of this study and forms the level of analysis in this chapter. This will be discussed in the next section. Then, secondly, we will discuss the features of infusion from the subsidiary network context into the MNC.

According to Ghoshal and Bartlett (1990) the MNC can be viewed as an interorganisational network. In such a network, the local subunit plays an important operative role since it controls linkages to the network it is embedded in. It is posed that different attributes of the MNC can be explained by »..selected attributes of the external network » (ibid. p.12). This is also the point of departure in our approach. We want to stress, however, that the network which a subsidiary considers important for its activities is not necessarily only a matter of business relationships external to the MNC. What matters is the system of relationships that the subsidiary is embedded in. As illustrated in Figure 1, this can very well include relationships which both are internal and external to the MNC.

Thus we cannot exclude relationships between sister units from the subsidiary network context (Holm, Johanson and Thilenius, 1995). Although there may be differences in what actors and relational dimensions influencing the internal and the external parts of the network, this means that we regard the subsidiary network context as one single system independent of the legal borders of the MNC. This also means that the relationships in the subsidiary's network context, internal as well as external, are viewed as business relationships. Of course, this is an effect of using the subsidiary network context as the level of analysis.

Empirical studies have showed that a limited number of such business relationships are more important to the firms involved than most of the ordinary market-exchange relations (Hallén, 1986; Håkansson,

---

85. Parts of this section originate from a description of network contexts in Holm, Johanson and Thilenius (1995, pp. 99-102)

Figure 1. The Network Context of a Subsidiary.

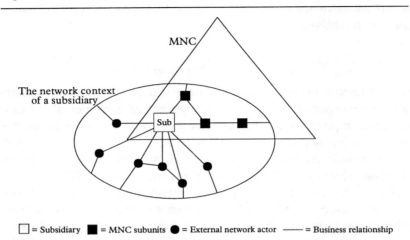

☐ = Subsidiary   ■ = MNC subunits   ● = External network actor   ―――― = Business relationship

1987; Cowley, 1988; Perrone, 1989). A firm's business relationships may be important because of business volume with a partner, the financial return from the relationship, the technological development driven by the interaction with a partner or because a particular relationship provides access to other important actors or market segments.

It has also been demonstrated that such business relationships have complex interfirm contact patterns (Hallén, 1986). The contact structures consists of managers on several organisational levels – including top management and shop floor personnel in addition to the middle managers – and specialists from all branches of the firms: marketing, purchasing, manufacturing, research and development, quality, planning, finance, etc. (Cunningham and Homse, 1986). These interfirm social structures typically involve contact between 10-20 managers and 5-10 face-to-face meetings per year. The contact patterns indicate that the interaction between the firms is not only – and, in many cases, not even primarily – a matter of selling and buying. The interaction comprises information exchange concerning the interacting firms' needs, capabilities, and strategies with regard to manufacturing, logistics and development. Thus, the interaction is often a matter of coordinating activities and resources between the firms involved.

Frequently, such co-ordination means that interdependent manufacturing, logistics, development or administrative activities and resources are modified and adapted in order to bring about a better match between firms. Often, such adaptations mean that one of the firms – sometimes both – modify their products, processes or systems according to the demands of the counterpart. The adaptations may, for example, result in specific interfirm product development and coordinated just-in-time logistic systems. Although the adaptations are discrete in many cases, such as with the installation of new equipment or systems, or with changes of products, they are more often gradual because the firms adapt over time to each others' ways of doing business, when performing current business activities.

This means that business relationships are not created overnight, but instead evolve gradually through interaction. To the extent that both counterparts respond, the interaction evolves sequentially, with mutual commitments gradually being made. During that process, the counterparts increase their knowledge of each other as well as their trust in each other whilst simultaneously the initial unilateral dependence of one of the parties on the other is transformed into a growing mutual interdependence. Thus, this time-consuming process changes the initial ordinary market relation into a dyadic business relationship, in which the firm and some of its business partners are strongly tied to each other, and, to a certain extent, share interests concerning future developments. Evidently, these working business relationships contain a strong element of mutual knowledge of which some is of a tacit nature and cannot be transferred to others (Kogut and Zander, 1992). From the perspective of a firm, it can be expected that some, but not all, of its business relationships provide knowledge of business and technology which is critical for long term survival in the market. For example, a number of studies have demonstrated that business relationships are critical in the technological development of the firm (von Hippel, 1988; Håkansson, 1987; Laage-Hellman, 1989; Lundvall, 1988).

According to business network findings, a firm bases its actions on a limited set of close and complex business relationships with suppliers, customers, cooperative firms and public agencies considered relevant by the firm. This set of directly and indirectly interconnected relationships form the network context (Håkansson and Snehota, 1989). Evidently, each firm's network context is unique, since it comprises a specific set of interconnected relationships considered relevant by the particular firm. Thus, the network perspective implies that, rather than operating in an environment which is common to all competing firms in a market, each firm has engagements and operates in a unique network context. Moreover, the relationships with the counterparts in the network context are unique. Each relationship in the network context has its own function for the firm. While one relationship may be important mainly because of the business volume with the counterpart, another may be important because of its technological competence and a third because it provides access to new business opportunities.

From a network perspective on the MNC this means that the network context is multifunctional. Some functions are primarily related to current operations, while others are more important from a developmental point of view. Although stable, the network context changes all the time because of the interaction between the network actors. Furthermore, the network context is invisible to outside observer. It is a matter of trust, knowledge and interpretations based on social interaction, all of which have evolved gradually over time. Thus it can only be understood by those directly involved in the interaction. Therefore we conclude that the network context is important and in several ways, unique, changing and incomprehensible to outsiders.

3. Network Infusion in the MNC

The business development of an MNC is often described as a matter of exploiting the firm's specific internal knowledge at the market. This knowledge is developed and controlled by the firm, and its exploitation is made possible through market imperfection (Calvet, 1981; Dunning, 1993; Hymer, 1976; Kindelberger, 1969).

Likewise, the way a firm should deal with a certain market segment is often described as a matter of combining and offering a particular price, product, place and promotion (Kotler, 1984). Here, the market is the »target« against which the firm acts and, afterwards, evaluates its performance (Porter, 1980). In this perspective, the firm explicitly or implicitly develops and adapts its technology and business through the evaluation of responses from the customer segment and by comparing its own success with that of competitors (ibid.).

Although evaluating external market reactions it is evident that what matters in these perspectives is the internal ability to create and control knowledge which gives the firm an advantage over other market actors. The contrast to this »from within« view, is that the concept of network infusion stresses mutual interaction with specific partners over time as a driving force for business and for the technological development of an MNC.

From a network perspective of the MNC, the subsidiaries are especially important as they are the units which work at the operative frontier and handle the day-to-day work through engaging in business relationships. Network infusion in an MNC can, for example, be traced to a subsidiary's interaction with a certain customer. Imagine a situation in which a subsidiary produces and develops a product which serves as equipment used in the customer's production. Over a long period of time, the customer has had an interest in increasing the productivity of its production and the subsidiary has been interested in developing equipment in accordance with that. So, now and then the parties cooperate and engage in solving this mutually important issue. The result is the making of adjustments and the development of equipment with greater efficiency that is customised to the partners requirements. During the process, the subsidiary turns to a supplier – within the MNC – which is affected by this development. Together they start interacting to achieve the necessary development of an important component which is sold by the supplier and installed by the subsidiary when manufacturing the equipment. Since the customer of the subsidiary buys large quantities, this is something that the supplier also considers important. Furthermore, since the supplier delivers components on a world-wide basis to several MNC subsidiaries, the improved component quality may be introduced in several business contexts and become important to the whole MNC.

The example above illustrates how product development in a customer relationship corresponds to technological development and business development within an MNC. It can be said that the more the behaviour of the internal supplier that steams from the subsidiary business relationship with the customer, the more infusion there is into the MNC. This means that we define network infusion as the interaction process which makes the corporation carry out its operative functions in accordance with the character of operative functions of specific subsidiary network contexts.

This definition is based on two relational components. First there is the impact of the network context on the subsidiary's operations and, second, there is the impact of the subsidiary on the operations of the MNC. Infusion appears when the importance of the network and the importance of the subsidiary in the MNC correspond. Note that the effect of the subsidiary's importance comprise the MNC as a unit, not only the subsidiary and its local operations.

There is, however, no one to one connection between a subsidiary network context and infusion in the corporation. Rather, since an MNC consists of several subsidiaries and consequently several subsidiary network contexts, we can assume there to be several infusion-forces. It should be an impossible task for a corporation to fully fit the demands of all subsidiaries, but the variation in the importance and characteristics of subsidiary network contexts suggests at least two things: First, it can be argued that, if a subsidiary network context is considered to be of local importance for the subsidiary and/or of overall importance for the corporation, there is a prime basis for infusion into the corporation. Second, different subsidiary network contexts carry different kinds of infusion. While one subsidiary network may infuse strongly in terms of technology another may infuse in terms of important knowledge about the market, etc.

Moreover, infusion can appear in different ways. Most obvious is the case of infusion from the subsidiary network through exchange relationships between the subsidiary and its sister units within the corporation. Another way is when headquarters come to recognise the importance of a certain subsidiary business network and use their authority to manage other subunits into a direction which corresponds to the characteristics of that network.

4. Network Infusion – an Empirical Illustration

In our illustration of network infusion, data from 61 subsidiaries in 13 divisions, all involved in international operations in Swedish MNCs, have been used. The data consists of information about the importance of certain operative functions in the subsidiary's network context for the subsidiary itself, together with information about the subsidiary's importance in the corresponding functions for the division as a whole. The main reason behind the choice of division as the level of analysis is the fact that the divisional level of the corporation is closer to the network context of the subsidiary. This enhances the possibility of identifying network infusion, since the divisional management has not only a strategic function vis a vis the subsidiary, but also operational responsibilities. This level, rather than an MNC level, is also an appropriate choice for analysis since divisions of an MNC are generally operationally separated from each other.

The number of subsidiaries studied per division varies between three and ten, and includes a wide range of industries (hard materials, paper, packaging, power, retailing, transportation services and telecommunications). The subsidiaries vary in size from 50 to over 5000 employees. It is important for the quality of data gathered about business relationships that the chosen subsidiaries are well established in their respective markets. In our sample, the average time the subsidiaries have been operative units is close to 38 years. All subsidiaries, with the exception of one in Mexico and another in Turkey, are located in Europe.

The data collection was carried out through personal interviews in a two-stage procedure. First, for each subsidiary, data concerning its most important relationships were gathered through interviews with subsidiary managers. Second, interviews with representatives of the divisional headquarters were conducted to ascertain the importance of each particular subsidiary for the division.

4.1 Measuring the importance
of functions in the subsidiary network context

When investigating network contexts some boundary has to be set to the network to restrict the amount of data collected. By its very nature, the setting of boundaries in a network analysis imposes several problems that have to be handled explicitly (Laumann et al., 1983). First, the network context of the subsidiary is defined by the people, within the subsidiary, who are involved in the interactions (Forsgren and Johanson, 1992). Second, theoretically the network context includes all actors who affect the business activities of the subsidiary (Snehota, 1990). In this respect it has to be recognised that all boundaries delimiting the network are arbitrary and subjective, but for analytical purposes suitable boundaries can be drawn.

In this study the network boundaries were set to include three customer relationships, three supplier relationships and three other relationships considered most important by the subsidiary, i.e., at most nine relationships. The choice of a limited set of relationships as the empirical base is supported by other studies which have shown that there is a limited number of business relationships which the corporation considers to be of greater long-term importance than most of the ordinary market exchange relations (Cowley, 1988; Håkansson, 1987; Perrone, 1989). The limit of three relationships in each category can also be considered to be somewhat arbitrary, however one of the objectives of our study was to let the most apt people choose the important relationships. In order to achieve internal consistency in the study and give the respondent a frame of reference, the limitation was set for each respondent's own choice of relationships. Accordingly, to select and assess the three most important customer relationships the sales manager or his colleagues at the subsidiary's sales department were interviewed. The interviews followed a similar procedure for the three most important supplier relationships. The three other types of relationships were estimated through interviewing the top management for each subsidiary. These included any other relationship besides those with customers or suppliers, for instance with governmental agencies, trade unions, research institutes, business associations etc., with the restriction that they must be considered to be important. In the following, we refer to them as »other relationships«.

Thus, the choice of important relationships was made by the respondents solely within the limits set. However, this approach means that in some cases fewer than nine relationships were selected. Of course, a subsidiary always has more than just a few relationships with counterparts, but their importance may vary greatly. In our study, we chose not to put pressure on the respondents to select further relationships when they had clearly stated that, for example, there was just one supplier that they regarded as significantly more important than the others.

All in all, we have network data concerning 398 important relationships on the subsidiary level classified as customer relationships (170), supplier relationships (152) or other relationships (76). The majority of these, 301 in all, are the ones that subsidiaries have with actors external to the division, while the remaining 97 are claimed to be important relationships with sister units in the division. The lowest number of relationships specified for a subsidiary was four and the average is just over seven. Initially, the respondents were asked to choose relationships that are important for any reason at all. Thus the empirical base consists solely of important relationships, but within this general criterion the importance of the relationships has been estimated for different functions, all being more or less important depending on the specific business and the history of the relationship.

A relationship, though, can be important in various ways. According to Håkansson (1989), von Hippel (1988) and Laage-Hellman (1989), it may be of importance for technological development (questions 1 and 2 in Table 1). Another area is the flows of goods and knowledge in the business activities (questions 3-7 in Table 1). Furthermore, a relationship can be of importance for the maintenance of other relationships within the network context (questions 8 and 9 in Table 1, cf. Astley and Zajac, 1991; Cook and Emerson, 1984). Finally we include an indicator (question 10 in see Table 1) for the actors' possibilities of creating new and valuable business contacts as a result of the relationship (Blankenburg, 1995). This is of concern for the evolution of current business. All in all, this amounted to ten questions determining the importance of relationship functions with specific counterparts of the subsidiary (see Table 1). Although other importance indicators could have been included, those used represent both the maintenance and the development of current business activities.

Table 1. Indicators of the Importance of the Subsidiary's Business Relationships

To what extent is this counterpart important for you concerning ...	
1. Product development?	6. Sales volume?
2. Production development?	7. Continuity and security in delivery
3. Technological information?	8. Maintenance of internal relationships?
4. Information about market activities?	9. Maintenance of external relationships?
5. Information about governmental restrictions	10. New, important business contacts?
Answers on this five-point scale: 1=Not at all, 2=Little, 3=To some extent, 4=Much, 5=Very much	

As a consequence of the design of our study and the relatively large sample, we are able to compare subsidiaries over several divisions. There is, of course, the problem that divisional HQs may have different frames of reference when assessing the importance of a subsidiary. If it had been possible to compare subsidiaries in only one division, the estimates of the variability of importance among the subsidiaries would probably be more accurate. However, one should not overestimate this problem. First, by using highly standardised questions related to rather well-defined problem areas, the similarity of the frame of reference among the respondents probably increased. Second, several studies indicate a rather high internal consistency among different sources when reputational measures of importance are used (Brass, 1984; Krackhardt, 1990). Nevertheless, this limitation must be kept in mind in the further discussion.

Our unit of analysis is the subsidiary's network context rather than a single relationship. In order to receive a valid measure of the importance for all ten functions on a network context level, the data on importance were summed for each function. The sums were then weighted by the actual number of relationships the respondents had chosen as most important (i.e., at the least, four up to a maximum of nine) leaving us with ten variables all measuring the importance of ten defined functions in the network context for the subsidiary.

4.2 Measuring the importance of subsidiary divisional roles

As mentioned in the introduction, the objective of the empirical illustration is to find out whether there is a correspondence between functions in the subsidiary's network context and the subsidiary's divisional roles. Subsidiary roles have been defined and measured in various ways. Gupta and Govindarajan (1991) use the degree of inflow and outflow of knowledge to define four roles, while Bartlett and Ghoshal (1990) base their roles on the strategic importance of the subsidiary's local environment in combination with its level of resources and capabilities.

There are two traits that are commonly brought up in the discussion of subsidiary roles: First, the assignment of roles to a subsidiary is a managerial task, i.e., it is a management task to define the subsidiary role according to its situation. Second, the assignment of roles is mainly based on the operational characteristics of the subsidiary independent of the roles formally given by headquarters.

The objective of our illustration is not to estimate how these roles are established, but, rather, to decide to what extent subsidiary roles can be traced back to attributes of the subsidiary network context. This requires that, e.g., the importance of a subsidiary's network context for its product development can be compared with its role for the division's product development. Thus, the estimation of the importance of the subsidiary's network context and the subsidiary's role in the division is based on similar indicators. This implies that the questions used for indicating the importance of subsidiary roles focus on the same operational areas as are used for the subsidiary's network context (See Table 1).

It is important, though, to emphasise that in the first case the data are based on assessment made by the subsidiary, while in the second case, they are based on the assessment of managers at the division headquarters. This accounts for the separation of the two measures and that any correspondence between them should be considered as an indication of network infusion.

4.3 Investigating the existence of network infusion

The purpose of using empirical data in this chapter is mainly descriptive rather than conclusive. Therefore, we have chosen to indicate infusion using a correlation analysis. Correlation analysis provides a measure of the degree of conformity in a group of variables. In this analysis, we employ the 20 chosen variables, ten measuring the importance, for the subsidiary, of the functions in a subsidiary network context, and ten measuring the importance of subsidiary roles for the division for the same functions. To the extent that we find positive signs which are significantly separated from zero, in the correlation matrix, it can be said that network infusion is indicated among the functions concerned. The resulting correlation matrix (see Table 2), has been reduced to include the relevant parts.[86]

The general pattern indicates that network infusion is rather common in the sense that 45 of the 100 cases given in the table are significant. We can therefore conclude that the characteristics of the subsidiary's network context are often transmitted into the role that the subsidiary exerts in the division. For instance, the more important the network is for the subsidiary's own *product development* the more important is the subsidiary's role in the *product development* of the whole division (correlation coefficient 0,318; significant on five per cent level).

As is evident from the table, such direct links between the subsidiary's network function and its divisional role also exist in terms of *information about market activities, maintenance of internal and external relationships and new important business contacts*. In these cases there is a significant correlation (on at least a one per cent level) between the network's importance for the subsidiary and the subsidiary's importance for the division within one and the same function. This is what we call straight-functional infusion.

---

86. The complete correlation matrix is available on request from the authors.

Table 2: *Correlation Matrix (reduced)*

Subsidiary division role	Importance of Network functions										No:s
	1	2	3	4	5	6	7	8	9	10	
1. Product development	318*	271*	214	341**	243	254*	331**	322*	330**	358**	8
2. Production development	150	47	-248	168	208	-90	46	141	181	267*	1
3. Technological information	163	100	213	289*	3	201	189	199	219	246	1
4. Information about market activities	187	294*	285*	444***	174	404**	360**	99	235	531***	6
5. Information about governmental restrictions	-9	-36	63	242	86	160	214	139	136	234	0
6. Sales volume	344**	172	230	351***	346**	376**	203	248	246	354**	5
7. Continuity and security in delivery	412***	158	236	222	249	342**	246	210	153	299*	3
8. Maintenance of internal relationships	419***	299*	240	386**	263*	190	330**	434***	344***	426***	8
9. Maintenance of external relationships	278*	144	225	279*	249	188	189	351**	360**	351**	5
10. New, important business contacts	230	293**	322**	432***	233	309*	435**	379**	355*	425***	8
No:s significant cases	5	4	2	7	2	5	4	4	4	8	45

* p<.05, ** p<.10, *** p<.001

Note: Decimal points omitted

But the table also reveals other interesting patterns: On one hand, the importance of a function in the subsidiary's network seems to »spill over« into subsidiary roles in the division in terms of *other* functions, i.e., cross-functional infusion. This is especially apparent for the functions *information about market activities and new important business contacts* which are spread into subsidiary roles in the division within a majority of the other functions. But we can note that such a »spill over« effect also exists in other functions. For example, the *product development* function of the network also gives the subsidiary a more dominant role also in terms of the division's *sales volume, continuity and security of delivery and the maintenance of internal and external relationships.*

On the other hand, the subsidiary's role in the division can be traced back to several functions in the network. This is especially the case for *product development, maintenance of internal relationship and new, important business contacts.*

A general observation concerning straight- and cross-functional infusion is that the network functions with low straight-functional infusion are basically the same as those with low cross-functional infusion. Likewise, it seems that network functions with significant straight-functional infusion are more frequent in terms of cross-functional effect.

5. Managerial Implications

In general, the results indicate that network infusion is an important phenomenon in an MNC. In many cases there seems to be a significant connection between the characteristics of the subsidiary network and the role that the same subsidiary plays in the division. But the results also indicate that the degree of infusion varies between the different functions of the network. Some functions have no, or only a limited, impact on the subsidiary's role in the division. This seems to be the case for production development, technological information and information about governmental restrictions. Even though these functions in the subsidiary network can be very important for the subsidiary's own business, they do not transmit into a more dominant role for the subsidiary in the division. There is a striking difference between, on one hand, product development and information about market activities and, on the other hand, production development and technological information. The former lead to network infusion, while the latter do not. Maybe, a reasonable hypothesis is that the subsidiary's ability to develop new products has a wider applicability for the whole division than its ability to develop new production processes that are more likely to be adapted to local conditions. A similar argument would explain why information about market activities, including information about new products and competitors, has wider applicability than technological information which is more related to the production process. It is also apparent that information about governmental restrictions is primarily of relevance to the local business and therefore leads to a low degree of network infusion.

What, then, are the managerial implications of the existence of network infusion? Firstly, the subsidiaries of an MNC can play different roles in the formulation and implementation of strategy at the division and corporate level. These roles are, to some degree, reflected in the characteristics of the business network surrounding the subsidiary. Secondly, the possibility of the corporate and division managers to implement a strategy so that the subsidiary roles will be shaped in accordance with their capabilities is dependent on knowledge about the subsidiaries' networks (Krackhardt, 1990). The managers must have an understanding of the most important relationships in the network and why they are important. Some relationships can have a wider applicability than others, so, the better the knowledge about these relationships, the better the ability of formulating the roles.

Thirdly, the network infusion in an MNC, exerted by different subsidiary network contexts, is heterogeneous and contradictory. Different subsidiaries have different types of business relationships. One subsidiary's network can be crucial for the R&D in the MNC, while another's network can be important for information about competitors and new products. But the subsidiaries' networks can also be important within one and the same function, for instance R&D, and therefore to some extent compete with each other in terms of network infusion within the MNC. The degree of importance – of a specific subsidiary network function – for the division will affect that subsidiary's possibilities of prevailing in this competition.

But the corporate and division managers can have nothing but an incomplete knowledge about the business networks, and therefore will also have limited ability to »optimize« the infusion in terms of controlling the roles of the subsidiaries. And the manager's control of the strategy process within the MNC is dependent on its ability to understand the functions of the subsidiary network. In any case, these functions will play an important role in the actual behaviour of the MNC through network infusion.

6. Some Issues for Future Research

Although our study is illustrative and the results are to be regarded as tentative, the phenomenon of network infusion in the MNC exposes several research questions. For example, is there a connection between the subsidiaries' engagement in dynamic and important business relationships and the strategic knowledge within in the »whole« corporation? If so, this means that the MNC and the subsidiary are mutually interdependent and, consequently, that the subsidiary has possibilities to influence long term investments and the strategic direction of the corporation. An underlying issue to study is therefore if the characteristics of the subsidiary network context can explain this influence.

Another, and related issue is the studying of management in MNCs, given that network infusion can be observed. How do corporate or divisional managers handle different, and more or less competitive, infusion forces that emerge into the corporation? We can assume that this is a phenomenon which affects and delimits the managerial possibilities of headquarters. We can also assume that top managers regard various kinds of infusion differently. Some infusion bring new competence into the corporation and fits the interests of managers and are therefore sanctioned. Other kinds of infusion forces are regarded as disturbing the structure and activities of the corporation and are therefore neglected or opposed by top management. The main underlying questions here are: Why are some infusion forces sanctioned by managers and to what extent are managers actually able to control the process of network infusion?

References

Astley, Graham and Edward Zajac, 1991. »Intraorganizational Power and Organizational Design: Reconciling Rational and Coalitional Models of Organization«, *Organization Science*, Vol. 2, No. 4, 399-411.

Bartlett, C. and S. Ghoshal, 1989. *Managing Across Borders – the Transnational Solution.* Harvard Business School Press, Boston, MA.

Blankenburg, Désirée, 1995. »A Network Approach to Foreign Market Entry«, in D.T. Wilson and K. Möller, (eds.). *Relationships and Networks – Theory and Application.* PWS Kent, Belmont.

Brass, Daniel J., 1984. »Being in the right place: A structural analysis of individual influence in an organization«, *Administrative Science Quarterly*, Vol. 29, 518-539.

Calvet, L., 1981. »A Synthesis of Foreign Direct Investment Theories and Theories of the Multinational Firm«, *Journal of International Business Studies*, Spring-Summer, 43-59.

Cook, Karen and Richard Emerson, 1984. »Exchange networks and the analysis of complex organizations«, *Sociology of Organizations*, Vol. 3, 1-30.

Cowley, P.R., 1988. »Market Structure and Business Performance: An Evaluation of Buyer/Seller Power in the PIMS Database«, *Strategic Management Journal*, Vol. 9, 271-278.

Cunningham, Malcolm and E. Homse, 1986. »Controlling the Marketing-Purchasing Interface: Resource Development and Organizational Implications«, *Industrial Marketing and Purchasing*, Vol. 1, No. 2, 3-26.

Doz, Yves and C. K. Prahalad, 1993. »Managing the DMNCs: A Search for a New Para digm«, in S. Ghoshal and E. Westney, (eds.). *Organization Theory and the Multinational Corporation.* S:t Martins Press, New York.

Dunning, J., 1993. *The Globalization of Business.* Routledge, London.

Egelhoff, W. G., 1988. *Organizing the Multinational Enterprise. An Information-Processing Perspective.* Ballinger Publishing Company, Cambridge, MA.

Forsgren, Mats and Jan Johanson, 1992. »Managing Internationalization in Business Networks« in M. Forsgren and J. Johanson, (eds.). *Managing Networks in International Business.* Gordon and Breach, Philadelphia.

Galbraith, J. R., 1973. *Designing Complex Organizations.* Addison-Westley, Reading, MA.

Ghoshal, Sumantra and Christopher A. Bartlett, 1990. »The Multinational Corporation as an Interorganizational Network«, *Academy of Management Review,* Vol. 15, No. 3, 603-625.

Ghoshal, S. and E. Westney, 1993. *Organization Theory and the Multinational Corporation.* S:t Martins Press, New York.

Gupta, Anil K. and Vijay Govindarajan, 1991. »Knowledge Flows and the Structure of Control within Multinational Corporations«, *Academy of Management Review,* Vol. 16, No. 4, 768-792.

Hallén, L., 1986. »A Comparison of Strategic Marketing Approaches« in P.W. Turnbull and J-P. Valla, (eds.). *Strategies for International Industrial Marketing.* Croom Helm, London.

Holm, Ulf, Jan Johanson and Peter Thilenius, 1995, »Headquarters' Knowledge of Subsidiary Network Contexts in the MNC«, *International Studies of Management and Organization,* Spring-Summer, Vol 25, No 1-2, 97-119.

Håkansson, H., 1987. (ed.). *Industrial Technological Development – A Network Approach.* Croom Helm, London.

Håkansson, H., 1989. *Corporate Technological Behaviour – Cooperation and Networks.* Routledge, New York.

Håkansson, Håkan and Ivan Snehota, 1989. »No Business is an Island: The Network Concept of Business Strategy«, *Scandinavian Journal of Management,* Vol. 5, No. 3, 187-200.

Hymer, S., 1976. *The International Operations of National Firms: A Study of Direct Foreign Investment.* Ph.D. dissertation, M.I.T. (published by M.I.T. Press).

Kogut, Bruce and Udo Zander, 1992. »Knowledge of the Firm, Combinative Capabilities, and the Replication of Technology«, *Organization Science,* Vol. 3, 383-397.

Kindleberger, C. P., 1969. *American Business Abroad: Six Lectures on Direct Investments,* Yale University Press, New Haven, CT.

Kotler, P, 1994. *Marketing Managment: Analysis, Planning and Control,* Prentice-Hall, Englewood Cliffs, NJ.

Krackhardt, David, 1990. »Assessing the Political Landscape: Structure, Cognition, and Power in Organizations«, *Administrative Science Quarterly,* Vol. 35, 342-369.

Laage-Hellman, J., 1989. *Technological Developement in Industrial Networks.* Department of Business Studies, Uppsala University.

Laumann, Edward O., Peter. V. Marsden and David Prensky, 1983. »The Boundary Specification Problem in Network Analysis« in R. S. Burt, M. J. Minor and sociates, (eds.). *Applied Network Analysis: A Methodological Introduction*, Sage, Beverly Hills, CA.

Lawrence, P. R. and J. W. Lorsch, 1967. *Organization and Environment*, Division of Research, Harvard Business School, Boston, MA.

Lundvall, B-Å., 1988. »Innovation as an Interactive Process: From User-Producer Interaction to National System of Innovation«, in Dosi et al., (eds.). *Technical Change and Economic Theory*. Pinter Publishers.

Nohria, Nitin and Sumantra Ghoshal, 1994. »Differentiated Fit and Shared Values: Alternatives for Managing Headquarters-Subsidiary Relations«, *Strategic Management Journal*, Vol. 15, 491-502.

Nohria, Nitin, Ranjay Gulatti and Sumantra Ghoshal, 1994. »The N-Form: Re-conceptualizing Structure and Innovation in Multinational Corporations«, Working Paper, Harvard University, Northwestern University and INSEAD.

Perrone, V. (ed.). 1989. *Dettagli, Orizzonti and Ingrandimenti*. Osservatori Organizzativo, CRORA, CRORA-Bocconi University, Milan.

Pfeffer, J and G. R. Salancik, 1978. *The external control of organizations – A resource dependence perspective*. Harper and Row Publishers, New York.

Porter, M, 1980. *Competitive Strategy*. Free Press, New York.

Scott, R.W., 1987. *Organizations – Rational, Natural, and Open Systems*. Prentice-Hall, Englewood Cliffs, New Jersey.

Snehota, I., 1990. *Notes on a theory of business enterprise*. Doctoral dissertation. Department of Business Studies, Uppsala University, Uppsala.

von Hippel, E., 1988. *The Sources of Innovation*. Oxford University Press, Oxford.

Yuchtman. E. and S. E. Seashore, 1967. »A System Resource Approach to Organizational Effectiveness«, *American Sociological Review*, Vol. 32, No. 6, 891-903.

The Authors
Presentation of the Authors

Poul Houman Andersen, Ph.D. is Assistant Professor at the Aalborg University and University Lecturer (ext.) at Aarhus University. His current research interest encompasses the internationalisation of small- and medium sized enterprises, industrial marketing, resource-based theory and interorganisational theory. Recent publications include: Collaborative Internationalisation of SMEs (1995). He is associated with the DRU-ID-Program (Danish Research Unit in Industrial Dynamics) headed by Professor Bengt-Åke Lundvall, Aalborg University.

Ulf Andersson is Lecturer and Doctoral Student in the Department of Business Studies at Uppsala University. He is participating in the project Managing International Networks headed by Professors Mats Forsgren and Jan Johanson.

Gabriel R. G. Benito is currently a Visiting Associate Professor at the Institute of International Economics and Management, Copenhagen Business School. He is also affiliated with the Department of Marketing and Logistics at the Norwegian School of Management, Oslo. A graduate from the Norwegian School of Management, he received his Master and Doctoral degrees from the Norwegian School of Economics and Business Administration. His main research interest are in foreign market entry behaviour and MNE theory. His previous work has appeared in a number of journals, including *Journal of International Business Studies, International Journal of Information Management, Journal of International Marketing*, and *Journal of Business Research*.

Ingmar Björkman is a faculty member in the Department of Organisation and Management at the Swedish School of Economics in Helsinki, Finland. During the last few years, his research has focused on the operations of Western Companies in China. Recent articles include: »The board of directors in Sino-Western joint ventures« (*Corporate Governance,* 1995), »Social relationships and business networks: the case of Western companies in China« *(International Business Review,* 1995 – with Sören Kock), and »The sequence of operational modes used by

Finnish investors in Germany (*Journal of International Marketing*, 1996 – with Michael Eklund).

Per Blenker is Assistant Professor at the Department of Management, School of Economics and Management, University of Aarhus. His research interests are: Internationalisation of subcontractors, entrepreneurship and small business development.

Poul Rind Christensen is Professor of International Business, The Southern Denmark Business School. He is head of the Centre for Small Business Studies. His research is focused on the internationalisation of small and medium-sized enterprises. Recent research include responsibility of a Danish country study on the globalisation of economic activity and international development of SMEs (OECD, 1993) and a major study on the use of subcontractors by international contractors. Current research is centred around interorganisational perspectives on the internationalisation of vertical supply chains.

Lee Davis is an Associate Professor in International Business at the Institute of International Economics and Management, Copenhagen Business School. Her research interests include the strategic management of technology in international business, knowledge creation and diffusion, appropriability, and incentives to invention and innovation. She is currently engaged in a research project on cross-border buyer-supplier collaboration on R&D, focusing on the activities of foreign MNE »centres of excellence« in Denmark, and Danish MNE centres of excellence abroad.

Mats Forsgren is a Professor of International Business at the Institute of International Economics and Management, Copenhagen Business School. The author of several books and articles on international business, for instance, Managing the Internationalisation process – The Swedish Case (1989, Routledge), Managing Networks in International Business (1992, Gordon and Breach, co-editor) and Divisional Headquarters og Abroad – A Step in the Internationalisation of Multinational Corporations (1995, Journal of Management Studies, co-author), he currently heads two research projects: Managing International Networks (together with Jan Johanson) and Developing Centres of Excellence in Multinational Firms (together with Lee Davis and Torben Pedersen).

Désirée Blankenburg Holm is Research Assistant and Lecturer at the Department of Business Studies, Uppsala University. She is involved in the IMP-project and her research topics are the foreign market entry process and the impact of connected relationships on that process. Her publications include *Managing Network Connections in International Business* (together with Jan Johanson, Scandinavian International Review, 1992) and *A Network Approach on Foreign Market Entry* (in Wilson and Möller, 1995)

Ulf Holm is Ph.D. in international business and Lecturer at the Department of Business Studies, Uppsala University. He is involved in the project »Managing International Networks« and his main research interests are business networks and management of HQ-subsidiary relationships. His publications include *Division Headquarters go Abroad – A Step in the Internationalisation of the MNC* (1995, Journal of Management Studies) and *Headquarters' Knowledge of Subsidiary Network Contexts in MNCs* (1995, International Studies of Management and Organisation, together with Jan Johanson and Peter Thilenius).

Jan Johanson is a Professor of International Business at the Uppsala University, Department of Business Studies. He has an extensive publication record within the international business field. He is a founding member of the International Marketing and Purchasing Group which has conducted research on international business relationships and networks. Professor Johanson is currently heading a project called Managing International Networks (together with Mats Forsgren).

Tine N. Langhoff has a B.Sc in Business Administration and Management Research from The Southern Denmark Business School and a M.Sc in Economics and Business Administration from Odense University. She is currently a Research fellow (Ph.D student) in International Marketing at the Department of Marketing at Odense University. Her research focuses on the significance of competence development for the internationalisation process of firms with special emphasis on intercultural relations.

Jorma Larimo Lecturer in International Marketing at the University of Vaasa, Department of Marketing. Main research interests: internationalisation behaviour, foreign direct investment behaviour and performance.

Rebecca Marschan is an Associate Professor in International Business at the Helsinki School of Economics and Business Administration. Her research and publications are on the subject of organisational structures, communication networks and information flows in multinationals.

Sara McGaughey (MBA) is a Doctoral Student at the University of Tasmania, Australia. Her research focuses on the internationalisation of SMEs.

Jarmo Nieminen is an Assistant Professor in International Economics in Turku School of Economics and Business Administration and works currently in the School's Institute of East-West Trade. He is also a vice president of the International Management Development Association. His research covers marketing and management issues in East-West business, especially FDI investment behaviour.

Cecilia Pahlberg is Research Assistant and Lecturer at the Department of Business Studies, Uppsala University. She is involved in the project »Managing International Networks« and her main research interests are HQ-subsidiary relationships in MNCs with focus on cultural differences, autonomy and subsidiary influence.

Torben Pedersen is an Assistant Professor at the Institute of International Economics and Management, Copenhagen Business School. His research interests are related to the international operations of Danish firms and to corporate governance issues. Recent writings include: »Nationality and Ownership: The 100 largest Companies in six European Nations«. *(Management International Review,* 1996 – with Steen Thomsen), and »The Impact of Foreign Acquisition on the Evolution of Danish Firms: A Competence-based Perspective«, (chapter in a book from *Routledge,* 1996 – with Finn Valentin).

Bent Petersen is an Assistant Professor in International Business at The Institute of International Economics and Management, Copenhagen

Business School. His research interests are related to the internationalisation process of the firm and to market servicing modes, in particular export market penetration via independent, foreign intermediaries. (Ph.D. thesis subject). Writing on these topics have been published in Danish business journals, international proceedings and anthologies.

Trond Randøy is an Associate Professor at the Center for International Economics and Shipping at Agder College, Norway. His main research focus is in the area of international business strategy and international competitiveness.

Dr. D. Deo Sharma is the Professor of Marketing and International Business, Department of Business Administration, University of Umeå, Sweden. He completed his Ph.D. in 1981 from the University of Uppsala. His research interest lies, among others, in the areas of host government-TNCs interaction, the internationalisation process of firms, international strategic alliances, and international marketing.

Peter Thilenius is Research Assistant and Lecturer at the Department of Business Studies, Uppsala University. He is also involved in the project »Managing International Networks« and his research focus mainly on the importance of subsidiaries' network contexts. His publications include *Headquarters' Knowledge of Subsidiary Network Contexts in MNCs* (1995, International Studies of Management and Organisation).

Steen Thomsen is Associate Professor at the Institute of International Economics and Management, Copenhagen Business School where he teaches courses in corporate governance, managerial economics and industrial organisation. Present research projects include studies of ownership structure and economic performance, company life cycles and the contribution of big business to economic growth. He has served as a consultant for the Copenhagen Institute for futures studies, the EU Commission, the Danish Ministry of Industry and a number of large Danish companies.

Jan-Åke Törnroos is a Professor of Corporate Geography at the Swedish School of Economics and Business Administration in Helsinki, Finland. He has been a Research Fellow at Cambridge University, U.K. and a former Head of Department at Åbo Akademi University (Department of Economic Geography and International Marketing). His research covers international industrial marketing, Corporate geography, image-studies and industrial networks and interaction.

Carolina Wallström-Pan is a graduate student at the Department of Business Administration, University of Uppsala, Uppsala, Sweden.

Denice Welch (PhD) is Associate Professor of International Management, Norwegian School of Management, Oslo. Her research interests cover international human resource management, multinational management, and international strategy, and has published widely in these fields.

Lawrence S. Welch (PhD) is Professor of International Marketing, Norwegian School of Management, Oslo. He has published widely on internationalisation issues since the late 1970s, including extensive work with Nordic scholars in this field.

Ivo Zander is Assistant Professor at the Institute of International Business (IIB), at the Stockholm School of Economics. He received his Ph.D. from the Stockholm School of Economics in 1994. His research focuses on innovation and entrepreneurship in multinational corporations.

Udo Zander is Assistant Professor at the Institute of International Business (IIB), at the Stockholm School of Economics. He received his Ph.D. from the Stockholm School of Economics in 1991. His research interests include international entrepreneurship and management.